# THE CLASSICAL ECONOMISTS

# The Classical Economists

*by* D. P. O'BRIEN

CLARENDON PRESS
OXFORD
1975

*Oxford University Press, Ely House, London W.1*

GLASGOW  NEW YORK  TORONTO  MELBOURNE  WELLINGTON
CAPE TOWN  IBADAN  NAIROBI  DAR ES SALAAM  LUSAKA  ADDIS ABABA
DELHI  BOMBAY  CALCUTTA  MADRAS  KARACHI  LAHORE  DACCA
KUALA LUMPUR  SINGAPORE  HONG KONG  TOKYO

ISBN 0 19 877015 4

© *Oxford University Press 1975*

*Printed in Great Britain.*
*By Richard Clay (The Chaucer Press) Ltd*
*Bungay, Suffolk*

# Acknowledgements

This book was written partly in Belfast and partly in Durham. The book was begun in Belfast and the first five chapters written there. I owe a particular debt to the environment of the Department of Economics, Queen's University of Belfast, which was so favourable to the pursuit of work in the history of economic thought and in particular to Professor R. D. C. Black. Since the book is a study of Classical Economics, it grew out of my earlier work in this field which resulted in *J. R. McCulloch* and in *The Correspondence of Lord Overstone* and so I owe a debt of gratitude to those who guided me in the earlier stages of my interest in the history of economic thought especially Lord Robbins, Professor Marian Bowley, Professor T. W. Hutchison, and Professor R. S. Sayers, as well as Professor Black.

I must thank too those in the libraries of Queen's University, Belfast, and Durham University who coped with my demands upon them, especially in the matter of inter-library loans.

Sheila Drake typed and retyped the successive drafts of the book and I owe her a deep debt of gratitude for coping with a lengthy typescript many times over in a busy departmental office. Finally I must thank my wife for her help with the checking of typescripts and most of all for putting up with the condition which can best be described as 'author's pregnancy'. Since authors generally have a gestation period well in excess of that of the elephant this indicates a very considerable degree of forbearance.

# Contents

# Introduction

This book is a general treatment of Classical economics designed both for the economist interested in the history of economic thought and also for the economic historian. It is designed to be read as a continuous text and for this reason the notes have been assembled separately. I have tried to cover all aspects of Classical economics and to provide a guide, in the bibliographies appended to the chapters, for further reading. The latter have unavoidably been selective for the Classical economists' writings have generated a very considerable secondary literature. At the same time, despite this process of selection, the reader is bound to find differences of emphasis, sometimes considerable differences, in the references given as compared with the text of the book. Nevertheless, considering the enormous diversity of the Classical writings it is remarkable how far a degree of consensus has emerged amongst the various commentators.

The book builds upon the research work embodied in the monographs and articles listed in the bibliographies. What I have attempted to provide is a text which pulls together many of the main threads in the secondary literature. It seems that it is time that this was attempted. There is at present no general text that I know of that attempts to do this. The excellent book *Ricardian Economics* by Professor Mark Blaug does not, by design, cover either the same range of subjects as this volume or as long a period of time. The same author's major text *Economic Theory in Retrospect* similarly limits itself, this time by dealing with specific authors; and this is the path pursued by writers of general texts in the history of economic thought who feel that they want to include everything from Moses to Patinkin in one volume.

Before going on to look at the contents of the book however there is one point which should be dealt with. Marx is not discussed in this volume. Although his analytical apparatus was borrowed entirely from Classical economics and cannot be understood without a knowledge of Classical economics, it seems to me doubtful whether Marx was himself a Classical economist. It seems to me that his writings, like those of Henry George, are one of the off-shoots of Classical economics rather than a part of it. Certainly an attempt to integrate what he had to say with a general discussion of Classical writing would produce a hopeless muddle. Marx is better studied on his own; and there is a superb chapter in Mark Blaug's *Economic Theory in Retrospect* as a starting-point.

In Chapter 1 we have a look at the era of Classical economics and at the actors on the Classical-economic stage, looking briefly at their education and professional backgrounds and addressing ourselves to the question of whether or not they formed a scientific community. The chapter concludes with an all-too-brief look at the economic history of the Classical age. This chapter is designed to set the scene for the book; it is very easy to talk airily about Classical economics without explaining who or what was involved— and the result is often confusion, if not downright misrepresentation.

Chapter 2 continues the process of outlining the over-all picture by look- ing at the roots of Classical economics, initially in terms of the seventeenth- and eighteenth-century intellectual environment from which the subject sprang, especially the natural-law roots, as well as considering the importance of Utilitarianism, before proceeding to look at the two great sources for Classical economics, the works of Adam Smith and David Ricardo, especi- ally the *Wealth of Nations* and Ricardo's *Principles*. The relative importance of these two sources is considered together with the way in which the ele- ments from these two great writers were blended and developed by later economists, especially J. S. Mill.

Chapter 3 then completes the development of an over-all view of Classical economics by looking at some of the preconceptions of the system—the macro-economic and policy orientation of the literature, the central place afforded to views on population growth, and the Classical views on method. It proves possible to give some over-all indication of the elements involved here, despite the sharp divergencies between the views of different writers on both population, where we have Malthusians and anti-Malthusians, and on method—where we have both inductive and deductive methodological ap- proaches.

We then turn from our over-view to some more detailed considerations. Chapter 4 begins this process with an examination of the Classical theories of value—the cost of production, Ricardian and subjective value theories, as well as the related problems of a measure of value.

From value we turn in Chapter 5 to distribution dealing with the Classical theories of wages, profit, and rent, and with the Classical views on the likely long-run trends of relative shares.

Chapter 6 takes us into the Classical monetary theory—a truly exciting area where the achievements of the Classical economists were enormous. The same is true of the subject of Chapter 7, the development of Classical inter- national-trade theory from Adam Smith's absolute advantage approach through the comparative cost developments of Torrens and Ricardo to the formulation of the theory of reciprocal demand by Torrens and J. S. Mill. In this chapter it has been necessary to be much freer with modern technique than elsewhere. It is only through such techniques that the importance and subtlety of what was being argued by the Classical writers can be appreciated, as the misguided efforts of some relatively modern critics who did not them- selves use the techniques have made clear. But the techniques should not be allowed to hide the extent to which the older looser Classical formulations allowed a much greater range of considerations within the analysis, in particular in relation to the origins of comparative advantage.

In Chapter 8 we deal with the Classical theory of growth. Classical economics was really all about growth, so in a sense the whole book is about growth. But there is enough to make a separate treatment of the key elements in the growth engine a sensible proposition even though the rest of the book is necessary fully to understand the significance of this chapter.

Finally we come to the role and finance of government. In Chapter 9 we deal with the subject almost universally omitted from texts on the history of economic thought—the Classical theory of public finance. The omission of this is all the more surprising when one considers the importance attached to it by the Classical writers—it occupies nearly one-third of the *Wealth of Nations* and of Ricardo's *Principles* as well as a substantial text—the *Treatise On Taxation*—by McCulloch. The chapter goes through the general principles of public finance including Adam Smith's once famous maxims of taxation, then deals with direct and indirect taxes and debt finance. In Chapter 10, having established the basis of government finance in the previous chapter, we look at the Classical theory of public policy, dealing with the general question of the legitimate role of government and then focusing on such areas as factory legislation, mechanization, the Poor Law, education, trade unions, Ireland, and colonies. In this discussion a conscious attempt has been made to steer between the Charybdis of over-generosity to the Classical economists and the (much more frequently struck) Scylla of painting them as vicious reactionaries.

At the end of all this the reader should be left with a fairly coherent overall picture of the Classical economists. If he pursues the matter further (and it would be nice if the book helped to keep alive interest in the Classical economists) then he is unlikely to agree with everything in this book. But if it has stirred him to look at Classical economics for himself it will have done its job.

# 1. The Classical-Economic Stage

## i. THE PERIOD OF CLASSICAL ECONOMICS

In any detailed discussion of a particular body of ideas it is perhaps helpful to begin by indicating to the reader the period during which those ideas were of importance.

There can be little doubt that the hey-day of Classical economics was during the years 1800–50. Delineation of the period during which Classical economics developed as a body of thought, came to be the ruling approach to economics, ultimately experienced a measure of stagnation and decay, and was finally supplanted by the young and vigorous development of neo-Classical economics in the 'marginal revolution' is however a good deal less easy.

At one end it is usual to date the era of Classical economics as beginning in 1776 with the publication of Adam Smith's mighty *Wealth of Nations*. Such an approach has a strong *prima facie* appeal, but closer examination raises doubts about it. On the one hand Classical economics owed a great deal to David Hume in certain critical areas, especially that of monetary theory. The relevant part of Hume's *Essays* was published in 1752: and it is therefore doubtful if too much weight can be placed on the year 1776. Indeed the influence of Hume upon Smith cannot be ignored: they were close friends and Hume was appointed by Smith to be his literary executor. In addition the work of Adam Smith himself did not suddenly spring from nothing in 1776. He lectured in Edinburgh from 1748 and was a professor there from 1751 to 1763. Of course he covered other subjects in addition to economics: but there is a set of notes on his lectures taken in 1762–3—and their editor Edwin Cannan has pointed out many passages in them which are parallel to passages in the *Wealth of Nations*. Indeed it is apparent that quite a lot of the book was substantially in existence before Smith resigned his chair. Moreover there is evidence that his influence as a lecturer was considerable.

At all events we cannot date the Classical era as starting any later than 1776 and there are strong arguments for taking 1750 as its starting-point. But at the same time it must be emphasized that during these early years the Classical approach certainly did not dominate economics. The Physiocratic system of the French economists was still very much in its full strength. Indeed the beginning of the school is usually dated from the publication of the articles 'Fermiers' and 'Grains' by its leader Quesnay in 1756 and 1757. Mirabeau's *L'Ami des hommes* appeared in 1756–60 and the famous *Tableau économique* in 1758–9. The intellectual influence of the Physiocrats is however generally agreed to have been at its zenith in the 1760s, declining quite fast after 1770. Nevertheless the famous *Réflexions sur la formation et la distribution des richesses* of Turgot did not appear until 1771 and this was far from being the last Physiocratic work.[1]

But Classical economics did become the ruling system, and for half a century up to 1850 it completely dominated economic thought. Although there can be little doubt that its influence declined from that date, delineation of the end of the era is, again, far from easy. It is tempting to select the year 1870 and there are certainly persuasive arguments for this. Jevons, who has a strong claim to be regarded as the progenitor of the neo-Classical economics which succeeded the Classical system, published his *Theory of Political Economy* in 1871. In a sense this was a watershed in the development of economics. In the ten years up to its publication Jevons had, largely unsuccessfully, attempted to interest people in his theory of value, first published as a paper read to the British Association in 1862.[2] At that time it had attracted no attention, and Jevons seems to have become discouraged. But by 1870 he was President of the Statistical Section of the British Association and, in the ten years which followed, the marginalist approach of neo-Classical economics was clearly making extremely rapid strides.

At the same time Classical economics, and all it involved, did not suddenly come to an end in 1870. What was probably the last significant work of Classical economics, J. E. Cairnes's *Some Leading Principles of Political Economy Newly Expounded*, did not appear until 1874, a year which also saw the fourth edition of Henry Fawcett's *Manual of Political Economy* (first published in 1863). Classical economics did not go without a fight. In the preface to the second edition of his *Character and Logical Method of Political Economy*, published in 1875, Cairnes attacked Jevons's whole employment of mathematics in economics; and as late as 1895 when the young Winston Churchill set out to teach himself some economics it was to Fawcett's work that he turned.[3] But if it did not go without a fight it still went; and 1870 will accordingly be treated as the end of the era, although not in any rigid sense—some significant works published after that date will be considered as falling within the subject matter of this book.

## ii. THE PERSONNEL OF CLASSICAL ECONOMICS

Economists with no special interest in the history of economic thought tend, on hearing the word 'Classical', to think rather vaguely (if they think of anything) of Smith and Ricardo—and to leave the matter at that. Yet, although these two writers were undoubtedly the twin pillars of Classical economics, they were but two out of a great number of writers; and it may be helpful to indicate the extent of the army of the Classical economists.

Perhaps the best way to approach this exercise is to place the writers of the Classical school into three groups. Like all groups these involve arbitrariness; and no doubt the inclusion of particular writers in one or other group will cause some readers to feel that less (or more) than justice is being done to the individual concerned. This may well be the case; but the device of grouping is intended as a purely clarificatory one, not as a system of ranking on merit.

Group I consists, conveniently, of just two men, Adam Smith (1723–90) and David Ricardo (1772–1823). These two writers were without doubt the two major figures of Classical economics in terms of the influence they exercised. They were however not of the same kind. Smith, who as author of the *Wealth of Nations* has strong claims indeed to be regarded as the most influential economic author for 160 years after its publication, was a writer who covered virtually the whole field of economic inquiry. His great work, though at times straying off into lengthy digressions, has a strong claim to be one of the most influential ever written, extending its sway well beyond those who wrote on economics. It was often well argued and shrewd; yet it was capable of containing several different theories of the same economic phenomena without any real attempt to resolve the differences between them. But herein to some extent lay the secret of Smith's influence: for the *Wealth of Nations* was thus able to suggest many extremely interesting lines of inquiry to different people.

One of these people was David Ricardo. He started reading Smith's great work while bored when visiting Bath for his wife's health; and the outcome of his reading was to be highly significant. For Ricardo was of a very different cast of mind from Smith. He was the pure theorist *par excellence*. To the raw material of Smith's book he applied his analytical technique; and the result was the development of a method of reasoning and an approach to economic problems which is with us today. He seems to have followed what was his own instinctive method of procedure, although he had some limited study of natural science. It consisted of making a number of extremely limiting assumptions and proceeding to reason closely to a conclusion on the basis of these assumptions, often with no more than token reference to the real world. A perfectly legitimate device in itself, it has become known as 'model-building'; but it is a procedure much open to abuse when from the results of the exercise are drawn startling policy conclusions. Ricardo was to be guilty of this, and Schumpeter in his great *History of Economic Analysis* named this 'the Ricardian Vice'.[4] But for a while, though for nothing like as long as was the case with Smith, Ricardo's influence, both with respect to his theories *and* to the conclusions for policy drawn from them, was enormously strong. This was at least true of his influence with economic writers; the general public were less impressed and at one stage it was suggested in the House of Commons by Henry Brougham that Ricardo must have 'descended from some other planet'[5] so oversimplified did his view of the working of the economic system appear.

Nevertheless his influence with economic writers was, for a while, very considerable. It must be stressed here that it *is* on the score of influence that Smith and Ricardo are included in Group I. No arbitrary judgement about the quality of what they wrote, as compared with the writers in other groups, is implied. Indeed many of the writers in these other groups had extremely important contributions to make, and offered insights which were later to prove very significant. But it is difficult to contest the view that the influence of Smith and Ricardo (though that of the latter was by far the less of the two) stands out clearly when Classical-economic literature is viewed as a whole.

Nevertheless many of the writers in Group II were extremely important. They include T. R. Malthus (1766–1834) who, building on Smith's foundations, managed to disagree with Ricardo on practically everything and who was, without a doubt, a major figure in Classical economics, even if attempts to make him into a forerunner of Keynes have been unsuccessful. It was Malthus who supplied the population theory which for long exercised great influence amongst the Classical economists, and which was incorporated by Ricardo into his basic model of economic progress.

Another significant figure included in Group II was a correspondent of both Malthus and Ricardo, the French economist J. B. Say (1767–1832). His own work, like that of Malthus, was much influenced by Smith; but it included the important (though subsequently much abused and misrepresented) Say's Law, and a subjective theory of value. Included in Group II also is James Mill (1773–1836) a disciple of the Utilitarian Jeremy Bentham, and a man who found the Ricardian style of reasoning congenial. He was undoubtedly Ricardo's closest follower. His son, also in Group II, was the famous John Stuart Mill (1806–73) 'the leading intellectual of his day' but much less closely Ricardian than his father, and in many ways closer to Smith both in general approach and conclusions.

In addition to the two Mills there was John Ramsay McCulloch (1789–1864), Nassau Senior (1790–1864), Robert Torrens (1780–1864), Thomas Tooke (1774–1858), and, perhaps the last true representatives of Classical economics, J. E. Cairnes (1823–75) and Henry Fawcett (1833–84). McCulloch was considerably influenced by Ricardo, although he had begun his career very much under the influence of Smith and Malthus, and although the influence of Ricardo on him was to prove largely transitory. He was the author of a highly successful textbook, but his output was enormous because he for long lived by his pen. He wrote extensively on economic policy, and was a pioneer in the collection and publication of economic data. Senior was the first to lead the revolt against Malthus's population theory. He was the architect of the New Poor Law of 1834 and a value theorist in a different mould from either Smith or Ricardo. Robert Torrens, a one-time Royal Marine commander with a stormy military career, pursued a career as economist and controversialist, on such matters as money and banking and international-trade theory and policy, which was to prove almost equally stormy. In many ways his life was one continuous conflict: and his battles with successive governments for financial compensation for what he considered wrongs are a story in themselves. But Torrens was possibly the best pure theorist amongst the Classical economists, apart from Ricardo: indeed in some respects he was arguably superior. Tooke is chiefly remembered for his monumental *History of Prices*. This, and an earlier work on *High and Low Prices*, must establish Tooke as the greatest collector of monetary data in the nineteenth century and as a formidable monetary controversialist. His insights in the latter respect were particularly important; but he made significant contributions in other fields, notably his clarification of the concept of profit in his *Considerations on the State of the Currency*. Cairnes and Fawcett are perhaps the least important figures in Group II, not so much because they contributed little that was new—although this was arguably the case—but because, judged by the criteria of influence their importance, coming as they did at the end of an era, was necessarily limited. In many ways it was upon them that the marginal revolution fell. Fawcett has long been regarded as a regurgitator of J. S. Mill. This is perhaps a little unfair in that he was alive to some of the differences between experience and the expected theoretical conclusions; and in any case there can be little doubt that by virtue of his position as professor at Cambridge he was in a position to exercise influence. Cairnes, as a professor at University College London, was also in such a position: and his work had perhaps more to offer than that of Fawcett. In his work on method and subsequently in his *Leading Principles* he raised a number of questions about the central doctrines of Classical economics which, if he had pushed on to find answers to them, might have prolonged the vitality of the system.

Yet it is difficult to escape the feeling that Fawcett and Cairnes, included in Group II here because of an influence stemming partly from their academic positions, were analytically inferior to many, if not most, of the writers in Group III. The common characteristic of the latter is that they were men of considerable intellectual ability, sometimes highly influential over a narrow field of thought and policy, but men who did not attempt to exercise a broad general influence over large areas of economics and did not, with one or two exceptions, attempt comprehensive treatises, unlike virtually every writer in Group II except Tooke.

The common characteristic of the writers in Group III is that their contributions were highly specialized. They were confined to a considerable
extent (though not entirely) to monetary economics (including foreign
exchanges) and to value theory. Very many writers contributed to the public
debates on these subjects as well as to such popular matters of controversy
as the Corn Laws, protection in general, colonies, and the Poor Laws. Any
selection of the specialist writers becomes, then, highly arbitrary; and no
doubt the selection included here will displease some readers. But it must
be recognized that, on the one hand, no picture of Classical economics can
be complete which omits entirely the specialist writers; and on the other,
no complete coverage of such writers is possible in anything less than
encyclopedic dimensions. In defence of the particular selection offered here
it should be said, firstly, that most of them contributed several publications
of interest on a particular subject—they were not 'one-shot' economists;
and, secondly, that what they did have to say was, almost without exception, of considerable analytical interest.

The monetary writers form the largest group. They include Henry
Drummond (1786–1860), Thomas Joplin (*c.* 1790–1847), George Warde
Norman (1793–1882), Samuel Jones Loyd, Lord Overstone (1796–1883),
Henry Thornton (1760–1815), William Blake (*c.* 1774–1852), Francis Horner
(1778–1817), John Wheatley (1772–1830), William Newmarch (1820–82),
and Richard Page. Drummond and Joplin, together with Page and
McCulloch and one James Pennington, can claim to be the originators of
the principle of 'metallic fluctuation' which was to prove so important in
nineteenth-century monetary controversy. G. W. Norman and Overstone
(Loyd), particularly the latter, provided the basic theoretical framework
for the Bank Act of 1844 (though drawing on Ricardo's exposition) both
before its introduction and during its operation when attacks against it
required frequently to be repulsed. Norman, in addition, wrote on taxation
and on international-trade theory. Thornton has a strong claim to be the
greatest monetary theorist of the nineteenth century and indeed one of
the greatest of all time. One of the major figures in the Bullionist controversy
in the period of Bank of England inconvertibility during the French wars,
he expounded a form of bullionism which was far removed from the rigid
simplicity of the Ricardian version of the analysis. His form incorporated
many of the subtleties of much later monetary theory. The same may be
said to some extent of William Blake whose work on exchanges was certainly important. Thornton, Francis Horner, and William Huskisson were
the joint authors of the Bullion Report of 1810, one of the most amazing
analytical documents ever to emerge from a Parliamentary Select Committee.
John Wheatley was another contributor to the Bullion controversy, and
one who drew particular attention to the role of country-bank issues in
the money supply, a point neglected by theorists like Ricardo and which

had to be rediscovered by McCulloch and Overstone. William Newmarch was important, not only as Tooke's co-author (indeed probably the principal author) in the writing of the last two volumes of the *History of Prices*, but also in his own right as an investigator into the monetary significance of bills of exchange, and, with Tooke, as one of the leading opponents of the Currency School and the Bank Act of 1844.

Also included amongst the monetary writers in Group III, for the purposes of this study, is the great David Hume (1711–76). Hume is of course one of the great figures in any history of ideas, and his significance extends far outside the field of economics. But his two Essays, 'Of Money' and 'Of the Balance of Trade' form nothing less than the foundation of Classical monetary economics.

The remaining writers in Group III were principally (though by no means exclusively) of significance through their writings on value theory. They were Thomas De Quincey (1785–1859)—chiefly famous to the general public as the opium eater but important here as Ricardo's only other close disciple apart from Mill—Samuel Bailey (1791–1870) author of a brilliant if negative survey of value theory, and Mountifort Longfield (1802–84). The last named, a writer with a combination of penetration and compactness which was at times almost in the same class as David Hume, wrote not only on value theory but on transmission of international remittances, wages, and other matters.

Sir Edward West (1782–1828), *inter alia* one of the formulators of the Ricardian rent theory also comes into this group. There was in addition, George Poulett Scrope (1797–1876), one of only two writers in Group III to attempt a comprehensive treatise (in his *Principles of Political Economy* of 1833). He wrote on value and distribution, monetary economics and economic fluctuations, population, and the Poor Law. He was strongly opposed to much of Classical economics, yet his methods and conclusions were essentially Classical. Although many of his charges were simply based on failure to understand the full subtleties of his opponents' position, no discussion of Classical economics which ignored him could be regarded as complete. The other writer who attempted a comprehensive treatment of the subject was Samuel Read, who in 1829 published his *Political Economy, An Enquiry into the Natural Grounds of Right to Vendible Property or Wealth*. He also wrote on money and the bank-restriction laws and taxation. He was a close follower of Adam Smith's *Wealth of Nations*. Finally there were James Maitland (1759–1839) 8th Earl of Lauderdale, chiefly famous for his writings on the National Debt, and John Barton (1789–1852), who managed to change Ricardo's mind on the effects of machinery.

These then were the most important of the men who together constituted the Classical economists. Obviously the sort of grouping employed here is arbitrary both in its inclusions and in its exclusions. But it should at least give the reader who wants to find out who the Classical economists were some guidance as to where to look, after his initial halt at Smith and Ricardo.

The Classical economists are often considered, and indeed referred to, as the 'English' Classical economists. This is something of a misnomer. In so far as they have one common fount it is the Scot Adam Smith. The Scottish tradition of economic and social inquiry continued well on into the nineteenth century, mixing fact and theory and attempting to test the one against the other. Several English writers followed the same path, to some extent, notably Tooke and Newmarch. But in so far as there was a more directly native English tradition, this was essentially that of Ricardo, followed by De Quincey, the Irishman Torrens, and the Scot James Mill. The latter's son, John Stuart Mill, really straddled these two main parts of the Classical development. Classical economics was essentially a development of intellectual thinking throughout the whole British Isles. (Thus although Torrens was close to Ricardo on a number of theoretical issues, he retained a number of distinctively Irish characteristics including a marked concern with the need for Catholic emancipation. He wrote novels depicting their condition; and for those who cannot stomach the originals there are delightful summaries by Lord Robbins.)[6] It also extended its influence into France (where Say was an important exponent) and even Germany. Indeed in time Classical economics became a body of thought which was, for practical purposes, the common possession of the economically educated, both in the British Isles and elsewhere, for three-quarters of a century and more.

iii. THE BACKGROUNDS OF THE CLASSICAL ECONOMISTS

The student of economics is accustomed to regard it as an academic subject, and to accept that its practitioners will be academics. This is a perfectly reasonable assumption in our own time, and indeed it has been essentially reasonable since the beginning of this century and probably since the 1890s. It was a characteristic of neo-Classical economics that its practitioners, from the 1870s onwards, were largely academic both by employment and (to some extent at least) by cast of mind.

But all this was not true of the Classical economists. One of the most important distinguishing characteristics of the Classical economists is that they formed, educationally and professionally, a remarkably good cross-section of the educated classes of their age.

This characteristic is strongly borne out by the contrast between the two towering figures of Classical economics, Smith and Ricardo. Smith was an academic by profession, and received university education in both Glasgow and Oxford. He was Professor of Logic (and later of Moral Philosophy) at Glasgow 1751–64. Although he lived later on a Ducal pension (supplemented still later by a Customs salary) he was essentially an academic. Ricardo, by contrast, was a stockbroker who retired early. He was to a considerable extent self-educated, both in the natural sciences, in which he was interested before taking up economics, and in the latter subject itself.

We find similar contrasts when we look at the other Classical economists. On the one hand there are those with a university education and background. Malthus was educated at Cambridge and was both academic—as Professor of History and Political Economy at the East India College at Haileybury—and cleric. Cairnes was educated at Dublin University and was at various times a professor at Dublin, Galway, and University College London. Fawcett, Cambridge educated, was a professor there for twenty-one years. Senior, an Oxford Fellow, was Drummond Professor there 1825–30 and 1847–52. Henry Drummond himself was educated at Oxford, as were Scrope, De Quincey, West, Lauderdale, and Wheatley. Overstone was educated at Cambridge. Hume was twice an unsuccessful candidate for professorial chairs in Scotland and was keeper of the Advocates' Library in Edinburgh. Longfield, Dublin University educated, was professor there, firstly of political economy and then of law. McCulloch, educated like James Mill (and Lauderdale) at Edinburgh University, was an unsuccessful candidate for a chair there in 1825, and was professor at London University 1828–37. Say was a public lecturer in Paris in 1815 and subsequently appointed to chairs at the Conservatoire des Arts et Métiers (1819) and the Collège de France (1830).

On the other hand many of the Classical economists had neither university education nor employment. James Mill, though he had university education and was *inter alia* an educational theorist and one of the founders of London University, never had university employment. But many had not even university education. Even his son J. S. Mill, one of the leading figures of his age, was educated by his father.[7] Thomas Tooke, who started work at fifteen, was largely self-educated, as was his collaborator William Newmarch (who rose from the position of bank clerk to be a force in the City of London) and his adversary Robert Torrens—Major and finally Colonel in the Royal Marines. So very probably was Thomas Joplin, and so certainly was George Warde Norman who spent a good deal of his life trying to repair the educational deficiencies of Eton. Samuel Bailey seems to have fallen into this category also.

Of course all these figures were to a considerable extent—usually entirely —self-educated in the subject of economics even where they had formal university education. For although Adam Smith's teaching in Glasgow was followed by that of Dugald Stewart in Edinburgh, the first chair of economics outside Scotland—indeed the first chair anywhere in the British Isles formally concerned with economics as distinct from Moral Philosophy[8] —was not established until 1825 when the Drummond Chair at Oxford was founded. The pioneering efforts of McCulloch as a public lecturer and private tutor should not be disregarded;[9] and amongst his pupils was Overstone. But by and large these men were self-educated in the subject which they helped to advance.

Two other educational characteristics are perhaps worthy of mention. On the one hand there were those (admittedly not very many) with a pronounced interest in natural science. They include in particular Scrope, Ricardo, Overstone, and Norman. The last two had a particular interest in geology, while Scrope was a leading geologist and Secretary of the Geological Society, which awarded him its Wollaston Medal in 1867. But, except in Scrope's case, the scientific interest lacked the backing of formal education in the subject. Formal education especially at university level, tended to be in classics, philosophy, mathematics, or law, for most of those under consideration here. It is the last named which indicates a second educational characteristic of the Classical economists worthy of mention. For a remarkable number of them had at least legal training. Senior was a barrister of Lincoln's Inn, and a Master in Chancery 1836–55. Cairnes was an Irish barrister, and Fawcett studied law as a student of Lincoln's Inn after leaving Cambridge. Francis Horner was called to the Scottish Bar in 1800 and to the English Bar in 1807. Hume studied law and, as already noted, became librarian of an important law library. Longfield was not only Professor of Law at Dublin 1834–84 but a judge of the Landed Estates Court 1858–67. West was Recorder of Bombay and became, in 1823, Chief Justice. Wheatley too was a lawyer, called to the Bar in 1797, though he seems to have practised little. Lauderdale too was trained as a lawyer.

The legal training provided both a common element in the educational background of some of the Classical economists and also a common professional interest. However the professions of the group taken as a whole were highly varied. Nevertheless various members of the groups are found to have had some occupational interest in common. Some, as already noted, became academics, though they did not usually spend their working lives as such. Many relied on their pens to a greater or lesser extent. Thus James Mill, J. S. Mill, Torrens, Francis Horner, Richard Page, De Quincey, and, above all perhaps in this sphere, McCulloch, were to some extent journalists in that they gained a part, in some cases a significant part, of their income from working for periodical publications. In addition, Torrens was a newspaper proprietor, and the Mills were instrumental in the setting up of the *Westminster Review*, while McCulloch edited the *Scotsman* in the years 1817–21.[10]

Another common thread was provided by government employment, whether full time or occasional. Thus both Mills were also effectively (as employees of the East India Company) civil servants. Smith was in his later years a Customs Officer. McCulloch was a full civil servant for the last twenty-six years of his life, in his capacity as Comptroller of the Stationery

Office.[11] Senior did work for government in his preparation of the enormously influential Poor Law Comission Report of 1834 and in other ways. Torrens was a member of the South Australia Commission. Fawcett became Paymaster-General under Gladstone. George Warde Norman was an Exchequer Bill Commissioner. Say was a member of the tribunat under Napoleon though he was dismissed by the latter. David Hume was a British diplomat in Paris during 1765. Longfield was appointed an Irish Privy Councillor in 1867.

A number of the writers considered here were also members of Parliament. Ricardo was member for the Irish seat of Portarlington 1819–23. John Stuart Mill was M.P. for Westminster 1865–8. Torrens was M.P. for Ashburton 1831–5 and Fawcett become M.P. for Brighton. Drummond was an M.P. for many years, as were Henry Thornton and Scrope. Overstone and Francis Horner were also M.P.s while Samuel Bailey was an unsuccessful Parliamentary candidate, and Lauderdale was a member in the years 1780–9.

A number of these writers apart from Ricardo had financial careers, especially in banking. Overstone was an immensely wealthy and influential banker; George Warde Norman was a timber merchant and, more importantly, a Director of the Bank of England for more than fifty years.[12] Joplin founded the National and Provincial Bank in 1833. William Newmarch rose to be manager of the bank of Glyn, Mills, & Co., while Thomas Tooke was a merchant, a partner in the firm of Astell, Tooke, & Thornton, Chairman of the St. Catherine's Dock Company, and Governor of the Royal Exchange Assurance Corporation 1840–52. Say was employed in business after his disgrace by Napoleon until the Restoration in 1815. Samuel Bailey worked for his father, a Sheffield master cutter, for a while, and was later chairman of the Sheffield Banking Company which he helped to found.

The Classical economists, then, formed a very diverse group of men both in respect of their educational backgrounds and their professions. Yet, partly because many of them filled several different roles, there were important elements in all this which would have helped to bring them together, given a common interest in economics. It is therefore of some interest to ask whether they in any sense constituted a 'scientific community'.

iv. A SCIENTIFIC COMMUNITY?

The question of the extent to which the Classical economists constituted a scientific community is interesting on two counts. Firstly, the extent to which a group of thinkers forms such a community will have considerable influence on the way that the ideas that they hold are refined and developed to meet the test of criticism, and on the degree to which anything like a consensus emerges. Secondly, those who are interested in the structure of 'scientific revolutions' regard a community as a prerequisite for a revolution. This second aspect will not be pursued here, although references are given at the end of the chapter so that the interested reader may pursue the matter. But the first aspect is of considerable general interest.

It has already been stressed that the Classical economists formed something of a cross-section of society. It is then interesting to find that they still managed to form what was in the circumstances a surprisingly close-knit group. The links which bound them together were of two main kinds, institutional and periodical.

The institutional links were basically four, the Political Economy Club, the (Royal) Statistical Society, the British Association and the Royal Society. Of these the Political Economy Club was by far the most important as a link. The vast majority of those whom we have included in our three groups were members, and a number were indeed founder members of the Club. The latter included Ricardo, Malthus, James Mill, Torrens, Tooke, and G. W. Norman. J. S. Mill, McCulloch, Senior, Cairnes, Fawcett, Newmarch, Overstone, and Blake were also members. J. B. Say was elected an honorary member in 1822 and visited the Club in 1828; and although it could not contain Henry Thornton, who died before its foundation, it did include his close associate Zachary Macaulay, father of T. B. Macaulay.

The Club was founded in London in 1821 at a dinner attended by some of the founder members, and seems to have taken its origin from the luminous and magnetic personality of Ricardo, and his desire to talk with other economists. But it should be emphasized that the Club was not guilty of being some kind of society for the propagation of Ricardo's views or any-one else's. It has been accused both of this and of being a means of disseminating the views of a small number of Utilitarians. Examination of both the membership and the questions discussed, and also of the records of the discussions kept by J. L. Mallet, shows this to be a wholly false view. The enormous strength and vitality of the Club, which would certainly have withered if it had been merely a propaganda institution is itself a testimony to this. The most that can be said is that the membership accepted as a general basis the kind of economics to be found in the *Wealth of Nations* —and this is hardly enough on its own to establish any significant degree of unanimity, as the discussions bear witness. The significance of the Club was that it was truly a debating forum; and because it was this it has great significance as providing a vital link for a scientific community.

The membership was far wider than that merely of the Classical economists. Apart from the latter, there were many who were on the fringe of Classical economics, although not included in any of the three groups here. Looking at those elected up to 1840 we find in this category such names as Walter Coulson, Robert Mushet, Sir Henry Parnell, James Pennington, John Horsley Palmer, and Perronet Thompson. There were also very many who were important in government, politics, or business. They include G. G. de Larpent, J. G. S. Lefevre, John Abel Smith, Henry Warburton, Lord

Althorp, William Whitmore, W. B. Baring, Poulett Thomson, Wilmot Horton, Lord Monteagle, Charles Hay Cameron, J. D. Hume, James Morrison, Edwin Chadwick, Charles Buller, and Sir William Clay. George Grote too was a member. Significant elections beyond that date include Robert Lowe, Sir G. C. Lewis, Rowland Hill, Stafford Northcote, Goschen, Gladstone, and W. E. Forster.

The procedure of the Club was to hold a dinner on the first Monday of every month from December to June. (July was substituted for January from 1832.) By prior arrangement one member would speak to a particular question, and the discussion of the question would then go on for several hours. The questions themselves covered an enormous range. In only the first two years they included such theoretical and practical questions as the duty on corn, gluts, the effect of machinery, tax theory, Poor Laws, the colonial system, the demand for labour, profits and the rate of interest, the national debt, tithes, monetary theory, trade policy, value, and the improvements in political economy since the *Wealth of Nations*.

The Royal Statistical Society was founded, as the Statistical Society of London, in February 1834. The founders included such men as Charles Babbage, Richard Jones, Malthus, and William Whitmore. It too helped to provide an institutional means of welding the Classical economists into a scientific community. Malthus was the only original member from amongst our three groups, but later members included Overstone, Norman, Tooke, Newmarch, Torrens, Scrope, McCulloch, and Senior. It also included men not in our three groups though they wrote on economics, including Babbage, J. W. Gilbart, Jones, Frederick Hendriks, Thorold Rogers, W. L. Sargant, Leone Levi, Herman Merivale, and G. R. Porter who, with McCulloch, must rank as the chief economic statistician of his age—even Tooke and Newmarch, incomparable though they were in their particular field, did not cover such a wide area. The Statistical Society was not as important as the Political Economy Club in linking the economists: for one thing, it was not founded until 1834. But it reinforced the effects of the Club and some of the economists—including Overstone who was President 1851-3—were active in supporting its meetings. But the biggest guns do not seem to have involved themselves greatly in the Society: it was mainly dominated by men like G. R. Porter, and the 'fringe' economic writers listed above. Newmarch however came in time to dominate the Society—he presented a great many papers to the Society, was its Secretary and editor of its Journal, and its President 1869-71. Tooke too was prominent in the Society and on his death it endowed a Chair of Economics at King's College London and a Tooke Prize. But the fact that most of the big guns were little involved was important; apart from anything else it meant that the *Journal* of the Society, which could have become a professional journal for the economists never took on this role.

The Society had grown out of the Statistical Section of the British Association, itself only dating from 1833. The annual meetings of the Association provided the opportunity for a further link between the economists. However it for long mainly involved men like G. R. Porter together with some writers on economics outside our groups such as Gilbart and Hancock of Dublin. Gradually a few of the more important names appeared; Overstone took the chair in 1852 (when Gilbart, Hancock, and the historical economist Cliffe Leslie were also present). In 1853 Tooke was a Vice-President and in 1854 President, while Newmarch was one of the Secretaries of the Section. He began increasingly to contribute papers to this section and to assume great importance in it. By 1857 Cairnes had joined Newmarch as a Secretary, and Hancock and Leslie were both on the Section's Committee, together with another historical economist J. K. Ingram. Cairnes too became a frequent contributor of papers, as did Leslie and Fawcett, the latter becoming a member of the Committee and a Vice-President. Strangely enough the central figures of Classical economics participated only in old age. Senior was President in 1860 (succeeded the following year by Newmarch) and in 1863 and 1864 Torrens was a member of the Comittee and contributed papers.

The last institution linking the Classical economists was the Royal Society. This, dating from the 1650s, was designedly a society of natural scientists, but it contained for many years a number of those eminent in other fields—indeed they were for long in the majority. The natural scientists resented this and in the 1820s and 1830s they made attempts to alter it, although it was not until 1847 that they achieved any real success. Thus it was that it numbered amongst its members Malthus, Tooke, Newmarch (incidentally elected long after the reform of 1847), William Blake, and Scrope (the last however elected for his natural science work). The Society also included a number of 'fringe' economists, notably G. R. Porter, J. W. Gilbart, and Babbage.

Probably equal in importance to the institutional links between the Classical economists were those afforded by periodical literature. In our own day scientific and other kinds of academic communities are linked to a considerable extent, and their subject matter develops and is refined, through the publication of articles in professional academic journals. For the economist this means such publications as the *Economic Journal* and the *American Economic Review*. But during the era of Classical economics such publications simply did not exist. Fortunately however there was something else which filled the role admirably. This was the circulation of the various reviews.

The senior of them, in terms of foundation, influence, and content was undoubtedly the *Edinburgh Review*. It was founded in 1802 by Francis Horner and two other men once celebrated, Sidney Smith and Francis

Jeffrey. Several of the early contributors had studied under Dugald Stewart
at Edinburgh, and the *Review* had a decidedly economic bent from its
earliest days. Its circulation approached 14,000 at times and there may have
been up to five readers for every copy. It was widely read by the middle and
upper classes, and it provided an important outlet for economic articles and
summaries for its readers of the current state of economic debate on an
enormously wide range of issues. The contributors included McCulloch (who
had a major share of economic articles for nearly twenty years), Horner,
Malthus, James Mill, Torrens, Senior, and J. S. Mill. Professor F. W. Fetter,
the leading authority on these reviews, has pointed out that fifteen members
of the Political Economy Club wrote for the *Edinburgh*, compared with six
for the *Westminster Review*, four for the *Quarterly Review*, and none for
*Blackwood's Edinburgh Magazine*; and that by 1850 the *Edinburgh* had
published about 250 economic articles with known authors. Of these seventy-
eight were by McCulloch, fifty-four by other members of the Club, and
some of the remainder by friends of members. By contrast the *Quarterly*
carried 200 such articles up to 1850—but only seven were by Club members.

The *Quarterly Review* was started by the Tories in 1809, in order to
oppose the Whig *Edinburgh*. To do this it found itself printing many economic articles. Apart from writers basically opposed to Classical economics
its authors included Huskisson, Malthus, Scrope, Senior, and the latter's
friend Archbishop Whately.

*Blackwood's Edinburgh Magazine* was founded in 1817 by the Edinburgh
ultra-Tories. It was strenuously contemptuous of economics and published
articles full of vulgar ridicule and coarse abuse directed at economists—
above all at McCulloch. Very different from this, and far more important,
was the *Westminster Review* founded in 1824 by Jeremy Bentham. It was
designed to promote the views of the utilitarians and the philosophical radicals, and James Mill and (later) J. S. Mill were much involved in it. But it
also carried articles by Scrope and by 'fringe' economists such as W. R.
Greg, Gilbart, and Perronet Thompson. Unlike the *Quarterly* and *Blackwood's* it worked within the general framework of Classical economics and
it was an important source of economic literature. Its circulation was small:
compared with 14,000 *Edinburgh*'s it sold 2,000 to 3,000 while the *Quarterly*
sold 10,000, and even *Blackwood's* managed 6,000. But its economic output
was of excellent quality—significantly better than anything the *Quarterly*
or *Blackwood's* had to offer—and amongst the Classical economists it was
well read.

Of course articles in the Reviews were not the limit of the Classical economists' contributions to periodicals. There were also newspapers. J. S. Mill
was involved with one called the *Examiner*, and Torrens was a major
proprietor of the *Globe and Traveller* for which he also wrote. J. R.
McCulloch contributed in the years 1817–27 a significant number of

economic articles, often on theoretical subjects, to the *Scotsman*, the front
page of which he frequently occupied. Many of the original formulations of
his ideas appeared in the paper. He later contributed to the *Courier* and
*The Times*; and Overstone published some important material in the paper
under the pen name 'Mercator' in the years 1855–7. James Wilson, one of the
arch-opponents of the Bank Act of 1844, founded and wrote for *The
Economist*.

There were also other reviews, including the *Foreign Quarterly Review*,
which carried seven articles by McCulloch in the years 1829–33, and the
short-lived *London Review* for which Senior wrote. There was also the
*Foreign and Colonial Quarterly Review* and the *North British Review* for
which an economic writer a little outside the Classical fold, Thomas
Chalmers, wrote articles in the years 1844–7.

Of course all these articles were anonymous. But at the time they were
written their authorship was pretty well known to their readers; or if not
known exactly, the readers would have a short list of perhaps three or four
people who were likely to have written the article. Sometimes their identification might be erroneous: but on the whole it was strong enough for the
Reviews to add to the sense of community. Indeed it should be clear from
the material of this section that the Classical economists *did*, to some extent,
constitute a 'scientific community', a fact which is further borne out by their
published correspondence, although there is not space to detail that here.

V. THE ECONOMIC HISTORY OF THE CLASSICAL AGE

What the Classical economists wrote and believed, the body of ideas they
developed, was influenced to a considerable extent by the discussion of those
ideas within their community. But it can hardly have been independent of
the momentous events of the economic history of their age. What follows
is a highly compressed attempt to indicate the most important threads of
this.

The Classical economists wrote and worked through an explosion of
economic growth for which there was no historical precedent, and which
they were faced with explaining and analysing. Population and income began
to grow together in the mid-eighteenth century. The population expansion
began in the 1740s and reached a growth rate of $3\frac{1}{2}$ per cent per decade by
1751–61. By 1810–20 the staggering figure was 16·9 per cent. The population
of England and Wales which had been less than 6 million in 1700 had
reached 22·7 million by 1871. At the beginning of the eighteenth century
national income was probably less than £50 million. By 1871 it had risen
nearly four times in the course of seventy years to £916·6 million. Despite
the population increase G.N.P. per head increased at greater than 1 per
cent per annum in the years 1801–71. Yet it is doubtful (though not impossible) that there was any significant rise in real wages up to about 1820.

From that date however wages did improve significantly, especially from 1840 onwards.

The period under consideration also saw a revolution in policy towards, and the volume of, trade. Policy largely followed a trend of liberalization (with the exception of the war years) after the publication of the *Wealth of Nations*. Pitt attempted reform of the customs in 1784–6 and Huskisson and Robinson pursued trade liberalization in the 1820s. However the most important reforms were those of Peel who, starting in 1842, began an important review of British tariffs culminating in the budget of 1845 (which saw duties on over 400 items removed) and the repeal of the Corn Laws in 1846. The volume of trade rose enormously; U.K. imports which were valued at £39·6 million in 1796 had risen to £103·0 million by 1853, with domestic exports increasing from £30·1 million to £71·4 million. This involved a great broadening of the range of commodities traded as the British economy expanded and diversified and it became sensitive to economic changes throughout the whole trading world.

Closely bound up with this was a fundamental change in the balance of the British economy. Agriculture, which accounted for 40–45 per cent of national income in the years 1700–76, had declined to only 26 per cent by 1821 and to 14 per cent by 1871. Between 1801 and 1871 its share of the labour force fell from 36 per cent to 15 per cent. It became increasingly unreasonable to reason in terms of a basically agricultural economy.

The role of the agricultural innovations in all this cannot have been insignificant—either for agriculture, or for the history of ideas. The agricultural labour force was about 1·7 million in 1801 and 1·8 million in 1871; during the same period agricultural output rose from £75·5 million to £130·4 million.

The rise of the manufacturing sector to predominance was impressive; probably the most impressive single factor to contemporary economic writers. Accounting for 24 per cent (£30·3 million) of G.N.P. in 1770 it accounted for 38 per cent (£348·9 million) by 1871. The great staple industries grew up in this period; output of the cotton industry rose from £0·6 million in 1760 to £104·9 million in 1871. Parallel with all this, and inseparable from it were changes in transport. There were only 70 miles of railway open as late as 1826–30; by 1864 there were nearly 11,000 miles. The special position of the railways forced the State to intervene in their running; and this was but one aspect of the great growth of effective state power in this era, even though much state regulation (largely dating from the Tudor and Stuart eras, and more honoured in the breach than the observance) was swept away. This is reflected in the rise in state spending from £14 million in 1776 to nearly £70 million in 1870.

Other significant economic changes took place during the period, notably in the monetary sphere, and though there is not space to detail them here they undoubtedly exercised a strong influence on the thinking of contemporaries. The interested student may pursue some of the references at the end of this chapter. But having surveyed the Classical-economic stage it is now time to examine the roots from which Classical economics sprang.

## NOTES

1. See R. L. Meek, *The Economics of Physiocracy* (London, 1962).
2. 'Notice of a General Mathematical Theory of Political Economy' (1862), printed in the *Journal of the [Royal] Statistical Society*, 29 (1866). See R. D. C. Black, Introduction to Jevons, *The Theory of Political Economy* (London, 1970), pp. 12 ff.
3. Randolph Churchill, *Winston S. Churchill* (London, 1967), *Vol. I Companion*, Pt. I, p. 585.
4. J. A. Schumpeter, *History of Economic Analysis* (London, 1954), p. 473. See also Chapters 2 and 3 below.
5. See Ricardo's *Works*, ed. Sraffa, V. 85.
6. They are contained in the appendix to Lord Robbins, *Robert Torrens and the Evolution of Classical Economics* (London, 1958).
7. James Mill was particularly doubtful about education in the ancient universities: see D. P. O'Brien, *The Correspondence of Lord Overstone* (Cambridge, 1971), ii. 486, n. 2. But he played an important part in the founding of London University.
8. See Schumpeter, op. cit., p. 159, for earlier chairs in Continental Europe.
9. See D. P. O'Brien, *J. R. McCulloch, A Study in Classical Economics* (London, 1970), Ch. IV.
10. Ibid., Ch. III.
11. Ibid., Ch. VI.
12. See D. P. O'Brien, *Lord Overstone*, i. 5–8, 10–47, and *passim*.

## BIBLIOGRAPHY

The bibliography for a chapter in a work of this sort can only skim the available literature. What follows is an attempt to indicate some further references bearing on the material in the text. The two great source books of economics are fortunately available in excellent editions. See Adam Smith, *An Inquiry into the Nature and Causes of the Wealth of Nations*, ed. E. Cannan (London, 1904), and D. Ricardo, *Principles Of Political Economy and Taxation*, which is Vol. i of the magnificent *Works and Correspondence of David Ricardo*, ed. P. Sraffa with M. H. Dobb (Cambridge, 1951–5). The most important works of the Group II writers are as follows: T. R. Malthus, *Principles of Political Economy, Considered with a View to their Practical Application* (London, 1820 and 1836); James Mill, *Elements of Political Economy* (London, 1821), rep. in D. Winch (ed.), *James Mill, Selected Economic Writings* (Edinburgh, 1966); J. S. Mill, *Principles of Political Economy*, ed. W. J. Ashley (London, 1909); J. R. McCulloch, *The Principles of Political Economy with a Sketch of the Rise and Progress of the Science* (4th edn. Edinburgh, 1849); R. Torrens, *The Principles and Practical Operation of Sir Robert Peel's Act of 1844, Explained and Defended* (3rd edn. London, 1858); J. B. Say, *Traité d'économie politique* (Paris, 1803, 4th edn. trans. C. R. Prinsep, rep. New York, 1964); N. W. Senior, *Selected Writings on Economics* (A. M. Kelley, New York, 1966); T. Tooke (with W. Newmarch), *A History of Prices and of the State of the Circulation from 1793* (London, 1838–57); H. Fawcett, *Manual of Political Economy* (London, 1863); J. E. Cairnes, *Leading Principles of Political Economy Newly Expounded* (London, 1874). It is perhaps unnecessary in a work of this kind to detail the leading works of the Group III writers though mention may be made of D. Hume's *Essays and Treatises on Several Subjects* of which there have been many edns. since their first appearance in 1752 (and of which there is a useful selection in D. Hume, *Writings on Economics*, ed. E. Rotwein, Madison, Winsconsin, 1955) and J. R. McCulloch's *Select Collection of ... Tracts ... on Paper Currency* (London, 1857, rep. New York, 1966), which includes the most important works of Thornton and Blake as well as the Bullion Report. General secondary references abound: the two best are probably J. A. Schumpeter's mighty *History of Economic Analysis* (London, 1954), and M. Blaug, *Economic Theory in Retrospect* (London, 1961). See also A. L. Macfie, *The Individual in Society* (London, 1967), for a discussion of the Scottish tradition. Those interested in the delineation of the era of Classical economics should consult the introduction to Adam Smith's *Lectures on Police, Justice, Revenue and Arms*, ed. E. Cannan (London, 1896), and to his *Lectures on Rhetoric and Belles Lettres*, ed. J. M. Lothian (Edinburgh, 1963), as well as R. L. Meek, *The Economics of Physiocracy* (London, 1962). For the other end of the chronology see R. D. C. Black's introduction to Jevons's *Theory of Political Economy* (London, 1971). An excellent general survey is provided within a brief compass by Donald Winch, *The Emergence of Economics as a Science* (London, 1971).

There are many articles and a number of books about individual economists. See in particular Lord Robbins, *Robert Torrens and the Evolution of Classical Economics* (London, 1958), which includes a superb bibliographical summary of each of Torrens's works; M. E. A. Bowley, *Nassau Senior and Classical Economics* (London, 1937); S. Leon Levy, *Nassau W. Senior 1790–1864* (New York, 1970); D. P. O'Brien, *J. R. McCulloch, A Study in Classical Economics* (London, 1970); Ricardo's *Works*, ed. Sraffa (Vol. x contains biographical material); P. Schwartz, *The New Political Economy of J. S. Mill* (London, 1972). See also O. St. Clair, *A Key to Ricardo* (London, 1957) (the best guide to what Ricardo actually said) and M. Blaug, *Ricardian Economics* (New Haven, 1958). There are a number of biographies of economists; interesting material will be found in John Rae, *Life of Adam Smith*, rep. with a fascinating introduction by Jacob Viner (New York, 1965); A. Bain, *James Mill: a Biography* (London, 1882), and J. Bonar, *Malthus and his Work* (London, 1885). There are also two important autobiographies, that of J. S. Mill, which is available in many edns. and that of De Quincey in his *Confessions*. De Quincey in fact left a lot of biographical material—see Vols. 1–3 of his *Works*, ed. Masson (London, 1896). There are also a number of articles about particular economists; see in particular F. W. Fetter, 'Robert Torrens: Colonel of Marines and Political Economist', *Economica*, 29 (1962), 152–65; and the same author's 'The Life and Writings of John Wheatley', *Journal of Political Economy*, 50 (1942), 357–76; R. L. Meek, 'Thomas Joplin and the Theory of Interest', *Review of Economic Studies*, 18 (1950–1), 154–63; R. Opie, 'A Neglected British Economist: George Poulett Scrope', *Quarterly Journal of Economics*, 44 (1930), 101–37. Edns. of the writings of economists other than Smith and Ricardo are becoming increasingly available: see for instance D. Winch, *James Mill: Selected Economic Writings* (Edinburgh, 1966) (this contains much valuable biographical material and commentary); F. W. Fetter, *The Economic Writings of Francis Horner* (London, 1957); F. A. Hayek's edn. of Henry Thornton's *Enquiry into the Nature and Effects of the Paper Credit of Great Britain* (1802; London, 1939); R. D. C. Black, *Economic Writings of Mountifort Longfield* (New York, 1971); D. P. O'Brien, *J. R. McCulloch: Treatise on Taxation* (Edinburgh, 1974). There is also a magnificent new edn. of the works of J. S. Mill appearing from Toronto University Press: and the introductions to his *Essays* (by Lord Robbins) and the *Principles* (by V. W. Bladen) are especially valuable.

The student interested in pursuing the idea of the Classical economists as a community should start with the following references: F. W. Fetter's 'The Authorship of Economic Articles in the *Edinburgh Review* 1802–47', *Journal of Political Economy*, 61 (1953), 232–59; 'The Economic Articles in the *Quarterly Review* and their Authors, 1809–52', *Journal of Political Economy*, 66 (1958), 47–64, 154–70; 'Economic Articles in 'Blackwood's', *Scottish Journal of Political Economy*, 7 (1960), 85–107, 213–31; 'The Economic Articles in the *Westminster Review* and their Authors, 1824–51', *Journal of Political Economy*, 70 (1962), 570–96; 'Economic Controversy in the British Reviews, 1802–1850', *Economica*, 32, (1965), 424–37. The great general source for authorship of review articles is now W. Houghton *et al.*, *The Wellesley Index to Victorian Periodicals* (Toronto, 1966). Vols. vi to ix of Ricardo's *Works* contains his correspondence with his contemporaries amongst economists; Vol. ii of the same edn. contains his *Notes on Malthus*. See also *The Correspondence of Lord Overstone*, ed. D. P. O'Brien (Cambridge, 1971)—this also contains letters throwing light on Torrens's battles with authority. J. S. Mill's correspondence is also being published in the Toronto edition of Mill: see *The Earlier Letters of John Stuart Mill 1812–1848*, ed. F. E. Mineka, 2 vols. (Toronto, 1963).

The Political Economy Club's *Centenary Volume* (London, 1921) contains the necessary source material on the Club; on the institutions see *Annals of the Royal Statistical Society* (London, 1934); O. J. R. Howarth, *The British Association ... A Retrospect* (London, 1922); and *The Record of the Royal Society of London* (London, 1940).

Those wishing to get a broader view of the literature than that presented here should see the catalogues of the Kress Library (Boston Mass. 1940–67) and the Goldsmith Library (London 1970) and R. D. C. Black, *A Catalogue of Pamphlets on Economic Subjects ... 1750 ... 1900 in Irish Libraries* (Belfast, 1969). There is also a valuable work by one of the Classical economists, J. R. McCulloch's *The Literature of Political Economy* (London, 1845).

Three references on the whole question of scientific revolutions will suffice here. The origin of the approach is to be found in T. S. Kuhn, *The Structure of Scientific Revolutions* (Chicago, 1962); see also A. W. Coats, 'Is there a "Structure of Scientific Revolutions" in Economics', *Kyklos*, 22 (1969), 289–96; and M. Bronfenbrenner, 'The "Structure of Revolutions" in Economic Thought', *History of Political Economy*, 3 (1971), 136–51.

Finally there is the economic history of the age, of which only the briefest sketch was offered above. The most useful references here are W. H. B. Court, *A Concise Economic History of Britain from 1750 to Recent Times* (Cambridge, 1954), P. Deane, *The First Industrial Revolution* (Cambridge, 1965); P. Deane and W. A. Cole, *British Economic Growth 1688–1959* (Cambridge, 1964); B. R. Mitchell with P. Deane, *Abstract of British Historical Statistics* (Cambridge, 1962). The figures given in the text above are drawn from these sources. There is also the great work by Sir John Clapham, *An Economic History of Modern Britain*, 3 vols. (Cambridge, 1926–38).

# 2. The Roots of Classical Economics

## i. INTRODUCTION

This chapter is called the Roots of Classical Economics but the roots from which the system emerged are only a part of what it will be necessary to consider here. The subject may be likened to the examination of a fully matured and unpruned tree. First we shall look at the roots from which Classical economics sprang and the soil which nurtured those roots. Next we shall examine the main trunk—the system produced in the *Wealth of Nations* which provided *the* great foundation for all the Classical economists, not least Ricardo. Then we shall look at a major branch which grew from the main trunk—Ricardo's system, a branch which grew up alongside the main trunk but which itself produced branches which intertwined with those of the main trunk. Finally, we shall try to make some tentative generalizations about the predominant strands in the work of the Classical economists who came after Smith and Ricardo.

Because economics grew out of so many other subjects, particularly philosophy, its roots were enormously widespread and any attempt to be all-inclusive must fail at the outset. In a sense we need to know the roots of British education in the eighteenth century. But it is still possible to say something sensible about the origins of Classical economics. Smith and Ricardo are the two great founders of Classical economics and their work, especially that of Smith, pervades all of Classical economics. But they did not write in a vacuum, cut off from all other influences. In particular, Smith was a highly educated man. We therefore need to look not only at pre-Classical economics but also at the general intellectual influences to which a highly educated man was subject, including the work of the natural-law philosophers.

## ii. THE INTELLECTUAL ENVIRONMENT

The intellectual currents which produced Classical economics were of two main kinds. On the one hand there were the philosophers. These included not only the recognized natural-law philosophers such as Grotius, Pufendorf, and Adam Smith's teacher Hutcheson, but also David Hume, who was critical of much of natural law, and Comte. The other important intellectual current which produced Classical economics was the output of economic writings of the pre-Classical economic writers; the mercantilists (and their free-trade critics) and, of particular importance, the Physiocrats, as well as the work of brilliant individual writers such as Cantillon and Petty.

Apart from the intellectual currents which produced Classical economics there were also important historical and institutional influences. These included such factors as population growth, the rise of the nation state, the development of bourgeois society, the Industrial Revolution, and, at least partly because of the pressures produced by these developments, a growing discontent with such regulations as the Navigation Laws and the Corn Laws. Such influences as these cannot be wholly disregarded; indeed it is important to recognize that many, if not all, the major developments in economics have owed a significant debt to such outside influences. But having said that, it has also to be recognized that, with the exception of the Corn Laws and their influence on Ricardo, which will be returned to below, there is often very little that the historian of theory (as distinct from the historian of opinion) can point to as *specific* examples of the operation of such influences. The treatment here will then concentrate on the intellectual influences.

Of these the most important by far, at least for Adam Smith (and through him for Classical economics in general) was the influence of the natural-law philosophers. Any natural-law system involves four basic propositions; and it may also, though it does not necessarily do so, involve several others. The four basic propositions are as follows: that there is an underlying order in material phenomena; that this underlying order is discoverable either by reasoning from observed phenomena or from innate moral sense; that discovery of the underlying order leads to the formulation of natural laws which, if followed, lead to the best possible situation; and that positive legislation should reflect these natural laws. A natural-law system may also involve the following further propositions: that natural laws are productive of immutable forces which man cannot deflect or impede—this will be called *determinism*; that if freedom is accorded then society will progress harmoniously to a better state—this will be called *harmony theory*; and that therefore the operation of natural laws requires a great degree of freedom to achieve their ends—this will be called the *natural liberty* doctrine.

Now the European tradition of natural-law philosophy, though it had its roots in the Ancient Classical writers, especially Aristotle, stemmed mainly from medieval Scholasticism—which means essentially the writings of St. Thomas Aquinas and those who followed him in the fourteenth, fifteenth, and sixteenth centuries. The Scholastic version of natural law involved a theological adaptation of Aristotle. If the natural law, as discovered by St. Thomas and his followers, were adhered to then men would progress towards their ideal fulfilment. It was thus what is called an optimistic teleology. The direct influence of the Scholastics on Classical economics was probably negligible. But they did have a direct influence on the Physiocratic conception of natural law, as we shall see; and through the successive adaptations of their system by the Protestant natural-law theorists, especially Grotius, Pufendorf, and Hutcheson, they exercised an indirect influence on Adam Smith.

The medieval theory was a theological theory. It contained the belief that the natural laws were of God's making—the Maker's instructions for the operation of worldly affairs. When we come however to the Protestant natural-law philosophers we find that God's role in the formulation of these laws becomes a good deal less prominent. A process of securalization of the natural law was beginning. Hugo Grotius (1583–1645), who advanced a theory of international relations based on natural law, stated the concept in the following terms:

The law of nature is a dictate of right reason, which points out that an act, according as it is or is not in conformity with rational nature, has in it a quality of moral baseness or moral necessity; and that, in consequence, such an act is either forbidden or enjoined by the author of nature, God.

But God is essentially a fifth wheel in this formulation. If natural laws are to be derived in this way then whether or not God is their author is not immediately relevant. As the quotation shows the seventeenth-century writers were reluctant to commit themselves to such a separation; but their writings suggested it, and the free-thinking David Hume was to make the proposition quite explicit in the next century. Grotius is now generally recognized as having made the first attempt to obtain a principle of right and a basis for society and government outside the Church and the Bible. Natural law was connected by him with a social instinct supposedly possessed by all men as an intrinsic part of their nature. Samuel Pufendorf (1622–94) in his *De Jure Naturae et Gentium* started with the theories of Grotius and sought to develop them in the light of the writings of Hobbes and of his own ideas. The natural law was to be derived through reasoning from experience and to be applied to the regulation of conduct between men in this world. Though the state of nature was not one of war (as Hobbes had argued) but one of peace, it was a feeble and insecure peace which thus needed regulation.

Thomas Hobbes (1588–1679) himself is chiefly significant in the particular context under discussion not because of his concept of a social contract based on fear for which he is chiefly famous, but because both he and John Locke offered as part of their natural-law apparatus a theory of a right to property acquired through labour—a fundamental idea in Classical economics which regarded security of property as of central importance for economic motivation and economic growth. Locke (1632–1704) also offered a sense psychology; and although, like most such writers, he offered a list of senses, these boiled down to motivation by seeking of pleasure and avoidance of pain, which was to become, in various guises, a common property of eighteenth-century natural-law writers.

One of these writers was Francis Hutcheson (1694–1746) Professor of Moral Philosophy at Glasgow from 1729. Building on the work of another English natural-law philosopher, Shaftesbury, he produced an idea of natural law as being in accord with an innate moral sense—his principle of 'benevolence'. Although Adam Smith was critical of this in his *Theory of Moral Sentiments* it is easy to see how it led to the principle of 'sympathy' which provided the basis for morals in Smith and of which more will be said below. Unlike Hobbes's, Hutcheson's theory was not deterministic; men were free to act according to their moral sentiments. At the same time it was a harmony theory. Such a non-deterministic harmony version of natural law was to be of great importance for the development of Classical economics. Hutcheson also held a utilitarian theory—he regarded as natural laws those rules of conduct which tended to promote the greatest happiness of mankind; and his natural law, despite frequent references to God (who had implanted the principle of benevolence in human beings) was a secular one, developed from the works of Grotius and Pufendorf. It was because of these characteristics of his philosophy indeed that in 1738 he was accused before the Glasgow Presbytery of teaching two 'false and dangerous doctrines': that the standard of moral goodness was the promotion of the happiness of others; and that it was possible to have a knowledge of good and evil without a knowledge of God. Both these doctrines were fundamental to the view of natural law which Adam Smith was to develop and which Classical economics inherited.

It is in the sixteenth- and eighteenth-century natural-law writers that the *harmony* element, which was to characterize much of Classical economics appears most strongly. However an important point must be made here. The Classical economists from Smith onwards recognized fundamental flaws in the harmony of the unregulated natural order. Ultimately they believed that harmony could be achieved only through the creation of a legal and non-legal framework within which men had to operate. The physical scientists were trying to find a harmony in nature through empiricism and the experimental method; and the natural-law philosophers tried to find the same in society. The economists who followed the philosophers were however much less convinced of the inherent harmony. But economics grew out of the natural-law systems; it was for long treated as part of a comprehensive social science—Moral Philosophy. This included natural ethics, natural jurisprudence, police (policy)—the latter included economics—and revenue (public finance). Thus it was that Adam Smith's lectures, in which most of the fundamental ideas of the *Wealth of Nations* are to be found came to be *Lectures on Justice, Police, Revenue and Arms.*[1] Both the *Wealth of Nations* and Adam Smith's other great work *The Theory of Moral Sentiments*[2] were part of a larger whole, and Adam Smith also contemplated, though he probably never completed, a separate work on *Justice.* It is only with the developments founded on the *Wealth of Nations* that economics became too large to be incorporated into the whole.

Given that the later natural-law writers had laid down so much not only in their view of society but also in their utilitarianism and their sense psychology, it is easy to see that the independent contribution of Utilitarianism proper, stemming from the writings of Jeremy Bentham (1748–1832), was limited. Writers on the history of ideas have been rather free with the label 'Utilitarian' (and also with the associated one, 'Philosophical Radical') but there is little justification for according Utilitarianism a major independent role in relation to the development of Classical economics. The pain/pleasure psychology was common eighteenth-century property and indeed all that the Utilitarians did was to turn it into a tautology—by definition a man was motivated by pursuit of pleasure and avoidance of pain, so any action, however benevolent in appearance, must be undertaken for the pleasure it gave or the avoidance of (psychological) pain which would be associated with an alternative course of action.

The Benthamite welfare criterion of the greatest happiness of the greatest number had already been supplied by Hutcheson who had even used that precise phrase.[3] Moreover such an approach was not confined to those who were primarily natural-law philosophers; the Physiocrats' writings had a highly utilitarian character—for them, ascertaining the precepts of nature meant ascertaining what was necessary for the greatest general good—and Adam Smith too adopted a similar position, particularly in making the judgement, thenceforth fundamental to economics, that the interests of (numerous) consumers should prevail over those of (less numerous) producers. The harmony elements in the Benthamite writings were borrowed from the natural-law philosophers, and the Benthamite stress on the necessity of security of property was common amongst natural-law philosophers at least from the time of Locke's development of the idea of right to property through labour, and is certainly to be found in Smith.

Moreover when we ask ourselves who, amongst the Classical economists, can be classed as Utilitarians, we find that only the two Mills, apart from Bentham himself, were really Utilitarians, and the younger Mill rejected Utilitarianism for a while although he later came back to it at least to the extent of endorsing the 'greatest happiness' principle. Ricardo, though he was sympathetic, was not a Utilitarian.

The great contribution of the Utilitarians was in the field of policy. They were deeply committed reformers, and Bentham in particular produced an ambitious programme of reform. They supplied the radical element in Classical economics; but this was not a theoretical contribution. Their only significant theoretical contribution was J. S. Mill's tax theory developed in terms of equal sacrifices of utility. Bentham himself, who wrote on economics for eighteen years, could have produced an important and subtle monetary theory—but he did not, and he seems to have influenced Ricardo's *Principles* not at all.

If the influence of Utilitarianism has been occasionally over-emphasized a little, that of A. Comte (1798–1857) on the other hand is not always perhaps sufficiently recognized. Even though he directly influenced only one Classical economist, that one was J. S. Mill. His peculiar use of the terms 'statics' and 'dynamics', the former indicating the equilibrating mechanisms of non-evolutionary phenomena, and the latter the behaviour of evolutionary phenomena in society, was taken over by J. S. Mill. In couching a lot of his treatment of economic problems in terms of such dynamics, Mill essentially adopted the approach to be found in the *Wealth of Nations*, where allocative problems are treated in a context of onward-moving growth.

The position of David Hume (1711–76) is of special importance. His intellectual development proceeded with (or perhaps somewhat ahead of) that of Adam Smith himself, and contact with Hume was to prove of great importance to Smith. His psychology, which was a variant of the pain/pleasure approach—man is motivated by a desire for pleasure, or for action, stimulation, or gain, all of which give pleasure—was perhaps not of great importance to Smith because Smith's own psychological approach could well have been developed from other sources, and there is indeed a distinct contrast between Hume's view of pleasure derived from activity and the Classical emphasis on disutility of labour. Moreover his explanation of the sense of justice as due to a sense of the social utility of compelling men to respect the rights of their fellows and to sympathy with the general happiness thus protected, conflicts with Smith's own explanation of the sense as deriving from sympathy with the feelings of others. But his complete freeing of a theory of the origin of laws from Divine planning helped to prepare the way for the separation of a theory of economic behaviour from Moral Philosophy; and, most important of all, his philosophy was productive of contributions to economic theory which are of fundamental importance in their own right. We shall see, when we come to examine the Classical monetary theory, that Hume's analysis provided its very foundations. But his economic writings also covered interest theory (and the real interest theory of Classical economics stems largely from his work and that of Turgot), growth theory, trade theory (including the role of trade in growth), taxation, and debt policy.

Of course Hume was not the only one of the philosophers to write on specifically economic matters. The Scholastic writers had advanced a subjective value theory and a theory of money, although there is no real evidence of their influence on Classical economics in these matters. Grotius had argued that free trade was a natural right and pointed to the benefits of territorial division of labour. Pufendorf, following the Scholastics, distinguished value in use and value in exchange, and argued that the latter depended on relative scarcity of goods and money but gravitated towards cost of production, thus indicating the just price. Indeed he has been hailed by Schumpeter as producing 'an embryonic *Wealth of Nations*'.

The inheritance of Classical economics from the natural-law philosophers was then of fundamental importance. Its inheritance from the primarily economic writers who came before the *Wealth of Nations* is much more doubtful. The inheritance of Classical economics from the mercantilists was slight: indeed the *Wealth of Nations* was a mighty blow against the whole mercantilist ethic. Although the concept of economic man is common among the mercantilist writers (which is perhaps hardly surprising since they were largely pleading special cases themselves) it was something which Adam Smith could be expected to have arrived at when dealing with pain/pleasure psychology in an economic context. When we look at the leading features of mercantilism—bullion and treasure as the key to wealth, regulation of foreign trade to produce a specie inflow, promotion of industry by inducing cheap raw-material imports, protection against imported manufactures, export encouragement, trade viewed as a zero-sum game—we realize that the mercantilist system was the complete antithesis of Classical economics.

The influence of Sir William Petty 1623–87) on Classical economics, although he was not a mercantilist but a brilliant and isolated original, was also limited. Though his work was known to Smith and the other Classical writers, his pioneering quantitative efforts produced more admiration than imitation, and the other key concepts which he had, such as the division of labour, were derived by Smith from Hutcheson. But there is probably a case to be made out, as we shall see when looking at the Classical views on public finance, for his having exercised some influence in the matter of tax theory, especially on Adam Smith.

The influence of Richard Cantillion (1697–1734) is still more problematical. Although the writing of his great *Essai*[4] predates the *Essays* of David Hume[5] it was published later—as late as 1755—and the elements of his thought which were to prove important in the development of Classical economics—notably in monetary theory—had very largely been independently developed and published by Hume. But his discussion of relative wages in different occupations[6]—and also his discussion of market and natural price—foreshadows what Smith had to say quite closely. However if Smith's treatment was derivative here, it was undoubtedly superior.

The influence of the free-trade writers who came before Smith was probably not important. Professor Jacob Viner in his exhaustive *Studies in the Theory of International Trade*[7] was able to find only five genuine free-trade writers before Smith. Of these two, Sir Dudley North,[8] and the anonymous author of *Considerations on the East India Trade*[9] were little known, and one, Gervaise,[10] was virtually unknown. There is no evidence that the other two—Paterson[11] and Whatley[12]—exercised any real influence on Smith or the other Classical writers.

The importance for Classical economics of a number of writers who had dealt with the subject of population was however more substantial. Although the population doctrine normally associated with Classical economics stems initially from Malthus's *Essay on Population* of 1798[13] he had a number of precursors, and the general idea of some sort of population mechanism, although not in anything like such a deterministic form as that advanced (initially at least) by Malthus, was to be the common property of eighteenth-century writers. The doctrine stems at least from Botero writing in 1589[14] and is to be found in such eighteenth-century writers as Wallace and Townsend and also in David Hume.[15] Smith incorporated the general idea into the *Wealth of Nations* although he followed the non-deterministic pre-Malthusian pattern.

But with the exception of the population writers, the importance for Classical economics of most pre-Classical *economic* (as distinct from philosophical) writing is questionable. However there can be no question about the importance of the first great school of economic writers, the Physiocrats. Their system involved two main elements: a natural-law framework, and a theory of economic relationships within that framework. The first of these was arguably not important for Classical economics because Smith developed his own natural-law framework independently. Their own natural-law context owed a great deal to the Scholastic tradition. The natural law was to be discovered by reasoning on the basis of conduct observed where freedom already existed. The institutions of *L'ordre naturel* were to conform to the principles of *Droit naturel*. Maximum freedom under the monarchy and judiciary, both being guided by knowledge of natural law, was what was required. This did not involve inaction; thus for instance education was to be an important function of the State. But it did involve a great deal of freedom; and it was deterministic in that following the natural law was the only effective path. Within this natural-law framework men were to pursue their self-interest. Quesnay taught the idea of the individual pursuing his self-interest and thus maximizing general welfare. Men, being endowed with reason and free will, could adjust themselves to their environment so as to secure its benefits and avoid the incidental evils. They had to discover by reason the course laid down by Nature for optimization.

Now although there are obviously important parallels (as well as differences) between this and the harmony theory underlying Classical economics, it is arguable that Adam Smith's independent evolution of such a system (and there is no doubt it was independent because it is incorporated in the *Lectures* he gave before he ever went to France) was more important for Classical economics. But parts of their theory of economic relationships are of undoubted significance. Their concept of economic activity involved the idea of a circular flow of income between the three classes of landlords, farmers, and manufacturers. Only the farming class produced a 'produit net', viz. a total product greater than inputs (including its own subsistence). This concept of a circular flow was very probably the origin of Say's Law of Markets which was central to Classical macro-economic thought. The division into social classes suggested to Smith the need for a theory of distribution; and the concept of annual product and advances from this to get next year's production under way undoubtedly influenced Smith not least in providing him, either directly or through Turgot's *Réflexions* with a theory of capital. On other matters such as their recommendation of a single tax, they were less influential. But of the importance of the Physiocrats for Classical economics there can be no doubt.

We have now reviewed the soil and the roots from which Classical economics sprang. It is now time to look specifically at the great trunk of the Classical economic tree, the work of Adam Smith.

### iii. ADAM SMITH

Adam Smith, as an eighteenth-century philosopher and teacher of high standing, was a man well versed in a wide range of subjects. It is important to remember that he lectured not only on economics but also on broad philosophical questions and on literature. His knowledge of the ancient writers of Greece and Rome was obviously considerable, as was his acquaintance with the work of his contemporaries, especially Montesquieu, and his friend David Hume. But having said that, it is clear that, eclectic though Smith was, his whole approach developed out of the natural-law foundations outlined in the previous section.

The *Wealth of Nations* was in fact the first fully systematic quasi-natural-law treatment of economics. It is important to stress that it was a secular natural-law system which Smith was building on, following the tradition of Grotius and Hutcheson. He recognized variation of moral rules with time, place, and circumstance, in a somewhat similar way to Montesquieu in his great *Esprit des lois*. The contrast with the Physiocratic view of natural law is evident enough. The Physiocrats were much closer to the Scholastics in their view of the natural law and much more absolutist. It is true too that Adam Smith's theory involves no social contract, although such an idea was a hallmark of British natural-law philosophers. But if Adam Smith's system was different to that of the Physiocrats, and even, in some respects, to that of his English and Scottish predecessors, it was developed from a natural-law system none the less. One of Adam Smith's major claims to fame, in some ways his greatest, is his development of a unified concept of an economic system with mutually interdependent parts. His development of this came well before the *Wealth of Nations*: it is in the *Theory of Moral Sentiments* of 1759 and the Lectures of 1762–3. It was a very considerable achievement; and it was recognized as such by his successors. Thus it was that McCulloch who counted Adam Smith as his 'great economical chief' wrote of the *Wealth of Nations* that it was 'a work which has done for Political Economy what the Treatise of Grotius *de Jure Belli ac Pacis*, did for public law'.[16]

Adam Smith's underlying theory was a harmony theory. There was (or could be arranged) a beneficent order manifesting itself in the way in which phenomena interacted. The well-known phrase 'the invisible hand' which Smith uses in the *Wealth of Nations* is only one of several phrases for guiding Providence, in the *Theory of Moral Sentiments*. The exposition in the *Wealth of Nations* is much more particularized than that in the *Moral Sentiments* and much more reliance is placed on specific examples of harmony. It occurs through the beneficial results of the pursuit of self-interest (within a framework of law and custom) and manifests itself in such phenomena as the division of labour (with its origin in the propensity to barter), money, savings and investment, and trade. This developed out of a teleological view of the universe which Smith held and which is expounded in the *Moral Sentiments* (Part II, Section ii, esp. Ch. 3); although by the time he came to write the *Wealth of Nations* he was more concerned to stress the extent to which harmony required law.

The harmony view of natural phenomena, even though that harmony was recognized to be incomplete without the erection of a framework of law and custom as will be noted below, implied that resource allocation would be optimized by the workings of natural forces. The main motive force in resource allocation was self-interest.[17] It followed from Adam Smith's view of psychological motivation in an economic context. This was simple pursuit of self-interest, a view of human nature hilariously characterized by Bagehot as assuming 'a Scotsman in every man'. The pursuit of self-interest ensured (subject to an appropriate framework) optimal resource allocation. Thus Adam Smith wrote:

It is not from the benevolence of the butcher, the brewer or the baker that we expect our dinner, but from their regard to their own interest. We address ourselves, not to their humanity but to their self-love, and never talk to them of our own necessities but of their advantages.

Every individual is continually exerting himself to find out the most advantageous employment for whatever capital he can command. It is his own advantage, indeed, and not that of society, which he has in view. But the study of his own advantage naturally, or rather necessarily leads him to prefer that employment which is most advantageous to the society.[18]

Fundamentally involved in this was a view of competition between individuals, pursuing their self-interest, as providing the mechanism by which resources were allocated. Though it is true that such a view had been put forward earlier by Boisguillebert there is no reason for doubting that Adam

Smith's view of the competitive process was his own. Competition provided the means through which the pursuit of economic self-interest optimized the allocation of resources, and its *modus operandi* was the price system, Adam Smith's vision of which has stayed with economics ever since. Competition was central to the determination of prices, numbers of producers, knowledge, and resource mobility. But it is important to stress that it was not *perfect* competition that Smith was discussing, but atomistic competition: large numbers but with possibly significant, if localized, market imperfections, and with competitive activity taking place within a framework of growth not of fixed and known resources and technology. With Smith as with Marshall, trying to force what he has to say into a *perfectly* competitive framework is not helpful. The fundamental point about competition in Smith is that it ensures the elimination of excess profits and allocates capital (and hence other resources commanded by capital) when the technology of products and processess, tastes, and total resources are all in a state of flux. Competition is itself also part of the growth process; it widens the scope of the market and extends division of labour, increasing the productivity of that labour and leading to further capital accumulation.

But it must be stressed very strongly that all this presupposes the *framework* of Justice set out in the *Theory of Moral Sentiments*. Natural Justice sprang from sympathy in each man with the feelings of others. Sentiments of justice evolved in men's minds by the play of sympathy in their contacts with other men. Sympathy thus gave rise to private rules of behaviour. It also led to the formulation of positive laws. By the eighteenth century natural law was being increasingly derived not from human reason and observed phenomena alone, but from human reason and innate natural feelings and sentiments. Smith's view of natural law was of this kind; and the requirements of Justice were to be learnt in this way. Justice was entirely necessary because otherwise flaws in the unregulated order would manifest themselves. There were certain conflicts of interest if each person's self-interest was not regulated by Justice, for competition could not always be relied on to optimize. Thus there was a conflict of interest between masters and workmen over the level of wages and a tendency for conflict to arise if the masters colluded to depress wages.

Smith also found other flaws in the natural order; in general, positions of market power might be abused. Such characteristics of the order are given more prominence in the *Wealth of Nations*; and there is even the implication there that, because of its effects on moral character, division of labour is not to be strictly applauded. But there is no real conflict between the *Wealth of Nations* and the *Moral Sentiments* even though there are certainly differences of emphasis. One work offers a theory of the way in which both public and private laws limit the operation of individual interests where these may conflict with social interests.[19] The other offers a theory of the way in which individual interests, *thus limited*, produce optimal resource allocation for growth.

Since, within the confines of Justice, Smith held a harmony version of natural law, natural liberty as a policy prescription was an obvious corollary. This is in fact to be found not only in Smith's predecessors, notably Pufendorf and Hutcheson, but also in Smith's own *Lectures*. His material on the beneficial effects of freedom in fact dates from as early as 1751[20] and the *Lectures* set it forth clearly. Here we find the need for agricultural freedom, and for the removal of barriers not only to trade in agricultural goods but also to trade in agricultural resources. Progress in the arts (technology) and commerce is hindered by all duties, regulations, monopolies, corporations, apprenticeships, and similar devices. Regulation of price is condemned and protection is shown to distort the allocation of resources.

The exposition of the natural-liberty requirement in the *Wealth of Nations* is derived from examination of the operation of self-interest in the economic system, and the effects of government interference. But this is particularizing from the general system of the *Lectures*: and its roots are in the natural-law philosophers.

The stress on natural liberty left government with, on the face of it, a fairly circumscribed role. Adam Smith gives the three duties of the sovereign as defence, justice, and public works and institutions. At first sight this is very limited, and Smith undoubtedly tended to play down the role of government because he was interested in ending *mercantilist government* interference. Like Locke he believed that government's main function was protection of property: and although, in accord with the particularizing of the *Wealth of Nations*, he condemned government interference in specific instances, there was the underlying idea, which pervades the work of his Classical-economic successors, that the individual knew his self-interest better than government.

But closer examination of the *Wealth of Nations* does show that Smith's view of government was nothing like so negative as it might seem at first sight. Defence itself was recognized as sufficiently important to permit of interference with commerce; and in the interests of Justice, regulation of contracts, truck, and monopolies, might be undertaken. The issue of paper money could be a government function as could highways, bridges, canals, harbours, coinage, the Post Office, education, public health, regulation of mortgages, and colonial laws to check engrossing of land. Even the Usury Laws for regulating the maximum rate of interest on loans were approved by Smith. Indeed Adam Smith does devote one whole book of the *Wealth of Nations* (Book V) to taxation and public finance.

The great treatise which provided the foundations (and much of the superstructure) of Classical economics was set out in the form of five such books. Book I, entitled 'Of the Causes of Improvement in the productive

Powers of Labour, and the Order according to which its Produce is naturally distributed among the different Ranks of the People', covers division of labour, money, value, and distribution. Book II 'Of the Nature, Accumulation, and Employment of Stock' contains not only Smith's capital theory, but also the major part of his monetary theory, the latter being largely derived from Hume and from Harris. Book III 'Of the different Progress of Opulence in different Nations' is an historical treatment of growth much influenced by Hume's great eight-volume *History of England*. Book IV 'Of Systems of political Economy' reviews mercantilism and protectionism in general (including colonialism) and Physiocracy. Finally comes Book V 'Of the Revenue of the Sovereign or Commonwealth', a treatise on public finance covering both taxation and debt policy as well as the role of government.

The analysis contained in this work was pre-eminently a real analysis. The rise of Classical economics on the basis of the *Wealth of Nations* marks a sharp shift in the balance of economic writing towards real as distinct from monetary analysis, despite the purely monetary effects which Hume had suggested in his analysis of inflation, and those later advanced by Malthus. Smith himself did not draw on this part of Hume's analysis, possibily because inflationism was not very satisfactory in an overwhelmingly agricultural economy, possibly because he was influenced by the Aristotelian and Scholastic doctrine of the sterility of money. The *Wealth of Nations* did contain a quantity theory of money which owed much to Joseph Harris as well as to Hume: but oddly enough it did *not* contain the price-specie-flow mechanism linking international price level relationships and the money supply, which had been formulated by Hume and Cantillon and which Smith himself had expounded in his *Lectures*.[21]

The treatment of interest was in real terms, following the expositions of Massie and of Hume who had both advanced a theory of the rate of interest as depending on investment demand and consumption demand on the one hand and on the supply of loanable funds on the other, the latter being a function of total income, income distribution, and past saving.

Such a treatment of interest followed also from Smith's capital theory. He offered the distinction, accepted by all the Classical economists, between fixed and circulating capital. Savings derive from decisions to postpone consumption by investing in production, either by purchasing goods (circulating capital) or machinery. This capital theory, which is French in its ancestry, provided the essentials of nineteenth-century capital theory both Classical and even, to some extent, neo-Classical.

Such a capital theory was entirely appropriate for a work whose focus and overriding interest is undoubtedly economic growth. Smith was quite explicit about this. In the introduction to Book IV he says:

Political Economy, considered as a branch of the science of a statesman or legis- lator, proposes two distinct objects: first, to provide a plentiful revenue or sub- sistence for the people, or more properly to enable them to provide such a revenue or subsistence for themselves; and secondly, to supply the state or com- monwealth with a revenue sufficient for the public services. It proposes to enrich both the people and the sovereign.[22]

Economics is seen as providing the statesman's guide to economic growth, and in all this division of labour is given a central role as the mechanism of growth. This idea, which is in Locke, Petty, and Mandeville but which was almost certainly obtained by Smith from Hutcheson, is in the *Lectures* as well as the *Wealth of Nations*. Division of labour is dependent on capital to support it, and it does not occur in rude society where this capital is lacking. An enormous load is placed on division of labour, and, via 'progress in the arts' which proceeds with it, and results from it, it covers virtually all forms of technical progress. National income per head is then dependent on division of labour and the quantity of capital—the former (which deter- mines the skill with which labour is applied) depending on the latter which also determines the proportion between productive and unproductive labourers.

This last distinction (only the former contribute directly to economic growth) was accepted by most of the Classical economists who followed Smith. It is a distinction between activity which gives rise to products which support future production, and that which does not, and it comes in two versions. These are the storage version, where productive labour produces tangible material commodities, and the value version where productive labour produces a total output greater than total inputs (including its own subsistence) thus producing a surplus (in the form of rent and profits) from which capital can be accumulated. Both these versions shade into another version, the investment version, where labour is productive when it is realized in something which gives rise to further production.

The wealth which labour produces is quite clearly identified with annual product. Thus Smith identifies growth of wealth with economic growth as it has been understood ever since Smith, rather than as it was understood by the mercantilists who thought in terms of accumulation of wealth through trade surplus. There is a contrast here indeed not only with the mercantilists but also with Cantillon. Even Turgot regarded the riches of a country as being the annual value of land multiplied by the number of years' purchase plus the value of movable goods. Only Petty and the Physiocrats had really taken the same view as Smith was to take. Smith also made a significant step forward in substituting wealth per head for wealth in the aggregate; the latter was more obvious to the mercantilists with their strategic pre- occupations, but the welfare implications of Smith's concept are far more apparent—and far more relevant to a book concerned with economic growth.

Essential to growth was security of property, an emphasis which stems from the British natural-law tradition, especially Locke and Hutcheson. Smith had emphasized this in his *Lectures* and it remains a permanent assumption of his work—so permanent and so generally accepted that he felt little need to support his presumption with lengthy argument.[23]

Even given security of property however, economic growth would not continue indefinitely. Smith, like most of the Classical writers, had a theory of eventual economic stagnation, arising in his case from exhaustion of investment opportunities. But for Smith the approach of a stationary state in which growth had ceased does not seem to have been an immediate problem. Rather the focus of the *Wealth of Nations* is on removing the obstacles to getting growth fully under way.

But if the *Wealth of Nations* is a book about growth and the requirements for, and mechanisms of, this, it is also important for the presentation of a comprehensive case for freedom of trade which was to be historically of the greatest significance. The basic arguments stem from the *Lectures*. Firstly, trade is grounded in absolute advantage; it can never pay an individual to produce what he can obtain more cheaply from someone else. Secondly, it is absurd to see trade as a zero-sum game in which what one party gains the other loses. Both parties to an exchange gain by obtaining a collection of goods which they prefer to their previous one. Finally trade must be seen as important to growth—it produces a means of disposing of surplus produce resulting from division of labour, in exchange for goods which are preferred (the 'vent for surplus' doctrine); and since division of labour is limited by the extent of the market, trade which increases the size of the market increases division of labour and hence growth.

In offering this free-trade case, which was grounded in the natural law and liberty foundations of his thought, Smith was offering a powerful critique of mercantilism. Although he concentrated on mercantilist policy (Chs. 2–8 of Book IV) rather than mercantilist theory Ch. 1), and although he perhaps was less than completely fair to the mercantilist writers in his stress on their confusion (usually implied) between money and wealth, he had, together with Hume, destroyed their theoretical foundations. In the *Lectures* he had shown how Hume had torpedoed the balance of payments doctrine by means of the price-specie-flow mechanism: now in the *Wealth of Nations* Smith supplied the general free-trade case.

Three further elements in Smith's production need to be noted at this stage. Firstly, Smith offers a theory of value in the work which departs, probably quite deliberately, from the subjective value tradition of Pufendorf and Hutcheson[24] and settles on cost of production. Smith distinguishes short-run market price from 'natural' or long-run normal price—the latter being determined by cost of production. Obviously he was assuming a constant cost supply curve to get his supply-determined price: and this was possibly in part because he thought that focus on costs was suitable in a growth context but mainly for reasons we shall see in Chapter 4.

Secondly, and coupled with this, was a labour standard of economic welfare, clearly directed towards the evaluation of the welfare effects of changes in the prices of corn or money. It is presented in Book I, Ch. 5, 'Of the real and nominal Price of Commodities, or of their Price in Labour, and their Price in Money'. Smith was concerned to relate changes in income to changes in welfare and to view them as variations in the amount of 'toil and trouble' (disutility) necessary to obtain a given amount of real income as relationships within the system changed. This followed from his switch from national income in the aggregate to national income per head already noted. We return to the question of this standard, which has received various interpretations, later.

Thirdly, and linked with the theory of value which Smith advanced, was a theory of distribution. The 'natural' levels of rent, wages, and profits make up 'natural' price. Smith's theories of each of these rewards were not fully or consistently developed; but basically, wages were determined by the interaction of population and capital advanced (the origins of the wage-fund approach), rent was, though a price-determined surplus in the aggregate, a price-determining element in the cost of any particular good, and profit was treated as interest adjusted for risk and distinguished from wages of management. Smith's general treatment of the distributive shares not only laid down the pattern for the Classical economists but also contained sufficient material for them to develop the theory of distribution in several ways.

In all this a number of intellectual debts are apparent. Those to Cantillon and Harris (and Grotius, to whom Smith paid tribute in the *Moral Sentiments* and the *Lectures*) have been mentioned already. Smith's debt to Hutcheson has also been noted: but it is worth emphasizing that it is to him that Smith owed his basic approach as well as such specific concepts as division of labour as a source of growth. This is true even though Smith criticized Hutcheson in the *Moral Sentiments* for thinking too little of self-love. To Petty Smith owed more than a little in the field of taxation.[25] To Hume he owed much of his theory of international trade (and of its interaction with growth) even though he had modified what he drew from Hume in the light of his own independent thought, and had proceeded much further along a free-trade path than Hume who remained mildly protectionist. Smith also drew from Hume such specific ideas as that of urban business zeal improving the country's economic welfare (*Wealth of Nations*, Book III, Ch. 4).

To the Physiocrats Adam Smith owed the identification of produce with wealth, the idea of an annual produce distributed annually (as in the *Tableau économique*), and the stimulus to develop a theory of distribution

—both Hutcheson's and Smith's lectures are innocent of such a theory. Smith also owed to them his distinction between productive and unproductive labour although, as with just about everything else that he borrowed, he improved it—the Physiocratic concept had been confined to labour employed in agriculture. Less usefully Smith also drew from the Physiocrats a certain tendency to exalt the role of agriculture in economic development,[26] although he was critical (Book IV, Ch. 9), of governments which had deliberately favoured agriculture—this meant depressing manufactures and, given the interdependence of the economic system, thereby depressing agriculture also.

To Turgot Smith may have owed his theory of capital. On this last point there has been disagreement between two of the greatest scholars who have written on the history of economic thought. Cannan believed that Smith's treatment was parallel to that in Turgot's *Réflexions*—an independent development of suggestions of the Physiocrats. He pointed out that the *Réflexions* were published after Smith left France and that he does not seem to have owned the book. Viner, benefiting from later information on Smith's library, has argued that our knowledge of Smith's collection of books is incomplete and that he certainly had some of, and may have had the whole run of, a journal called the *Ephémerides* in which the *Réflexions* was first published. Certainly Smith's theory of capital is of French ancestry though whether the debt is to the Physiocrats or to Turgot will probably never be completely resolved.

The greatest independent development after the *Wealth of Nations* was to be Ricardo's *Principles*. This was the other great source of Classical economics and it is to this that we now turn.

## iv. DAVID RICARDO

It is particularly necessary to be clear about the most important elements in Ricardo's work, not only because of his influence on Classical economics but also because different commentators have seen different aspects of his work as the core of his system.

Ricardo's system was, if not entirely the first, certainly the first sweepingly successful example of economic model building. Its essence was the 'corn model' of aggregate economic relationships. This viewed the economic system as a single-output model, producing corn by applying labour and capital to land. The corn model was in real terms—in corn terms in fact. Inputs, outputs, and distributive shares were all stated in corn. The transition to money was normally made on the assumption of zero elasticity of demand so that all price changes related directly to changes in the supply price at the margin. The term 'corn' was used sometimes to mean not only grain but all agricultural wage goods. When this was done however the underlying assumption was that these commodities were in fixed proportions in the wage-good basket so that the factor-pricing problems associated with commodity substitution did not arise.

Since land was not homogenous, diminishing returns arose from applying increasing quantities of labour and capital to grades already under cultivation; while from bringing into cultivation land which was less fertile than that already cultivated, there were decreasing returns to scale. The average product and the marginal product of the labour and capital both declined as a result of these effects. What Ricardo was concerned with was, in the main, decreasing returns to scale with one input non-homogeneous. But since he also considered the case of applying increased inputs of labour and capital to land already under cultivation, and since in any case the total supply of land was fixed, there was also the problem of diminishing returns to the variable inputs of labour and capital as they were applied to the fixed factor, land.

The demand for wheat, and via this, the extension of cultivation, were treated as functions of population. Population itself was determined according to what might be called the Mark I version of Malthus's population mechanism (this will be discussed more fully in Chapter 3). Adam Smith, like most of the writers of his time, had recognized some sort of interaction of population, growth, and wage levels, but he did not attach any great significance to it. But after the publication of Malthus's *Essay*, and the extension of the domestic cultivation of corn during the Napoleonic Wars, the problem came into much greater prominence. The mechanism involved two forces: the desire for procreation and the need for subsistence. The former of these ensured that population always expanded to the level which could be supported at subsistence wages. If wages rose above subsistence, population would expand and wages would fall again to the subsistence level. If they fell below subsistence, population would contract through starvation and wages would rise again to subsistence. 'Subsistence' itself is sometimes treated as a psychological requirement which is variable: but usually Ricardo speaks as if it is a physical concept of what is necessary to sustain life—which was consistent with his general theoretical approach because unless subsistence was a physical concept the death-control mechanism would not operate.

The model also incorporated the theory of rent which had been first developed by James Anderson in 1777 and which Malthus and Sir Edward West had published in 1815.[27] Ricardo had apparently developed it independently. This theory treated rent as an intra-marginal surplus: price of the product (corn) was determined by the supply price (given Ricardo's assumption of zero elasticity of demand this was valid) at the margin of cultivation, and total rent was the sum of the differences between price and cost of production on all the intra-marginal cultivation. The argument is shown in Fig. 1. Put slightly differently in terms of the average and marginal pro-

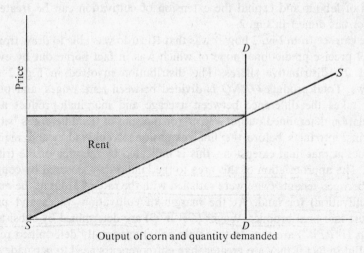

Output of corn and quantity demanded

**FIGURE 1**

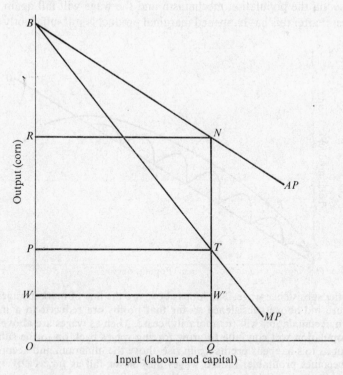

Input (labour and capital)

**FIGURE 2**

ducts of labour and capital the extension of cultivation can be treated, as Kaldor has done,[28] in Fig. 2.

We can see from Fig. 2 how it was that Ricardo was able to draw from his model precise predictions (none of which was in fact borne out by events) about the distributive shares. The distribution involved in Fig. 2 is as follows. Total product *ORNQ* is divided between rent, wages, and profits. Rent takes the difference between average and marginal product at the population determined output *PRNT* (or the sum of the differences between marginal products before the final extension of cultivation and marginal product at that final extension—this is indicated by the area of the triangle *PBT*. The appropriation of this area to the landlords is ensured by competition between tenants (who were satisfied with the rate of profit at the margin of cultivation) for land. At the margin of cultivation wages and profits exhaust marginal product. Wages (*OWW'Q*) are determined by subsistence. Profits (*WPTW'*) are thus (rather unhappily) apparently determined residually. But in fact if they are greater than entrepreneurs need to persuade them to 'wait', i.e. to abstain from consuming capital, they will compete for labour and thus bid the wage above subsistence. If they do this population will increase via the population mechanism and the wage will fall again to subsistence. If after this has happened marginal product is still sufficiently large to

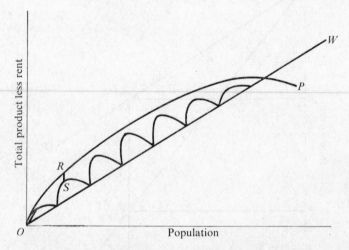

*OW* is the subsistence wage. The loops above are the line of market wages. When wages are bid above subsistence so far that profits are reduced to a minimum *RS* then accumulation will (temporarily) cease. Then as wages are above subsistence population will continue to grow forcing wages back on to the subsistence line. But as this happens profits again rise above the minimum and accumulation again becomes profitable. Indeed wages may never fall as far as *OW* until the stationary state is reached.

FIGURE 3

afford profits greater than necessary, entrepreneurs will again bid wages above subsistence. The whole process, which has been illustrated diagrammatically by Baumol,[29] is shown in Fig. 3. It will continue until marginal product has fallen so far that profit levels no longer afford the incentive to further accumulation—abstinence from consumption—and bidding for labour. At this point, which is likely to be at some minimum level of profits rather than zero, accumulation will cease, population will cease to grow, wages will be at subsistence, and the economy will have reached the stationary state.

Now this is the core of Ricardo's system and it is important to be clear about this. The corn model is quite clearly the fundamental concern of Ricardo's *Principles*. It is a model designed to prove one central proposition: that the existence of the Corn Laws, which hindered the import of corn, caused resort to inferior land at home, involving a fall in the average and marginal products of labour and capital and hence bringing about a stationary state in the not very distant future. Smith had envisaged a stationary state, but it was nothing like imminent and its achievement was not mechanical. Ricardo on the other hand had provided a mechanical model to establish its fairly immediate likelihood. *(see p. 55)*

But it should be stressed that some commentators have seized on other aspects of Ricardo's thought as being of key importance. A front runner is Say's Law of Markets—the doctrine of impossibility of failure of effective demand, stated usually in barter terms—that production of commodities constituted demand for commodities. Since this was in fact borrowed by Ricardo from Say and James Mill the attribution to this idea of key importance in relation to Ricardo is rather dubious. But the point needs to be made if the reader is to understand the literature. Keynes in particular saw neglect of aggregate demand as a fundamental characteristic of Ricardianism. In fact Ricardo did make use of Say's Law; but only because it provided a means of establishing that the mechanism of his model which produced declining profits was in fact the *only* mechanism which could produce declining profits, and that over-production theories could not explain a decline in profits.

But Say's Law cannot, for all that, be regarded as a fundamental part of Ricardo's contribution to economics.

Ricardo's monetary theory is another (dubious) contender. In fact Ricardo's monetary theory was entirely unoriginal: in the words of Professor Fetter:

What Ricardo did, in the heat of controversy over the credit policy of the Bank of England, was to strip from existing theory Thornton's refinements on Hume and come up with a simplistic proposition that had a tough cutting edge in the polemics of the day: depreciation of English money on the foreign exchanges was entirely the result of the expansion of the note issues of the Bank of England.[30]

But precisely because monetary theory was treated in this way by a first-class theorist *and* controversialist it provided a focus of ideas which had originated with other writers, and it greatly influenced the Currency School in the Currency and Banking controversy in the 1830s and 1840s. But it has to be stressed that this monetary theory was not the core of Ricardo's system: it was not even Ricardo's own. To regard a rigid quantity theory approach to policy problems as the essence of Ricardo's contribution to economics is then doubly misleading.

Strangely enough Ricardo's international-trade theory, in which his formulation of the theory of comparative advantage has strong (if not incontestable) claims to originality, has received little attention in the efforts to identify the nub of Ricardianism. Adam Smith had explained the advantage to be derived from trade in terms of absolute cost differences. Ricardo however showed that with input (labour) productivity higher in both commodities in one country than another trade would still be advantageous. His treatment was incomplete because it was still necessary to explain how this advantageous possibility would actually be realized, a task which was largely left to Senior and J. S. Mill. But Ricardo had made a very real and fundamental contribution here. Nevertheless its neglect by those seeking the core of Ricardianism is perfectly correct because it was the Corn Model which was at the centre of the system.

But if the Corn Model does constitute the core of Ricardo's system there is another characteristic of his work which *is* of great importance and which has to be taken account of in estimating his contribution to Classical economics. For Ricardo's deductive method, his model-building, was to be of the greatest importance. Ricardo essentially invented these techniques. His procedure not only contrasts strongly with Adam Smith's basically inductive approach, but, as a process of heroic abstraction, it not only neglects the frictions in the economic system but also habitually reasons in terms of the immediate relevance of the long run. Both these characteristics were to be of far greater importance for economics after the end of the Classical era: but that they left their scars on Classical economics there can be no doubt.

They left their mark on Classical economics not only because economists thenceforth had learnt to reason deductively but because they led to another characteristic which Schumpeter has aptly named 'the Ricardian Vice'.

His interest was in the clear-cut result of direct, practical significance. In order to get this he cut that general system to pieces, bundled up as large parts of it as possible, and put them in cold-storage—so that as many things as possible, should be frozen and 'given'. He then piled one simplifying assumption upon another until, having really settled everything by these assumptions, he was left with only a few aggregative variables between which, given these assumptions, he set up simple one way relations so that, in the end, the desired results emerged almost as tautologies. The habit of applying results of this character to the solution of practical problems we shall call the Ricardian Vice.[31]

In deriving his method and constructing his system, Ricardo drew on remarkably few sources. His main source was undoubtedly the book which first interested him in economics—the *Wealth of Nations*. The order of the chapters in his *Principles* coincides closely with the order of topics in the *Wealth of Nations*. This is no coincidence. For with Ricardo, as with Marx, criticism was his method of working: and it is to the raw material contained in the *Wealth of Nations* rather than to specific theoretical positions that Ricardo is indebted for all that is characteristic of his analysis. It is true that the underlying view of the allocative mechanism in Ricardo is entirely from the *Wealth of Nations*: and, except for Ricardo's pessimism about profits and progress, and the implications of this for the relationship between the landlord's interests and those of the rest of society, the harmony view of this mechanism, together with the self-interest psychology of the *Wealth of Nations* is accepted. But these are not what we think of when we think of Ricardianism. The central parts of Ricardianism were obtained by approaching critically the raw material of the *Wealth of Nations* and reconstructing it in terms of a corn model.

The system which Ricardo did construct out of the raw material of the *Wealth of Nations* was arguably a detour from the mainstream of development of Classical economics, which was in essence not a model building phenomenon. But it was not a very serious detour. For the full Ricardian apparatus attracted hardly any disciples. By 1831 at the latest it is probably true that no writers apart possibly from James Mill and Thomas De Quincey could accurately be called Ricardian in the sense that they thought in terms of the Corn Model. Whereas Adam Smith influenced every Classical economist, Ricardo's influence was both more uneven and more transient. McCulloch was much impressed with Ricardo's personality but did not think in terms of the Corn Model: rather he tried to incorporate effects derived from that model into Smith's system. Torrens, who became in time, on questions of monetary economics, Ricardo's closest follower, had analytical ability on a par with that of Ricardo himself but did not follow him through the Corn Model. J. S. Mill had moved a long way from pure Ricardianism by the time he came to write his *Principles* although just how far he made clear neither to his readers nor even (probably) to himself. Ricardo's general theorem of declining agricultural profits was paid lip service by a number of writers, but it was so heavily qualified by them as entirely to lose its predictability. Thus the emphasis of McCulloch and of Jones on agricultural improvements (which Ricardo had largely assumed away but to which they accorded great importance), and the attitude of Senior and McCulloch to population (they rejected Malthusianism) entirely removed the system's determinacy. Even De Quincey came to be convinced of the idea that profit could fall for other reasons[32] and that the rate of profit was not declining for the reasons Ricardo gave.[33] By the 1830s there was agreement amongst his fellow economists assembled in the Political Economy Club that Ricardo's system was no longer at all generally accepted.[34]

When we look at the case put for the repeal of the Corn Laws in the 1840s we do not find Ricardo's model looming large, although the Corn Laws were the bull's-eye in the centre of the target at which his model was aimed. McCulloch's attack on the Corn Laws in particular, and this is singularly instructive since he has often been labelled as 'Ricardian', was far more broadly based.[35] But in any case the general Classical free-trade case had Smithian rather than Ricardian roots—thus the Merchants' Petition of 1820 was drawn up by Tooke on the basis of the case for free trade in the *Wealth of Nations*.[36]

Moreover, Ricardo's theory of limited social conflict between landlords and the rest of society exercised only a limited influence even in this context. Opponents of the Corn Laws tended to argue that the landlords had mistaken their real interest—again this is particularly true of McCulloch. The Ricardian theory of conflict was really more influential with socialist writers and with Marx than with the Classical economists. Amongst the latter Adam Smith's outlook was dominant.

Say's Law—the denial of the possibility of a failure of effective demand —continued to rule throughout the Classical period. The rebels, with the exception of Malthus, were usually lightweights. But two points should be made in this connection. Firstly, as already noted, it was not Ricardo's; secondly, it was not used to prove that the only way profits could decline was through the rising difficulty of procuring subsistence, but to establish that growth could be pursued without fear of impediment—in other words for the same purpose as Smith had used a somewhat similar formulation.[37]

Ricardo's influence in these areas was then neither comprehensive nor long lasting. When we come to the more obscure and knotty parts of his analysis, especially his value theory, we find its influence even smaller. Ricardo tried to develop a labour theory of value beyond the 'early and rude stages of society' but clearly realized this was impossible, so he settled for what might be called an 'empirical' labour theory of value with '93 per cent' of value explained by direct and indirect labour input. (The reasoning involved in this will be dealt with in Chapter 4.) But inextricably linked with all this in Ricardo's mind was the desire to find some way of judging the progress towards the stationary state: and for this he attempted to construct an invariable measure of value in terms of which agricultural goods would rise and manufactured goods would fall. This effort virtually began and ended with Ricardo. By 1830–1 Ricardian value theory had effectively disappeared.[38] Even J. S. Mill produced a 'cost of production' theory of value. Nor did Ricardo's essays in such areas as tax theory, treated in terms of the Corn Model, find more favour with the Classical economists who were, in this field as elsewhere, more interested in concrete tax problems, usually in a Smithian growth context, than in *a priori* theorizing, however elegant.

Only in the case of Ricardo's treatment of comparative advantage do we find an unbroken continuation, development, and refinement of his work, through J. S. Mill and Torrens, and even beyond the era of Classical economics to Marshall and Edgeworth.

But having said all this it is vital to be clear about one thing. Though the influence of Ricardo has been shown to have been extremely limited, it was entirely necessary to discuss his system. For his tremendous intellectual vitality had burnt deep scars on to the Classical-economic consciousness. *It simply is not possible to read the Classical economic literature and understand it unless we know the system in which those scars originated.* A brief look at the work of some of the other Classical writers, in particular the great J. S. Mill, will help to make this clear.

## V. THE LATER CLASSICAL ECONOMISTS

By the 1830s then the magic of Ricardo's influence had waned. But his theorems, though so modified as to alter completely their character as compared with their original formulation, continued to appear in the work of the later Classical economists.

This is notably true of J. S. Mill who was the most important of these economists, a man who made significant theoretical contributions in his own right. To Mill we owe such contributions as the theory of reciprocal demand in international trade, the idea of non-competing groups, a treatment of the problem of joint products, opportunity costs, economies of scale within the firm, supply and demand treated in terms of schedules rather than amounts, and a discussion of Say's Law which not only made some steps towards clarifying the underlying assumptions, but also improved the analysis of the circularity of the economic system.[39] But he was theoretically eclectic and hence it was that he tried to incorporate Ricardo's work into his own, though in so doing he emasculated the former more or less completely. Thus he still had the concept of diminishing returns in agriculture—but modified it so much by the possibilities of technical progress that it ceased to be a fundamental proposition. It was, he believed, only a valid proposition in a given state of technical knowledge; and he gave many reasons why it should be offset by changes in technical knowledge. He also expressed the opinion that it had not been operative since about 1825[40] because of the effects of improvements. He still had the inverse relationship of wages and profits: but this was not linked with the invariable measure (which he did not use), but, in distinguishing wages and the cost of labour he destroyed its meaning—for him, wage cost per unit of output need not inexorably rise with the progress of population as wage cost depended on money wages, the efficiency of labour, and the price of wage goods.[41] Again, he offers the basic Ricardian thesis[42]—but no longer regards it as determinate, and instead suggests submitting it to statistical test. Moreover in his treatment of public debts he seems to envisage an alternative explanation for declining profits—the Smith–Wakefield thesis of exhaustion of investment opportunities.[43] In one chapter[44] he considers a number of possible cases of progress, with population increasing faster than capital, capital increasing faster than population, both population and capital increasing at the same rate, and both population and capital constant, but technical change reducing the necessary inputs. His treatment of population again shows the ambiguity of his work: while he apparently accepted the basic Malthusian concepts, he so modified them as to produce not only a prediction that subsistence will rise in time (as Smith had believed) but that limitation of population—neo-Malthusianism—was desirable to bring this about. Nevertheless he still has a stagnation thesis—but replaces Ricardo's pessimistic view of this with an optimistic one. The stationary state would be happy.[45]

There were other influences on J. S. Mill which were important, notably that of Comte whose ideas on a science of society so impressed Mill that he produced a book which resembled the *Wealth of Nations* in the breadth of its treatment. Another influence was Utilitarianism. Mill rebelled against this but then returned to it substantially.[46] At least it is true that he returned to the greatest happiness principle even if he found the pleasure/pain psychology too limited. It gave him not only his reforming zeal but his stress on security of property, and his refined tax theory which called for equal sacrifices of utility on the basis of diminishing marginal utility of income.

Partly because of these other influences Mill's treatment of some subjects is fundamentally opposed to Ricardo's. Thus his production and distribution dichotomy, treating the latter as variable and as a partly social phenomenon, is in sharp contrast to Ricardo who made one depend entirely and rigidly on the other. His treatment of production itself is really a development of both Ricardian and Smithian elements. He distinguished productive and unproductive labour, the former being maintained by capitalists out of a wage fund, this fund depending on the abstinence of capitalists. Thus demand for commodities is not demand for labour—Mill's famous fourth proposition on capital. The others were that employment is limited by capital, that capital is the result of saving, and that saving is spending—and the roots of each of these can be found in Adam Smith, while they bore the scars of Ricardo's formalization. But Ricardo's conclusion that the employment of machinery can bring about permanent unemployment of labour did not find favour with Mill.

The treatment of distribution—basically a wage-fund approach combined with Senior's abstinence theory of interest, and the treatment of relative wages which follows Adam Smith, is a summary of the whole Classical approach to distribution. Mill adopts the later developments notably Bailey's and Senior's generalization of the rent concept to all factors in less than perfectly elastic supply, though pointing out that rent enters into costs when factors have alternative uses, and adds his own modifications, especially the concept of non-competing groups.

Mill's general views on growth are very much in the Smithian mould: instead of reliance on a narrow model there is a broad sweep to the discussion which is reminiscent of the *Wealth of Nations* and represents a reworking of the analysis in that great book in the light of developments in Classical economics and in the economic history of the years since 1776.[47]

His value theory, though representing the best of its type in its discussion of zero elasticity of supply, infinite elasticity of supply, and rising supply price, and in its recognition of joint costs, was of the conventional Classical type, that is treating value as determined by supply and demand in the short run and by cost of production in the long run. At the same time it should be emphasized that Mill went beyond most of the Classical economists (not excepting Ricardo) in stating his argument in terms of *schedules* of supply and demand rather than quantities.

His notable contributions to tax theory were not in terms of a corn model but were the result of treating the kinds of approach to tax theory to be found in the *Wealth of Nations* in terms of Utilitarianism. His savings theory (in which savings are made a function of the rate of interest) was built directly on Senior's work. His monetary theory was rather more subtle and complex than Ricardo's. He realized (as had Thornton and others before him) that the demand for cash balances could alter relative prices: and it was partly because of this that he adopted a much less than mechanistic approach to the theory of monetary policy, in the great Currency and Banking controversy around the Bank Act of 1844. There was certainly a number of writers who were much closer to Ricardo at that time, notably Overstone and Torrens.

On the other hand his trade theory, which involved important contributions to pure theory, built entirely on Ricardo's foundations. He provided an analysis of the determination of the barter terms of trade which, as later presented geometrically by Marshall, is familiar to every student now in the form of offer curves. But it was a contribution, as we shall see in Chapter 8, which was formulated precisely to fill a gap in Ricardo's analysis.

J. S. Mill's contribution has been dealt with at some length because of his great importance. Space does not permit such lengthy discussion of the other Classical writers but a little may be said without being misleading. Torrens's contribution has been dealt with in detail and with great clarity and elegance in a separate study.[48] In general it may be said that Torrens never accepted the Ricardian position on value. Having a strong claim himself to be the independent author and originator of the theory of comparative costs it can hardly be said that his later work on international trade (which in any case led in a very different—protectionist—direction) wholly derived from Ricardo; and although he was one of the very few Classical economists with the undoubted ability to think consistently in terms of the Corn Model, he did not do so. But it is true that from the 1830s he accepted Ricardo's formulation of monetary theory.

Nassau Senior's contribution has also been illuminatingly analysed in a full-length study,[49] and it is clear from this that Senior was not a Ricardian. He accepted neither the basic Ricardian progress and distribution thesis, nor the associated value theory. Indeed he was the leader amongst the Classical economists in the rejection of Malthus's doctrine, a doctrine which was essential if the distribution implications of the Ricardian theorems were to hold; and he believed, like virtually all the later Classical economists, that technical progress in agriculture could indefinitely offset diminishing returns. He was himself the formulator of a quasi-subjective value theory, and he also provided an important contribution to the theory of capital in the form of his abstinence theory of interest.

The present writer has dealt with McCulloch's writings in detail elsewhere[50] and the reader requiring detailed treatment of the subject is referred to that source. But in summary it may be said that McCulloch successively discarded the bits of Ricardo (since he never thought in terms of the latter's Corn Model) that he had attempted to incorporate into a Smithian framework.

Other writers persevered with their own independent developments from the trunk of the *Wealth of Nations*—Malthus and Tooke are both examples here—while Samuel Bailey provided a damaging critique of Ricardo's value theory though he had relatively little positive to contribute himself. James Mill on the other hand followed Ricardo as closely as he was able: but he wrote only one book on economics after Ricardo's *Principles*, his *Elements*.

Classical economics then continued its own developments in the years after Ricardo's death, with an independence of thought on the part of the protagonists which ensured that they were the slaves of no system. Essentially the developments stem largely from the great trunk of the *Wealth of Nations* but they were made in the shade of Ricardo's *Principles* and could not remain unaffected by that work even though they disagreed with most of its conclusions. As separate aspects of Classical theory are dealt with in succeeding chapters, it will be possible to be more specific about the elements making up the totality of Classical thought on any one topic. But before we proceed to that stage it is necessary to look at some of the common characteristics and preconceptions of Classical economics.

## NOTES

1. *Lectures on Justice, Police, Revenue and Arms delivered in the University of Glasgow by Adam Smith, reported by a student in 1763,* ed. E. Cannan (Oxford, 1896, repr. New York, 1964).

2. Adam Smith, *The Theory of Moral Sentiments; or an Essay Towards an Analysis of the Principles by which Men Naturally Judge concerning the Conduct and Character, First of Their Neighbours and afterwards of Themselves* (first publ. London, 1759).

3. F. Hutcheson, *Inquiry Concerning Moral Good and Evil,* Section 3.

4. R. Cantillon, *Essai sur la nature du commerce en général,* written about 1729–30, first published 1755, ed. H. Higgs (London, 1931).

5. D. Hume, *Essays and Treatises on Several Subjects* (Edinburgh, 1752). The edn. cited in this book is dated Edinburgh, 1809.

6. *Essai,* Chs. 7 and 8, Higgs edn., pp. 19–23.

7. J. Viner, *Studies in the Theory of International Trade* (repr. London, 1955), pp. 91–109, esp. p. 92.

8. Sir Dudley North, *Discourses upon Trade* (1691).

9. [Henry Martyn], *Considerations on the East India Trade* (London, 1701).

10. I. Gervaise, *The System or Theory of the Trade of the World* (London, 1720).

11. See William Paterson, *Writings of William Paterson,* ed. S. Bannister (London, 1858).

12. George Whately, *Principles of Trade* (1774). In the case of this writer his work predates only the *Wealth of Nations* not Smith's development of his free-trade theory, and he may have owed his liberation to Physiocratic influence.

13. T. R. Malthus, *An Essay on the Principle of Population, as it affects the future improvement of Society* (London, 1798).

14. See J. Bonar, *Theories of Population from Raleigh to Arthur Young* (London, 1931), p. 38.

15. R. Wallace, *A Dissertation on the Numbers of Mankind in Ancient and Modern Times* (Edinburgh, 1753); Revd. J. Townsend, *A Dissertation on the Poor Laws* (London, 1786); D. Hume, op. cit. 'Of the Populousness of Ancient Nations', p. 400.

16. See McCulloch's 'Introductory Discourse' to his edition of the *Wealth of Nations* (Edinburgh, 1863 edn.), p. xlv. The reference to Adam Smith as his 'chief' comes from McCulloch's *A Catalogue of Books, The Property of a Political Economist* (1862), p. vi.

17. Cannan in his introduction to the *Wealth of Nations* (pp. xliii *et seq.*) has raised the possibility that appreciation of the role of self-interest may have been suggested to Smith by Mandeville's writings. But Smith was critical of Mandeville in his *Moral Sentiments* and the stress on self-interest could well have come about through Smith's attempts to rectify deficiencies in Hutcheson's system—the latter had indeed implicitly recognized such deficiencies by extending benevolence to 'self-benevolence'.

18. *Wealth of Nations,* ed. Cannan, i. 16, 419. See also ibid., 421 and ii. 43.

19. See esp. *Moral Sentiments,* Pt. III, Chs. 4 and 5.

20. See Cannan's introduction to the *Wealth of Nations,* pp. xxxiv–xxxv.

21. An interesting possible explanation for this is to be found in J. M. Low, 'An Eighteenth Century Controversy in the Theory of Economic Progress', *Manchester School,* 20 (1952), 311–30.

22. *Wealth of Nations,* 1. 395.

23. See *Lectures,* pp. 222 ff. 'Of the Causes of Slow Progress of Opulence'; *Wealth of Nations,* ii. 207; and Cannan's introduction, p. xxxvii.

24. In fact Hutcheson had simply followed Pufendorf's treatment in Ch. xii, Bk. II of his *Short Introduction to Moral Philosophy,* 'Concerning the Values or Prices of Goods'.

25. This is not simply because Petty was a pioneer writer on public finance. Compare Hull's edition of Petty (Sir William Petty, *The Economic Writings,* ed. C. H. Hull (Cambridge, 1899), p. 91), and Cannan's edition of the *Wealth of Nations,* ii. 310.

26. See *Wealth of Nations*, i. 266, 343–4, 356. See however ii. 162. The stress on agriculture may help to explain a certain neglect of fixed capital in the book.

27. J. Anderson, *Observations on the Means of Exciting a Spirit of National Industry* (Edinburgh and London, 1777); T. R. Malthus, *An Inquiry into the Nature and Progress of Rent and the Principles by which it is Regulated* (London, 1815); Sir E. West, *Essay on the Application of Capital to Land, with Observations Shewing the impolicy of any Great Restriction of the Importation of Corn* (London, 1815).

28. N. Kaldor, *Essays on Value and Distribution* (London, 1960), p. 212.

29. W. J. Baumol, *Economic Dynamics* (2nd edn., New York, 1959), p. 19. The diagram given here is different from Baumol's original formulation which was incorrect as it showed wages being bid up until they exhausted total product less rent.

30. F. W. Fetter, 'The Rise and Decline of Ricardian Economics', *History of Political Economy*, 1 (1969), 67–84, 74.

31. Schumpeter, op. cit., pp. 472–3.

32. *Blackwood's Magazine*, 52 (1842), 468–9.

33. T. De Quincey, *Logic of Political Economy*, repr. in *The Collected Writings of Thomas De Quincey*, ed. D. Masson (Edinburgh, 1897), ix. 293–4.

34. Political Economy Club, *Centenary Volume* (London, 1921), pp. 223–5.

35. See D. P. O'Brien, *J. R. McCulloch, A Study in Classical Economics* (London, 1970), pp. 378–95.

36. See T. Tooke, *Free Trade. Some Account of the Free Trade Movement ... with the petition of the Merchants of London, presented to the House of Commons on May 8 1820* (London, 1853).

37. *Wealth of Nations*, ed. Cannan, i. 320–1.

38. See e.g. S. Read, *Political Economy* (Edinburgh, 1829), p. 203; C. F. Cotteril, *An Examination of the Doctrines of Value* (London, 1831), p. 8.

39. See G. J. Stigler, 'The Nature and Role of Originality in Scientific Progress', *Economica*, N.S. 22 (1955), 293–302.

40. J. S. Mill, *Principles*, ed. Ashley, pp. 193, 704.

41. Ibid., Bk. II, Ch. 15, Section 7.

42. Ibid., Bk. IV, Ch. 2.

43. Ibid., pp. 77–8, 873–6.

44. Ibid., Bk. IV, Ch. 3.

45. Ibid., Bk. IV, Ch. 6.

46. See J. Viner, 'Bentham and J. S. Mill: The Utilitarian Background', in *The Long View and the Short* (Glencoe, Illinois, 1958).

47. See esp. Mill, ed. Ashley, op. cit., Bk. I, Chs. VII, VIII, and XIII. But, like the *Wealth of Nations*, the discussion of growth is continually appearing, against a background of institutional and historical considerations, throughout the book.

48. Lord Robbins, *Robert Torrens and the Evolution of Classical Economics* (London, 1958).

49. M. E. A. Bowley, *Nassau Senior and Classical Economics* (London, 1937).

50. D. P. O'Brien, *J. R. McCulloch*.

# BIBLIOGRAPHY

The reader wishing to pursue the question of the roots of Classical Economics should start with Schumpeter's *History*. Pt. II, Ch. II is perhaps the central chapter, but the whole of Pts. I and II and the first three chapters of Pt. III are all relevant here. See also W. Letwin, *The Origins of Scientific Economics* (London, 1963). Two elements on which Schumpeter is particularly illuminating are the Scholastics and the Natural Law Philosophers. On the former see also R. de Roover, 'Scholastic Economics: Survival and Lasting Influence from the Sixteenth Century to Adam Smith', *Quarterly Journal of Economics*, 69 (1955), 161–90. On the mercantilist background see M. E. A. Bowley, *Studies in the History of Economic Theory before 1870* (London, 1973). On the natural-law background there are two classic articles by O. H. Taylor, 'Economics and the Idea of Natural Laws' and 'Economics and the Idea of Jus Naturale', in the *Quarterly Journal of Economics*, 44 (1929–30), 1–39, 205–41, as well as the same author's *Economics and Liberalism* (1955). On one particular source see also W. R. Scott, *Frances Hutcheson* (Cambridge, 1900). W. L. Taylor shows how the Scottish philosopher Gershom Carmichael acted as the link between Grotius and Pufendorf, and Hutcheson, 'Gershom Carmichael: a neglected figure in British political economy', *South African Journal of Economics*, 23 (1955), 251–5. For Montesquieu's economics see N. Devletoglo, 'Montesquieu and the Wealth of Nations', *Canadian Journal of Economics*, 29 (1963), 1–25. The influence of Benthamite Utilitarianism can be pursued in a number of sources: J. Viner discusses 'Bentham and J. S. Mill—The Utilitarian Background', in *The Long View and the Short* (Glencoe, Illinois, 1958), and there is an illuminating discussion of Mill's Utilitarian tax theory in R. A. Musgrave, *The Theory of Public Finance* (New York, 1959). On the influence of Benthamite reformism there is R. D. C. Black, *Economic Thought and the Irish Question* (Cambridge, 1960) and Lord Robbins's magisterial *The Theory of Economic Policy in English Classical Political Economy* (London, 1952). On Bentham's influence as an economist see T. W. Hutchison, 'Bentham as an Economist', *Economic Journal*, 66 (1956), 288–306.

Five references on the economic writers who provided roots for Classical economics will suffice. Schumpeter is, as always, stimulating, even though occasionally prone to rather strong opinions. Viner, *Studies*, covers the mercantilist and pre-Smithian free-trade writers brilliantly and exhaustively. Rotwein's introduction to Hume, *Economic Writings*, sets the latter's economic writings in the general context of his thought extremely well; and E. A. J. Johnson, *The Predecessors of Adam Smith* (New York, 1937), may be consulted not only in relation to Hume but also to Petty and other writers such as Sir James Steuart.

All these references given so far contain a lot, either explicitly or by implication, about the origins of the *Wealth of Nations*. But on this particular subject there are some most illuminating references. Schumpeter, though he plays down Smith's importance, cannot be ignored: and there are two superb essays by Cannan dating from the beginning of this century but which have stood the test of time wonderfully well. They are his introductions to Adam Smith's *Lectures* and to the *Wealth of Nations*. There is also a fine article by the same author, 'Adam Smith as an Economist', *Economica*, 6 (1926), 123–34. N. Rosenberg, 'Some Institutional Aspects of the Wealth of Nations', *Journal of Political Economy*, 68 (1960), 557–70, is also a most valuable contribution.

On the question of Smith's indebtedness (or otherwise) to Turgot the reader should consult not only these sources but also J. Viner's introduction to John Rae, *Life of Adam Smith* (repr. New York, 1965), and P. D. Groenewegen's splendidly balanced and scholarly 'Turgot and Adam Smith', *Scottish Journal of Political Economy*, 16 (1969), 271–87. The influence of Natural Law on Smith is questioned, though on the basis of a rather restricted view of what constituted Natural Law, in H. J. Bitterman, 'Adam Smith's empiricism and the Law of Nature', *Journal of Political Economy*, 48 (1940), 487–520, 703–34. This should be read in conjunction with the two articles by Taylor already referred to. J. Viner's 'Adam Smith and Laisser Faire' in *The Long View and the Short*, is also interesting in this respect although he sees much more opposition than the present writer between the contents of the *Moral Sentiments* and the *Wealth of Nations*. These two works are also discussed in A. L. Macfie, *The Individual in Society* (London, 1967), and in two earlier articles by Macfie (*Oxford Economic Papers*, 11 (1959), 209–28, *Scottish Journal of Political Economy*, 8 (1961), 12–27) as well as in W. F. Campbell, 'Adam Smith's theory of justice, prudence, and beneficence', *American Economic Review*, Suppt., 1967, pp. 571–7. An intriguing discussion of Smith's source for the division of labour is to be found in R. Hamowy, 'Adam Smith, Adam Ferguson, and the division of labour', *Economica*, N.S. 35 (1968), 249–59.

The Physiocratic influences on Smith have been mentioned above: the interested reader should also see R. L. Meek, 'Physiocracy and Classicism', in *The Economics of*

*Physiocracy*, and Smith's own view as put forward in the *Wealth of Nations*, Pt. IV, Ch. IX. On the contents of Smith's work see especially Cannan's essays already cited, and M. Blaug, *Economic Theory in Retrospect*, Ch. 2. For an excellent discussion of Smith's view of competition see P. J. McNulty, 'A Note on the History of Perfect Competition', *Journal of Political Economy*, 75 (1967), 395–9.

For a survey of the contents of Ricardo's writings, see Schumpeter, Pt. III, Blaug, *Ricardian Economics*, Ch. 2, and *Economic Theory in Retrospect*, Ch. 4. Attention should also be directed to the superb introduction to Vol. i of Ricardo's *Works*, ed. P. Sraffa. There has been a great deal of discussion as to the extent of Ricardo's influence, a question which cannot be decided without being clear about the important elements in his economic system. On this the reader should see S. G. Checkland, 'The Propagation of Ricardian Economics in England', *Economica*, N.S. 16 (1949), 40–52, and R. L. Meek, 'The Decline of Ricardian Economics in England', ibid., 17 (1950), 43–62. See also Schumpeter, Pt. III, especially Ch. 4, Blaug, *Ricardian Economics*, Chs. 3, 8, and 9, and F. W. Fetter, 'The Rise and Decline of Ricardian Economics', *History of Political Economy*, 1 (1969), 67–84.

Finally, references have already been given which should help the reader to see how the work of the other Classical economist related to their main sources: but, specifically in relation to J. S. Mill see Blaug, *Economic Theory in Retrospect*, Ch. 6, and the whole of Schumpeter, Pt. III. But, perhaps with Mill above all, it cannot be stressed too often that there is no substitute for the original.

# 3. The Characteristics and Pre-conceptions of Classical Economics

## i. THE FOCUS OF CLASSICAL ECONOMICS

To the student concerned with the kind of economics forming the core of first-year economics courses the matters which primarily concerned the Classical economists will appear somewhat unfamiliar. The core of neo-Classical economics is the theory of micro-economic allocation, to which the student is introduced in his first year in an elementary and largely intuitive form and which receives increasingly sophisticated statements during succeeding years of study. On top of this, as a sort of icing on the cake, comes the Keynesian macro-economic theory of income determination, with, in little attached boxes so to speak, theories of growth and trade appended. But the approach of the Classical economists was the very reverse of this. For them the central propositions of economics concerned macro-economic problems. Their focus above all was on the problem of growth, and the macro-economic distribution conclusions which followed from their view of growth. On the one hand international trade, at least for Smith, was inextricably bound up with all this: on the other, the micro-economic problems of value and micro-distribution took their place as subsets of the greater whole. We have already seen that the content of Smith's *Wealth of Nations* was distinctly growth orientated, with distribution as part of the first book which is itself primarily concerned with 'the Causes of Improvement in the Productive Powers of Labour'. The same is true of virtually all the other Classical writers.

Of course it is true that the Classical writers were concerned with the problem of allocation: and one of Adam Smith's greatest achievements was to show how individual micro-economic decisions could work, in general, to optimize allocation. But it was allocation within a growth context. Again, in so far as the Classical economists were concerned with maximizing behaviour (and Adam Smith's enlightened self-interest ultimately lies behind *all* such models) they were concerned with dynamic, not static, maximization. It is perhaps ironic that a dynamic view of economic phenomena, taken for granted in the Classical writings, disappeared from view with the marginal revolution of the 1870s and had to be rediscovered by Schumpeter, Galbraith, and others in our times. The Classical view of competition was also a dynamic one and it is misleading to interpret their

writings in terms of a perfectly competitive model. The view of the allocative process which is contained in Book I of the *Wealth of Nations* or in
Book I of J. S. Mill's *Principles* is a view of the mechanism of allocation
taking place within a framework of changing technology and changing
resources. To anyone living through one of the greatest explosions of economic growth in the history of mankind, such a view was the one most likely
to make sense. It was because of the dynamic nature of this competition that
owners of capital were able to exploit *new* profit opportunities, sell *new*
commodities, obtain supplies from *new* sources, and sell in *new* markets.

The student will find correspondingly that the analytical procedures to
which he has become accustomed are rather different from those of the
Classicists. It is true that the method of comparative statics which forms
the staple of undergraduate micro-economics teaching is also to be found
in the Classicists, above all in Ricardo: but the comparative-statics method
was principally employed at a macro-economic level. Although it certainly
makes its appearance it was far from exclusively used by the Classical
economists who were in general at least as much interested in the dynamic
problems of the path between successive equilibria as in the equilibria
themselves. Moreover, they did not as a matter of habit (again Ricardo is
the main exception though J. S. Mill, Torrens, and Cairnes, amongst others,
also employed this device at times) take refuge in *ceteris paribus* assumptions, inappropriate as these were to an analysis of onward-moving growth.
They were concerned in particular with situations in which technology,
tastes, and incomes were *not* fixed, and with problems framed against a
moving background of these variables rather than with static maximization.

Another characteristic of their writings which distinguishes them quite
clearly from the neo-Classical economics which triumphed with the marginal
revolution, and also to some extent from the neo-Keynesian developments
of Keynes's work (though decidedly not from the work of Keynes himself)
was their concern with formulating analytical propositions which had a
more or less immediate policy implication. It is possible to see the reforming zeal of the Benthamites as lying behind this: and there can be no doubt
that they were a powerful voice in seeking reforms although these were at
least as much legal and political as economic. But if Benthamism gave the
policy-orientated characteristics of Classical economics added strength, this
characteristic did not originate with Benthamism. For Adam Smith's *Wealth
of Nations* was itself a highly policy-orientated document, with its fundamental anti-étatiste, anti-mercantilist, and anti-restrictionist message. The
review of 'Systems of Political Economy' in Book IV of the *Wealth of
Nations* is not done for its intellectual interest. It is done quite clearly with
the object of showing what was wrong with the theory (Ch. 1) but above
all the *policy* (Chs. 2–8) of mercantilism. There are exceptions to this generalization about Classical economics. The main ones are probably Ricardo's

treatment of taxation, and J. S. Mill's contribution to the pure theory of international trade. Even those writers who denied the existence of what they were pleased to call 'the art of economics' wrote quite a lot of material which had immediate policy implications—this is particularly true of Nassau Senior. Ricardo's tax chapters were essentially exercises in thinking through the corn model: yet even here Ricardo showed signs of believing, particularly with regard to the proposition that taxes on wage goods must be passed on, that his writing had immediate policy relevance, even if what he said had nothing to do with the tax system of his day. In any case Ricardo's *whole* system (which was outlined in Chapter 2 above) was policy-orientated. It was designed to prove one fundamental proposition: that unless the Corn Laws were repealed the rate of profit would decline, accumulation would cease, and the economy would cease to grow. Indeed it was with Ricardo most of all that the policy orientation was allowed to obscure the limitations of the analysis—hence Schumpeter's remarks about the Ricardian Vice referred to in the previous chapter, and the *simpliste* nature of his monetary theory already noted. The policy orientation of Classical economics strikes us even more strongly when we realize that Torrens's Cuba Case (a theorem about reciprocal demand in international trade which few of his contemporaries understood, to judge from their efforts to overturn it) was not advanced as a theoretical possibility but as an argument against free trade and indeed as an attack on the free-trade policy of the government of the day.

The monetary writing was almost entirely policy-orientated. It is only with the neo-Classicists' attention being directed to money later in the century that what was in some ways a rather unfruitful academicization of monetary theory began. From Hume, concerned to establish that the policy of attempting to secure a specie inflow was self-defeating, to Overstone and Torrens defending the operation of the Bank Act of 1844, the monetary writers were concerned with the theory of monetary policy. More than this, many of those contributing to the debates had first-hand knowledge—notably as bankers, whether private or governmental—of the operation of the monetary system, while others, such as Torrens and McCulloch, had free personal contact with such professionals.

The policy orientation of Classical economics was partly responsible for, and partly assisted by, the willingness of the Classical economists to make value judgements. Of course present day economists are also fairly willing to do this, but they usually go through the motions of separating the value judgements from the analysis. The Classicists did not. Some of their value judgements we still accept, as for instance the one already noted that the interests of (less numerous) producers were subordinate to those of (more numerous) consumers. Others, such as the benefits of continuing growth, had their critics amongst the Classical economists (notably J. S. Mill) as they have their critics today. Others, such as that sometimes implicit, that more work was better than less work (paupers should be made to work), and that the choice between income and leisure was not a subject for analysis, have dropped out of sight as neo-Classical analysis was extended to cover this kind of problem. But the student will find plenty of value judgements in the Classical writings.

In this section then an attempt has been made to indicate some of the leading characteristics which made the whole tenor of Classical economics different from that which the student encounters today. There is however one other characteristic of Classical economics which has not yet been mentioned. This is that the central analytical propositions took for granted (and often relied on) a theory of population, at least from the time of Malthus's first edition. This is such a fundamental characteristic that it deserves a section to itself.

### ii. POPULATION

Although the Classical population theory, at least for the majority of Classical writers, stemmed quite directly from the writings of Malthus, it would be misleading if the impression were given that Malthus was advancing new ideas. As he himself increasingly recognized in subsequent editions of his *Essay*, all his basic ideas are to be found in earlier writers. Although a review of such writers is beyond the scope of this section[1] it is possible at least to indicate three important sources on which the Classical economists could have drawn in the absence of Malthus.

Firstly, there is David Hume. His statement of the forces involved is so complete that it is worth quoting at length.

For as there is in all men ... a desire and power of generation, more active than is ever universally exerted, the restraints, which they lie under, must proceed from some difficulties in their situation, which it belongs to a wise legislature carefully to observe and remove. Almost every man, who thinks he can maintain a family, will have one; and the human species, at this rate of propagation, would more than double every generation. How fast do mankind multiply in every colony or new settlement; where it is an easy matter to provide for a family; and where men are nowise straitened or confined as in long established governments? History tells us frequently of plagues, which have swept away the third or fourth part of a people: Yet in a generation or two, the destruction was not perceived; and the society had again acquired their former number ... And, for a like reason, every wise, just, and mild government, by rendering the condition of its subjects easy and secure, will always abound most in people, as well as in commodities and riches.[2]

Hume was not without his critics in the Scotland of his time, with regard to his writings on population; yet one of the most important of these critics, Wallace, was in agreement with Hume on this fundamental view of the population mechanism.

It is not, owing to the want of prolific virtue, but to the distressed circumstances of mankind, that every generation does not more than double themselves ... Through various causes there has never been such a number of inhabitants on the earth at any one point of time as might have been easily raised by the prolific virtue of mankind. The causes of this paucity of inhabitants and irregularity of increase are manifold. Some of them may be called physical, as they depend entirely on the course of nature, and are independent of mankind. Others of them are moral, and depend on the affections, passions, and institutions of men ... To this last article we may refer so many destructive wars which men have waged against one another; great poverty, corrupt institutions, either of a civil or religious kind, intemperance, debauchery, irregular amours, idleness, luxury, and whatever either prevents marriage, weakens the generating faculties of men, or renders them negligent or incapable of educating their children and cultivating the earth to advantage.[3]

The debate between Wallace and Hume took place in Scotland, and it would be surprising indeed if it had left Adam Smith unaffected. Accordingly we find in the *Wealth of Nations* the proposition that population is dependent on the means of subsistence not so much because fertility varies with the means of subsistence as because the survival rate does so.

Every species of animals naturally multiplies in proportion to the means of their subsistence, and no species can ever multiply beyond it. But in civilised society it is only among the inferior ranks of people that the scantiness of subsistence can set limits to the further multiplication of the human species; and it can do so in no other way than by destroying a great part of the children which their fruitful marriages produce.[4]

For the mass of the people then population is limited by subsistence, a characteristic which is fortunate in that it ensures that an increased demand for labour, which is manifested in the form of increased wages, increases the supply of that labour.

The liberal reward of labour, therefore, as it is the effect of increasing wealth, so it is the cause of increasing population. To complain of it, is to lament over the necessary effect and cause of the greatest public prosperity.

It deserves to be remarked, perhaps, that it is in the progressive state, while the society is advancing to the further acquisition, rather than when it has acquired its full complement of riches, that the condition of the labouring poor, of the great body of the people, seems to be the happiest and the most comfortable.[5]

Other writers could be cited but what has been quoted here should be sufficient to indicate that the interaction between population and subsistence was hardly unknown before Malthus.

The basic population model which is to be found in Classical economics is however that which appeared in a work by T. R. Malthus entitled *An Essay on the Principle of Population as it affects the Future Improvement of Society*, the first edition of which was published in 1798. The basic model is contained in the first two chapters of this book. We begin with two propositions: 'First, that food is necessary to the existence of man. Secondly, that the passion between the sexes is necessary, and will remain nearly in its present state.'[6] This is followed by four more propositions. These are firstly, 'that the power of population is indefinitely greater than the power in the earth to produce subsistence for man'; that 'Population, when unchecked, increases in a geometrical ratio. Subsistence increases only in an arithmetical ratio'; thirdly, that 'By that law of our nature which makes food necessary to the life of man, the effects of these two unequal powers must be kept equal'; and fourthly, that 'This implies a strong and constantly operating check on population from the difficulty of subsistence. This difficulty must fall somewhere; and must necessarily be severely felt by a large portion of mankind.'[7] The checks are of two kinds, 'preventive' and 'positive'. The former consists in abstinence from marriage to avoid depressing the standard of living.

A man of liberal education, but with an income only just sufficient to enable him to associate in the rank of gentlemen, must feel absolutely certain, that if he marries and has a family, he shall be obliged, if he mixes at all in society, to rank himself with moderate farmers, and the lower class of tradesmen. The woman that a man of education would naturally make the object of his choice, would be one brought up in the same tastes and sentiments with himself, and used to the familiar intercourse of a society totally different from that to which she must be reduced by marriage. Can a man consent to place the object of his affection in a situation so discordant, probably, to her tastes and inclinations? Two or three steps of descent in society, particularly at this round of the ladder, where education ends, and ignorance begins, will not be considered by the generality of people, as a fancied and chimerical, but a real and essential evil ... These considerations undoubtedly prevent a great number in this rank of life from following the bent of their inclinations in an early attachment.[8]

This preventive check however receives relatively little stress in Malthus's first edition where the main emphasis is on the positive checks on population which come under the heading of 'Misery' and 'Vice'. The former involves control of the size of population through increased mortality, especially infant mortality. The latter involves moral licentiousness taking the place of marriage.[9] It is probably worth emphasizing that both the positive and the preventive checks do appear in the first edition of Malthus's *Essay* because Malthus himself gave the impression that the preventive check was introduced only in the second edition of his *Essay*. But the main emphasis throughout the *Essay* is on the positive checks to population which result in population always pressing against the means of subsistence.

A great deal of emphasis is placed by Malthus on the supposed mathematical necessity of his result. He asserts that population increases in geometrical ratio—giving the numbers, 1, 2, 4, 8, 16, 32, 64, 128, 256, 512, in illustration, while subsistence only increases in arithmetic progression— the corresponding numbers are 1, 2, 3, 4, 5, 6, 7, 8, 9, 10. Population, he says, will double in about 25 years if unchecked (the parallel with Hume is interesting here) but if subsistence is doubled within 25 years it can only be increased by the same absolute amount in the next 25 years.[10] Algebraically the two progressions are: $a, a + d, a + 2d, a + 3d$ with the $n$th term $a + (n - 1)d$ and $a, ar, ar^2, ar^3$ with the $n$th term $ar^{n-1}$. The argument about the geometric and arithmetic progressions is however rather a fraud. It is one of the earliest examples in the history of economic thought of giving spurious precision by the employment of mathematics to an idea which was

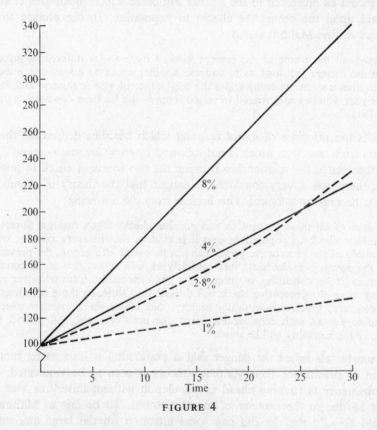

FIGURE 4

widely accepted in an approximate form before the mathematical formulation.

If we look at the diagram (Fig. 4) we can see that the two lines calculated at 4 per cent simple interest (the arithmetic progression assumed by Malthus) and at 2·8 per cent compound interest (the geometric progression implied by Malthus's arithmetic) do in fact intersect at 25 years and beyond this point that population is running ahead of subsistence thereby implying the need for operation of the checks to population. But on the same diagram we also have the comparison of two other arbitrarily selected arithmetic and geometric progressions—simple interest at 8 per cent and compound interest at 1 per cent. These two lines do not in fact intersect on the graph and would not intersect until 334 years. In other words the use of the ratios *qua* ratios proves nothing whatever about the relative states of population and subsistence at any particular moment in time.

The population model in the first edition of Malthus's *Essay*, with its stress upon the positive checks to population, was however modified by the model as presented in the second edition in which much greater stress is laid upon the preventive checks to population. In the preface to the second edition Malthus stated:

Throughout the whole of the present work, I have so far differed in principle from the former [edition], as to suppose another check to population possible, which does not strictly come under the head either of vice or misery; and, in the latter part, I have endeavoured to soften some of the harshest conclusions of the first Essay.[11]

This is the principle of *moral* restraint which Malthus defines as 'the restraint from marriage which is not followed by irregular gratifications'.[12] As Malthus stated the relationship between the two forms of check to population, there was a very considerable danger that the theory of population would become tautological. This is clear from the following:

The sum of all these preventive and positive checks taken together forms the immediate check to population; and it is evident that in every country where the whole of the procreative power can not be called into action, the preventive and the positive checks must vary inversely as each other; that is, in countries either naturally unhealthy, or subject to a great mortality, from whatever cause it may arise, the preventive check will prevail very little. In those countries, on the contrary, which are naturally healthy, and where the preventive check is found to prevail with considerable force, the positive check will prevail very little, or the mortality will be small.[13]

Obviously this raises the danger that if population is seen to be running ahead of subsistence then Malthus's theory is seen to be vindicated; and if subsistence is running ahead of population without misery or vice this must be due to the exercise of moral restraint. To be fair to Malthus it should be said that he did pay some attention (in the large amount of evidence which he gathered on population in different countries) to such indications of moral restraint as marriage rates and birth rates. But too often the argument, particularly in the hands of his successors, degenerated into the assertion that if subsistence was running ahead of population this must be due to moral restraint—whereas in fact, as we have seen above, it could quite simply be due to the fact that the adoption of arithmetic and geometric ratios did not mean that population necessarily ran ahead of subsistence.

Malthus's mechanism was taken over by Ricardo who made it, at least by implication, even more mechanistic than it had been in the first edition of Malthus's *Essay*. It provided him with a 'cost of production' theory of wages. 'The natural price of labour is that price which is necessary to enable the labourers, one with another, to subsist, and to perpetuate their race, without either increase or diminution.'[14] Wages will conform to this level.

However much the market price of labour may deviate from its natural price, it has, like commodities, a tendency to conform to it.

It is when the market price of labour exceeds its natural price, that the condition of the labourer is flourishing and happy, that he has it in his power to command a greater proportion of the necessaries and enjoyments of life, and therefore to rear a healthy and numerous family. When, however, by the encouragement which high wages give to the increase of population, the number of labourers is increased, wages again fall to their natural price, and indeed from a reaction sometimes fall below it.

When the market price of labour is below its natural price, the condition of the labourers is most wretched: then poverty deprives them of those comforts which custom renders absolute necessaries. It is only after their privations have reduced their number, or the demand for labour has increased, that the market price of labour will rise to its natural price, and that the labourers will have the moderate comforts which the natural rate of wages will afford.[15]

It is true that Ricardo talks as if subsistence is a conventional rather than a physical concept; but the references in Ricardo to population expanding until wages fall to a constant, and to privation reducing numbers, seem to imply that he thought in terms of physical subsistence, even though as enlightened and liberal men both he and Malthus would have preferred it to be otherwise.[16] But in terms of the basic purport of his model it *could* hardly be otherwise. If wages did rise to a level which afforded conventional rather than physical subsistence then, as we have seen in looking at Ricardo's system in Chapter 2, though the stationary state would be reached earlier, it would be a happy state with high wages—and Ricardo's case against the Corn Laws would then have been partially destroyed.

In the hands of the later Classical economists however the Malthusian mechanism ceased to have the clear implications that it had had both for Malthus and for Ricardo. Robert Torrens and Nassau Senior led the revolt against the basic Malthusian doctrine. Although his own statements were phrased so as to conceal the differences between himself and Malthus, there is no doubt that Senior in particular held two beliefs which were fundamentally opposed to the Malthusian thesis. Firstly, the main thesis of his *Lectures on Population*, which was also introduced into his *Outline*, was that the desire of man to better his position in the world is at least as important as the desire to procreate.

It appears, therefore, that habits of considerable superfluous expenditure afford the only permanent protection against the population pressing so closely on the means of subsistence, as to be continually incurring the misery of the positive checks ... As wealth increases, what were the luxuries of one generation become the decencies of their successors. Not only a taste for additional comfort and convenience but a feeling of degradation in their absence becomes more and more widely diffused. The increase, in many respects, of the productive powers of labour, must enable increased comforts to be enjoyed by increased numbers, and as it is the more beneficial, so it appears to me to be the more natural course of events, that increased comforts should not only accompany but rather precede, increase of numbers.[17]

The second thread in the *Lectures* is the idea that improvements in agricultural skill may increase with population and so offset diminishing returns[18]—Malthus's successors were forced to rely upon this idea, rather than the arithmetic and geometric ratios, as giving any substance to the idea of population running ahead of subsistence. Now it is true that, as we shall see, the principle of population is one of Senior's four 'postulates': and the question then arises as to how this is consistent with his attitude towards Malthusian doctrine. In his *Lectures* Senior simply met the problem by substituting in the statement 'That the population of a given district is limited only by moral or physical evil or by deficiency in the means of obtaining those articles of wealth', the phrase 'the apprehension of a deficiency' for the word 'deficiency'. He states:

My reasons for this substitution are: first, that the actual deficiency of necessaries is a branch of physical evil; and, secondly, that it is not the existence of a deficiency but the *fear* of its existence which is the principal check to population, so far as necessaries are concerned, and the sole check as respects decencies and luxuries.[19]

Although the postulate concerning population was reproduced in the *Outline* without this modification, the treatment of population in that work is consistent with the modification in the *Lectures*.

The great preventive check is the fear of losing decencies, or, what is nearly the same, the hope to acquire, by the accumulation of a longer celibacy, the means of purchasing the decencies which give a higher social rank. When an Englishman stands hesitating between love and prudence, a family actually starving is not among his terrors; against actual want he knows that he has the fence of the poor-laws. But, however humble his desires, he cannot contemplate without anxiety a probability that the income which supported his social rank, while single, may be insufficient to maintain it when he is married; that he may be unable to give his children the advantages of education which he enjoyed himself; in short, that he may lose his caste. Men of more enterprise are induced to postpone marriage, not merely by the fear of sinking, but also by the hope that in an unencumbered state they may rise. As they mount the horizon of their ambition keeps receding, until sometimes the time has past for realising those plans of domestic happiness which probably every man has formed in his youth.

It is by this desire of decencies, as distinguished from necessaries, that long-settled civilized Countries are preserved from the evils of a population greatly exceeding the means of comfortable subsistence.[20]

Senior's rejection of the basic Malthusian thesis was followed chronologically by that of McCulloch. In his early writings McCulloch had followed Malthus's model of the second edition, including both preventive and positive checks, and seems to have accepted that the latter would be important. However, even at this stage, and despite his emphasis on the positive checks, he seems to have been much less able to regard subsistence as a physical concept than either Ricardo or Malthus, and much more inclined to stress, like Adam Smith, the fluid nature of the concept. Following Senior's attack on Malthusianism, McCulloch adopted a different view. He no longer accepted that man was so moved by animal passion as to be a procreating automaton. He was also aware that those who continued to advocate the straightforward Malthusian doctrine were inclined to take refuge in use of the word 'tendency'. If population was outrunning subsistence then the Malthusian doctrine was vindicated; if, on the other hand, population was not outrunning subsistence, then the Malthusians fell back on asserting that there was a *tendency* for population to outrun subsistence but that moral restraint must be in operation to prevent the overt manifestation of this tendency:

it might be correctly laid down as a general principle that the necessity of a supply of food on the one hand, and the difficulty of getting it on the other, have a tendency to make every man die of hunger. Happily, however, the countervailing influences are so very powerful that, though many die of repletion, not one individual in ten thousand dies of want; and such being the case, a theory, or a work on the subject, which should in great measure overlook these influences, would not, we imagine, be considered good for much. And this, we apprehend, is the case with the 'Essay on the Principle of Population'.[21]

Probably influenced by John Barton, McCulloch made play with a statistically important fact neglected by Malthus, viz. that changes in the death rate were of more importance than birth- or marriage-rate changes; and moreover the latter showed that prudential restraint had operated. Indeed in time McCulloch came to be satisfied that subsistence had historically increased faster than population.

All this is worth noting, not only because McCulloch became an anti-Malthusian, but because he did so largely on the basis of the available evidence, rather than on a predominantly deductive basis as was the case with Senior. The significance of this will be clear when we have looked in the following section at the question of method in Classical economics.

Despite Senior and McCulloch however, J. S. Mill continued to advance the Malthusian position. He asserted, quite incorrectly, that Malthus had not attached great importance to his arithmetic and geometric progressions.

Some, for instance, have achieved an easy victory over a passing remark of Mr. Malthus, hazarded chiefly by way of illustration, that the increase of food may perhaps be assumed to take place in an arithmetical ratio, while population increases in a geometrical: when every candid reader knows that Mr. Malthus laid no stress on this unlucky attempt to give numerical precision to things which do not admit of it, and every person capable of reasoning must see that it is wholly superfluous to his argument.[22]

Mill in fact laid some stress upon the positive checks and seems to have been influenced by Ricardo in his treatment of the problem.

But whatever be the causes by which population is anywhere limited to a comparatively slow rate of increase, an acceleration of the rate very speedily follows any diminution of the motives to restraint. It is but rarely that improvements in the condition of the labouring classes do anything more than give a temporary margin, speedily filled up by an increase of their numbers. The use they commonly choose to make of any advantageous change in their circumstances, is to take it out in the form which, by augmenting the population, deprives the succeeding generation of the benefit. Unless, either by their general improvement in intellectual and moral culture, or at least by raising their habitual standard of comfortable living, they can be taught to make a better use of favourable circumstances, nothing permanent can be done for them; the most promising schemes end only in having a more numerous, but not a happier people.[23]

Nevertheless, elsewhere in the book, Mill did allow that, with education and progress, conventional subsistence was rising. Hence it was that he was able, unlike Ricardo, to see the stationary state as a potentially happy existence.[24] He was aware too that improvements in technology could run ahead of population[25] and that the price of corn had fallen even before the repeal of the Corn Laws. But he took refuge in the *tendency* of population to catch up with and overtake agricultural progress.

Senior, McCulloch, and J. S. Mill were all writers in the main stream of Classical economics. But there were also a number of writers who should be classed, especially on this question of population, as rebels. They were more outspoken critics of the whole population thesis. There was for instance M. T. Sadler who, in his book *The Law of Population: a Treatise in Six Books, in Disproof of the Superfecundity of Human Beings and developing the real Principle of their Increase*,[26] advanced the thesis that fertility varied inversely with the density of population. But Sadler was arguably a lightweight: certainly he was dismissed without much sign of respect by those anti-Malthusians who were within the main stream of Classical economics, like McCulloch. But G. P. Scrope, on the other hand, was a more substantial figure. He believed that, under good government, skill (i.e., technology) increased in relation both to population and to capital. In his *Principles* he traced the progress of population through history showing agricultural technology moving through hunting, pastoral, and cultivation stages,[27] and he pointed to the existence of large uncultivated tracts of land.

Misery and vice enough, indeed, have there been. But these evils have never been occasioned by 'the tendency of population to press against the means of subsistence'. That tendency has been productive of incalculable good and of no evil that might not with the utmost facility have been avoided. There was always at hand more than one simple, easy, and effectual resource for keeping the means of subsistence level, *at least*, with the wants of any possible population. The misery and wo, the vice and starvation that have exhibited themselves in such frightful frequency among men, have been ever the effect of tyranny and crime, of misgovernment, of the indulgence of their evil passions ... Enough has been said, we think, to prove that there OUGHT to be no deficiency of food in a civilized community—that there CAN be none in any whose home resources are well and prudently managed, and where, when these incline to fail, a provident use is made in time of the great natural resource of emigration.[28]

Another critic outside the main Classical fold was Samuel Read who attacked the basic Malthusian thesis from a slightly different angle, arguing that good government, which provided security, liberty, and education, would provide a sufficient incentive for people to abstain from procreation.

It is, therefore, maintained, that wherever good government is once established and advanced to a certain point of improvement, education will be speedily introduced and widely extended, and the principle of improvement, the desire of bettering their condition, will be extended in like proportion, and become effectual for its purpose, down to the very lowest ranks of the people, and that the necessary consequence must be, that the natural wages of labour, 'the custom of the country', and 'habits and modes of life', will begin and continue universally and indefinitely to improve and increase throughout the whole extent of the labouring population.[29]

But despite such dissent the population doctrine, however qualified as we have seen it was in the case of J. S. Mill, remained a continuing thread in Classical economics. The manner of its survival is perhaps best appreciated by looking at Cairnes's *Logical Method of Political Economy*, Lecture VII of which contains a lengthy defence of the Malthusian doctrine. There are two main points to be noted here. Firstly, Cairnes regards the Malthusian doctrine as fundamental to economics.

One of [the] doctrines ... quite fundamental in the science of Political Economy, though impugned and controverted in several recent publications, is the doctrine of population as expounded by Malthus ... What Malthus asserted ... is this— that, regard being had to the powers and propensities in human nature on which the increase of the species depends, there is a constant tendency in human beings to multiply faster than, regard being had to the actual circumstances of the external world, and the power which man can exercise over the resources at his disposal, the means of subsistence are capable of being increased.[30]

Now having taken the position that this doctrine was fundamental to economics Cairnes was faced with the problem that it was contradicted by the available evidence. This leads us on to the second point. This was Cairnes's view that the nature of economic laws was such that they could not be subject to empirical disproof.

From what I have already said of the character of an economic law, as well as from the terms of the proposition itself, you will at once perceive that it is not here asserted that population *in fact* increases faster than subsistence: this would of course be physically impossible. You will also perceive that it is not inconsistent with this doctrine that subsistence should *in fact* be increased much faster than population.[31]

Cairnes's defence of the Malthusian thesis (in which incidentally he avoided the more powerful critics of Malthus and concentrated his fire against a rather obscure incumbent of the Drummond Chair at Oxford) itself raises some rather serious questions about the methodology of Classical economics; and we shall now consider this in the final section of the chapter.

### iii. THE METHOD OF CLASSICAL ECONOMICS

In looking at the attitude of the Classical economists towards the method of economics it is important to bear two things in mind. Firstly, debates over economic method are very much alive today and the problems which troubled the Classical economists are still live matters today, though different terms are used for basically similar problems. Secondly, the sources for our conclusions about method have to be much wider than methodological writings. Jacob Viner said that 'economics is what economists do': and economic method, in the last resort, can only be learned from perceiving how it is that economists do what they do. This is true even in the case of economists such as Say, McCulloch, Senior, Torrens, J. S. Mill, and Cairnes, who left explicit methodological discussions: but it is a matter of necessity when we are dealing with writers who committed their thoughts on methodology to paper obliquely, if at all.

But by reliance both on what economists said they did, and on what they were seen to do, we can discover that there were in fact two opposing strands in the methodological positions of the Classicists. On the one hand there were those who believed that the method of the physical sciences should be applied to the social sciences and whose approach may be called basically inductive ('basically' because neither side were methodological purists); and on the other were those whose approach was basically deductive. In the first group we have, in the Scottish and Continental traditions, writers who took Bacon's and Newton's views on method as their guide, notably Hume, Smith, McCulloch, and Say. In the second group we have Ricardo and those who came after him, including Senior, Torrens (despite earlier criticism of such an approach), and Cairnes. J. S. Mill, if judged primarily on his methodological pronouncements, comes into this group also, although when we look at what he actually 'did' in his *Principles* we find that in some ways he straddled both traditions.

The Scottish school may be said to take its rise from the Scottish Historical School which included such writers as Adam Smith, Adam Ferguson, William Robertson, and John Millar, as well as more peripheral figures such as Lord Kames. This in turn owed much to Continental influences especially that of Montesquieu. The members of this school were concerned to base their social and economic generalizations on firm historical facts, and were opposed to abstract speculation and conjecture. A significant influence was David Hume who produced two important works in this genre, the Essay 'Of the Populousness of Ancient Nations' which was a major step forward in the treatment of population matters on a factual basis, and the *Treatise on Human Nature* which sought to distil the essential human qualities, revealed by experience of behaviour, as laws of behaviour in particular situations. History could be interpreted in terms of these laws: and in turn history had provided sufficient evidence to enable reasonably reliable generalizations to be produced.

The process common to all these writers was what was called induction. It was essentially one of formulation of premises on the basis of empiricism, and the derivation of empirical laws: reasoning on the basis of the generalizations thus established, and testing the results thus obtained against other historical data, was the next stage, and this testing procedure itself suggested points of departure for further reasoning. The process may be summarized as: empiricism—deduction—verification—empiricism and so on. Writers outside the Classical school also followed this method: and a notable example is that of Sir James Steuart whose method of fact collection, establishment of principles, reasoning on the basis of those principles, and then returning to the facts, was entirely in the eighteenth-century Scottish mould.

Such a method was a natural one for men concerned to establish the existence of a basic order and logical structure in social phenomena in parallel with that established by the natural scientists. It was noted in Chapter II that this description fits Adam Smith particularly well: and it is unfortunate that he did not treat the subject of methodology directly. His method has to be discovered mainly from what he 'did' in the *Wealth of Nations* and also from the posthumously published *Essays on Philosophical Subjects*, especially the Essay on the History of Astronomy in which the Newtonian method of investigation is extolled.[32] Having little respect for metaphysics and for the dialectial method of Socrates and Plato, he believed that both ethics and economics could and should be studied empirically. The laws of behaviour were to be formulated in this way. At each stage of investigation the conclusions had to be fitted together with others into a system which implied conclusions which were then subject to verification. Results might be tentative but they would rest on a solid body of facts and would not be speculative conclusions from speculative premises.

McCulloch's method follows from this. He essentially continued the Scottish tradition. McCulloch was quite explicit in his belief that economics was a science of fact and experiment, differing from the physical sciences only in that its conclusions held in a majority of cases but not all. An occasional errant fact need not upset a theory; but a theory must be able to explain a uniform and consistent result.[33] In the preface to the 1843 edition of his *Principles* he was critical of deduction from dubious assumptions. Thus he said of Senior:

He lays it down, for example, as a general principle, or rather axiom, that, supposing agricultural skill to remain the same, additional labour employed on the land will, speaking generally, yield less return. But though this proposition be undoubtedly true, it is at the same time quite as true that agricultural skill never remains the same for the smallest portion of time; and that its improvement may countervail, for any given period, the decreasing fertility of the soils to which recourse is necessarily had in the progress of civilization. It would, indeed, be easy to show, that the worst lands now under tillage in England, yield more produce per acre, and more as compared with the outlay, than the best lands did in the reigns of the Edwards and the Henrys. It is, therefore, to no purpose to say, that the science rests on principles of this description. They, no doubt, form a part of its foundation; but as they are modified in different degrees by others, the only general principles of any practical value are those deduced from observations made on their combined action; or, in other words, on the phenomena really manifested in the progress of society.[34]

Indeed he regretted the lack of evidence available to test some parts of economic theory.[35] Where McCulloch differed from the main Scottish tradition was that, coming under the influence of Ricardo, he attempted to incorporate Ricardian and other conclusions, often (especially in the case of Ricardo) based on non-empirical premisses, into his system. But he did not neglect the need for verification; and thus it was that he came to change his mind on a number of issues. In particular, he was satisfied that the fundamental generalization of Ricardian economics concerning diminishing returns in agriculture was not supported by the available evidence; that another fundamental underpinning of the Ricardian system, the Malthusian thesis, was contrary to the available evidence; and that evidence collected about foreign corn prices suggested that the case against the Corn Laws had been greatly overstated.[36]

The final writer in the inductive group who will be considered here is J. B. Say. Say was quite clear about the necessity of following the Baconian method, that political economy had a factual basis, and that economics was an inductive subject in the sense of the chain of processes already described.[37] But mention should also be made of Richard Jones, who attempted to develop economics as an inductive subject as entirely as possible, and urged economists to avoid formulating economic laws without taking full account of the sociological constraints and implications.[38] But Jones was really not a member of the mainstream inductive school in Classical economics but an outsider.

The fundamental pillar of the second group of economists and in many ways its most extreme member was Ricardo himself. Whenever a member of the former group wanted an example of over-abstraction they usually cited Ricardo. Ricardo himself wrote virtually nothing explicitly on method so that we are largely forced back on what he 'did' to understand his procedure. But comments in two of his letters are instructive. Thus he wrote to Malthus:

After the frequent debates between us, you will not be surprised at my saying that I am not convinced by your arguments on those subjects on which we have long differed. Our differences may in some respects, I think, be ascribed to your considering my book as more practical than I intended it to be. My object was to elucidate principles, and to do this I imagined strong cases that I might show the operation of those principles. I never thought for example that practically any improvements took place on the land which would at once double its produce, but to show what the effects of improvements would be undisturbed by any other operating cause, I supposed an improvement to that extent to be adopted, and I think I have reasoned correctly from such premises.[39]

To this may be added Ricardo's remark to Trower that:

it is one of my complaints against him [Malthus] that he does not answer your principle but wishes to shew that you have taken your case so wide, that it could under no circumstances exist; but however limited might be your case, the same principle is involved, and it is that which should be answered.[40]

Ricardo's method has in fact already been indicated in dealing with the 'Ricardian Vice'. Essentially it involved taking hypothetical premises, deducing conclusions from these premises, and making no attempt to verify the results. It has remained the method of the pure theorist ever since. Ricardo's deductive system gave rise to a number of testable propositions— secular diminishing returns, the decline of profits, the dependence of profits on wages, of wages on wheat prices, and of wheat prices on protection— and it depended on others, especially the Malthusian mechanism and the tendency of wages to subsistence. But the whole tenor of Ricardo's approach was opposed to verification. The message which his successors took from his procedure was that if a conclusion was reached logically from plausible premises it was correct even if the available data contradicted it.

The influence of this on subsequent methodological writings was extremely powerful. Torrens had originally been critical of this line of approach,[41] but he came to adopt it wholeheartedly. In his introduction to the *Budget* he accepted Ricardo's deductive method.

In the works of that profound and original thinker, more than in those of any other writer of our times, Political Economy is presented as an abstract science. All his reasonings are hypothetical. His conclusions are necessary truths ... under the premises assumed, and enabling us, if we will make the necessary corrections for the difference between the hypothetical circumstances and the circumstances which actually exist, to arrive at conclusions practically true under all the varying conditions of society.... The impression that his conclusions are at variance with facts ... involves a misconception. His conclusions are in strict conformity with the facts which he assumes; and, modified by the proper corrections, on account of the difference between the assumed and the existing facts will be found to be in tried conformity with existing facts.[42]

Torrens still believed that errors in economics stemmed from over-hasty generalization: but he believed that though Ricardo had sometimes been guilty of this, his opponents had fallen into a greater error by using modifying circumstances to disprove abstract propositions. He had now become an apostle of the deductive approach, and, following the arguments used by J. S. Mill (which will be discussed below), he emphasized what he saw as the limitations of the inductive approach compared to the much greater generality of the deductive. Indeed he expressed the belief that the latter would make economics perfect. This was despite the fact that he showed signs of discontent with not only the Malthusian prediction—he saw reproduction declining as *per capita* income increased—but indeed with the whole Ricardian thesis.[43]

Senior too, despite rejection of the two fundamental props of the Ricardian system, the Malthusian population thesis and secular diminishing returns in agriculture, acknowledged that Ricardo's analysis was formally correct.[44] He adopted the position that the whole of pure economics (and exactly what was pure we shall see below) was deduced from four postulates. These came after a definition of wealth as goods and services yielding utility and being scarce. The four postulates were:

1  That every person is desirous to obtain, with as little sacrifice as possible, as much as possible of wealth.
2  That population is limited only by moral or physical evil or fear of deficiency of conventional subsistence.
3  That the powers of labour and of other wealth-producing instruments may be indefinitely increased by using their products as a means of further production.
4  That with fixed technology in agriculture diminishing returns will appear.

The basis of these postulates was not exclusively empirical. The first postulate was arrived at by introspection and the others were, he usually held, a matter of observation.[45] There were in his view three sources of premiss: (a) observation, (b) consciousness (introspection), and (c) hypothesis. The physical sciences relied on (a) and (c), particularly (a), while mathematics relied on (c). But for the 'mental sciences' (and for him Political Economy was a mental science most emphatically) introspection was the source of premisses.[46] It was also the means by which 'experiments' could be conducted —we could imagine ourselves in a particular situation. Yet Senior was aware of the dangers of this position and in his later lectures he pointed to Ricardo as illustrative of these dangers. The premisses must have some contact with reality: and introspection seems to have been the way of keeping in contact that he saw as desirable. His attitude to facts was that their collection was necessary but that it did little to improve the laws of economics. The Baconian method was inapplicable to economics and there must be reliance on introspection because of the impossibility of experiment.

In fact when we look at what Senior 'did' we find that his writings were not in practice totally deductive. But this was partly because, in accordance with his emphasis on scientific purity as he saw it, Senior distinguished strongly between the 'science' and the 'art' of economics, as Cairnes was also to do. The 'science' embraced the propositions of pure theory arrived at deductively, the general laws of economics which were few in number and wide in generality. It was, he held, capable of as much certainty as any science not founded exclusively on definition (i.e. mathematics). It was only in this branch of economics that the accuracy of, for instance, logic or mechanics was to be expected. The 'art' included the analysis of all particular cases and the application of the general principles to these cases, including the giving of advice to the legislator. Senior's hostility to the 'art' varied. In his Introductory Lecture of 1826 he was prepared to allow that economists should be concerned with both art and science. In his *Outline* of 1836 however he limited economics to the field of pure theory and denied the existence of an art of economics on the grounds that it was beyond the bounds of human capacity to study all the other branches of knowledge necessary to apply economic conclusions to particular cases or give advice on policy, at the same time as mastering economic theory. But by 1852 Senior was prepared again to allow the existence of an art of economics although he still felt that the conclusions of this art were not arrived at in the strict scientific role of the economist.[47] It was in the 'art', into which he sometimes permitted himself excursions, that the non-deductive elements mainly appeared—and here Senior did some extensive work.[48]

A purist attitude was of course unlikely to find much sympathy with the inductive school. McCulloch expressed himself robustly on this point.

The economist who confines himself to the mere enunciation of general principles, or abstract truths, may as well address himself to the Pump in Aldgate, as to the British public. If he wishes to be anything better than a declaimer, or to confer any real advantage on any class of his countrymen, he must leave general reasoning, and show the extent of the injury entailed on the community by the neglect of his principles; how their application may be best effected; and the advantages of which it will be productive. This science has its practical as well as its theoretical portion; and the economist will abdicate his principal functions if he does not call the public attention to every institution or regulation which appears, on a careful enquiry, to be adverse to the increase of public wealth and happiness. Unless he do this, he can be little else than a mere ideologist, about whose speculation most people will, very properly, care little or nothing.[49]

But Senior, himself undoubtedly a major figure in the development of Classical economics, had an important ally. J. E. Cairnes, in his *Logical Method of Political Economy*, adopted a very similar position on this as on a number of issues. On the 'science and art' question, Cairnes's view was that it was necessary to limit economics to a science of wealth that was above policy. Economics should be neutral between different plans of social organization as mechanics was between different plans of railway construction. He followed Senior too in his procedure of establishing premises and then making deductions from these. The premises were:

1 The existence of a desire for physical well-being and, as a consequence of this, of a desire to obtain wealth at the least possible sacrifice.
2 The (Malthusian) principle of population as derived from the psychological character of man and his mental propensities.
3 The existence of certain physical qualities of the natural agents, more especially land, on which human industry was exercised.[50]

Now it is true that Cairnes asserted that the premises from which political economy was deduced were empirical. He argued that political economy was a deductive science with empirical premises—as long as the premises were empirical this made hypothetical procedures satisfactory.[51] But it is highly doubtful how far these three premises could be described as empirical. Indeed Cairnes treats introspection of premises as apparently superior to induction and regards the establishment of hypothetical cases as a substitute for experiment.[52]

Statistical verification was not only not necessary; it was positively misleading. 'The severe and logical style which characterized the cultivators of the science in the early part of the century has ... been changed ... results are now appealed to instead of principles.'[53] The inevitability of diminishing returns was a physical law which could not be refuted on a statistical basis.[54] If the conclusions of political economy did not correspond with the facts that was not because the conclusions were wrong but because of disturbing causes.[55] When conclusions reached by deduction were contradicted by the available evidence there must be underlying tendencies which accorded with the conclusions.[56] His attitude to induction was hostile—indeed he regarded it as futile[57]—and he viewed the Baconian method as applied to the social sciences as of no use, because economic facts always had a multiplicity of causes. He also advanced the rather startling theory that while Baconian induction was necessary in the physical sciences because mankind had no knowledge of ultimate physical principles, the economist started with a knowledge of ultimate causes in his branch of inquiry so that he was compensated for the inability to experiment by the possibility of introspection.[58]

Cairnes's attitude, and in particular his comments on induction, did not only derive from Senior and Ricardo. J. S. Mill's formal statements on method were in very much the same mould. Not only did Mill ostensibly distinguish between the science and the art of economics[59] but he saw the basic method in the social sciences as what he called the 'Concrete Deductive Method'.[60] This involved deductive analysis from premises drawn from introspection and observation. In its most extreme form this is to be found in an article in the *Westminster Review* of 1825 when, in reply to Malthus who had objected that those associated with Ricardo had altered the theories of Adam Smith on the basis of pure speculation, Mill replied that it would have been surprising if they had altered them on any other basis.[61] The stress on this method is also particularly marked in his *Essay* (in which it is called the *a priori* method). In Mill's writings on method there is a good deal of ambiguity on two fundamental points—the nature of premises (whether hypothetical or empirical—Mill seems to switch between one and the other)[62]—and the need for verification.[63] The latter point was however taken care of to some extent by Mill's introduction in his *Logic* of the 'Inverse Deductive or Historical Method' to supplement his primary method.[64] This method was not however directly concerned with verification but with providing empirical generalizations in complicated situations where the powers of the deductive method accurately to predict the course of events were limited. But he was generally hostile to such empirical laws which he regarded as generalizations behind which we needed to find the causes. Real scientific truths were not empirical but were the causal laws that explained the observations. Nevertheless Mill did attempt to steer a middle course. On the one hand he condemned what he called 'The Chemical or Experimental Method' in the social sciences because the impossibility of experiment made isolation of causes impossible;[65] on the other hand he was also hostile towards purely deductive reasoning from hypothetical premises to hypothetical conclusions—which he called the 'Geometrical Method'.[66]

The end result of all this was somewhat of a hybrid however. On the one hand Mill defended Ricardian theorems, established by something at least very like the 'Geometrical Method' as 'tendencies' when they were contradicted by the available evidence as it was gathered by such writers as McCulloch and G. R. Porter. On the other, when one takes the contents of the *Principles* as a whole—in other words when we see what Mill 'did'—it is impossible to deny Schumpeter's view that Mill's formal stress on deduction is excessive.[67] For the *Principles* is almost as wide ranging as the *Wealth of Nations*. Mill's aim was to update the *Wealth of Nations* both with regard to its theory *and* its facts. As Schumpeter points out Mill's readers got factual material to the extent of about one-sixth of the book.[68] This is less than Smith's readers got: but it still presents an enormous contrast when compared with Ricardo's *Principles* which contains hardly a fact at all. But in any case if we agree with Schumpeter that Mill was relying on the factual and straightforwardly inductive work of Babbage as being available to his readers then, on this basis, more than two-thirds of the book is factual.[69] As Viner concluded, the *Principles* has no single methodological character.[70]

We have now finished our survey of the distinguishing characteristics of Classical economics and it is time to examine the Classical formulations in specific areas of theory, beginning with the theory of value.

## NOTES

1. For a review of these writers see J. Bonar, *Theories of Population from Raleigh to Arthur Young* (London, 1931).
2. Hume, *Essays* (1809 edn.), i. 400–1.
3. R. Wallace, *Dissertation on the Numbers of Mankind* (1753), quoted in E. Cannan, *A History of the Theories of Production and Distribution in English Political Economy* (London, 1903), pp. 126–7.
4. i. 81.
5. i. 83.
6. Malthus, op. cit., p. 11.
7. Ibid., pp. 13–14.
8. Ibid., pp. 64–5. (1st Essay )
9. Ibid., pp. 15, 71–2, 139–41.
10. Ibid., 21–5.
11. Preface to 2nd edn. repr. in 4th edn. (London, 1807), p. ix.
12. Ibid., p. 19.
13. Ibid., pp. 21–2.
14. Ricardo, *Works*, ed. Sraffa, i. 93.
15. Ibid., p. 94.
16. Ibid., pp. 94, 101, 104, 125–6, 164, 292, 407.
17. N. W. Senior, *Two Lectures on Population* (1829), repr. in *Selected Writings on Economics* (A. M. Kelley, New York, 1966), p. 35. For Torrens see the Appendix to the 1829 edn. of his *Essay on the External Corn Trade*, pp. 473–7. The analysis therein actually dated from an unpublished MS. of 1826.
18. See also N. W. Senior, *Outline of the Science of Political Economy* (repr. London, 1938), pp. 85–6.
19. *Lectures on Population*, p. 2. Compare *Outline*, pp. 26 and 36.
20. *Outline*, p. 38.
21. Quoted in O'Brien, *J. R. McCulloch*, p. 317.
22. J. S. Mill, *Principles*, ed. Ashley, p. 359.
23. Ibid., p. 161. See also ibid., pp. 156–61, 561, 702–4, 721–2.
24. Ibid., Bk. IV, Ch. VI, pp. 746–51.
25. Ibid., pp. 191–3.
26. London, 1830.
27. G. P. Scrope, *Principles of Political Economy* (London, 1833), Ch. XI.
28. Ibid., pp. 278–9.
29. S. Read, *Political Economy* (Edinburgh, 1829), pp. 173–4.
30. Cairnes, op. cit. (2nd edn. London, 1875), pp. 149–50.
31. Ibid., pp. 150–1.
32. Newton's four principles were as follows:

    1 We are to admit no more causes of natural things than such as are both true and sufficient to explain their appearances;
    2 therefore to the same natural effects we must, as far as possible, assign the same natural causes;
    3 the qualities of bodies which admit neither intension nor remission of degrees, and which are found to belong to all bodies within the reach of our

experiments, are to be esteemed the universal qualities of all bodies what-soever;

4 in experimental philosophy we are to look upon propositions collected by general induction from phenomena as accurately or very nearly true, not-withstanding any hypothesis that may be imagined, till such time as other phenomena occur, by which they may either be made more accurate or liable to exceptions.

33. See O'Brien, *J. R. McCulloch*, pp. 96–8.
34. McCulloch, op. cit., repr. in *Principles* (1849 edn.), pp. xi–xii.
35. O'Brien, ibid.
36. Ibid.
37. Say, *Treatise on Political Economy*, trans. C. R. Prinsep (repr. A. M. Kelley, New York, 1964), pp. xvii–xviii.
38. *Introductory Lecture at King's College* (London, 1833).
39. Ricardo, *Works*, ed. Sraffa, viii. 184.
40. Ibid., pp. 234–5.
41. R. Torrens, *An Essay on the Production of Wealth* (London, 1821), (repr. A. M. Kelley, New York, 1965), p. iv.
42. R. Torrens, *The Budget* (London, 1844), p. xiii.
43. R. Torrens, *Essay on the External Corn Trade* (5th edn. London, 1829), p. 473; *On Wages and Combination* (London, 1834), pp. 30–1.
44. Compare Senior's *Outline*, pp. 86, 193. See also M. E. A. Bowley, *Nassau Senior*, pp. 173–4.
45. N. Senior, *An Introductory Lecture on Political Economy* (London, 1827, repr. A. M. Kelley, New York, 1966), p. 36. But see also Senior's *Outline*, pp. 26–7.
46. N. Senior, *Four Introductory Lectures on Political Economy* (London, 1852, repr. New York, 1966), pp. 26–7.
47. Ibid., pp. 18–19.
48. See Bowley, op. cit., Pt. II.
49. McCulloch, *Principles* (1849), p. x.
50. Cairnes, *Logical Method*, pp. 59–60.
51. Ibid., pp. 51–4.
52. Ibid., pp. 76–7.
53. Ibid., p. 5.
54. Ibid., p. 35.
55. However Cairnes does sometimes indicate a recognition of the need for verification (op. cit., pp. 80, 84–5).
56. Ibid., pp. 94, 99.
57. Ibid., p. 63.
58. Ibid., pp. 66–8, 70, 75.
59. J. S. Mill, *Essays on Some Unsettled Questions of Political Economy* (London, 1844, 3rd edn. London, 1877), pp. 123–4.
60. J. S. Mill, *Logic* (7th edn.), Bk. VI, Ch. IX.
61. *Westminster Review*, 3 (1825), 213.
62. Contrast *Logic*, ii. 501, *Essay*, pp. 142–3 and 143–4, 149.
63. Contrast *Logic*, ii. 488, 503, and *Essay*, pp. 142–3, 152–4.
64. See *Logic*, Bk. VI, Ch. X and esp. pp. 488–9.
65. *Logic*, Bk. VI, Ch. VII.
66. *Logic*, Bk. VI, Ch. VIII.
67. Schumpeter, op. cit., p. 537.
68. Ibid., p. 541.
69. See ibid., p. 542 for a long list of factual topics covered in the book.
70. Viner, *Long View and Short*, p. 329.

## BIBLIOGRAPHY

The focuses of Classical economics—the general interests and orientation of the Classical writers—can really only be appreciated by reading the works of those writers. But a stimulating general survey is contained in Pt. II (Ch. 3, Section 4e, and Ch. 5) and Pt. III (especially Chs. 4–7) of Schumpeter's great *History*. See also Ch. 8 of Blaug's *Economic Theory in Retrospect* for a bird's-eye view of the changes in direction produced by the marginal revolution. For the Classical view of competition see the article by McNulty already cited in the bibliography to Ch. II.

On population there is a wide range of primary and secondary references. The brilliant and original critique of Malthus is to be found in E. Cannan, *History of the Theories of Production and Distribution* (London, 1903), and the same author's *Review of Economic Theory* (London, 1929), pp. 69–74. See also Blaug, *Retrospect*, pp. 61–71, and *Ricardian Economics*, Ch. 6. Another source (which we will have occasion to refer to again) is the classic article by G. J. Stigler, 'The Ricardian Theory of Value and Distribution', *Journal of Political Economy*, 60 (1952), 187–207. See also I. Bowen, *Population* (Cambridge, 1954). For more sympathetic treatment see J. Bonar, *Malthus and his Work* (London, 1924), and G. F. McCleary, *The Malthusian Population Theory* (London, 1953).

Malthus's name in our own day has been frequently used in contexts of which he did not approve. On the campaigners for artificial limitation of family size ('neo-Malthusianism') during the era of Classical economics see N. E. Hines's two articles in *Economic History* for 1928 and 1929 and two more articles from the same author, in the *Quarterly Journal of Economics* 1928 and the *Journal of Political Economy* 1929.

On anti-Malthusianism amongst the Classical economists see Bowley, *Senior*, Ch. III, and O'Brien, *McCulloch*, Ch. XIII. Robert Torrens claimed to have led the movement away from Malthusianism (*Letters on Commercial Policy* (London, 1833), p. 43, and cited the Appendix to the 1829 edn. of his *Essay on the External Corn Trade*. Although the dating might be considered as giving him a place beside Senior on this issue Torrens's claim seems doubtful. The wage analysis contained in the appendix does, it is true, actually date from early in 1826 (see D. P. O'Brien, 'Torrens on Wages and Emmigration', *Economica*, 33 (1966), 336–40). But it certainly does not read like anti-Malthusianism. On J. S. Mill see P. Schwartz, *The New Political Economy of J. S. Mill* (London, 1972), Ch. 3. The full-scale rebels were Sadler and Scrope whose work has been referred to in the text: see McCulloch's *Literature of Political Economy*, Ch. XII, for a full range of references. Comparing the quality of what Sadler and Scrope had to offer with Malthus's own *Essay* (the 1st and 6th are the important edns.) it is not altogether surprising that the former had relatively little impact. At the same time the defects in the latter are fairly obvious: and the reader will find instructive warning in the tautological attempts at preservation of the Malthusian thesis especially that in Cairnes's *Logical Method*. For Ricardo's use of the population model see O. St. Clair, *Key to Ricardo*.

The range of references on method is even wider. On the Scottish school see R. L. Meek 'The Scottish Contribution to Marxist Sociology' in J. Saville (ed.), *Democracy and the Labour Movement* (London, 1954), A. Skinner, 'Economics and History: The Scottish Enlightenment', *Scottish Journal of Political Economy* 12 (1965), and in the same volume (pp. 267–80) 'Economics and the Problem of Method: an Eighteenth Century View', as well as the same author's introduction to Sir J. Steuart's *Inquiry into the Principles of Political Economy* (Edinburgh, 1966). There is also H. F. Thompson, 'Adam Smith's Philosophy of Science', *Quarterly Journal of Economics*, 79 (1965), 212–33. See also E. Rotwein's introduction to D. Hume, *Economic Writings* and O'Brien, *McCulloch*, pp. 96–8. On the deductive school see Bowley, *Senior*, Ch. I, and M. Blaug, 'The Empirical Content of Ricardian Economics', *Journal of Political Economy*, 64 (1956), 41–58. General discussions of the problem will be found in Schumpeter, *History*, pp. 527–84, and Viner, *Long View and Short*, pp. 327 ff. See also the article by Bitterman referred to in the previous chapter, pp. 497–507. The most important primary references have been indicated in the text: but to get some flavour of the immense appetite of some Classical economists for economic facts see J. R. McCulloch, *Dictionary of Commerce*, which ran through ten edns. from 1832.

# 4. Classical Value Theory

In this chapter it will be necessary to examine three kinds of value theory, all of which are to be found in the Classical writings. These three kinds are, firstly, the 'cost of production' theory of value which, so far as Classical economics is concerned, originated with Adam Smith; secondly, the Ricardian theory of value; and thirdly the subjective value theories associated especially with the work of J. B. Say. The contributions of Smith and Ricardo will be dealt with first since an understanding of these is necessary to an understanding of the significance of the other Classical writings on value.

## i. ADAM SMITH

Adam Smith laid the foundations for Classical value theory. What he did, and the way he did it, were to prove extremely important because he seems deliberately and consciously to have rejected the value theory which he inherited. He inherited a subjective value theory: and instead of developing this he largely substituted for it a cost of production theory of value. A developed subjective value theory was available in the works of Pufendorf, Smith's teacher Hutcheson, and Hutcheson's teacher Carmichael. These writers had made value dependent on usefulness and relative scarcity—just as it has done in economic literature since the marginal revolution of the 1870s. Adam Smith had himself advanced a somewhat similar value theory in his *Lectures* and there solved the paradox that water is very useful but valueless while diamonds are useless but valuable on the basis of relative scarcity. But in the *Wealth of Nations* we find, as we shall see, that Smith advanced a 'cost of production' theory of value, and relegated all the material from the earlier writers to a discussion of short-run market fluctuations. Various reasons have been advanced for this change, notably the idea that the 'cost of production' theory was more suitable for a work dealing with growth; and it has been (rather uneasily) linked with an attempt to see a welfare theory in Smith's value theory—more will be said of this last below. But there is one rather obvious explanation which seems to have escaped the commentators. As noted in Chapter 2, Smith's *Wealth of Nations* contained a theory of distribution, though his *Lectures* did not. Without the concept of marginal productivity there was no very obvious way of linking distribution to value except by a cost of production theory of value. Having thought it necessary to introduce a theory of distribution, Adam Smith had to rework his value theory.

Having decided on a 'cost of production' value theory Smith then offered it in two forms. The first was the case of a labour-only economy.

In that early and rude state of society which precedes both the accumulation of stock and the appropriation of land, the proportion between the quantities of labour necessary for acquiring different objects seems to be the only circumstances which can afford any rule for exchanging them for one another. If among a nation of hunters, for example, it usually costs twice the labour to kill a beaver which it does to kill a deer, one beaver should naturally exchange for or be worth two deer. It is natural that what is usually the produce of two days or two hours labour, should be worth double of what is usually the produce of one day's or one hour's labour.[1]

Smith recognizes that allowance has to be made for the hardship of different kinds of labour and for particular skill and ingenuity, in comparing different quantities of labour but he makes no allowance for the fact that it will take longer to bring the beaver to market than the deer. But, in any case, this only relates to a hypothetical Robinson Crusoe type of economy. In the normal case there are three inputs to be rewarded. After capital has been accumulated some of the price of a good is made up of amortization and of profit —the latter is distinguished from wages of management on the basis of an example which takes the *rate* of profit as determined exogenously. When land has all become private property rent constitutes a third component of price.

In every society the price of every commodity finally resolves itself into some one or other, or all of those three parts; and in every improved society, all the three enter more or less, as component parts, into the price of the far greater part of commodities.[2]

Of course such a formulation encounters the very real difficulty that unless the author offers a theory of the pricing of the productive services whose costs enter into value he is not really offering a theory of value. But we have already seen that the theory of distribution was in fact the whole rationale of Smith's value theory in the *Wealth of Nations*. Distribution itself is dealt with in the next chapter.

All this relates to what Adam Smith called Natural Price, and which may be loosely equated with Marshall's Long Run Normal Price. But it is special because what we have here is supply-determined price in the long run. In every society there is an average rate of wages, profits, and rent, to pay which a commodity is sold at its natural price or cost of production.

When the price of any commodity is neither more nor less than what is sufficient to pay the rent of the land, the wages of the labour, and the profits of the stock employed in raising, preparing, and bringing it to market, according to their natural rates, the commodity is then sold for what may be called its natural price.[3]

The dismissal of utility as a determinant of value is justified by reference to the 'diamonds and water' paradox[4] although, as we have seen, Smith solved this in the *Lectures*. It is interesting to see that Smith so far purges his analysis of the subjective elements as to redefine utility. As understood by Hutcheson and Smith's other predecessors, utility was subjective; and this was also the view adopted by the other Classical economists from Ricardo onwards. But for Adam Smith 'having utility' meant not being productive of subjective satisfaction but having objective usefulness. Thus when Smith said that diamonds had no utility he did not mean that they did not give satisfaction but that they were not useful.

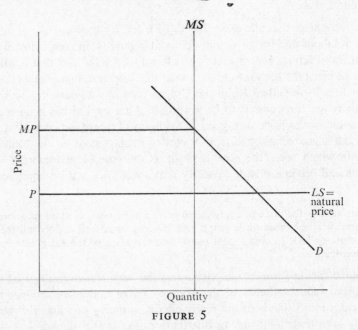

FIGURE 5

But even though utility was dismissed from the Long Run determination of value, it was treated in the short-run determination of value which Smith dealt with in Book I, Ch. VII. This contained Smith's treatment of market price. It was an important part of his total value theory because he saw natural price as something around which *actual* price fluctuated according to the prevailing balance of demand and supply.

Market price (*MP*) was regulated by the quantity brought to market (*MS*) and by 'effectual demand'—the latter being the demand of those willing to pay the natural price. When the quantity fell short of the effectual demand, i.e those willing to pay the natural price, competition between buyers would cause price to rise (Fig. 5). When the quantity exceeded effectual demand (thus defined) competition between sellers would lower price (Fig. 6). When quantity brought to market supplied effectual demand at the natural price

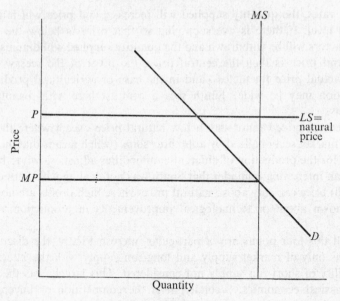

FIGURE 6

the competition of sellers would oblige them to accept the natural price but
no less (Fig. 7).

Smith has here advanced a market analysis which provided the basis for
the market analysis in virtually all the Classical writers. The quantity of a
commodity brought to market according to this analysis adjusts itself to
the effectual demand. This adjustment is achieved through the effect on
factor rewards. If there is a shortfall so that the market price is greater than
the natural price, factors producing the good will receive more than their

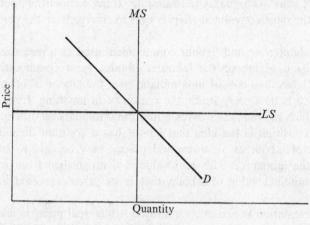

FIGURE 7

natural rates, the quantity supplied will increase, and price will fall to the natural level. If there is oversupplying so that price is below the natural level, factors will be withdrawn and the quantity supplied will diminish.

Natural price is then the central price, the pivot of the seesaw around which actual price fluctuates—and in the case of agricultural produce this fluctuation may be wide.[5] Smith sees a contrast here with manufactured products.

In general price cannot stay below natural price except where there is a labour market sectionalized by apprenticeships (which means that the labour supply for the production of different commodities adjusts slowly): but (and this is an interesting reminder that Smith was not dealing with Perfect Competition) price can stay above natural price where high profits are not generally known about or technological improvements in production are kept secret.

In all this four points are of particular interest. Firstly, the discussion is in terms only of market supply and long-run supply with the intermediate possibility of short-run supply not considered. This largely sets the pattern for Classical economics. Secondly, it is the competition of buyers where price is above normal, and of dealers at and below normal price which clears the market. Thirdly, we see that market clearing is achieved in the market period by price variation and in the long run by quantity variation. The former is Walrasian; the latter Marshallian. Fourthly, although we now know that negative feedback is insufficient for stability, Adam Smith's assumption that it was set the pattern for more than 150 years.

This completes the discussion of Adam Smith's main value theory as set out in Chapters VI and VII of the *Wealth of Nations*. But we cannot leave the subject without turning our attention to Chapter V, 'Of the Real and Nominal Price of Commodities, or of their Price in Labour, and their Price in Money', which is arguably (and despite strong competition, notably from Ricardo) the most convoluted chapter ever to emerge from the pen of a great economist.

In this chapter we find 'labour commanded' used as a measure of riches. After division of labour the labourer obtains most commodities by exchange. Riches then consist in command over the labour of others. Labour commanded is then, says Smith, the real price of anything. Its real value is the toil which the purchaser saves himself and imposes on others. The basis of this proposition is the idea that labour has a constant disutility; 'equal quantities of labour at all times and places, may be said to be of equal value to the labourer'.[6] This real value is distinguished from what Smith calls the nominal value of labour, that is its price expressed in terms of money.[7]

The presentation is extremely confused—thus 'real price' is used in three apparently different senses. It is used firstly as disutility embodied in a commodity, secondly in the sense that the term is now used, i.e. after adjustment for changes in the value of money, and finally as the subsistence of the labourer.[8] Because of this the chapter has presented commentators with a very real problem. Some have seen Smith as trying to provide a welfare index.[9] The 'real value' of a commodity is its labour price, i.e. the units of disutility it commands. They see Smith as concerned to find the improvements in welfare associated with a reduction in the labour disutility involved in obtaining a given amount of real income. If this were to make sense however, we should expect to find Smith offering some measure of welfare over time, pointing for instance to real wages per head as increasing with growth. In fact he does not do this but argues that the corn wage is in the long run effectively a constant. Earlier writers, especially Ricardo, have seen Smith as having become hopelessly confused between labour embodied and labour commanded as determinants of value. Obviously when there are other claimants apart from labour so that rent and profit take some of price, disutility embodied will be less than disutility commanded where the commodity is exchanged for a more or less labour intensive one.

In fact however Smith is wrestling in this chapter with two different problems. On the one hand there is the welfare concept. The quantity of subsistence which the labourer's (constant) disutility commands, varies over time: so the real value (disutility command) of commodities varies over time as their command over (varying) subsistence changes although the labourer has to part with a constant amount of disutility to obtain his subsistence, what ever level that may be at.

The subsistence of the labourer ... is very different upon different occasions; more liberal in a society advancing to opulence, than in one that is standing still; and in one that is standing still, than in one that is going backwards. Every other commodity, however, will at any particular time purchase a greater or smaller quantity of labour in proportion to the quantity of subsistence which it can purchase at that time.[10]

This is a *different* question from that dealt with earlier[11] in which command of a given money payment over other commodities varies over time because of debasement. In the first case the difference is because of the varying progressiveness of society which determines, for Smith, the level of subsistence of the labourer: in the second it is because of variations in the value of money. But this latter *is* a major preoccupation of the chapter: and it is significant that in a chapter of seventeen pages, the last nine pages are taken up with a discussion of changes in the value of the precious metals and are thus concerned with the second source of variation.

The two however come together. They are linked in the sense that both ultimately produce variation in command over labour disutility. But they do so for different reasons. Because, *in the long run*, the subsistence of the labourer varies with the price of corn, variation 1 can best be dealt with by a corn deflator: and because corn is more stable than money[12] the corn deflator is still better for dealing with variation 2. Thus in illustration we may cite the following:

A rent therefore reserved in corn is liable only to the variations in the quantity of labour which a certain quantity of corn can purchase. But a rent reserved in any other commodity is liable, not only to the variations in the quantity of labour which any particular quantity of corn can purchase [variation 1], but to the variations in the quantity of corn which can be purchased by any particular quantity of that commodity [variation 2].[13]

In so far as this constitutes a welfare standard, what is involved is a sectional, not a general or national, welfare standard. Adam Smith expressly says that because the value of subsistence does not vary directly with the price of corn *in the short run*, it is *advantageous* (i.e. in terms of command over labour—other men's sweat) to specify rents in corn.[14] Both the sources of variation identified above are concerned with a common problem: variations in command over labour disutility, which is the essence of wealth. But this is *not* used as a welfare standard for the community but for sectional interests, especially rent receivers who are the burden of Adam Smith's concern here. He does *not* go on to deal with the ratio of national income to total disutility which would provide a *general* welfare standard.

That concludes our examination of Adam Smith's theory of value. As we shall see it provided the framework for all the developments in Classical value theory; but before we go on to consider the other writers who also held a specifically 'cost of production' theory of value it is necessary to consider Ricardo's contribution.

## ii. RICARDO

Ricardo is often credited with having advanced a labour theory of value. Although this is not, as we shall see, a strictly accurate description of what he produced, his writings on value are sufficiently different from what the other writers had to offer to require a separate section. Two things are indisputable about Ricardo's value theory: that a primary role was given to labour; and that recognition was given to the complications caused by capital. Older writers on the history of economic theory took the view that Ricardo conceded the latter reluctantly in successive editions; while more recent interpretations, especially that of Mr. Sraffa, made in the light of Ricardo's correspondence, suggest that Ricardo recognized the problem all the time and that the modifications to the treatment of the problem in successive editions of his *Principles* are designed to minimize its importance.

Undoubtedly Ricardo's first approach is to offer a labour theory of value. The heading to the first section of Chapter 1 of his *Principles* reads 'The value of a commodity, or the quantity of any other commodity for which it will exchange, depends on the relative quantity of labour which is necessary for its production, and not on the greater or less compensation which is paid for that labour'. The problem of capital arose because once labour was not the only input, relative labour inputs would not explain relative values if capital/labour ratios for the production of different commodities varied. This could still have been dealt with if the capital involved had earned no profit. In that case depreciation would simply have been treated as wages— the wages of *indirect* labour—with the amount of these wages inversely related to the durability of equipment. Ricardo did in fact treat capital in this way and we find Section III of his first chapter headed 'Not only the labour applied immediately to commodities affect their value, but the labour also which is bestowed on the implements, tools, and buildings, with which such labour is assisted'. It would still be possible to talk of value as determined by total labour, adding remuneration of direct and indirect labour together. This obviously was not satisfactory however. There was no reason why a man should, for instance, spend capital employing labour to produce machines rather than to produce directly saleable commodities unless he received some compensation for his inability to get his capital back straight away. Ricardo in fact thought that this necessity of compensation for waiting was both a necessary and a sufficient condition for the emergence of profit. On this he was confused, because, as McCulloch pointed out, there was no profit to be made from storing wine which was already mature. In other words, in the simple Ricardian model, both waiting and productivity were necessary if a premium was to emerge.

But although Ricardo was confused over why a premium emerged, he was clear enough about the fact that it did emerge and that value could not be resolved into payment for direct and indirect labour. The reason that it could not had two aspects, as Mr. Sraffa has pointed out.[15] Firstly, the existence of profit meant that price did not resolve itself completely into payments to direct and indirect labour and that, as we shall see, unless the durability of capital was the same in the production of all commodities, labour input alone, counting both direct and indirect labour, was not sufficient to explain relative values. Secondly, a wage rise would alter relative values. This effect has been called the 'wage/durability-of-capital theorem' by the present author in another context and that is the term which will be used here, although the reader should note that it is also known as the 'Ricardo effect'. What was involved can be seen from the following example. Suppose that wages and profits move inversely (as they do in the Ricardian system) and that both are made uniform by competition. Then take three commodities *A*, *B*, *C*, where *A* is labour intensive, *C* is capital intensive, and *B* has the 'average' labour/capital ratio. Suppose that *A* employs £1,000 in circulating capital with profits at 10 per cent, final product value £1,100. Suppose that *B* employs £500 fixed and £500 circulating capital (the latter expended on wages), final product value £1,100. Suppose that $C$ employs £750 fixed capital and £250 circulating capital, final product value £1,100. Suppose that wages rise by 5 per cent. $A$'s wage bill becomes £1,050 and his profits 5 per cent. $B$'s wage bill becomes £525 and his profit $7\frac{1}{2}$ per cent. $C$'s wage bill becomes £262·50 and his profits 8·75 per cent. Product prices must now alter so as to equalize profits. The relative price of $C$ will fall and that of $A$ will rise. If we had assumed that $C$ had *no* wage bill so that his profits stayed at 10 per cent, profits would finally have settled at $7\frac{1}{2}$ per cent with $B$ as the average commodity. As we have assumed that $C$ has *some* wage bill they will settle slightly below $7\frac{1}{2}$ per cent.[16]

It is important to note in all this that in terms of this model a rise of wages cannot bring about a general rise of prices because the value of money is held constant. Ricardo achieved this partly by making money a commodity which would be affected like other commodities by a wage rise,[17] and partly by an assumption about the production period of money which we will see below.

The problem of capital in fact manifested itself in four different forms. Firstly there were straightforward differences in the amounts of fixed and circulating capital and hence (since the latter largely represented wage payments) in capital/labour ratios. Secondly there was the unequal durability of fixed capital. Thirdly there were variations in the length of time before a product could be brought to market. Finally there were differences in the rapidity with which capital was returned to the employer. These last two are particularly important to note. The former is the period of production and the latter the turnover rate of capital. Obviously one is the reciprocal of the other. Ricardo in fact saw quite clearly that all of these differences between commodities reduced to the common problem of time. Because of this common problem he recognized that relative values could be altered independently of differences in labour inputs. He played this down however, averring that it would not be of the order of more than 6 or 7 per cent[18]— hence Stigler's reference to Ricardo's 93 per cent labour theory of value. The same author has made the point that Ricardo, having clearly recognized the problem of capital, could be said to hold an *empirical* but not an *analytical* labour theory of value—labour input roughly, but not precisely, determined relative values.[19]

Even on this level there were however a number of complications of which Ricardo took insufficient notice. The first was the problem of rent. Now Ricardo simply 'got rid of' rent. He did this by treating it as a price-determined surplus. Such a procedure was only legitimate if land had no alternative uses so that its earnings in alternative occupations were zero. Ricardo implicitly got round this by making the workers' 'corn' a basket of wage goods in fixed proportions: if there was no commodity substitution then corn-growing land did not have a necessary supply price to the farmer which

*Marginalia (handwritten, left margin):*

This is not quite right. B determines general rate of profit ⊐ $1,100 - (500 + 525) \div 1025 = 7.32\%$ The other industries will adjust price with that π-rate.

had to be paid to it to prevent it switching to potatoes. But Ricardo's solution is only implicit in his examples: he never really faced this problem.

The second major difficulty was valuation of the labour input. Relative quantities of labour, as Viner pointed out, could in fact only mean relative quantities of wages.[20] But a given amount of wages would only represent a given amount of common labour if wage differentials between common labour and skilled labour were fixed *and* unchanging. If they changed then relative values would change (because different commodities used different amounts of skilled and unskilled labour) without labour inputs (reduced to a common denominator) changing. Now Ricardo did recognize this problem: and his solution was simply to say that differentials were fixed,[21] and that the price of common labour (which, as we have seen in considering Adam Smith's value theory, had to be explained if it was in turn to explain relative prices) was explained by his subsistence theory of wages. In fact such an argument ran into serious difficulties. Relative wages depended not only on relative disutility (agreeableness) of different occupations (possibly constant), but also on costs of training (and *profit* on the capital invested in this training as well as in premiums to persuade labour to undergo training during which it earned little or nothing), and on rents of ability as well. Ricardo's theory was then hardly satisfactory.

But all this of course relates to the problem of the determination of relative exchangeable values at any moment in time. It would however be entirely misleading to leave the reader with the impression that this was either the only or even the main concern of Ricardo's value theory. In fact his value theory was constructed so as to revolve around the central problem of his model—agricultural progress, diminishing returns, and the decline of profits. His value theory was, in other words, subservient to his distribution theory.

It is here that the most important part of Ricardo's value theory, the invariable measure of value, comes into its own.[22] He distinguished between exchangeable value and absolute value, the latter being value measured in terms of the invariable measure. The invariable measure was a commodity produced with an average capital/labour ratio—in fact the average derived from finding the total capital/labour ratio for the whole economy. It thus used the average period of production for the economy. It was then a pivot around which changes in value moved. Following the wage/durability-of-capital theorem, a rise in wages would raise the price of all commodities produced with a period of production of less than the average, and lower the price of all commodities produced with a period of production greater than the average. Now Ricardo made a number of important steps to produce his result. The first was the constant price level assumption already noted in dealing with the wage/durability-of-capital theorem. A change in wheat prices could not then be due to a change in the general value of money.

The next step was to decide (arbitrarily) that gold was produced with an average period of production. The next step, one which is fundamentally important yet nowhere explicitly stated in the *Principles* although implied by the examples, was the decision that the period of production of gold was one year and that this was the *same* as the period of production in agriculture. In this way Ricardo was able to isolate changes in the money price of corn which were due to changes in the input requirements of corn.

This can be made clear in the following way. Suppose that there exist diminishing returns in agriculture. Then inputs per unit of output rise with the progress of population. The relative price of wheat (determined at the margin) rises. Now according to Ricardo's theory of wages this would increase wages. Through the operation of the wage/durability-of-capital theorem the price of all goods with a period of production less than that of the invariable measure would rise and that of all goods with a period of production greater than the invariable measure would fall. Since wheat and the invariable measure have the *same* period of production, this cause of variation in wheat prices (expressed in the invariable measure, which is money) is removed. Wage increases *on their own* leave wheat prices constant. Hence any change in wheat prices in terms of the invariable measure must signal rising inputs for wheat production and thus, according to the basic Ricardian model, declining profits.

Quite apart from the arbitrary steps already apparent to the reader, there is a further difficulty arising from the relative cheapening of capital intensive commodities. As relatively capital-intensive products become relatively cheaper more will be produced and thus the average length of the period of production for the economy as a whole will be increased. This would mean that the invariable measure, in order to remain the average for the economy as a whole, would have to change and would no longer be invariable! Ricardo, by implicitly ruling out commodity substitution as we have seen, side-stepped this problem. But it is doubtful whether he was really conscious of its existence.

His sweeping assumptions had also ruled out other possible changes in the price of wheat. By making the price elasticity of demand for wheat zero and making the demand for wheat a function of the size of population he ruled out all the cobweb and demand problems with which we are now familiar in relation to agricultural products. This despite the facts that the cobweb theorem was already more or less in existence in the writings of McCulloch.[23] But if Ricardo knew of it, he ignored it.

We have now covered the core of Ricardo's value theory. In fact he had more than this to say on the subject of value, but in this remainder of his treatment he largely followed Smith.

The value of non-reproducible commodities was determined by demand.[24] Commodities which could not be freely increased in quantity obtained value from their scarcity. The treatment of demand and supply is generally close to Smith's. Chapter IV treats of the relationship between natural and market price and sees mobility of capital as equalizing profits. Thus in Figs. 8a and 8b a shift in demand from woollens to silks initially raising the market

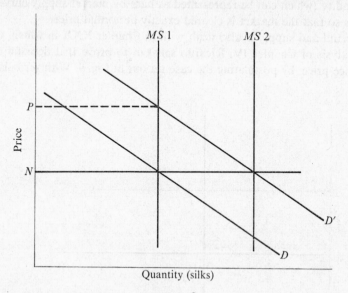

FIGURE 8a

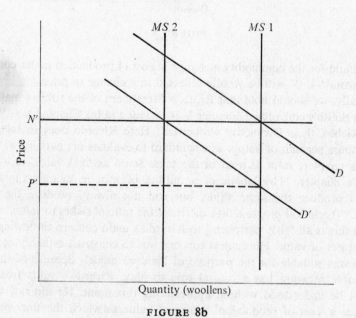

FIGURE 8b

price of silks above the natural price by the distance *NP* and lowering the market price of woollens below the natural price by the distance *N'P'* will result, in Ricardo's example, in a transfer of inputs from the manufacture of woollens to the manufacture of silks so that the amount supplied of each commodity (which can be represented as here by market supply curves *MS*) adjusts so that the market is cleared exactly at normal price.

Demand and supply is also dealt with in Chapter XXX in which, despite the analysis of Chapter IV, Ricardo sets out to prove that demand cannot influence price, by postulating the case set out in Fig. 9. With zero elasticity

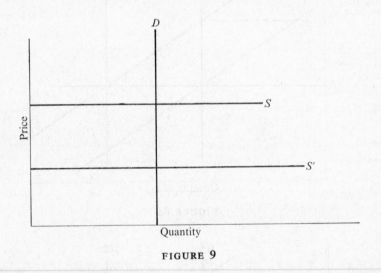

FIGURE 9

of demand for the commodity a change in cost of production under constant costs from *S* to *S'* will be wholly reflected in a change in price.

Finally, we should note that Ricardo's treatment of the subject matter of Adam Smith's convoluted Chapter V is included in his Chapter XX, 'Value and Riches, their Distinctive Properties'. Here Ricardo does in fact offer man-hours per unit of output as a standard to evaluate net national product. In this chapter, value is used in the same sense as 'real value' is used in Smith's chapter. 'The labour of a million of men in manufactures, will always produce the same value, but will not always produce the same riches.'[25] Technical progress then increases the ratio of riches to value.

But this is all fairly peripheral to Ricardo's main concern in dealing with the subject of value. His central concern was to construct a theory of value which was suitable for the purpose of his corn model. Because of this the invariable measure has a central role to play. Ricardo's value treatment cannot be understood without appreciating this point. He did not simply produce a 'cost of production' theory of value in which the star role was given to labour by the use of a rather specialized concept of capital, but he attempted to produce a theory of value which would serve him in his attempt to show the harmful effects of the Corn Laws.

We have now examined the value theories offered by both Smith and Ricardo. Before going on to deal with the subjective value theorists it is perhaps best to see what the other Classical writers on value who followed them made of the foundations they had laid.

### iii. 'COST OF PRODUCTION' THEORIES OF VALUE AFTER RICARDO

Although Ricardo did not set out to produce a 'cost of production' theory of exchangeable value in the same way as had Adam Smith, his own wrestlings with the problems of value for rather different purposes had a not inconsiderable influence on the way in which writers who came after him treated the formulation of a 'cost of production' theory of value, even though they were not attempting to solve the same problem as Ricardo at all but looked rather to Smith's example.

Samuel Bailey is chiefly famous as a critic of Ricardian value theory. He was indeed a merciless critic of Ricardo's verbal inexactititude and of the whole idea of absolute value and of an invariable measure. But the value theory which he himself advanced was a 'cost of production' theory of value (for commodities produced under competition) and he excluded rent from cost of production like all the Classical 'cost of production' writers after Ricardo.[26] Foreshadowing what Senior was to do he laid some emphasis on supply conditions of less than infinite elasticity, distinguishing monopoly and various forms of imperfect competition. But he had no proper demand theory, and he solved the 'diamonds and water' paradox by simply ignoring value in use.

Torrens's 'capital theory of value' should probably be included amongst the 'cost of production' theories of value although it is a little hard to see exactly where it does fit. The important point about his value theory is that while the normal 'cost of production' theories (and Ricardo's also) saw value as determined by total labour input of both direct and accumulated labour, Torrens saw value as determined by the latter only. He argued that the products of equal capitals must be of equal value or one entrepreneur would be earning lower profits than another. If this were so capital would be reallocated and the production of the more profitable commodity increased and that of the less profitable decreased until their relative values adjusted to equality giving the entrepreneurs the same profit as each other. The idea can be illustrated by one of Torrens's numerical examples. Take two entrepreneurs each with capital (accumulated labour) obtained by 50 days' labour. Suppose that one entrepreneur makes woollens and spends his capital on wages for 90 and material equivalent to wages for 10. The other entrepreneur, making silks, spends his capital on wages for 20 and on material equivalent to wages for 80. The labour, according to Torrens, direct plus indirect, in the woollens is 90 (direct) plus 50 (indirect) equals 140. The labour in the silks is 20 (direct) plus 50 (indirect) equals 70. The labour input of one is, says Torrens, twice that of the other. But this only shows him that the labour and 'cost of production' theory of values are wrong.

The question does not turn upon the quantities of labour required to procure our respective articles. Our capitals are each worth à hundred days' wages: they are equivalent and convertible; and, if you refuse to exchange their respective products upon equal terms, I can, at the same cost which fabricates my silk, obtain wages for ninety, with wool equivalent to wages for ten, and thus have wrought up for me the same quantity of woollens which I require of you. You cannot expect that I should accept in exchange for the product of my capital, a less quantity of any article, than that capital might at any time procure for me, if I chose to manufacture it for myself.[27]

There was one difficulty with this which Torrens clearly recognized: production periods might not be equal as they were assumed to be in this example, and if they were not the problem of durability of capital arose. Torrens's solution here was to say that the equality of value produced by equal capitals was the equality of the values of the products plus the residue of the capital still locked up.

This theory caused a great deal of confusion to the Classical economists. Both McCulloch and James Mill at various times seemed to think that it was the *same* as a 'cost of production' theory which counted both direct *and* indirect labour.[28] Even the usually clear-headed Samuel Bailey seems to have fallen into this trap, as did another writer Samuel Read, as we shall see.

But there was one fundamental difficulty with the theory in any case which made it completely useless. Ricardo saw this clearly enough. The problem was quite simply this: *what determined the value of the capitals?* As Ricardo wrote to McCulloch,

I would ask what means you have of ascertaining the equal value of capitals? ... These capitals are not the same in kind and if they themselves are produced in unequal times they are subject to the same fluctuations as other commodities. Till you have fixed the criterion by which we are to ascertain value, you can say nothing of equal capitals.

the means of ascertaining their equality or variation of value is the very thing in dispute.[29]

Samuel Read was another 'cost of production' value theorist, one who was quite consciously advancing the analysis of the *Wealth of Nations*. He dismissed analysis of value in terms of demand and supply without reference to labour or cost of production, and advanced the usual Classical analysis of Natural and Market price.[30] Price was made up of natural rates of wages, profits, and rent, as it had been for Adam Smith. However Read got himself into something of a tangle by attempting to reconcile this with Torrens's capital theory of value; and he concluded that capital expended in production regulated the price of a commodity. Nevertheless this price was made up of wages, profits, and rent.[31] This was *not* the same as the theory he had earlier advanced but he does not seem to have appreciated this.

The position of J. R. McCulloch as a 'cost of production' theorist was obscured by the fact that he also advanced a popular labour theory of value, and by his confusion over Torrens already noted. It was also rendered unsatisfactory by his attempts to treat costs as real costs, i.e. disutility, and by a confusion in the minds of both Ricardo and McCulloch over the necessary and sufficient conditions for the emergence of profit. Ricardo saw that waiting was necessary for the emergence of profit; and he seems to have thought that it was both necessary *and* sufficient. McCulloch on the other hand perceived that waiting without productivity would not produce profit but then seems to have gone on to the view that productivity itself was both necessary and sufficient. His version of the confusion led him to advance the argument that if maturing wine increased in value the labour embodied in the wine must go on working while the wine was maturing. In the second edition of his *Principles* however he adopted Ricardo's version of the confusion between necessary and sufficient conditions and it was not until the 1838 edition of his version of the *Wealth of Nations* that he finally made clear that both waiting and productivity were necessary.[32] But in the end he emerged with a 'cost of production' theory in which relative prices were determined by labour input (both direct and indirect) and profit, *at the margin of production* (thus affording a role to demand, in selecting the margin), with rent eliminated from cost in the usual post-Ricardian manner.[33] It was essentially a version of Smith, adjusted in the light of the West–Malthus–Ricardo rent theory and it was not a Ricardian theory of value—McCulloch was not interested in the invariable measure or in value in any other sense than relative value. Nevertheless his treatment was influenced by Ricardo in that acceptance of the wage/durability-of-capital theorem is to be found consistently throughout his writings on value, although, in a wider context, he became increasingly unhappy about the inverse relationship of wages and profits

G. P. Scrope should also probably be included amongst the 'cost of production' theorists because he accepted that in the long run cost determined value where competition existed.[34] 'It is quite evident that the cost of producing any article must in the long run determine its price (or selling value). For unless a price can be obtained sufficient to cover this cost, no one will continue to produce it for sale at that expense.'[35] Cost for Scrope meant direct and indirect labour plus time (a borrowing from Senior's abstinence theory of profit of which we shall have more to say in the next chapter). As with the other Classical economists, rent was a price determined surplus, not a cost. However Scrope's position, writing after Senior, took much more account of situations in which commodities were not produced under conditions of free competition.

Apart from Smith himself, the most important 'cost of production' value theorist amongst the Classical economists was J. S. Mill. He was clearly a 'cost of production' value theorist, and he rejected the whole idea of a measure of value.[36] Nevertheless his treatment of cost of production was influenced by Ricardo in that the mechanism of price equalization to cost is through capital mobility. Moreover he accepted the wage/durability-of-capital theorem in his treatment, although his inverse relationship of wages and profits is not derived from the invariable measure as we shall see it was for Ricardo. Mill gives an excellent summary of his theory of value in the short Chapter VI of Book III of his *Principles* and it is worth quoting at length.

I.   Value is a relative term. The value of a thing means the quantity of some other thing, or of things in general, which it exchanges for. The values of all things can never, therefore, rise or fall simultaneously. There is no such thing as a general rise or a general fall of values. Every rise of value supposes a fall and every fall a rise.

II.   The temporary or Market Value of a thing depends on the demand and supply; rising as the demand rises, and falling as the supply rises. The demand, however, varies with the value, being generally greater when the thing is cheap than when it is dear; and the value always adjusts itself in such a manner that the demand is equal to the supply.

III.   Besides their temporary value, things have also a permanent, or, as it may be called, a Natural Value, to which the market value, after every variation, always tends to return; and the oscillations compensate for one another, so that, on the average, commodities exchange at about their natural value.

IV.   The natural value of some things is a scarcity value; but most things naturally exchange for one another in the ratio of their cost of production, or at what may be termed their Cost Value.

V.   The things which are naturally and permanently at a scarcity value are those of which the supply cannot be increased at all, or not sufficiently to satisfy the whole of the demand which would exist for them at their cost value.

VI.   A monopoly value means a scarcity value. Monopoly cannot give a value to anything except through a limitation of the supply.

VII.   Every commodity of which the supply can be indefinitely increased by labour and capital, exchanges for other things proportionally to the cost necessary for producing and bringing to market the most costly portion of the supply required. The natural value is synonymous with the Cost Value; and the cost value of a thing means the cost value of the most costly portion of it.

VIII.   Cost of Production consists of several elements, some of which are constant and universal, others occasional. The universal elements of cost of production are, the wages of the labour, and the profits of the capital. The occasional elements are taxes, and any extra cost occasioned by a scarcity value of some of the requisites.

IX.  Rent is not an element in the cost of production of the commodity
     which yields it; except in the cases (rather conceivable than actually
     existing) in which it results from, and represents, a scarcity value. But
     when land capable of yielding rent in agriculture is applied to some
     other purpose, the rent which it would have yielded is an element in
     the cost of production of the commodity which it is employed to
     produce.

X.   Omitting the occasional elements; things which admit of indefinite
     increase, naturally and permanently exchange for each other accord-
     ing to the comparative amount of wages which must be paid for
     producing them and the comparative amount of profits which must be
     obtained by the capitalists who pay these wages.

XI.  The *comparative* amount of wages does not depend on what wages
     are in themselves. High wages do not make high values, nor low
     wages low values. The comparative amount of wages depends partly
     on the comparative quantities of labour required, and partly on the
     comparative rates of its remuneration.

XII. So, the comparative rate of profits does not depend on what profits
     are in themselves; nor do high or low profits make high or low
     values. It depends partly on the comparative lengths of time during
     which the capital is employed, and partly on the comparative rate of
     profits in different employments.

XIII. If two things are made by the same quantity of labour, and that
     labour paid at the same rate, and if the wages of the labourer have to
     be advanced for the same space of time, and the nature of the em-
     ployment does not require that there be a permanent difference in
     their rate of profit; then, whether wages and profits be high or low,
     and whether the quantity of labour expended be much or little, these
     two things will, on the average, exchange for one another.

XIV. If one of two things commands on the average, a greater value than
     the other, the cause must be that it requires for its production either
     a greater quantity of labour, or a kind of labour permanently paid
     at a higher rate; or that the capital, or part of the capital, which
     supports that labour, must be advanced for a longer period; or lastly,
     that the production is attended with some circumstances which re-
     quiries to be compensated by a permanently higher rate of profit.

XV.  Of these elements, the quantity of labour required for the production
     is the most important: the effect of the others is smaller, though none
     of them are insignificant.

XVI. The lower profits are, the less important become the minor elements
     of cost of production, and the less do commodities deviate from a
     value proportional to the quantity and quality of the labour required
     for their production.

XVII. But every fall of profits lowers, in some degree, the cost value of
     things made with much or durable machinery, and raises that of
     things made by hand; and every rise of profits does the reverse.

This is a comprehensive and clear statement of the developed Classical
'cost of production' theory of value. But this is not all there is to be noted
about J. S. Mill's writings on a subject which, as is well known, he considered more or less settled.[37] For he did manage to advance in Chapter

XVI, 'Of some Peculiar Cases of Value', a solution to the problem of joint costs. Demand and supply will set a price at which the quantity of each of the jointly produced commodities sold will cover their total costs. It should also be noted that although Mill advances a 'cost of production' theory of value he distinguishes quite clearly between cases of horizontal, vertical, and positively inclined supply schedules.[38] But he was not a subjective value theorist, and like all the 'cost of production' theorists he treated utility as merely a condition of value.

Mill's treatment in turn influenced that of Fawcett and of Cairnes. The former followed Mill closely in producing a 'cost of production' theory of value while distinguishing horizontal, vertical, and positively inclined supply schedules.

With Cairnes however the situation is more complicated. Although he apparently advances a 'cost of production' theory of value it becomes apparent[39] that by 'normal value' he does not mean just cost of production, and that where he does so he means by cost, real cost.[40] But it is in relation to the concept of normal value that he advances the most interesting ideas. Starting from J. S. Mill's fundamental proposition that there were also normal values for internationally traded goods whose values were determined by reciprocal demand because of factor immobility between countries, Cairnes extended this to the internal economy of a country in which he said that factor immobility produced non-competing groups. With reference to these groups he then went on:

the measure of the aggregate demand of each trading body will be the total of its productions, and the measure of its demand for the production of the bodies with which it trades will be the proportion of its total production which it desires to apply to the purchase of the productions of these bodies.[41]

Total output does not fluctuate much and therefore demand can be expected to remain stable. However this only gives a normal value over a wide range of commodities. Cost of production still has to determine relative values within the groups.

The writers so far considered in this group were all more or less clear that they were attempting to produce 'cost of production' theories of value. There remain however two writers who attempted to produce labour theories of value and in doing so believed that they were following Ricardo. These two writers were the elder Mill and De Quincey. Neither of them however advanced the invariable measure or treated value as other than exchange value. But they do deserve special treatment in that they were consciously attempting to follow Ricardo in respect of value theory.

We find J. Mill offering the usual theory that in the short run value was determined by demand and supply and in the long run by cost of production. The latter included both direct and indirect labour although, as already

noted, Mill became confused on this last point in relation to Torrens's
'Capital' theory of value. But he was consciously trying to produce a labour
theory of value, which he understood to have been Ricardo's aim. Not only
did he offer the argument (borrowed from McCulloch) that the labour embodied in wine goes on working while the wine is maturing, in order to
explain profits—profits were the wages of stored-up labour—but he also
appeared to confuse profit and amortization at times.[42] Moreover, although
he accepted the validity of the wage/durability-of-capital theorem he still
felt able to assert that this did not affect the principle that labour quantity
determined exchangeable value.[43]

Thomas De Quincey in his *Logic of Political Economy* advanced an
almost pure labour theory of value.[44] Capital was only admitted towards the
end of the treatment where the problem of capital durability was recognized
as modifying the labour-input theory of value.[45] In his earlier *Dialogues of
Three Templars* the treatment was even narrower.

*The ground of the value of all things lies in the quantity* (but mark well that word
'quantity') *of labour which produces them.* Here is that great principle which is
the corner-stone of all tenable Political Economy; which granted or denied, all
Political Economy stands or falls. Grant me this one principle, with a few square
feet of the sea-shore to draw my diagrams upon, and I will undertake to deduce
every other truth in the science.[46]

Interestingly enough, however, although De Quincey believed himself to
be following Ricardo, he not only rejected the invariable measure but even
credited Ricardo with doing the same.[47]

This concludes our examination of the 'cost of production' theories of
values in Classical economics. But although it is undeniable that the main
stream of Classical value theory was in fact of this kind, there was more to
Classical value theory than this. For there were a number of writers who
advanced a subjective value theory which bears a much closer resemblance,
at least superficially, to the value theory with which the reader is familiar,
and it is to these that we now turn.

## iv. THE SUBJECTIVE VALUE THEORISTS

It is not surprising that there should have been a subjective value stream
in Classical economics. The word 'utility' appears in all the Classical writers
although it does so in a variety of senses. It is used to mean both total
utility and the utility of one single amount of a good where this is all that
is available—the writers usually cited the utility of a single item of food to
a starving individual in this context. Utility was also used, as we have already
noted, both in an objective sense of usefulness (by Adam Smith) and also
in a subjective sense (by all the other Classical writers, and even by Smith
himself in his *Lectures*). Given that these Classical writers recognized the

concept of utility and recognized the so-called paradox of value—the diamonds and water problem—it is not surprising that various writers should have attempted to solve the paradox in similar ways to those employed by Adam Smith's predecessors. Indeed it is arguable that much of Classical subjective value theory was developed on the basis of the discussion of market price in the *Wealth of Nations*, although it must be recognized that there was an independent utility tradition in France stemming from the scholastic inheritance. The contrast then is between those writers, in the 'cost of production' camp, who saw the paradox of value as offering an insuperable bar to a subjective value theory, and those writers who felt that a useful theory could be constructed on such a basis. But even those in the last group by and large failed to carry the analysis through to the valuation of productive services. Even those who attempted it, such as Say, failed to produce a cohesive theory in this respect and so Adam Smith's basic reason for largely dropping the subjective elements in value theory and concentrating on cost of production remained effectively vindicated throughout the Classical period.

### 1. J. B. Say

Say's starting-point was that production was the creation of utility which was thus afforded a key role in value. All factors engaged in production, whether of goods or services, produced utility. Production created not matter but utility.[48]

Goods in order to have value had to have utility and to be limited in supply. This latter provision excluded 'natural wealth' (largely free goods) from the province of the economist who had only to be concerned with 'social wealth' which only had utility after the application of human agency.[49] The actual value of an article depended upon the relative strengths of supply and demand at any given time, although in any period other than the market period cost of production set a lower limit to price.

In some ways the whole approach is reminiscent of the post-1870 approach to value theory. The value of factor services is fixed by that of the final product—not the other way round, as was the case for both Smith and Ricardo.

Wherefore, there is a current value or price established for productive services as well as for products. For, if the agency exerted in the creation of a bushel of wheat can obtain, as its reward, in the way of exchange, either a bushel of wheat or seven pounds of coffee indifferently, what is there to prevent its obtaining in the same way any other equivalent product, say a yard of cotton cloth, five yards of ribbon, a dozen plates, or anything else? Should the bushel of wheat be exchangeable for a less amount of any of these commodities respectively, the productive agency exerted in the creation of wheat would be proportionately less rewarded, than that exerted in the creation of the specific commodity; and a portion of the former would be attracted to the latter branch of production, until the recompense of labour in each department should find its fair level ... thus it is obvious that the current value of productive exertion is founded upon the value of an infinity of products compared one with another.[50]

So the current value of the productive services is established on the same basis as that of everything else, i.e. supply and demand.[51] The demand originates in the value of the final product. Of course it is difficult to be sure how much sense this really makes. Without marginal productivity it is not at all clear what significance can be attached to valuation of factors by demand for the product. But at least the whole approach was heading in the same direction as the post-1870 writers.

Yet there are startling gaps in what Say had to offer. Although we have a downward-sloping demand curve and a rising supply curve, an explanation of the effect on value of changes in both demand and supply in the form of Say's distinction between real and relative price variations (see Fig. 10), and an explanation of the equilibration of demand and supply,[52] the striking fact is that the downward slope of the demand curve is derived from income distribution, not from utility.[53] Moreover, although Say at times appears to understand the distinction between total and marginal utility,[54] he does not seem to have grasped it very solidly because he claimed that price measured utility.[55] To this Ricardo was able to object that according to Say's treatment, if cost of production fell, utility fell.[56] The main-stream Classicists were at least able to point out that the utility approach without a properly developed total/marginal-utility distinction was unsatisfactory—and it was usually Say that they attacked in this respect.[57] But for all that, Say's analysis has much in common with post-1870 value theory.

## 2. N. W. Senior

Senior's approach to value theory in some ways provides a link between the main stream of Classical value theory and the more thoroughly subjective value theory of Say. This is essentially because there are two main strands in his analysis. On the one hand he insisted on the role of utility in value: but on the other, perhaps his main contribution was in clarifying the role of cost of production in relation to value.

Senior postulated that three conditions were necessary for a good to have value.[58] It had to have utility, to be transferable (from one individual to another), and to be limited in supply. Value in exchange depended on the causes which limited commodities in supply and gave them utility.

If we look at the treatment of utility we find that Senior recognized that there was 'an endless diversity in the relative utility of different objects to different persons, a diversity which is the motive of all exchanges'.[59] Senior in fact correctly formulated the principle of diminishing marginal utility though he did so somewhat misleadingly under the heading of 'Limitation in Supply'.

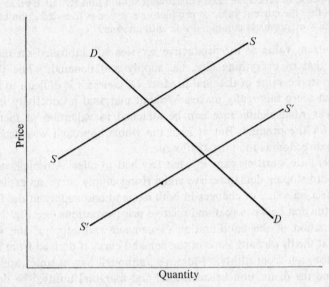

**Real Price Variation**

FIGURE 10a

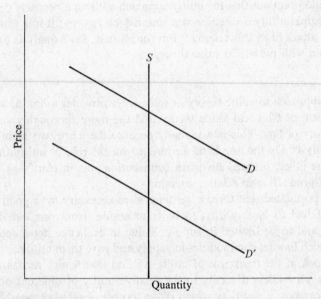

**Relative Price Variation**

FIGURE 10b

It is obvious. however, that our desires do not aim so much at quantity as at diversity. Not only are there limits to the pleasure which commodities of any given class can afford, but the pleasure diminishes in a rapidly increasing ratio long before those limits are reached. Two articles of the same kind will seldom afford twice the pleasure of one, and still less will ten give five times the pleasure of two. In proportion, therefore, as any article is abundant, the number of those who are provided with it, and do not wish, or wish but little, to increase that provision, is likely to be great; and, so far as they are concerned, the additional supply loses all, or nearly all, its utility. And in proportion to its scarcity the number of those who are in want of it, and the degree in which they will want it, are likely to be increased; and its utility, or, in other words, the pleasure which the possession of a given quantity of it will afford, increases proportionally.[60]

Yet ultimately, as the exposition proceeds, we find that Senior failed to relate this principle to the derivation of the demand curve. In particular we find that he attempts to equate demand with utility without making the transition to effectual demand in Smith's sense.[61]

Senior's contribution to the analysis of demand was then limited. However he had much more to say about the problem of supply. He recognized the necessity of explaining the scarcity of goods by cost of production.[62] The main limitation on supply was the need for factor input. Cost of production also provided the limits between which price could settle. The producers' costs provided the lower limit to which price, which must cover labour, amortization, and abstinence, could fall,[63] while the purchasers' potential cost of production set the higher limit to price—since if price rose above this then purchasers would become producers. In the special case of free competition the two costs of production would coincide and normalization of wages and profits through factor mobility would ensure the equalization of price and cost. Rent was eliminated in the usual Classical manner as a price-determined surplus.

But Senior was of the opinion that free competition was a special case.[64] There were many interferences with factor mobility and, because of these, cost of production was only a centre of oscillation. But in any case Senior seems to have seen quite clearly that cost of production could not determine value on its own except in the special case of constant costs. Nevertheless he explained much less clearly the need for the supply curve to be horizontal here than many other Classical writers. There is in fact some confusion between imperfection of competition and a rising supply schedule caused by technical characteristics of production, in his discussion: and we can only be certain that he had a horizontal supply schedule in mind for the case of free competition by reference to the other cases he discusses.

Senior in fact formulated five distinct cases of value.[65] The first was the case of constant costs. Here price must be equal to wages, amortization, and profits. The other four cases all came under the heading of 'monopoly', for Senior, like Bailey, used this term to cover any situation where supply was less than perfectly elastic, whatever the reason for this. Case two then was a 'monopoly' where one producer had some special advantage, for instance patent rights, which were not available to all producers. The monopolist was envisaged as producing under either constant costs or decreasing costs. The cost of production of the producer with the special advantage, and of the other producers, set the lower and upper limits to the price of the article. Under these circumstances the advantaged producer would extend his own production but would pursue a profit-maximizing policy so that price would not fall as far as his own costs of production. Exactly how he was to pursue this profit-maximizing policy is not clear—it is one of the examples of progress in economic theory that only since the Marginal Revolution can we begin to see what a profit-maximizing policy would involve. The third case that Senior considers is that of a monopolist in the normal sense of the term, that is, someone with no competitors, but whose cost curve is a reverse L shape. Here the horizontal section of the L sets the lower limit to price but there is no upper limit. However Senior then goes on to say that there *is* an upper limit, 'the will and the ability of the consumers'. His failure here to relate this to his earlier analysis of diminishing marginal utility is an indication of the incompleteness of his subjective value theory. The fourth case that Senior considers is again a monopoly but it is one with a definitely falling cost curve. (Senior instances the case of a publisher of a potentially very popular book such as a novel by Scott.) In this case the price set by the producer will be a profit-maximizing price—again just where this lies is left vague. The final case that Senior considers is that of a rising supply schedule caused by scarcity of a particular factor. Obviously what he has principally in mind here is agricultural produce. In such a case, price will coincide with cost of production at the margin—the margin being selected by demand.

This is about the extent of Senior's contribution. He did not go very far (certainly not as far as Say or Longfield) in carrying the subjective analysis over to the valuation of factors. Indeed his analysis is distinctly in the English Classical tradition. Although he firmly limited value to value in exchange,[66] he distinguished between 'intrinsic' and 'extrinsic' value in a way which clearly reflected Ricardo's preoccupation with the invariable measure. The demand for and supply of a commodity determined its intrinsic value while the demand for and supply of a commodity for which it was to be exchanged determined its extrinsic value.[67]

Although Senior's value theory was a good deal more satisfactory in many ways than the 'cost of production' theories it still left rather a lot to be said on the side of demand. Our next two writers did, to some extent, fill this gap.

### 3. M. Longfield

Longfield was an important subjective value theorist. Yet the reader of his *Lectures*[68] may at first find this a puzzling assertion. For he gave the impression of following Ricardo on many points, accepted that labour was the best measure of value,[69] appeared to agree that utility was only a preliminary condition of value, accepted the distinction between natural and market value,[70] and at times appeared to offer a labour theory of value. Thus we find him writing:

And it may be asserted as a general truth, subject to few exceptions, that no permanent change can take place in the relative values of any two commodities without its being occasioned by some alterations in the quantity, or nature, or value, of the labour required to produce one or both of those commodities; and hence the utility of frequently referring to labour as a measure of value.[71]

At other times Longfield seems to be offering a 'cost of production' theory of value. Thus we find:

the cost of production or natural value of any commodity always exercises a very considerable influence upon its price. The cost of production regulates the supply, and keeps it pretty nearly in that proportion to the demand which may produce a conformity between the exchangeable and the natural value. In some articles this tendency of the market price to conform to the cost of production is so strong, that a difference between them can only be produced by a very considerable and accidental disproportion between the demand and the supply.[72]

Moreover, Longfield gets rid of rent from cost in the normal Classical manner.[73] But for all this he arguably advanced the most complete subjective value theory of any writer during the Classical period. Despite the material we have referred to we find it stated quite explicitly later on in the lectures that value depends on demand and supply, that cost of production regulates supply, and that utility lies behind demand.[74] It is in this last area that Longfield's striking contributions were made. He developed, from the confused and uncertain start made by Malthus, the concept of 'intensity of demand'. This he related to utility, showing marginal utility varying with places and with persons and with varying wants of the same individual, and he related this all to price. In this way he strikingly derived the downward-sloping demand curve from intensity of demand rather than from income distribution as Say had done. The material in the *Lectures* containing all this is so striking that it is worth quoting at length.

it is to ... utility, ... that ... demand is to be entirely attributed.... The measure of the intensity of any person's demand for any commodity is the amount which he would be willing and able to give for it, rather than remain without it, or forgo the gratification which it is calculated to afford him. On this we may observe, in the first place, that there may exist a demand not sufficiently intense to exercise any influence upon price.... Still a demand may affect prices, although it be not sufficiently intense to lead to an actual purchase. Of this an example is, the demand of those who will not purchase at the existing prices, but who would come into the market and purchase, if a slight reduction should take place ...

But it is to be remarked, that there may be, and that in fact there generally is, an excess of intensity of demand, which exercises no perceptible influence upon the prices of commodities. This is the demand of those who, if necessary, would pay more than the existing prices, but who do not, because the state of the market enables them to procure the same commodities, or more desirable substitutes more cheaply ...

For provisions and other articles of greater or less necessity, the intensity of demand among different persons varies according to the sacrifices of other objects which they can conveniently afford to make; and yet all will effect their purchases at the same rate, viz. at the market prices, and this rate is determined by the sum which will create an equality between the effectual demand and the supply. Now if the price is attempted to be raised one degree beyond this sum, the demanders, who by the change will cease to be purchasers, must be those the intensity of whose demand was precisely measured by the former price. Before the change was made, the demand, which was less intense did not lead to a purchase, and after the change is made, the demand, which is more intense, will lead to a purchase still. Thus the market price is measured by that demand, which being of the least intensity, yet leads to actual purchases. If the existing supply is more than sufficient to satisfy all the demand equal or superior to a certain degree of intensity, prices will fall to accommodate themselves to a less intense demand.

But the intensity of demand varies not only in different places, and among different individuals, but in many cases the same person may be said to have in himself several demands of different degrees of intensity ... that portion which any person ceases to consume in consequence of a rise of prices, or that additional portion which he would consume if prices should fall, is that for which the intensity of his demand is less than the high price which prevents him from purchasing it, and is exactly equal to the low price which would induce him to consume it ... each individual contains as it were within himself, a series of demands of successively increasing degrees of intensity; ... the lowest degree of this series which at any time leads to a purchase, is exactly the same for both rich and poor, and is that which regulates the market price.[75]

This is all very striking. But one thing is strikingly missing here as well. Longfield had related intensity of demand to utility and he had related intensity of demand to price. He should then have been able to relate utility directly to price and provide an explanation of value in terms (on the demand side) of total and marginal utility. But this he did not do. Indeed at one point in the *Lectures* he apparently accepted Say's thesis that value measures utility.[76] He also stated, as we have seen, that people's intensity of demand could exceed the price they paid for the good.[77] He apparently did not see how utility could be used to explain the downward sloping demand curve. He had assembled all the building blocks for a satisfactory theory but he did not really take the final decisive steps.

## 4. W. F. Lloyd

The same is true of another author who offered a striking analysis of total and marginal utility, W. F. Lloyd. Lloyd in fact distinguished total and marginal utility more clearly than any writer before Jevons. After pointing out that an increase in quantity will at length exhaust the demand for any specific object of desire, he went on to show how each consumer had a scale of wants of varying importance, and that the utility of any particular good depended on the particular want on the scale which was satisfied. It was the importance of the last want satisfied which determined utility.

Let us suppose the case of an hungry man having one ounce, and only one ounce of food at his command. To him, this ounce is obviously of very great import-ance. Suppose him now to have two ounces. These are still of great importance; but the importance of the second is not equal to that of the single ounce. In other words he would not suffer so much from parting with one of his two ounces, re-taining one for himself, as he would suffer, when he had only one ounce, by part-ing with that one, and so retaining none. The importance of a third ounce is still less than that of the second; so likewise are the fourth, until at length, in the continual increase of the number of ounces, we come to a point when ... the appetite is entirely or nearly lost, and when, with respect to a single ounce, it is a matter of indifference whether it is parted with or retained ... The case is the same with respect to all other commodities.[78]

Lloyd distinguishes quite clearly between total utility and marginal utility and relates value to marginal utility. Yet the analysis is incomplete for all this. Value is made dependent on marginal utility without apparent refer-ence to the supply conditions[79] and the case of Robinson Crusoe is used to establish the proposition that value—meaning marginal utility—could exist without exchange or transferability. Since marginal utility alone was not value but subjective valuation with fixed supply, his argument would have seemed true but irrelevant to the other English economists including Senior.

## 5. Other Writers

Malthus probably belongs in this section of the chapter if only because of his formulation of the concept of 'intensity of demand'. It is not clearly expressed but it apparently means total purchasing power directed towards a commodity.[80] In fact the most sensible construction to put on his formula-tion is the outlay rectangle formed by perpendiculars from the price and quantity axes to the demand curve. It was used to explain the willingness of an individual to make a sacrifice to obtain a good. Yet he seems to have had no idea of the relation between willingness to pay and marginal utility. His interest in the short run also led him to stress supply and demand as determinants of value while agreeing that in the long run value depended on cost of production. We find him arguing that the value of the majority of commodities is determined by demand and supply only because at any moment of time existing market prices are likely to differ from cost of production through the process of market adjustments.[81]

It should also perhaps be mentioned that Malthus engaged in a long and unprofitable debate with Ricardo on the best measure of value, finally deciding that embodied labour was the best measure.[82] Recounting this will only confuse the reader—the important issues in the debate will be found embodied in Ricardo's final measure of value already discussed.

There were other subjective value theorists as well. There was John Craig who attempted to develop Adam Smith's distinction between value in use and value in exchange but ended up by deciding that they were the same thing although he seems to have been trying to get to the connection between marginal utility and value.[83] There was also Lord Lauderdale who followed Say's example, and John Rooke who saw value as determined by demand and by cost of production at the margin. Mention should also be made of Senior's friend Archbishop Whately, founder of the Chair occupied by Longfield, who advanced similar views on value to those of Senior.

## 6. Conclusion

After a survey of the writings on value from a subjective point of view which appeared in the Classical period, two main conclusions stand out. The first is that there was indisputably a stream of value theory which was different from that associated directly with the 'cost of production' theorists. To this extent the Marginal Revolution of the 1870s may seem somewhat less revolutionary than it is sometimes depicted. But the second and quite inescapable conclusion is that the performance of none of the writers considered was sufficiently complete to displace the orthodox value theory. This itself has two aspects. Firstly the very lack of completeness of the performances meant that the writers considered here had virtually no followers in their treatment of value. Senior certainly influenced other writers including Scrope but he had no direct followers. Say it is true was followed by Destutt de Tracey but the latter was a minor writer and Say's influence was on the whole limited at least in respect of his value theory. Only in Dublin, at Trinity College, was there a continuing tradition of subjective value theory, perhaps springing originally from the influence of Whately but continued by occupants of the Chair who followed Longfield.[84] The second aspect of the problem is that the writings of all the subjective value theorists exhibit varying degrees of cloudiness and inconsistency. Reading this literature it does seem clear that without calculus the obscurities and verbal ambiguities were unlikely ever to be cleared up. Indeed it is only with our post-1870 training that we are able to make sense of the kind of muddle that, for instance, Say was able to get into.[85] Yet if we take this view, we have to admit two things. Firstly Menger, one of the three principal writers who brought about the Marginal Revolution used nothing more complicated than straightforward arithmetic. Secondly a number of the writers that we have considered here had a good deal of formal mathematical training. Malthus certainly had such training, and both Longfield and Lloyd were adept mathematicians. Nor was the mathematical training confined to the subjective theorists' camp. McCulloch had mathematical training and Ricardo's mind was of a decidedly mathematical cast. There simply is no easy answer to the problem of the very partial and unsatisfactory analysis of value which is to be found in the Classical writings.

## NOTES

1. *Wealth of Nations*, ed. Cannan, i. 49.
2. Ibid., p. 52.
3. Ibid., p. 57.
4. Ibid., p. 30.
5. Ibid., pp. 60–1.
6. Ibid., p. 35.
7. Ibid., pp. 34–5.
8. Ibid., p. 37.
9. See especially H. M. Robertson and W. L. Taylor, 'Adam Smith's Approach to the Theory of Value', *Economic Journal*, 67 (1957), 181–98 (this also covers Smith's departure from the subjective value theory of his predecessors); M. Blaug, 'Welfare Indices in the *Wealth of Nations*', *Southern Economic Journal*, 26 (1959), 150–3.
10. *Wealth of Nations*, p. 37.
11. Ibid., pp. 35–6.
12. See ibid., Bk. I, Ch. XI, pp. 177–216, 'Digression concerning the Variations in the Value of Silver during the Course of the Four last Centuries'.
13. Ibid., pp. 37–8.
14. Ibid., p. 38.
15. Ricardo, *Works*, Vol. i. p. xlvii.
16. See also Ricardo's own example, ibid., p. 35.
17. Ibid., pp. 46, 48, 105, 110 n, 169.
18. Ibid., p. 36.
19. G. J. Stigler, 'Ricardo and the 93 per cent Labor Theory of Value', *American Economic Review*, 48 (1958), 357–67.
20. *Long View and the Short*, p. 400.
21. Op. cit., pp. 21–2.
22. Ibid., Ch. I, Section vi, pp. 43–7.
23. See O'Brien, *J. R. McCulloch*, p. 381.
24. Ricardo, op. cit., p. 12.
25. Ibid., p. 273.
26. S. Bailey, *A Critical Dissertation on the Nature, Measures, and Causes of Value* (London, 1825, repr. 1931), pp. 183 ff., esp. pp. 197–8, 205.
27. R. Torrens, *Essay on the Production of Wealth*, pp. 37–8. On Torrens's value theory see Lord Robbins, *Robert Torrens*, pp. 60–72. Torrens's results are not the same as the other Classical writers would have obtained from the data: they would have seen the costs of production of the two commodities resolved as follows: Woollens; wages (direct labour) 90 plus materials (indirect labour) 10 equals 100: silks; wages 20 plus materials 80 equals 100.
28. See O'Brien, *McCulloch*, p. 131.
29. Ricardo, op. cit., p. xlix.
30. S. Read, *Political Economy*, Ch. IV, pp. 231–43.

31. Ibid., p. 241.
32. See O'Brien, *McCulloch*, pp. 130–1, 141–3.
33. See the references to Buchanan and Samuelson in the bibliography to this chapter.
34. Scrope, *Principles*, pp. 174–6.
35. Ibid., p. 198.
36. *Principles*, Bk. III, Ch. XV.
37. Ibid., p. 436.
38. Ibid., pp. 444–5.
39. Cairnes, *Leading Principles of Political Economy* (London, 1874), pp. 46–7.
40. Ibid., p. 60.
41. Ibid., p. 103. For the reciprocal-demand treatment see ibid., pp. 98–109. Of course the analysis begs some rather fundamental questions in the last twenty words of the quotation.
42. J. Mill, *Economic Writings*, ed. Winch, pp. 261–3.
43. Ibid., p. 264.
44. Op. cit. (ed. Masson), pp. 118–294.
45. Ibid., Section vii, pp. 196–9.
46. Op. cit., p. 55.
47. Ibid., pp. 92–4.
48. Say, *Treatise*, pp. 62, 284.
49. Ibid., p. 286.
50. Ibid., p. 287.
51. Ibid., pp. 293–4, 314–15.
52. Ibid., pp. 289–90, 299.
53. Ibid., p. 288.
54. See paras 1 and 2, p. 295.
55. Ibid., p. 62.
56. Ricardo, op. cit., p. 181.
57. e.g. McCulloch (ed.), *Wealth of Nations* (1838 edn.), p. 818.
58. *Outline*, pp. 14–15.
59. Ibid., p. 7.
60. Ibid., p. 12.
61. Ibid., pp. 15–16.
62. Ibid., pp. 7–8.
63. Ibid., pp. 101–3.
64. Ibid., p. 102.
65. Ibid., pp. 101–5.
66. Ibid., pp. 14, 20–2.
67. Ibid., pp. 16–20.
68. M. Longfield, *Lectures on Political Economy* (Dublin, 1834 repr. London, 1931). Also repr. in *Economic Writings*.
69. Ibid., p. 31.
70. Ibid., p. 36.
71. Ibid., p. 32. See also ibid., p. 164.
72. Ibid., p. 47. See also ibid., p. 39.
73. Ibid., pp. 116 ff., esp. pp. 118–19.
74. Ibid., p. 110.
75. Ibid., pp. 110–15.
76. Ibid., pp. 27–8.
77. Ibid., p. 112.
78. W. F. Lloyd, *A Lecture on the Notion of Value* (1883), repr. in *Economic History*, 2 (1927), 168–83, 172–3.
79. Ibid., pp. 174–5.
80. Malthus, *Principles of Political Economy* (2nd edn. London, 1836, repr. 1936), Ch. II, pp. 60–9, esp. p. 63.
81. Ibid., pp. 69–72.

# Classical Value Theory

82. See ibid., pp. 83–111.

83. *Remarks on Some Fundamental Doctrines in Political Economy* (Edinburgh, 1821). On Craig and the other writers mentioned below see M. E. A. Bowley, *Nassau Senior*, and the same author's 'The Predecessors of Jevons—the Revolution that wasn't', *Manchester School*, 40 (1972), 9–29.

84. On this see R. D. C. Black, 'Trinity College, Dublin and the Theory of Value, 1832–63', *Economica*, N.S. 12 (1945), 140–8.

85. Say managed to assert that consumers sometimes paid more than the utility of a good, because of monopoly (*Treatise*, pp. 62–3.).

## BIBLIOGRAPHY

Adam Smith's value theory is discussed in Cannan, *Review of Economic Theory*, pp. 64–72, and (in much more detail) in Blaug's *Economic Theory in Retrospect*. See also the latter's 'Welfare Indices in the *Wealth of Nations*', *Southern Economic Journal*, 26 (1959). The question of welfare indices is also raised in an important article by H. M. Robertson and W. L. Taylor, 'Adam Smith's Approach to the Theory of Value', *Economic Journal*, 67 (1957). This is also most notable for its documentation of Smith's deliberate break with subjective value theory. But there is no substitute for reading Smith himself: see the *Wealth of Nations*, Bk. I, Chs. IV–VII.

Ricardo's value theory has been the subject of a good deal of discussion. The modern interpretation really started with J. M. Cassells 'A Re-interpretation of Ricardo on Value', *Quarterly Journal of Economics*, 49 (1935), and F. H. Knight, 'The Ricardian Theory of Production and Distribution', *Canadian Journal of Economics*, 1 (1935), 3–25, 171–96. It was continued and developed by Stigler in his 'The Ricardian Theory of Value and Distribution', *Journal of Political Economy*, 60 (1952), and his 'Ricardo and the 93 per cent Labor Theory of Value', *American Economic Review*, 48 (1958), as well as in M. Blaug, *Ricardian Economics* and *Economic Theory in Retrospect*. These references are also useful for James Mill and De Quincey. See also Mr. Sraffa's introduction to Vol. i of Ricardo's *Works* which clarifies some other issues. The question of Ricardo's '93 per cent' theory is also dealt with in H. Barkhai, 'The Empirical Assumptions of Ricardo's 93 per cent labour theory of value', *Economica*, N.S. 34 (1967), 418–23, and in G. W. Wilson and J. L. Pate, 'Ricardo's 93 per cent labor theory of value: a final comment', *Journal of Political Economy*, 76 (1968), 128–36.

For an older view see Cannan, *Review*, and J. H. Hollander, 'The Development of Ricardo's Theory of Value', *Quarterly Journal of Economics*, 18 1904, and *David Ricardo, A Centenary Estimate* (Baltimore, 1910).

Ricardo's convoluted value discussions are to be found in Chs. I, IV, XX, and XXX of his *Principles*. Apart from the writings already cited the reader will find O. St. Clair, *A Key to Ricardo*, of assistance here. But the Sraffa edn. of Ricardo is fairly essential.

On the invariable measure see also the paper on 'Absolute and Exchangeable Value', repr. in Vol. iv of Ricardo's *Works*, ed. Sraffa.

The Ricardian method of 'getting rid' of rent is illegitimate. On this the fundamental reference is D. H. Buchanan, 'The Historical Approach to Rent and Price Theory', *Economica*, 9 (1929). See also P. A. Samuelson, 'A Modern Treatment of the Ricardian Economy', *Quarterly Journal of Economics*, 73 (1959). On the importance of fixed proportions in the wage-good basket see L. Pasinetti, 'A Mathematical Formulation of the Ricardian System', *Review of Economic Studies*, 27 (1960).

On the other cost of production theories see Lord Robbins, *Robert Torrens*, Blaug, *Ricardian Economics*, and O'Brien, *J. R. McCulloch*. For a discussion of Malthus's value theory see M. Paglin, *Malthus and Lauderdale: the anti-Ricardian tradition* (New York, 1961), especially pp. 34–45. The same work also discusses Lauderdale's value theory, which was omitted from the chapter. Another discussion of Malthus is to be found in V. E. Smith, 'Malthus's theory of demand and its influence on value theory', *Scottish Journal of Political Economy*, 3 (1956), 205–20. See also Blaug, *Retrospect*, for a discussion of J. S. Mill's value theory. But Mill himself should be read: see his *Principles*, Bk. III, Chs. I–VI, XV, XVI. Just as the Sraffa edn. of Ricardo (and the Cannan edn. of Smith) are essential, the Ashley edn. of Mill (or the new Toronto University Press edn.) are similarly indispensable. See also Longfield's *Economic Writings*, ed. R. D. C. Black.

On the marginal-utility theorists see Bowley, *Senior*. See also the same author's excellent 'The Predecessors of Jevons—the Revolution that wasn't, *Manchester School*, 40 (1972), which is in many ways a valuable supplement to the older reference. See also E. R. A. Seligman's famous 'On some Neglected British Economists', repr. in his *Essays in Economics* (New York, 1925).

# 5. The Classical Theory of Distribution

The bare bones of the Classical theory of distribution have already been outlined in Chapter 2, particularly in the diagrammatic representations of the Ricardian system. However Classical writings on distribution, dealing with the subject within a framework of wages, profits, and rents, as the three returns to the three factors of labour, capital, and land (a treatment which derives from Adam Smith and the Physiocrats) had a good deal more than these bare bones to offer.

## i. WAGES

Virtually all the Classical wage theories stem from the varied approaches to wage determination to be found in Adam Smith's Book I, Chapter VIII. This contained elements of a wage-fund theory,[1] a productivity theory,[2] a residual theory (this stemmed from Natural Law—labour produced the whole product but had to submit to deductions in the form of profits and rent),[3] a bargaining theory,[4] and, although there was considerable ambiguity in Smith's view of the relationship between the price of provisions and the level of money wages, a subsistence theory.[5]

These approaches were not all mutually exclusive. A wage-fund theory needs productivity to explain why capital demands labour,[6] the residual theory explained wages as paid out of labours' product after deduction of profits and rent; this deduction of profits and rent might depend on bargaining strength in a non-competitive situation; and the subsistence theory was a long-run (or sometimes a secular) theory rather than a theory of the market determination of wages. But there was a rich profusion about the presentation which enabled others to quarry Smith's writings for further developments.

The bulk of Classical wage theory which evolved out of the *Wealth of Nations* concentrated on two particular aspects. For the short run it developed the Supply and Demand or wage-fund theory. For the long run it developed further the subsistence theory. Strictly speaking the wage-fund theory offered only a theory of the demand for labour. This took the form of pre-accumulated capital—often treated as pre-accumulated wage goods. These supported labour during production. The approach followed from the fundamental idea in the *Wealth of Nations* that division of labour rested on pre-accumulation of capital, and the further implication of this idea that the production process could be viewed as a discontinuous one. It also followed from another fundamental idea, the Smith–Say position that acts of saving and investment were identical. Abstinence from consumption was the source of capital, and capital was demand for labour; hence the dictum that 'What is annually saved is as regularly consumed as what is annually spent, and nearly in the same time too.'[7] Starting from these positions we can understand J. S. Mill's famous fourth proposition on capital—that demand for commodities is not demand for labour. The reasoning is clear enough once we see it in these terms; demand for labour depends on capital accumulation. (Nevertheless Mill recognized that demand for commodities affected the allocation of labour between industries; and as these have different capital/labour ratios there is a further difficulty which we will see again below.)

In the more careful treatments, wage capital was distinguished from total capital and working population from total population, although it is easy enough to find statements in the Classical literature which make neither distinction, particularly when the context is the need for limiting the advance of population.[8] Such discussions as these often obscured another fairly vital point: that the whole analysis implied productivity. It had to, because otherwise there was no motive for capital to demand labour. But the Classical economists, especially perhaps the Mills, tended to ignore all such ideas (and hence the associated one of an optimum population) in stressing the need to increase the ratio of capital to labour as far as possible.[9]

But these points were recognized. The discussion of the determination of the size of the fund—a rather vital point—was however a lot less clear. Most writers contented themselves with indicating that it depended upon the size of the total product and the capitalists' share of that product as well as on various parameters in the savings function. But the question was left rather imprecisely answered. Classical writers generally however tended to assume that, whatever size the fund might be, normal market-clearing adjustments would ensure that it was all employed. J. S. Mill however offered the view that it might not all be employed in the short run,[10] although without really explaining what this implied. But his was a minority view. The general Classical position was that decisions to save all constituted a demand for labour by providing capital which supported division of labour and hence increased productivity. The capital (or rather the variable part of it) was consumed during the process of production in the form of wage payments.

But it is important to stress that the wage fund was not of itself a theory of wages any more than the marginal productivity theory is a theory of wages. It was a theory of the demand for labour, and various assumptions could be made about the supply side. The crudest was that the supply of labour was equal to total population, and this was frequently made, although we have seen that total and working populations were also distinguished. However such a distinction does not take us very far because it leaves us with a supply curve of labour which has zero elasticity. Fortunately some of the Classical writers did go further. McCulloch probably treated the subject more satisfactorily than any of his contemporaries.[11] He envisaged four different supply functions: a rising short-run schedule (which Adam Smith had also offered);[12] two negatively inclined ones, the first where the supply of labour was temporarily increased as labour fought to survive and reduced as survival became easier, and the second involving the idea that as the price of food rose the actual size of the labour force would increase through the addition of women and children; and a fourth supply function (which did not relate directly to the wage-fund formulation) in the form of the population function doubling as a secular supply function. But a number of the other Classical writers were a good deal less careful about the analysis of the supply function. Nevertheless given that *some* positive assumptions about the supply of labour were made, the wage-fund theory of demand for labour then provided a view of the determination of the general wage level in the community in the short run. Since the theory has been much abused, and since J. S. Mill publicly renounced it in his famous recantation,[13] it is perhaps worth stressing that the approach was not entirely without merit. It has to its advantage that it can be regarded as offering a theory of the aggregate demand for labour (which neo-Classical economics did not do) and as being the precursor of modern aggregate analysis. Moreover when the theory came under heavy attack, some of the criticisms were at an extremely low analytical level.

But having said this, it has to be recognized that there were fundamental difficulties with the analysis. Firstly, there was the problem that since taxes on wage goods apparently raised wages *in the short run*, by an amount sufficient to pass on the tax, the size of the fund was indeterminate. Secondly there was a fundamental difficulty concerning the nature of the demand for 'unproductive labour'—J. S. Mill recognized this but then passed hastily by on the other side.[14] Adam Smith had, before the formalization of the wage-fund idea, added part of consumption expenditure to variable capital to obtain the total demand for labour.[15] But this dropped out of sight during most of the Classical period. Classical wage discussions tended to assume that capital was the only source of wage payments—which then left the nature of the demand for servants rather vague. This may have been because of the controversy with Malthus which made many of the Classical economists reluctant to admit the role of unproductive expenditure in demanding labour. Senior, by an arbitrary judgement which would find more favour with today's theorists than with his contemporaries, half-heartedly offered a solution—that rent constituted the demand for unproductive labour. Now this does in fact allow the market to be cleared.

Let $W$ be the wage fund, $N$ the productive (non-servant) labour force, $P$ the total labour force, $R$ the rent available for wage payments, and $w$ the wage rate. We are given $W$, $P$, and $R$. We then have two independent equations and two unknowns, $w$ and $N$.

$$\frac{W}{N} = w \tag{1}$$

$$N = P - \frac{R}{w} \tag{2}$$

$$\frac{W}{P - \dfrac{R}{w}} = w \tag{3}$$

$$W = w\left[P - \frac{R}{w}\right]$$

$$= wP - w\frac{R}{w} = wP - R$$

$$W + R = wP$$

$$w = \frac{W + R}{P}$$

But this was not taken up by his contemporaries perhaps because of its apparent circularity—at first sight the number of labourers that rent would employ as servants depended on the average rate of wages—or perhaps because of its arbitrary form.

There is also the fundamental criticism made by Wicksell that the wage-fund approach made wages depend on division of a given amount of capital into fixed and circulating, whereas the inverse relationship of wages and profits (which we have already noted in Chapter 4) made that division depend on the wage rate. Through the wage/durability-of-capital theorem, a rise in wages would produce a fall in the relative prices of capital-intensive goods. Demand for these goods would then increase relative to less capital-intensive goods and so the composition of output for the economy as a whole would rely more on fixed capital.

The difficulties with the approach can be seen most clearly if we look at a very interesting attempt by Professor S. Hollander to salvage it.[16] In a book called *On Wages and Combination* published in 1834 (and in an unpublished paper)[17] Torrens advanced a form of wage-fund theory which involved two things in particular. It took specific account of productivity, and it involved a fixed capital/labour coefficient. Torrens argued that there was a minimum of wages (psychological subsistence), a maximum of wages (total product less depreciation and minimum profit) and an actual wage rate determined between these limits by a wage-fund analysis. The wage fund was not the simple one used by such writers as J. Mill which ignored productivity and concentrated on the ratio of total capital to total population. An increase in labour and capital, even though their proportions remained the same, would cause resort to inferior soils, thereby lowering the maximum of wages. But the most interesting part relates to the fixed capital/ labour ratio. With full employment, a fixed labour supply, and a fixed capital/labour ratio, every new accumulation of capital will simply increase wages. But an increase in population will lower wages more than proportionately because some of the circulating capital will have to be turned into fixed capital. Now Hollander has, on the basis of this, developed an '*ex post w*age fund theory' which he distinguishes from the '*ex ante*' version. The latter involves a demand curve for labour of unit elasticity: the former does not but follows the Torrens formulation as we can see.

Let $P$ be the quantity of labour demanded, $C$ the aggregate capital stock, $\lambda$ the single capital/labour coefficient fixed for the whole economy (i.e. uniform between industries), $w$ the wage rate, and $M$ the fixed capital stock (which is taken as given here).

Total capital $$C = M + wP$$

But $$M = \frac{P}{\lambda}$$

Substituting: $$C = \frac{P}{\lambda} + wP = P\left(\frac{1}{\lambda} + w\right)$$

So the demand for labour $$P = \frac{C}{\frac{1}{\lambda} + w}$$

The supply of labour $S$ is given. In full employment by normal market-clearing assumptions $P = S$.

So $$\frac{C}{\frac{1+w}{\lambda}} = S$$

$$w = \frac{C}{S} - \frac{1}{\lambda}$$

This is contrasted with the *ex ante* wage fund where $C'$ is circulating capital and $w = \frac{C'}{S}$.

This is indeed ingenious and interesting; but it involves, in order to salvage the theory, a number of steps which the Classicists did not take, and is in the last resort unsatisfactory. There is of course the point that supply is taken as given—all the problems over the supply side are ignored.

But there are much more fundamental criticisms to be made than this. Space is limited, so we shall have to be brief; but some indication of the difficulties can be given. Firstly, according to this formulation $P = \lambda M$: quantity of labour demanded thus depends on the size of the capital stock, whereas Torrens makes the size of the capital stock depend on the size of the labour force; for him $M = \lambda S$. Secondly as Hollander points out, with a fixed coefficient the short-run elasticity of demand for labour is zero: taken in conjunction with the first point it then becomes difficult to see to what period the analysis refers. Thirdly, if taken to its logical conclusion, the theory would abolish wages if population increased sufficiently. Fourthly, if the capital/labour ratio differs between industries, wage-rate changes will lead to a change in the total quantity of labour demanded. Hollander recognizes this. But more importantly, if wages increase then relatively fewer labour intensive commodities will be demanded and so the *average* capital/labour ratio for the economy will change. In other words if the capital/labour ratio varies between industries then the average capital/labour ratio for the economy depends on the wage rate—and so we are back to Wicksell again. But such differences in capital/labour ratios between industries were recognized by the Classical economists and indeed they are of the essence of the wage/durability-of-capital theorem which they all recognized after Ricardo. Fifthly, we may add to this the point that the wage rate will affect the choice of technique within an industry. Sixthly, we can find passages in which Cairnes, who was the other writer apart from Torrens, most obviously to advance this analysis, recognized that the average capital/labour ratio varies with the wage rate.[18] We can also find such passages in the works of J. S. Mill[19] (whom Professor Hollander also cites) and Torrens.[20] Seventhly, in none of these writers is the total capital stock given. It depends on decisions to save out of total product, the size of the total product, and the difference between wages and total product (wages and profits moving inversely), and, as Cairnes recognized, because total capital is not fixed, wages and fixed capital both increase with the progress of the economy,[21] as one would expect them to in any analysis which does not entirely ignore productivity. Finally, learning, division of labour, and changes in the ratios of capital to labour in different industries, are central parts of the Classical system from Adam Smith onwards.

The discussion so far has related to the short-run determination of wages. Although Schumpeter's view that the short run got longer and longer throughout the Classical period has some truth in it, a long-run subsistence theory of wages is also to be found in Classical economics. For virtually all the Classical writers subsistence was a psychological rather than a physical concept, although a number of them, especially Ricardo and Malthus, often spoke of it as if it was a physical level—which indeed it had to be, if the argument they employed about population being reduced through death when wages fell below subsistence was to hold together. Ricardo did however follow Torrens elsewhere in making subsistence a psychological concept, although such a view of subsistence had also been present in the *Wealth of Nations*. Except in the case of Ricardo,[22] the level was not only psychological but a secularly rising one as it had been with Smith.[23] Thus for instance both McCulloch and J. S. Mill saw real wages rising over time—population took time to adjust to higher wages and during the interval the psychological subsistence level rose. Ricardo did however offer one clarification of the nature of subsistence in that he defined subsistence wages as the level which would keep the population constant.[24] But his treatment of the subject was markedly deficient in other respects, particularly as he made the level of subsistence wages depend upon the price of agricultural wage goods and made as little allowance as possible for the effect on wages of cheaper manufactures, by assuming fixed proportions in the wage-good basket. This was also consistent with his value theory which assumed constant rather than increasing returns in manufactures—although he sometimes assumed the latter[25] as did other Classical economists especially Senior.

It would be wrong to conclude this discussion of Classical wage-theory without making the point that there were other wage-theory formulations offered during the Classical period. Thus Sir Edward West believed that demand for labour depended on flows of consumption and investment expenditure and that there was no fixed fund.[26] He also pointed out that it was necessary to take account of the rate of turnover of wage capital. However J. S. Mill was able to concede that the wage bill was equal to the wage-fund times the turnover rate without having at that stage to abandon the wage fund. More importantly Say and Longfield offered explicitly productivity analyses which foreshadowed what was to come with the Marginal Revolution. Say did not take his analysis very far but merely demonstrated a parallel between demand for factor services and for goods.[27] Longfield[28] dispensed with discrete economics. The labourer was paid out of current sales and wages were governed by the supply of labour and the demand for labour, the latter depending on the utility of labour's product. He rejected a subsistence theory of wages and asserted that the standard of living depended on wages not the other way around. But his was not a complete performance basically because he was thinking in terms of physical productivity and thus was not able to cope with the problem of unproductive labour.[29]

All this relates to the general level of wages. However, although the presentation was normally in terms of wages of common labour, it was conceived of as covering the payments to all kinds of labour including wages of management and professional fees. This it was enabled to do by a theory of relative wages which was supplied for all of Classical economics by Adam Smith,[30] though modified by J. S. Mill and Cairnes. According to this theory, wages differed so as to equalize the net advantages of different employments. They differed according to the agreeableness of the work, the cost of learning the business, constancy of employment (this involved not just averaging wages over a long period but including compensation for anxiety although without making any allowance for diminishing marginal utility of income), the trust reposed, and the probability of success (though over-optimism made wages lower in uncertain professions than they should have been even on a straight average of success and failure). Observed differences in wages were due to these factors and also to imperfect liberty, i.e. obstructions to labour mobility including apprenticeships. For the equalization of net advantages not only was perfect liberty required but it was also necessary that employments should be well known and long established (new industries yielded higher wages to attract labour), the industry itself must be in equilibrium, the employment must be the principal employment of the labour involved, and there must be an absence both of corporations and privileges, and of subsidized training.

It is perfectly possible to be critical of all this. As the analysis was presented it often failed to make clear that it was only an analysis of factors affecting the *supply* of labour to different occupations; it failed to explain the problems arising from the fact that those who invested money in learning a business were different from those who received the compensation, it neglected the actuarial problem that returns to investment beyond twenty-five years were arguably not part of the supply price, it did not take sufficient account of the fact that risk might have positive utility for some, and it relied on a doubtful disutility of responsibility-bearing—J. S. Mill and Malthus pointed out that a shortage of suitable people to bear responsibility was possibly a more important factor than any disutility of responsibility-bearing.

Mill and Cairnes also pointed out that there were 'non-competing groups' in the labour market. There was not free entry to training; and labour was not homogeneous so that the worst grades for which there was least demand had to take the worst jobs. Mill also pointed out that there were special problems over the wages of women who were limited to particular employments which were oversupplied with their labour.[31] But despite these difficulties the wages of all kinds of labour related to the common denominator of basic labour through this framework, although some of the Classical writers (especially Senior) did recognize that wages could contain elements of rent.

ii. PROFITS

Profit was seen throughout the Classical period as primarily the return on capital. The nature of capital in Classical economics has already been indicated—it was accumulation as a result of abstinence from consumption.

It was usually seen in real terms as being a stock of products which took the form both of wage goods which increased productivity by lengthening the production process, and fixed capital which directly increased the productive power of labour. Little attention was paid to the origin of the distribution of the capital amongst capitalists even by J. S. Mill, although he wished to redistribute wealth holdings through severe legacy duties.

It was generally recognized, as we have seen in Chapter 2 and elsewhere, that profits had a fundamental role to play in resource allocation. Three questions had however to be answered; the nature of the profit reward, the reason for its existence, and the determination of its level.

Profit was distinguished by the Classical economists from wages of management from Adam Smith onwards.[32] It was identified by Smith as interest plus a risk premium,[33] and he offered the rule of thumb that the ruling rate of interest was about half the average rate of profit.[34] Further clarification was supplied by Tooke, followed by McCulloch.[35] They distinguished the following elements in gross profits: pure interest, payment for risk (McCulloch was particularly clear here that the risk involved was of the non-insurable variety), wages of management, return to skill, and advantages of situation or connection. McCulloch also deducted rent of market position from pure profit.

Pure profit was then isolated. But the exact source of this reward was for long unclear. A number of writers accepted Smith's point that capital, by supporting division of labour and by assisting labour, increased productivity, and apparently considered that physical productivity was sufficient to give rise to value productivity. Thus Lauderdale offered a pure productivity theory—the owner of capital invested in a machine received the wages that would otherwise have gone to the labour supplanted by the machine. Say implied a marginal-productivity analysis of the return to capital but his treatment was vague. The problem was that productivity will not give rise to value unless the supply of the agent increasing productivity is limited and not a free good like air. Adam Smith had implied negative time-preference—the 'desire for self-betterment'—which apparently ruled out the possibility that saving involved a cost. His own interpretation of profit contained both the idea that capital increases productivity and the further idea that the worker had to part with some of his product to capital in order to gain the benefits of capital's assistance. It was then almost an exploitation theory.

The problem was not cleared up for some time. Ricardo's and McCulloch's confusion between necessary and sufficient conditions for the emergence of profit has already been referred to in Chapter 4 and there is no need to repeat it here. Ricardo did recognize the concept of profits of innovation;[36] but on the more fundamental issue he remained confused. A considerable step forward was made by Samuel Bailey who established by introspection the existence of positive time-preference[37] and it was on this that Senior built a theory of the nature of the profit reward which is still essentially with us today.

Senior's theory was this. Capital increased labour's productivity by allowing the use of more roundabout methods of production—this followed from his third fundamental proposition that the power of labour and other instruments that produce wealth can be indefinitely increased by using their products as a means of further production. But creation of capital involved abstinence from present consumption. This abstinence involved a sacrifice because of the assumption of positive time-preference. This limited the supply of capital. So Senior had now established the interaction of demand for capital and its supply price. However he confined the analysis to savings out of current income and treated the return on inherited property as rent.

Senior was followed by J. S. Mill. Mill made two main modifications to the analysis. Firstly, Senior had implied that saving was carried out under conditions of constant disutility. For this Mill substituted conditions of increasing disutility with the rate of interest governed by the marginal-supply price of abstinence. He also developed the argument that saving depended not only on the motive for saving (the rate of interest) but also on the state of society, especially its security—these factors seem to determine the intercept of the savings function. Saving also depended on the productivity of labour and capital together, for this determined the size of the product from which saving had to be made. This was an assumption of Classical economics from Smith's time onwards, but it was to Mill's credit that he made the assumption quite explicit in this context. His work of pulling the threads of the Classical discussion together continued when he introduced the notion that there was a saving class and a non-saving class, thereby linking up with Adam Smith's treatment of entrepreneurial frugality while managing to retain the assumption of positive time-preference. Finally, his other modification to Senior's analysis was to use the term 'abstinence' to cover refraining from consumption of capital rather than merely the sacrifice incurred in new savings.[38]

The third question, the determination of the rate of profit, received four main answers in the Classical period. The first stems from Hume and Massie. These writers stressed that the rate of interest and profit was a real, rather than a monetary, phenomenon. It depended on the supply of 'riches' (which apparently meant both investment goods and loanable funds) and the demand for these. The demand came both from those who wished to use them productively and from those who were in need of consumption loans. Smith followed this path. Like Hume, Smith saw the demand for loans coming from consumption demand and from investment demand. The supply of loans for the former purpose was limited however not by the rate of interest (market clearing) but by the self-interest of the lenders which led to credit-rationing. (Smith also approved of the Usury Laws as a further check against prodigals bidding up the rate of interest and thus competing funds away from productive investment.) All the Classical productivity explanations of the rate of interest spring from these origins. In these formulations the rate of interest is determined by the productivity of new investment a result achieved by taking the supply of 'riches' as given, ignoring consumption demand for the moment (or treating it as insignificant), and thus ending up with a demand-determined rate, where the demand was investment demand.

This general path was followed by Tooke,[39] who added the further refinement that the rate of interest was governed on the demand side by *expected* profit. His full analysis of demand however involved three sources: those with the prospect of employment for funds greater than their own; those who had already invested all their own capital in a business and were in need of more to keep it going; and spendthrifts, including governments. Moreover Tooke did not entirely ignore the sources of the supply of 'riches'. According to him the sources of supply of funds was also of three kinds: those who had funds to invest but were precluded from making risky investments; persons willing to invest and to manage the funds but on a limited risk basis; and risk-incurring entrepreneurs.

A second answer to the determination of the rate of profit, one which was essentially a development along these lines, was supplied initially by Lord Lauderdale, but later on and better by Longfield.[40] It was essentially a marginal-productivity formulation. Longfield recognized both Senior's positive time-preference/abstinence formulation and also Adam Smith's negative time-preference. Taken together these could have given positive, negative, or zero time-preference depending on their relative strengths; and Longfield simply side-stepped the problem by assuming that the supply of capital was given but limited. He then said that capital had a diminishing marginal product which he explained by a non-homogeneous labour input (a sufficient but not a necessary condition) as well as by changing capital/labour ratios and by relative overproduction of capital-intensive goods. The rate of profit was then determined by the marginal productivity of capital.

All these explanations had in common that the main element in determining the rate of interest (pure profit) was general profitability in the economy: The third main answer however which stemmed from Ricardo, made the rate of profitability depend upon the productivity of marginal investment in one sector—agriculture. This idea runs, often in a camouflaged form (almost as if the writers were unaware of what they were advancing), right through Classical economics from his time onwards. It started from the basic Ricardian propositions of diminishing returns in agriculture (of which we will have more to say in considering rent in the next section), the resolution of marginal product in agriculture into profits and wages, and the determination of agricultural price by supply price at a margin determined by population size. From this, and from the Ricardian value theory with its invariable measure of value, followed two propositions. The first was the inverse relationship of wages and profits. The dependence of this on the measure of value can be seen in Ricardo's table.[41]

When wheat is £4 per quarter suppose wages to be £24 p.a. Suppose half wages are spent on wheat. Then, with wages adjusting to the rising cost of wheat, wages would be

TABLE 1.a

| £24. 14s. | | £4. 4s. 8d. |
|-----------|-----------|-------------|
| £25. 10s. | when wheat | £4. 10s. |
| £26. 8s. | was at | £4. 16s. |
| £27. 8s. 6d. | | £5. 2s. 10d. |

Now of an unvarying fund of £720 (sales receipts fixed in terms of the invariable measure) to be distributed between labourers and farmers.

TABLE 1.b.

| | £ | s | d | | £ | s | d | | £ | s | d |
|---|---|---|---|---|---|---|---|---|---|---|---|
| when the price | 4 | 0 | 0 | the [ten] | 240 | 0 | 0 | and the farmer | 480 | 0 | 0 |
| of wheat is | 4 | 4 | 8 | labourers | 247 | 0 | 0 | will receive | 473 | 0 | 0 |
| | 4 | 10 | 0 | will receive | 255 | 0 | 0 | | 465 | 0 | 0 |
| | 4 | 16 | 0 | | 264 | 0 | 0 | | 456 | 0 | 0 |
| | 5 | 2 | 10 | | 274 | 5 | 0 | | 455 | 15 | 0 |

Suppose the original capital of the farmer was £3,000, profits at £480 would be at 16 per cent. When profits fell to £473 the rate would be 15·7 per cent. With profits successively £465, £456, £445, the rates would be 15·5 per cent, 15·2 per cent, 14·8 per cent.

The important point to grasp is that the value of the labour of ten men with their requisite capital for a year is fixed at £720 in terms of the invariable measure. So as the price of wheat rises in terms of the measure because of increasing input requirements due to diminishing returns (and we have seen in Chapter 4 in discussing the invariable measure that this is the only reason it *can* rise in terms of the invariable measure) *then* wages rise by the subsistence mechanism and profits fall—a larger part of the £720 goes to labour and a smaller part to capital.

The second proposition started out in Ricardo's *Essay on Profits* as the proposition that the rate of profit in agriculture determines the rate of profit throughout the economy. Assuming diminishing returns and falling profits in agriculture there were in fact several possible ways in which this could have depressed profits in manufacturing.

1. The price of the manufacturing input—capital in the form of agricul-

tural wage goods—goes up with the rising price of corn and falling agricultural profits.

2. The price of the manufacturing labour input goes up with the rising price of subsistence.

3. Capital moves out of agriculture into manufacturing. This was ruled out normally by Ricardo's assumption that, without improvements, investment in agriculture was fixed by the size of the population which produced a totally inelastic demand for corn. (Ricardo was not however consistent about this.)

4. The purchasing power of cloth profits declines with a rise in the price of wheat.

5. A rise in the price of wheat in terms of the invariable measure will mean that the price of manufactures falls via the wage/durability of capital theorem, thereby depressing profits.

Explanations 1 and 4 appear in the *Essay* and explanations 2 and 5 appear in Ricardo's *Principles*. Explanation 3 appears fleetingly in the *Essay* as well.[42] But suppose there is a rise in profits in manufacturing. Now Ricardo denies that this can raise the profits of agriculture on the grounds that no capital can be withdrawn from agriculture—the assumption we have already seen. At the same time there cannot be two rates of profit in the economy so manufacturing profits must fall again to the agricultural level[43]—he seems to envisage this occurring through an influx of capital into the trades where the innovation has occurred. The trick (which seems to have escaped commentators) is that Ricardo here (and elsewhere when it suits him such as in dealing with the effect of agricultural improvements on rent) treats the agricultural sector as one giant farm, while disaggregating the manufacturing sector. Innovation in manufacturing therefore affects only one (by implication small) part of that sector, and capital can then flow from the remainder of the sector to depress profits again. Ricardo was unwilling to concede the reverse causality except in so far as recognizing that manufacturing innovation could reduce the price of non-agricultural wage goods and therefore the level of subsistence wages, which he put into a footnote in the *Essay*.[44] Because of his reluctance he kept skirting the problem and this is why, when he treated the problem of the introduction of machinery in the third edition of his *Principles*, he did so on the basis that after the introduction of the machine the manufacturer earned no greater profits than before.

In the *Principles* the proposition is more general; it is that marginal productivity in agriculture determines the rate of profit in the economy. Reliance is then placed on explanations 2 and 5. But an essential point to grasp in understanding all this is the following. Given that the rate of interest was assumed to be falling (as it was, from Adam Smith onwards) and given that it could not fall (because of Say's Law), for any other reason than falling marginal productivity in agriculture,[45] it could be said that the rate of profit in agriculture determined that elsewhere. This is really what Ricardo had in mind, and why he shirked the manufacturing-innovation problem.

J. S. Mill who, as we have seen, saw the reason for the existence of interest as lying in abstinence, linked up this idea with the Ricardian analysis and with sociological considerations derived from the work of John Rae, to produce a supply-and-demand theory of the rate of interest. One of the striking features of the majority of the other Classical writers is that they had virtually demand determined rates with a given supply: whereas Mill, through focusing on abstinence, managed to provide a more general analysis. According to his treatment all capital was the product of saving. The amount of saving depended on the amount of the fund from which saving could be made—this meant total product less rent, including wages greater than subsistence—and the strength of the disposition to save. Elasticity of saving was dependent on both circumstances and individuals—on mental states, the security of enjoying the fruits of accumulation, and the size of the saving class. These may be said to have affected the intercept of the savings function (though of course Mill used no such terminology) while the slope of the function depended on time-preference. In equilibrium the rate of interest was equal to the marginal supply price of abstinence —which varied according to security of property and the other considerations noted. It was also equal to the marginal productivity of investment which depended not only upon physical productivity but upon the level of wages which together gave the cost per unit of output. Before equilibrium was reached profits would be greater than the supply price of abstinence; but whenever this occurred accumulation would run ahead to bid up wages and reduce profits again to the supply price of abstinence. What we have here in fact is Mill's ideas expressed in terms of the basic Ricardian model of Chapter 2—and Mill repeatedly gives his argument a Ricardian gloss by reasoning in terms of the marginal productivity of investment in agriculture.[45a]

All this of course related to the common level of profits. Classical theory also offered a theory of relative profits to complement the theory of relative wages. But of the five conditions in the *Wealth of Nations* that affect wages, only two affect profits, agreeableness and risk.

### iii. RENT

The basic Classical ideas on rent have already been outlined in Chapter 2 in dealing with the Smithian and Ricardian systems. Rent, as we saw there, was, at least from the time of Ricardo onwards, viewed as an intra-marginal surplus. Competition between tenants (who were content to earn only normal profits) ensured that this surplus was appropriated by the landlords. This was pure rent which was distinguished from the return on capital invested in improvements—although, as Ricardo uneasily recognized in a footnote, if capital invested in land could not be *dis*invested its return was really rent.[46]

Agricultural production had two special characteristics which gave rise to this surplus: a feedback from production to demand through the population mechanism (this was stressed by Malthus) and rising costs associated with increasing output. This latter point was dealt with in the Classical literature under the heading of Diminishing Returns. Now every student is well versed in the distinction between diminishing returns to a variable factor combined with a fixed factor, and decreasing returns to scale. The Classical discussion called both of these diminishing returns, however, and confused the presentation still further by apparently relying on non-homogeneity of land input as the 'cause' of diminishing returns—the 'degrees of fertility' which characterized every Classical rent discussion. This was of course a sufficient but not a necessary condition for diminishing returns, as some writers, including Senior and Torrens, Longfield, Lloyd, and Bailey recognized. But Ricardo seemed to see differing grades as necessary.[47]

But the idea of diminishing returns in the modern sense was also recognized, and it was understood that the increase of output would involve equalization of the return to extra capital-and-labour employed on land already under cultivation (the intensive margin) and to extra-capital-and-labour employed on newly cultivated land (the extensive margin). The resort to inferior land was used to illustrate the existence of an intensive margin. This was reasonable because although it is possible to argue that returns to the plots already under cultivation might be increasing and that extension would still take place if returns were increasing even faster on the pieces newly brought under cultivation, the plots already under cultivation would go out of cultivation if this were the case. It was the extension of cultivation *and* the continued cultivation of 'old' land which established the existence of diminishing returns.

Average and marginal product were clearly distinguished in the Classical literature although it was wrongly believed that if marginal product was declining average product must also be, which is only true in the case of linearly declining returns which, in fact, the Classical arithmetical examples normally assumed. (The matter was not cleared up till Edgeworth.)[48]

The typical classical presentation was flawed in a number of ways. In particular most writers neglected to stress that, for rent to exist, land had to be productive (although the much abused Malthus did so), and, as noted in the value discussion, the transfer earnings of land were neglected. But the analysis was a significant achievement for all that. It had originated with four writers—West, Malthus, Torrens, and Ricardo, who all published more or less simultaneously in 1815.[49] Subjectively the analysis was theirs, though it has to be acknowledged that Turgot had already supplied the idea of the intensive margin,[50] and that James Anderson had provided, a year after the publication of the first edition of the *Wealth of Nations*, a more or less complete discussion of the idea of rent as a price-determined surplus due to diminishing returns, although it was couched largely in terms of the extensive margin.[51] Moreover, as was so often the case, the basic building blocks were to be found in that great quarry the *Wealth of Nations*. In fact Adam Smith had rent as both a price-determined surplus[52] and also as price-determining because of transfer earnings.[53] In some ways his discussion was superior to that of the later Classical writers because he explicitly took account of transfer earnings. But the lack of the marginal concept made Smith's discussion appear confused—he could have borrowed this from Anderson but he did not. So although he had rent varying with fertility and location, and although he realized that transport improvements reduced rent, he still left the subject in a confused state. But he had supplied almost all that was necessary for the formulation of a correct theory.

With Ricardo the rent analysis became a basic part of his analytical schema of class conflict—rent was maximized by high agricultural prices resulting from incurring diminishing and decreasing returns at home rather than importing cheap corn. The interests of the landlords were thus basically opposed to those of the rest of the community. Ricardo proceeded on this basis to argue that improvements in agricultural technology were also rent-reducing and thence against the interests of the landlord. His analysis envisaged two kinds of improvements, those which reduced the land necessary to produce a given output, and those which reduced the capital-and-labour inputs required to produce a given output. The essence of the distinction is supposed to be that the first kind of improvement will result in contraction of the extensive margin while the second will not. The distinction is however unsatisfactory. In the first case there will be a direct reduction in cultivation area; but in the second case there will also be a reduction in cultivation area because as capital and labour are now more productive (when combined with land) than before, factor combinations will now have to be readjusted to re-employ unemployed capital and labour. There will be a shift of output from the extensive to the intensive margin and cultivation area will also be reduced in the second case. (Remember we are continuing to make Ricardo's assumption of a totally inelastic demand for agricultural output.) Without doing much violence to the argument we can then regard the two kinds of improvement as equivalent. We can examine the effect of both in terms of an upwards shift in the marginal product curve of capital-and-labour.

The effects of improvements on rent can then be seen in Figs. 11 and 12.

Improvements which shift the marginal-product curve upwards by equal *absolute* amounts (as Ricardo usually but not always assumed) so that the new curve is parallel to the old one, will reduce corn rent (the landlords' share of output). Those improvements which increase marginal product by equal *proportional* amounts (as J. S. Mill assumed) will also diminish corn rent, given linearity of the productivity functions, if the change in the slope of the marginal-product curve increases the perpendicular of the rent triangle

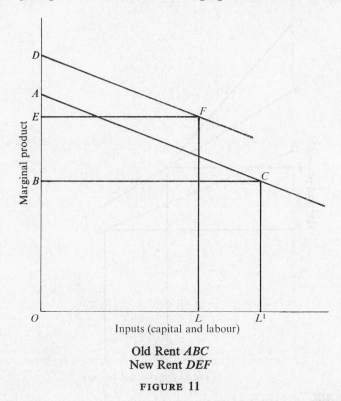

Old Rent *ABC*
New Rent *DEF*

FIGURE 11

by *proportionately* less than the diminution in its base. In Fig. 11 we have the absolute case and in Fig. 12 the two proportional cases. The rent triangle with hypotenuse 1 is greater than the rent triangle with hypotenuse II despite the proportional shift in the marginal-product curve. The rent triangle with hypotenuse III is equal to the triangle with hypotenuse I. Any steeper hypotenuse will increase corn rent.

Having seen the effect on corn rent (share of output) we can make the transition to money rents quite easily. As a result of an improvement the price of agricultural produce falls because marginal cost has fallen. Money rent must therefore fall unless corn rent increases in the same proportion as price has fallen. Money rent will therefore decrease with equal absolute shifts in the marginal-product function: but it can (although it will not necessarily) remain the same or even increase with equal proportional shifts in the marginal-product schedule.

Ricardo actually made the mistake of changing *inputs* rather than *output* by equal *absolute* amounts in his example and Cannan was able to show

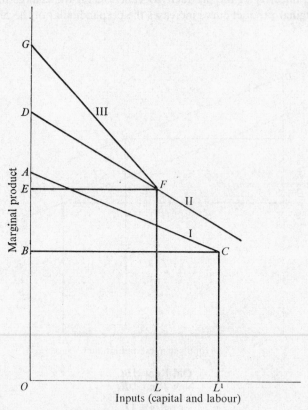

Rent    I *ABC*
Rent   II *DEF*        Triangle *ABC* is equal in
Rent  III *GEF*        area to triangle *GEF*.

FIGURE 12

that Ricardo's numerical example actually involved a rise in corn rent and a constant money rent, although Ricardo had thought that it would result in a constant corn rent and a falling money rent. He could however have got the result he wanted by altering *inputs* by equal *proportionate* amounts.

Ricardo posited a case in which four portions of capital, 50, 60, 70, 80, were employed with land to produce equal amounts of corn. He then assumed that as a result of an improvement the inputs necessary for this output were reduced to 45, 55, 65, and 75. He believed this would leave corn rent constant and reduce money rent. But if the output of each portion of capital is $x$ then the original corn rent will be as follows:

$$\frac{10}{80}x + \frac{20}{80}x + \frac{30}{80}x = \frac{3}{4}x$$

The 80 portion of capital (which regulates price) will pay no rent—it is the marginal input.* The 70 portion will pay $\frac{10}{80}x$, and so on.

After the improvement

$$\frac{10}{75}x + \frac{20}{75}x + \frac{30}{75}x = \frac{4}{5}x$$

$\frac{4}{5} > \frac{3}{4}$ so corn rent increases. Money rent will remain the same. If a quarter was worth £4 before the improvement and the improvement reduces inputs by $\frac{5}{80}$ or $\frac{1}{16}$, price, as determined by marginal cost, will fall from £4 to £3$\frac{3}{4}$.

But
$$\frac{3}{4} \cdot 4 = \frac{15}{4} \cdot \frac{4}{5} = 3$$

So money rent remains unchanged.

This example however raises a further difficulty with the analysis. As the reader will find for himself if he works out the marginal productivities from the Cannan figures, the productivity function is not linear but slightly convex towards the origin. We have so far confined ourselves to linear productivity functions. If however we use non-linear productivity functions the results become even less clear cut: only in the equal-absolute case is it true that even with the non-linear productivity functions an improvement will necessarily decrease rent. But of course we will not expect to get linear productivity functions unless the production function is quadratic.

Moreover there is a further difficulty with all this. It applies to any improvements which result in the unemployment of inputs (e.g. $L - L^1$ in Fig. 11) as they must necessarily do on Ricardo's (short-run) assumptions. Profit rates were equated between agriculture and manufacturing before the improvement. The improvement raises profits in agriculture, as we could see if we drew a subsistence wage constant into Fig. 11. But the unemployed labour and capital, in so far as they are not reabsorbed into agriculture through readjustment of the extensive/intensive margin balance will migrate to the manufacturing sector whose profit would be lowered. The Ricardian economy then has two profit rates, which Ricardo never tired of saying was impossible![54]

* Cost increases in proportion to input so the relative size of the portions of capital indicates relative costs. Thus the cost of producing $x$ on the second last extension of cultivation is only $\frac{7}{8}$ of the cost of producing it on the last grade so $\frac{1}{8}$ goes in rent.

The later Classical economists, who did not subscribe to Ricardo's class-conflict thesis, soon found that there was in any case plenty wrong with the apparently persuasive treatment. They pointed out that population and improvements tended to go hand in hand, the one stimulating the other, and that rents were kept up as population expanded to keep up with the improvements which its own pressure had brought about. They were quite clear that improvements and rent had historically marched in the same direction.[55] Even if they did not go hand in hand, however, Ricardo's argument was only a short-run one as population would expand in the long run and restore rents[56]—a point which Ricardo was forced to recognize, though he did so only fleetingly.[57]

Moreover, as McCulloch pointed out, there were alternative demand assumptions to Ricardo's that elasticity was zero. McCulloch himself suggested assuming that elasticity was equal to one so that, as price fell because of improvements, consumption increased in proportion. In this case demand would increase in the short run even without a population increase. The corn rent could then increase and the money rent remain constant. In addition, if improvements affected only the better grades (for which a plausible *a priori* case could be made), then rent would increase so long as the price-determining margin was not contracted. The extension of cultivation to inferior soils was no proof of universally diminishing returns to equal amounts of labour on equal amounts of land at a constant state of technique—diminishing returns are not proved to proceed at the same *rate* by this course of reasoning, and if they do not proceed at the same rate then the effect of improvements is unlikely to be the same on different pieces of land.

Finally, although none of the Classical economists seems to have recognized this (Senior came close),[58] the whole mechanism of the introduction of improvements had been obscured by Ricardo's 'collectivization'—the treatment of the agricultural sector as one giant farm. Once disaggregation is recognized then it is clear that it is in the interests of a landlord to introduce improvements because his rent will go up by more than the market price falls as a result of his improvement. Competition will then ensure that other landlords (who will in any case wish to gain the advantage of increased rents) also introduce the improvements. Thus micro-economic decision-taking in a disaggregated agricultural sector would ensure that landlords introduce improvements whatever the supposed conflict of interest.

Apart from their treatment of the problem of improvements the later Classical economists also extended the rent analysis. They generalized the rent concept to include any return which was greater than a necessary return —the concept we have in fact today. The process began with Craig (who extended the concept to income from fixed capital) and with Bailey. The latter pointed out that rent could exist without non-homogeneity of land input and extended the rent analysis to wages (though confusingly he made this result from non-homogeneity of labour input). But he seems to have been clear that rent could be earned by any factor in less than perfectly elastic supply. The process of generalization was more or less fully carried out by Senior who saw rent of land as a 'species of an extensive genus'.[59] He pointed out that, unlike profits and wages in his formulation, rent was a return for which no sacrifice had to be incurred—which was presumably what Adam Smith had meant by his dictum about landlords reaping where they had not sowed. He then said that any return which did not correspond to a sacrifice was rent; and he was thus able to include under this head payment for patent rights, payment to inherited property, fortuitous profits, and special payment earned by ability.[60] He also came close to a concept of quasi-rent[61] although he never seems to have got the short-run/long-run distinction sufficiently clear to sort the matter out properly.

## iv. RELATIVE SHARES

Since Classical economics was above all growth economics, and since it contained theories of distribution in the long run, it is necessary to examine what it had to offer concerning the trends of relative shares of total output.

In the *Wealth of Nations* we find a falling long-run rate of profit due to the exhaustion of investment opportunities in all forms of employment of capital including agriculture.[62] Increasing productivity, e.g. the cultivation of new colonial lands, raised profit for a while but the accumulation of capital depressed it again unless further new employments for it were opened. Malthus followed this line of argument and it appears later in the development of Classical economics during the discussions of colonialism. But a more general legacy was that from this time onwards there was a tendency simply to take it for granted that the rate of profit was falling.

Smith's treatment of the long-run trend of wages is indeterminate. In general he sees wages as at first rising and then falling back to subsistence as population catches up with capital accumulation. But because subsistence is a movable and a psychological concept the trend line for wages can follow one of several paths indicated in figures 13a, 13b and 13c. So the long-run trend of real wages in the *Wealth of Nations* is indeterminate.

The long-run trend of rent in the *Wealth of Nations* is also indeterminate. In one place Smith says that progress will cause rents to rise both in money and produce terms.[63] This does seem to be his main conclusion but he does not offer any reasoning to support it. Elsewhere he offers the view that rents diminish with progress;[64] and at one point[65] he suggests that the highest rates of profit will eat up all rent—a view which he does not explain, but since he cites the case of the East India Company in Bengal he may have had in mind a rather special situation where ordinary competitive forces were replaced by bilateral bargaining.

Ricardo offered quite clear predictions about the trends of all three shares. These can be seen not only in the diagrams in Chapter 2 but in Table 2 which is taken from his *Essay on Profits* and which exemplifies his procedure

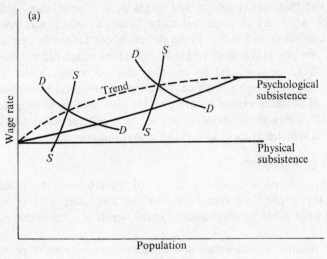

**FIGURE 13a**

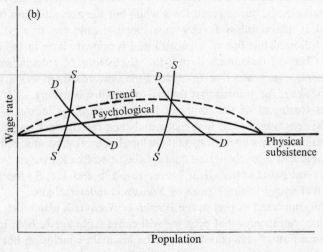

**FIGURE 13b**

of treating the economy as a giant farm in order to arrive at a clear-cut solution. The table is shown graphically in Figure 14. With wages tied to subsistence by the population mechanism and so constant in real (corn) terms though increasing in money terms, he saw rental share rising and profits falling. In fact, however, diminishing returns were a necessary but not a sufficient condition for the increase of the rental share. Rents rise as a share of output (corn rents) with economic progress only if returns diminish at a

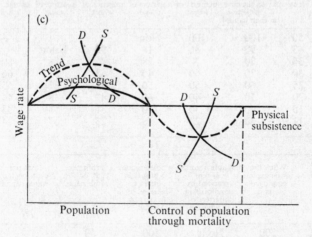

FIGURE 13c

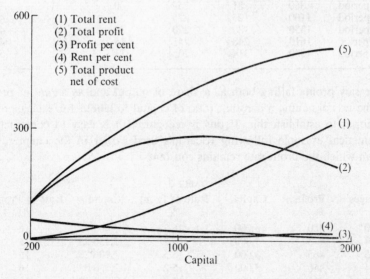

FIGURE 14

constant or increasing rate.[66] Ricardo's numerical example above and elsewhere implies constantly diminishing returns to the variable input. But his treatment was perfectly reasonable because in order to get a different result from his we need marginal product falling less fast than average product—which implies that diminishing returns will come to an end.

TABLE 2, *showing the Progress of Rent and*

| Capital estimated in quarters of wheat | Profit per cent | Neat produce in quarters of wheat after paying the cost of production on each capital | Profit of 1st portion of land in quarters of wheat | Rent of 1st portion of land in quarters of wheat | Profit of 2nd portion of land in quarters of wheat | Rent of 2nd portion of land in quarters of wheat | Profit of 3rd portion of land in quarters of wheat | Rent of 3rd portion of land in quarters of wheat |
|---|---|---|---|---|---|---|---|---|
| 200 | 50 | 100 | 100 | None | | | | |
| 210 | 43 | 90 | 86 | 14 | 90 | None | | |
| 220 | 36 | 80 | 72 | 28 | 76 | 14 | 80 | None |
| 230 | 30 | 70 | 60 | 40 | 63 | 27 | 66 | 14 |
| 240 | 25 | 60 | 50 | 50 | 52½ | 37½ | 55 | 25 |
| 250 | 20 | 50 | 40 | 60 | 42 | 48 | 44 | 36 |
| 260 | 15 | 40 | 30 | 70 | 31½ | 58½ | 33 | 47 |
| 270 | 11 | 30 | 22 | 78 | 23 | 67 | 24 | 56 |

| | When the whole capital employed is | Whole amount of rent received by landlords in quarters of wheat (1) | Whole amount of profits in quarters received by owners of stock (2) | Profit per cent. on the whole capital (3) | Rent per cent. on the whole capital (4) | Total produce in quarters of wheat, after paying the cost of production (5) |
|---|---|---|---|---|---|---|
| 1st period | 200 | None | 100 | 50 | | 100 |
| 2nd period | 410 | 14 | 176 | 43 | 3½ | 190 |
| 3rd period | 630 | 42 | 228 | 36 | 6¾ | 270 |
| 4th period | 860 | 81 | 259 | 30 | 9½ | 340 |
| 5th period | 1100 | 125 | 275 | 25 | 11½ | 400 |
| 6th period | 1350 | 180 | 270 | 20 | 13¼ | 450 |
| 7th period | 1610 | 248½ | 241½ | 15 | 15½ | 490 |
| 8th period | 1880 | 314½ | 205½ | 11 | 16½ | 520 |

He saw profits falling both as a share of output and as a *rate* of profit. But he was assuming a constant ratio of capital to labour for each increase in output to establish this. If this is recognized it is easy to construct an arithmetical example following Ricardo's used earlier in the chapter, but one in which the profit rate remains constant.

TABLE 3

| Wages. £ *s* | Profits. £ *s* | Capital. £ | Rate of Profit % | Capital. £ | Rate of Profit. % |
|---|---|---|---|---|---|
| 240 | 480 | 3,000 | 16 | 3,000 | 16 |
| 247 | 473 | 3,000 | 15·7 | 2,956·25 | 16 |
| 255 | 465 | 3,000 | 15·5 | 2,906·25 | 16 |
| 264 | 456 | 3,000 | 15·2 | 2,850·0 | 16 |
| 274 5 | 445 15 | 3,000 | 14·8 | 2,782·19 | 16 |

The result was pointed out by Cannan; and as early as 1825 McCulloch had made a similar point.[67]

Apart from this difficulty we have also to recognize that not only was there the possibility that manufacturing innovation could raise general profits, once we drop Ricardo's very special assumptions noted above, but it

*Profit under an assumed Augmentation of Capital*

| Profit of 4th portion of land in quarters of wheat | Rent of 4th portion of land in quarters of wheat | Profit of 5th portion of land in quarters of wheat | Rent of 5th portion of land in quarters of wheat | Profit of 6th portion of land in quarters of wheat | Rent of 6th portion of land in quarters of wheat | Profit of 7th portion of land in quarters of wheat | Rent of 7th portion of land in quarters of wheat | Profit of 8th portion of land in quarters of wheat |
|---|---|---|---|---|---|---|---|---|
| 70 | None | | | | | | | |
| 57½ | 12½ | 60 | None | | | | | |
| 46 | 24 | 48 | 12 | 50 | None | | | |
| 34½ | 35½ | 36 | 24 | 37½ | 12½ | 40 | None | |
| 25·3 | 44·7 | 26·4 | 33·6 | 27½ | 22½ | 27·6 | 12·4 | 29·7 |

could also quite specifically lower wage-good costs and thereby increase profits. Ricardo neglects this and implicitly minimizes (though he does not eliminate) its potential importance through his implied assumption of fixed commodity proportions in the wage-good basket.

Ricardo's approach to the matter of the trend of relative shares continued to hang over later Classical discussions of the problem. But the later writers did not find themselves tied to his particular results. Thus, J. S. Mill considered four cases.[68] Firstly, population might be increasing with capital constant. Wages would then fall and profits would rise. If, as a result of the fall of wages, the labour force economized on commodities other than food, so that the reduction in the demand for food from each member of the labour force was not in proportion to the reduction in his wages, then the increased population would require more food than the previous population which could only be supplied by extending the margin of cultivation, raising both money and corn rents. The second case that Mill considered involved a rise in capital, with population constant. Wages would then rise and profits would fall. There would be extra demand for wheat and rents would rise. In the third case population and capital were both supposed to rise with technology fixed. The price of corn would then rise as the margin was extended, rents would rise and profits would fall. But Mill recognized that in these circumstances the absolute amount of profits might rise even though the rate was falling. The fourth case that Mill considered involved the assumption that both capital and population were constant but that technology was improving. This leads to a discussion of the effect of improvements on rent, assuming equal proportional shifts in the productivity functions as we have already noted. Finally Mill considers a case with population and capital increasing and technology improving at the same time. This, the normal case of economic growth, is simply left with the remark that what happened would depend on the relative rates of increase under these three heads.

Mill had gone through a sort of Ricardian exercise here and it will have been noted that in his schema wages and profits move inversely. But this is in fact a shorthand for the proposition that, for Mill, profits depend on the *cost of labour* rather than on wages. The cost of labour is a function of the efficiency (productivity) of labour, the rate of money wages, and the price of wage goods. In other words Mill did not derive the theorem from the invariable measure and because he did not do so it lost a great deal of its certainty and its clear-cut nature. In addition to this, although Mill regarded diminishing returns in agriculture as a very important and indeed a self-evident proposition, he also ascribed great importance to technical improvements in agriculture which had, he asserted, offset diminishing returns since about 1825. He also ascribed great importance to increasing returns in manufacturing which reduced the cost of non-agricultural wage-goods. Finally, although he ostensibly subscribed to the Ricardian theory as a long-run proposition he turned it into the idea that a country with corn laws (i.e. a country which has suffered from diminishing returns to the point where growth stops) does not have a higher corn price and rental than a country without corn laws, but has the same corn price and rental with a smaller population because accumulation stops earlier. Moreover Mill also appeared at times to offer the Smithian explanation for the declining rate of profit— exhaustion of investment opportunities.[69]

Others were even less impressed by the Ricardian view of the trend of relative shares. Even De Quincey denied the existence of a declining rate of profit,[70] while McCulloch ultimately rejected the whole Ricardian vision. He doubted that the rate of profit *was* declining and decided that profits in Holland had fallen because of capital accumulation—in the same way as Smith had done. He accepted the role of technical progress in both the agricultural and manufacturing sectors and ultimately rejected also the Ricardian view of the inverse movement of wages and profits on the dynamic grounds, more typical of his later writings, that a wage rise would stimulate capitalists to extra enterprise and effort to maintain their profits.[71]

## V. CONCLUSION

We have now surveyed the Classical theory of distribution. Although it contains a number of disparate elements there is a sufficient number of coherent ones for it to be possible to speak of a Classical theory of distribution. Although it suffered from undoubted defects which have been indicated in this chapter it is indisputable that the Classical economists between them managed to produce something which was not only markedly superior to anything that had gone before but which also asked and indeed attempted to answer questions which were simply ignored by later economists.

# NOTES

1. Op. cit. (ed. Cannan), i. 71, 94.
2. Ibid., pp. 49–50, 94. See also p. 66—division of labour increased productivity and hence wages.
3. Ibid., pp. 50, 67.
4. Ibid., p. 68.
5. Ibid., pp. 69–70, 71–5, 82–3. See also pp. 348–51 where Smith's argument that taxes on wages are passed on seems to be based on a subsistence-wage mechanism. However Smith believed wages in Britain to be above subsistence. Compare also ibid., pp. 84–5 and 87–8, for the ambiguity in Smith's view of the relationship between the price of provisions and the level of money wages.
6. A further link is provided by Smith (ibid., p. 88) in that wages and productivity rose together as a larger stock of wage capital supported greater division of labour.
7. Smith, op. cit., Bk. II, Ch. III, p. 320.
8. See Blaug, *Ricardian Economics*, pp. 122–3 and O'Brien, *J. R. McCulloch*, p. 356.
9. See especially J. S. Mill, *Principles*, ed. Ashley, pp. 349–60, and Bk. I, Ch. XIII, Bk. II, Ch. XIII, and Bk. IV, Ch. VII. The productivity element in the *Wealth of Nations* had been somewhat obscured by the natural-wage idea although it reappeared in some other Classical writers, notably Senior.
10. See op. cit., pp. 344–5.
11. See O'Brien, *J. R. McCulloch*, pp. 360–6.
12. Op. cit., i. 83.
13. See Mill, op. cit., ed. Ashley, Appendix O.
14. Ibid., pp. 343–4.
15. Op. cit., i. 71. See also O'Brien, *J. R. McCulloch*, pp. 358–9.
16. S. Hollander, 'The Role of Fixed Technical Coefficients in the Evolution of the Wages-Fund Controversy', *Oxford Economic Papers*, 20 (1968), 320–41.
17. See D. O'Brien, 'Torrens on Wages and Emigration', *Economica*, 33 (1966), 336–40.
18. J. E. Cairnes, *Some Leading Principles of Political Economy* (London, 1874), pp. 202, 204–5.
19. See especially J. S. Mill, op. cit., Bk. I, Ch. VI, especially pp. 94–5, 96, 99. See also ibid., Bk. I, Ch. VIII.
20. Torrens clearly recognized that the capital/labour ratio varied between agriculture and manufacturing—see especially his *Essay on the Production of Wealth*, pp. 136–46. See also ibid., p. 90.
21. Cairnes, op. cit., pp. 206–7.
22. Ricardo did not believe that the labourer's lot would improve with economic growth. *Works*, i. 102–3, 112, 125. See also i. 93.
23. Smith, op. cit., i. 91.
24. Ricardo, *Works*, i. 93.
25. Ibid., pp. 97, 121–2.
26. Sir Edward West, *Price of Corn and Wages of Labour, with Observations upon Dr. Smith's Mr. Ricardo's and Mr. Malthus's Doctrines upon these Subjects* (London, 1826).
27. Say, *Treatise*, pp. 293–7. Say also offered a rising supply schedule of labour and quoted Smith in support of this—ibid., p. 340.
28. *Lectures*, pp. 200–21.
29. Ibid., p. 212.
30. Smith, op. cit., Bk. I, Ch. X.
31. See J. S. Mill, op. cit., pp. 388, 400–1.
32. Op. cit., i. 50, 55.
33. Ibid., pp. 97–8.
34. Ibid., pp. 98–9.
35. For references see O'Brien, *J. R. McCulloch*, p. 310.

36. *Works,* i. 386–7.
37. Bailey, *Critical Dissertation,* p. 218.
38. Senior had himself actually taken such a view of abstinence at one point (*Outline,* p. 140), but the narrower concept was the one he generally employed.
39. *Considerations on the State of the Currency* (2nd. edn. London, 1826).
40. Lecture IX, pp. 180–99.
41. *Works,* i. 116–17.
42. *Essay* in *Works,* iv. 12.
43. Ibid., pp. 23–4.
44. *Essay,* p. 26.
45. *Works,* i. 289–300.
45a. Mill, *Principles,* pp. 163–75, 405–21, 725–39.
46. Ibid., pp. 261–2 n.
47. Ibid., p. 75.
48. See G. J. Stigler, *Production and Distribution Theories,* pp. 112–16; see also the same author's 'The Ricardian Theory of Value and Distribution', *Journal of Political Economy,* 60 (1952), 187–207, especially 195–200.
49. Sir E. West, *Essay on the Application of Capital to Land* (London, [13 Feb.] 1815); T. R. Malthus, *An Inquiry into the Nature and Progress of Rent* (London, [3 Feb.] 1815); R. Torrens, *An Essay on the External Corn Trade* (London, [24 Feb.] 1815); D. Ricardo, *An Essay on the Influence of a Low Price of Corn on the Profits of Stock* (London, [24 Feb.] 1815. Mr. Sraffa has established the publication dates given in brackets.
50. See Cannan, *Production and Distribution Theories,* pp. 147–8.
51. See O'Brien, *J. R. McCulloch,* pp. 397–8.
52. Op. cit., i. 67, 145–7.
53. Ibid., pp. 57, 68, 150, 153, 159.
54. See Stigler, *Production and Distribution Theories,* pp. 90–1 n.
55. R. Jones, *An Essay on the Distribution of Wealth* (London, 1831), pp. 217–44, 287–8, 303–4; Longfield, *Lectures,* pp. 137–8, 224. The point was admitted by J. S. Mill (*Principles,* ed. Ashley, p. 719).
56. Senior, *Outline,* p. 138; O'Brien, *J. R. McCulloch,* p. 400.
57. *Works,* i. 81 n.
58. Senior, *Outline,* p. 138.
59. Appendix to R. Whately, *Elements of Logic* (London, 1826).
60. *Outline,* pp. 91–2, 115–16, 129.
61. Ibid., pp. 102, 219–20.
62. i. 93–4, 95–6, 335, 385.
63. Ibid., Bk. I, Ch. XI.
64. Ibid., Bk. II, Ch. III.
65. Ibid., i. 98.
66. See M. Blaug, *Economic Theory in Retrospect,* p. 97.
67. Cannan, *Production and Distribution Theories,* pp. 288–9; J. R. McCulloch, *Principles of Political Economy* (1st edn. Edinburgh, 1825), pp. 371–2; ibid. (4th edn. London, 1849), pp. 533–4.
68. *Principles* (ed. Ashley), Bk. IV, Ch. III.
69. Ibid., p. 727.
70. *Logic of Political Economy,* pp. 293–4.
71. See O'Brien, *J. R. McCulloch,* pp. 296–9.

## BIBLIOGRAPHY

The Classical treatment of the three factor rewards is the subject of incisive treatment in Cannan's *Production and Distribution Theories* and *Review of Economic Theory,* works which are still amazingly fresh and penetrating even though the first of these dates from 1893. But see also Viner's review of the latter work repr. in *Long View and the Short*. See also Blaug, *Ricardian Economics* and *Retrospect*, and Schumpeter, *History*, pp. 662–71, 645–52, 671–9. On Ricardo's treatment of distribution O. St. Clair is also helpful as is Stigler's 'Ricardian Theory of Production and Distribution', *Journal of Political Economy* (1952). On other writers there are particular commentaries also: Lord Robbins, *Robert Torrens*, M. Bowley, *Senior*, O'Brien, *McCulloch*: the reader should also see R. D. C. Black's introduction to *Economic Writings of M. Longfield*.

These general references cover all three of the factor rewards. On the specific question of wages and the wage fund see also J. Bonar, *Malthus and his Work* (London, 1924), F. Taussig, *Wages and Capital* (London, 1896), A. Plummer, 'Sir Edward West', *Journal of Political Economy*, 37 (1929), D. O'Brien, 'Torrens on Wages and Emigration', *Economica*, 33 (1966), and S. Hollander, 'The Role of Fixed Technical Coefficients in the Evolution of the Wages-Fund Controversy', *Oxford Economic Papers*, 20 (1968), as well as W. Breit, 'The Wages Fund Controversy Revisited', *Canadian Journal*, 33 (1967), 509–28. But the most illuminating discussion of all is probably that by S. Wood, 'A Critique of Wage Theories', *Annals of the American Academy of Political and Social Science*, i (1890). This should not be missed. The important primary references on wages have been indicated in the footnotes to the text: see in particular Smith, Bk. I, Chs. VIII and X, Ricardo, Chs. V and XVI; Longfield, Lecture X, and J. S. Mill, Bk. II, Chs. XI–XIV.

Additional references on profits are Sraffa's Introduction to Ricardo's *Works*, Vol. i, Stigler, 'The Ricardian Theory', V. Edelberg, 'The Ricardian Theory of Profits', *Economica*, 13 (1933), and G. S. L. Tucker, *Progress and Profits in British Economic Thought* (Cambridge, 1960). An old commentary but a major classic in its own right is E. v. Böhm-Bawerk, *Capital and Interest*, trans. W. Smart (London, 1890). The primary references should include not only Smith (Bk. I, Chs. IX and X and Bk. II), and Ricardo's *Principles*, Chs. V, VI, XV, XXI, but also Ricardo's *Essay on Profits*. It is doubtful whether it is possible to understand the *Principles* without knowledge of the contents of the *Essay*. See also Longfield, Lectures VIII and IX. J. S. Mill's discussion on profits (and relative shares) is scattered throughout the book: see Bk. I, Chs. IV–VII and XI,* Bk. II, Ch. XV,* Bk. III, Ch. XXVI, and Bk. IV, Chs. IV and V. (The asterisks indicate the most important chapters.)

Special references on rent relate mainly to the subject of improvements and rent. Apart from Cannan (see especially *Production and Distribution*, pp. 310–88) see J. H. Hollander's Introduction to Ricardo's *Notes on Malthus* (Baltimore, 1928), H. G. Johnson, 'An Error in Ricardo's Exposition of his Theory of Rent', *Quarterly Journal of Economics*, 62 (1948), and G. J. Stigler, *Production and Distribution Theories* (New York, 1941), pp. 90–1 and 326–30, as well as H. Barkhai, 'Ricardo's second thoughts on rent as a relative share', *Southern Economic Journal*, 32 (1966), 285–93. See also Marshall's *Principles* (8th edn. London, 1927), pp. 833–7. The best primary reference to start with is probably T. R. Malthus, *Inquiry into the Nature and Progress of Rent* (1815). See also Ricardo, Chs. II, III, IX, X, XXIV, XXXII, J. S. Mill, Bk. II, Ch. 16, Bk. III, Ch. 5, Bk. IV, Ch. 3, and Longfield, Lectures VI and VII. The most important part of Anderson's contribution is repr. in J. R. McCulloch (ed.), *A Select Collection of Scarce and Valuable Economical Tracts* (1859).

Finally although wages of management were widely recognized by the Classical economists they gave little attention to the role of the factor entrepreneurship. Say was the main exception here. See G. Koolman 'Say's Conception of the Role of the Entrepreneur', *Economica*, 38 (1971), 269–86.

# 6. Classical Monetary Theory

## i. THE HISTORICAL BACKGROUND

It is not possible within the confines of this chapter to provide any detailed material on the monetary history of the Classical era. But some indication of the salient features of the period is necessary to enable the reader to appreciate what the argument was about. Economic theory is never independent of the background against which it emerges: and this is particularly true of monetary theory.

Convertibility of the note issue into gold was suspended in 1797 and it was not resumed until the years 1819–21. The country experienced inconvertible paper and inflation in the intervening period. Destruction of the country-bank paper in 1814–16, as many of the country banks failed, had however a serious effect on the money supply in an opposite direction. Sharp deflation occurred, and its effects were reinforced by the resumption of cash payments, when the return to gold was undertaken at the old parity—a mistake to be repeated after World War I. As the economy gradually recovered from this, a fierce debate arose, following the monetary crises of 1825–6, 1836, and 1839. The blame for these was laid by many commentators largely on the Bank of England; and the subsequent Bank Charter Act of 1844 was designed to produce an automatic system of currency regulation by making the note issue behave exactly as an identically circumstanced metallic currency would. Although by no means a total failure the Act was suspended in 1847 and 1857 during monetary crises, and again in 1866, though without crisis on that occasion.

The latter part of the Classical era was that of the gold discoveries but throughout the entire period there was a great expansion in the money supply. If we take note issue as representative of the money supply (and it almost certainly understates the growth of the latter as normally defined) we find the Bank of England's note issue to have been £4·3m. in 1750, £8·6m. in 1776, £28·2m. in 1844, and £34·9m. in 1870. In addition there was a substantial note issue by the English country, Scottish, and Irish Banks, the majority of which grew up after 1776. By 1844 this issue had reached nearly £17·1m.

The changes in the money supply and the parallel changes in the national income involved significant price-level changes. Various prices indices are available; the figures calculated by Rousseaux[1] presented here take 1865 and 1885 as 100. The figures for our period then were:

| 1800 | 175⎱ inconvertible | 1840 | 128 |
| 1810 | 193⎰ paper | 1850 | 95 |
| 1820 | 132 | 1860 | 120 |
| 1830 | 109 | 1870 | 110 |

Having outlined the historical background we can now proceed to consider the content of Classical monetary theory.

## ii. THE NATURE OF MONEY

Although Classical economics was founded to a very considerable extent on the real analysis of the *Wealth of Nations* and was opposed to the monetarist tenor of mercantilist writings, it could not of course dispense with monetary theory. The Classical economists were insistent that the quantity of money itself was of no significance (at least in the sense that the mercantilists had apparently thought it was) and that it did not affect the rate of interest except transitorily.[2] Adam Smith implied that there had been a confusion in the minds of previous economic writers between money and wealth, and was insistent that money was *not* wealth but merely a generally acceptable commodity, and that there was no need for concern over the quantity of money, as a sufficient stock was easily acquired through international trade. Hume was prepared to concede the 'sinews of war' argument[3] but Smith was not even ready to go so far, arguing that, if a country had commodities, gold and silver could always be obtained for the purposes of waging war.[4] Nevertheless, despite all this, Classical economics managed to advance a number of reasons why the quantity of money was of great significance. However, before passing on to this, we need to examine the *nature* of money as seen by the Classical economists.

The essentials of the analysis came from the *Wealth of Nations*. Money was a commodity which came to serve a special role in the transition from a barter to a monetary-exchange economy.[5] It had to act as a standard of value, medium of exchange, and store of value.[6] In these capacities it enabled specialization and division of labour to proceed, and it thus had a fundamental role to play in economic growth. Indeed Adam Smith habitually referred to money as 'the great wheel of circulation and distribution'.[7] The precious metals had special qualities which made them very suitable for use as money. The particular qualities on which Smith focused (following Harris as in much of his treatment) were divisibility and durability.[8] But in fact, as Cannan pointed out,[9] the qualities enumerated by Jevons in 1875—utility, portability, indestructibility, homogeneity, divisibility, and stability of value —are all to be found in the Classical and pre-Classical writers from Pufendorf and Locke onwards. Despite the fact that these characteristics were possessed by several metals, only one of them could act as a standard. This point had been recognized since Elizabethan times and depended upon the fact that a double standard encountered the difficulty that market values would fluctuate around Mint values and that payment would always be made in the less valuable currency. The more valuable would be hoarded, and thus withdrawn from circulation. Whatever precious metals were used had to be stamped. Although their purchasing power was dependent on the metallic content of a portion and not its face value, a stamp of fineness was necessary to facilitate payment.[10]

Use of the precious metals as money did however involve considerable costs. Metallic money had a cost of production, either directly or in obtaining it through international trade in exchange for commodities, and a running cost in the form of wear and tear.[11] Adam Smith likened these expenses to the cost of installing a machine and then paying its running costs and depreciation. Because of this Smith believed (although he was opposed both by Hume and by Joseph Harris, a one-time Master of the Mint, on the grounds of inflationary danger)[12] that the substitution of paper for metal as money was a great advantage to the country—at least as long as the paper was convertible.[13] Paper money as a substitute for gold saved both cost of production and maintenance.[14] The gold and silver freed from circulation could be sent abroad either to supply the consumption of a third country with commodities bought from a second (in which case the profit would be an addition to national income) or to supply home consumption of either luxuries or implements and raw materials of production.[15] Because of what Smith judged to be the overwhelming force of prudence in the aggregate, the first and the last courses, especially the last, would be followed.

The recognition of the role of paper money was often linked with an appreciation of the growing importance of banks. Their position as 'financial intermediaries' and as institutions which increased the velocity of circulation was appreciated from the time of Cantillon onwards.[16] Adam Smith, who was well informed on banking practice, proclaimed the benefits of the Scottish invention of the overdraft which enabled traders to economize on capital by providing them with their necessary reserves of cash.[17] Banking was, Smith proclaimed, like 'wagonways through the air' which allowed highways to be turned to pasture.[18]

Nevertheless Smith recognized that the growth of banking involved dangers: and agreed that regulation of it was a perfectly proper violation of natural liberty.[19] He also showed some appreciation of the importance of having a lender of last resort.[20]

But for all this it is relatively late in the Classical period that we find the power of banks to *create* deposits through adherence to a fractional-reserve system being first appreciated. It is now conventionally recognized that if deposits increase by an initial fraction $\Delta C$ the final increase in deposits $\Delta D$ will be $\Delta D = \dfrac{1}{\beta} \Delta C$ (neglecting the complications of increased private cash holdings ($a$) which would give us a result $\Delta D = \dfrac{1}{a + \beta} \Delta C$). But this was not recognized until a private memorandum by James Pennington of 1826 and not really fully articulated until Torrens's *Letter to Lord Melbourne* of 1837.

Nowadays even the narrowest definition of the money supply includes demand deposits. But with the exception of a relatively few (Banking School) writers late in the period, deposits were excluded from the category 'money' by Classical writers. J. S. Mill, it is true, had an extraordinarily wide concept of 'purchasing power' which included virtually every form of credit available. It is true also that James Pennington (not a Banking School member) saw deposits and notes as equivalent. Even Torrens (a prominent member of the Currency School as we shall see) agreed that deposits performed the functions of money; but he did not agree that they *were* money and confined the term 'circulating medium' to currency. There was in fact widespread agreement that deposits substituted for money but little agreement to treat them as money. Thus Thornton and many other writers tended to regard deposits as increasing velocity of circulation rather than as part of the money supply. He made no allowance either for cheques or bills of exchange when discussing the relationship between the circulating medium and the price level. Even Tooke (who with Fullarton held that deposits were effectively money) attacked J. Hume for treating even Bank of England deposits as being *exactly* on a par with currency.

This was not entirely a semantic problem. The desire to exclude deposits, as well as other non-currency forms of payment, especially bills of exchange, from the category of money, was based upon two related propositions. The first proposition was that only currency had the power of finally closing a transaction.[21] Secondly, and because of this, deposits were not an independent variable but were a part of the means of payment entirely dependent upon the currency base.

Having looked at the Classical concept of money we must now turn to the basic theory of the operation of money in the economic system.

### iii. THE BASIC THEORY

The mercantilist writers, in their concern with the quantity of money, had, sometimes unwittingly, and never consistently, laid the basis for the central analytical core of Classical monetary theory. This contained three interlinked parts; a quantity theory of money, the 'price-specie-flow' mechanism, and the theory of the international distribution of the precious metals. Viner[22] delineated the following elements as necessary to produce these parts. Firstly, recognition that the quantity of money is a determinant of the level of prices; secondly, recognition that the volume of exports and the volume of imports depends on the relative levels of prices at home and abroad; thirdly, recognition that net international balances of payments must be paid

in metal; fourthly, integration of the three preceding propositions into a
coherent theory of a self-regulating international distribution of monetary
metal; and fifthly, realization that this theory destroyed the basis for the
mercantilist concern about adequacy of the metal supply.

Despite some (uneasy) recognition by various mercantilist writers of the
first point, the clear formulation of the quantity theory really stems from
the work of three writers: David Hume (who published first in 1752),
Richard Cantillon, and Joseph Harris.[23] All of these writers recognized the
basic proposition that the money supply, multiplied by its velocity of circulation and divided by the number of payments which have to be made,
determines the price level. The theory is now conventionally represented
in terms of Irving Fisher's formulation $MV = PT$ or the so-called Cambridge equation $M = kPT$ (where $k$, the demand for cash balances, is the
reciprocal of velocity). If we exclude transactions which do not relate to
goods and services then we can write $Y$ for income in place of $T$, and $V$
then becomes income velocity instead of transactions velocity. In this way
the price level and the money supply are related to real output. All these
formulations appear, verbally, in the Classical literature. There were also
attempts at algebraic formulation. One of the earliest (though not the
earliest) of such formulations was that by Sir John Lubbock.[24]

$$\Sigma ax + E = A + mB + nC$$

where $\Sigma ax$ = the sum of transactions $a$ at prices $x$ during a given period.
      $E$ = the sum of transactions not involving prices (gifts, tax pay-
          ments, etc.).
      $B$ = the total amount of bills of exchange during the period.
     $mB$ = total use of these bills to settle transactions during this period.
      $A$ = total payments by cheque.
      $C$ = total amount of cash.
     $nC$ = total use of cash during the period ($m$ and $n$ are thus velocity
          co-efficients).

This is particularly interesting because of its breaking down of the com-
ponents of money and near money. But many of Lubbock's contemporaries
would not have accepted this on the grounds, as we shall see, that only $C$
was an independent variable.

Given a clearly formulated quantity theory, the price-specie-flow mechanism then followed from this. It was clearly formulated by Harris, writing
probably some time before Hume, but it is the latter's formulation which
has remained deservedly famous to this day.

Suppose four-fifths of all the money in Great Britain to be annihilated in one
night ... what would be the consequence? Must not the price of all labour and
commodities sink in proportion, and everything be sold as cheap as they were

in [past] ages? What nation could then dispute with us in any foreign market, or pretend to navigate or to sell manufactures at the same price, which to us would afford sufficient profit? In how little time, therefore, must this bring back the money which we had lost, and raise us to the level of all the neighbouring nations? Where, after we have arrived, we immediately lose the advantage of the cheapness of labour and commodities; and the farther flowing in of money is stopped by our fulness and repletion.

Again, suppose that all the money of Great Britain were multiplied five fold in a night, must not the contrary effect follow? Must not all labour and commodities rise to such an exorbitant height, that no neighbouring nations could afford to buy from us; while their commodities, on the other hand, became comparatively so cheap, that, in spite of all the laws which could be formed, they would be run in upon us, and our money flow out; till we fall to a level with foreigners, and lose that great superiority of riches, which had laid us under such disadvantages?

Now, it is evident, that the same causes which would correct these exorbitant inequalities, were they to happen miraculously, must prevent their happening in the common course of nature, and must forever, in all neighbouring nations, preserve money nearly proportionable to the art and industry of each nation. All water, wherever it communicates, remains always at a level. Ask naturalists the reason; they tell you, that, were it to be raised in any one place, the superior gravity of that part not being balanced, must depress it, till it meet a counterpoise; and that the same cause, which redresses the inequality when it happens, must forever prevent it, without some violent external operation.[25]

The price-specie-flow mechanism then produced two ideas. The first was that of a self-correcting balance-of-payments surplus or deficit. This was the property not only of Hume but also of Harris and of Cantillon. Secondly it was productive of the idea of an equilibrium distribution of the precious metals which was most clearly formulated by Ricardo although he was only following the ideas laid down by Hume, his contemporaries, and his successors.

Gold and silver having been chosen for the general medium of circulation, they are, by the competition of commerce, distributed in such proportions amongst the different countries of the world, as to accommodate themselves to the natural traffic which would take place if no such metals existed, and the trade between countries were purely a trade of barter.[26]

In other words the interaction of balance-of-payments surpluses or deficits and relative prices in different countries will ensure that payments come into balance so that trade can be conducted in equilibrium, without need for settlement in metal.

Ricardo was in many ways the most powerful exponent of the quantity theory and there is no doubt that his formulation provided a focus for the Currency School later in the nineteenth century. But it is necessary to point out that in the process of abstract model-building Ricardo frequently talked of the value of metallic money as determined by its cost of production. Such an approach would follow from his value theory (see Chapter 4). Now although Hume's theory was strictly a theory of *distribution* of the precious metals, rather than of their long-run value, so that there was no fundamental conflict between the two theories, the stress on cost of production tended to obscure two salient facts about the precious metals: firstly that most of current consumption was not the result of current production, and secondly, that they were not commodities the supply of which could be indefinitely increased under conditions of constant cost. Although Ricardo did recognize this at times, we are still able to find straightforward 'cost of production' statements in which the annual production of metal is identified with the total supply.[27] He was followed in this argument by Senior who rested the argument on the ground that the Mint price (as proxy for equilibrium) was equal to the cost of producing new gold either directly, or indirectly through trade. If the quantity in a particular country increased, production would cease until wear and tear had reduced that quantity back to a level at which production was again profitable.[28] But the importance of this proposition depends not only on the time period we are considering (as Senior seemed to think) but on the elasticity of supply. If the increase in the supply of metal resulting from a rise in the value of the metal is a very small part of the total of a highly durable good the equilibration of the value of gold with its cost of production ceases to have much operational significance, not only because equilibrium is unlikely to occur, but because the forces making for equilibrium are very weak. Indeed in a sense the marginal cost of production in the gold-producing countries, under such circumstances, will depend upon the world value of gold, not the other way around. But in the event of substantial discoveries this would not be (and indeed in the event was not) true.

For all the Classical writers the analysis was coupled with a fairly complete understanding and exposition of the operation of the exchanges and in particular of the gold points.[29] There seems no doubt that the Classical writers had a good understanding of the basic operation of a metallic standard. But at this point we come to a puzzle in the history of economic thought. For the strange thing is that although Adam Smith undoubtedly understood the quantity theory,[30] and although it is clear from his lectures that he understood the price-specie-flow mechanism,[31] he nevertheless confined himself in his great *magnum opus* to vague generalizations about the 'channels of circulation overflowing' if the money supply was too great, without any reference to the internal price level.[32] He asserted that the amount of a paper currency could never exceed the metal which would have been required in its absence; but he did not explain why not, except to argue that over-issue would involve strains on the cash reserves of banks. The banks would then be involved in disproportionate expense in maintaining their cash reserves and would then realize that their output of banking services had passed the profit-maximization point. Care in banking would

take account of this, as the Scottish banks had eventually learned. To this end
it was necessary that they should avoid bills of exchange which did not
originate in transactions for goods and services, and should also avoid advancing the whole of a trader's capital. Beside Hume's performance this
was a pretty weak one and indeed a puzzling one.

It is probably explained however by the fact that Hume had used the
price-specie-flow mechanism to explain that manufacturers, seeking to get
away from the effects of wage inflation and growth in any one country,
would move the seat of their operations to less developed countries, thus
diffusing the benefits of growth.[33] Smith however was anxious to establish
that growth required limitation on neither commodity *nor* factor mobility
for its continuation within one country. He had originally replied to Hume
that, although wages would be higher in a rich country, the labour cost per
unit of output would be lower because of specialization and therefore that
rich countries would keep their manufactures.[34] But he may have preferred
to evade the issue in the *Wealth of Nations* rather than enter into lengthy
public controversy with his friend.

The basic theory which we have sketched in this section is of fundamental
importance to the two great monetary controversies of the nineteenth century, the Bullion controversy and the Bank Charter controversy. It is to an
examination of these that we now turn.

iv. THE BULLION DEBATE

The writers dealt with in the previous section established, virtually for all
time, the basic theory of a metallic currency, and went a long way towards
providing that of a convertible paper currency. We now turn to developments
in monetary theory which emerged in the course of the debates which took
place during the period of the Bank of England's suspension of the convertibility of its paper currency in the years 1797 to 1819. These debates essentially produced the next stage in the development of monetary theory by
providing the essentials of a theory of an inconvertible paper currency. The
participants in this debate have been divided by commentators into two
camps, the Bullionists and the anti-Bullionists. This is only partially satisfactory both on theoretical and policy grounds, but we shall continue to use
the terminology here, with some modifications.

The essential characteristics of the Bullionist position were that these
writers, with some reservations, accepted the rise in the price of gold bullion
above its Mint price, together with depreciation of the exchange, as a sign
that paper had been over-issued. The first test is easy enough to grasp:
essentially what was involved was the idea that the over-issue of paper had
reduced its value in relation to commodities so that a unit of it commanded
fewer commodities than an equivalent quantity of gold, if the test of equiva-
lence was the Mint price of gold. The second test is slightly more difficult

for the twentieth-century mind to grasp because it involves an expression of the rate of exchange which is not directly in terms of particular currencies in a well-ordered and sophisticated market, but in terms of the relative premium or discount on bills of exchange drawn on different financial centres. Thus if a merchant in London wished to make payment in Paris he would buy bills of exchange drawn on Paris in London: and if the merchant had to pay, say, 5 per cent more for the bills than the price arrived at in terms of the par of exchange (e.g. £1 containing the same gold as 25 francs) then the exchange was said to be 5 per cent against London. If the exchange continued against London for a long period then, the Bullionists argued, this was a sure sign that the paper pound had been over-issued and was no longer worth an amount of gold equal to 25 francs.

This is a bald summary of the position. In the limited space available however it is possible to give some indication of the diversity beneath. The Bullionists really divided into two classes. There were, on the one hand, the rigid Bullionists; Boyd, Wheatley, Lord King, and Ricardo. These, following the Cantillion–Harris–Hume theory of the distribution of the precious metals, saw the high price of bullion and the depressed exchange as clear symptoms of a high domestic price level in terms of paper currency.

Their position is best summed up in the Ricardian definition of excess, a most powerful tool in monetary controversy both at this time and subsequently. This definition was that an amount of currency in existence at a time when the exchange was depreciated and the price of bullion in the market was above its Mint price (or when, under a regime of convertibility, the Bank of England was losing gold) was by definition an excessive amount. If these symptoms were apparent *then* the domestic price level must be too high in relation to the price levels of other countries, resulting in balance of payments deficit and an adverse exchange. It was a definition arrived at by rigid application of the price-specie-flow doctrine and the quantity theory of money and by ignoring all other possible causes of such symptoms. There followed from it two conclusions of extreme importance in the monetary debates of the nineteenth century. The first was that if the symptoms of excess appeared then, by definition, the currency was in excess, and *must* be contracted. Secondly it implied for the rigid Bullionists that there was, for particular economic circumstances, a single unique correct supply of currency.

For these writers, and especially for Ricardo, the high price of bullion provided a unique way round the 'social science problem' that whatever the level of prices might be in any year under one regime (inconvertibility) we had no way of knowing what they would have been under another regime (convertibility) in that same year. For these writers the price of bullion provided a measure of the differences between the existing price level and that which would have prevailed under convertibility. On this basis

Ricardo felt able to dismiss the idea of using index numbers as measures of inflation.

The rigid Bullionists were however still faced with the problem of meeting the objections that the depressed exchange might be explained by an adverse balance of payments brought on by harvest failure or by payments to foreign governments. Both Wheatley and Ricardo offered explanations for this, and both these explanations involved the application to the short run of long-run adjustments, implying the power of an adverse exchange automatically, and more or less instantaneously, to correct itself. Ricardo simply assumed that a depreciated exchange, by making British exports cheaper, would automatically correct itself. Wheatley more ingeniously offered the argument that income adjustment would ensure payments balance.[35] If the home harvest failed then this would *pari passu* reduce our power to demand imports.

The moderate Bullionist group comprised Malthus, Blake, and the authors of the famous Bullion Report. These were Francis Horner, William Huskisson, and, above all, Henry Thornton.

The essential characteristics of these writers were twofold. On the one hand, while they accepted the high price of bullion and the depressed exchange as providing, *in the long run*, the best working test of over-issue,[36] they advanced a far more subtle and complex analysis of the relationship between the total stock of currency, the price level, the income level, the volume of transactions, the velocity of circulation, and the exchange rate. On the other, they were able to conclude from this analysis that there was *not* a uniquely correct stock of currency at any time because there were many other variables and these could not be held constant.

In the interests of brevity we shall concentrate largely on Thornton. Firstly, he saw velocity of circulation as variable with the state of confidence.[37] When the level of economic activity rose liquidity preference fell. When, however, the economy approached an economic crisis then liquidity preference rose. Secondly, he argued that the amount of paper currency which was appropriate was greater than the corresponding amount of metal because the velocity of circulation of coin was greater than that of notes.[38] Because of these two factors the note issue should try to accommodate itself to changes in velocity as well as to the price of bullion and the state of the exchanges.

To limit the total amount of paper issued, and to resort for this purpose, whenever the temptation to borrow is strong, to some effectual principle of restriction; in no case, however, materially to diminish the sum in circulation, but to let it vibrate only within certain limits; to afford a slow and cautious extension of it, as the general trade of the Kingdom enlarges itself; to allow of some special, though temporary, increase in the event of any extraordinary alarm or difficulty, as the best means of preventing a great demand at home for guineas; and to lean to the side of diminution, in the case of gold going abroad, and of the general exchanges continuing long unfavourable; this seems to be the true policy of the directors of an institution circumstanced like that of the Bank of England.[39]

Not only did variations in velocity of circulation affect the price level but there was also the role of bills of exchange to which Thornton devoted quite a lot of attention[40] despite the fact that he neglected the importance of Bank deposits.

Thornton was quite clear that the symptoms of a high price of bullion and a depressed exchange could certainly arise from over-issue of paper currency. But they could also very well arise in his view from other causes. In particular there was the possibility of an extraordinary home demand for metal—'an internal drain'—and the possibility of an unfavourable balance of payments which was not caused by over-issue. Notably there were remittances to foreign governments fighting on our behalf, and the effects of two successive bad harvests.[41]

Because of these considerations, immediate and unremitting reductions in the note issue when faced with inflationary symptoms were not the best or even a good course.[42] As there was no uniquely correct currency supply in his analysis, and in particular because liquidity preference rose in time of crisis, contraction could produce catastrophic economic collapse.[43] Moreover although Thornton accepted Hume's basic analysis, he also stressed income adjustments to balance-of-payments deficits. He saw price adjustments as limited by inelastic demand for imports (which we now know of course not to be a sufficient condition for exchange instability on its own) and difficulties of contraction. He therefore argued that imports and exports came into balance through each individual adjusting his expenditure to his income.

The income of individuals is the general limit [to importation] in all cases. If, therefore, through any unfortunate circumstance, if through war, scarcity or any other extensive calamity, the value of the annual income of the inhabitants of a country is diminished, either new economy on the one hand, or new exertions of individual industry on the other, fail not, after a certain time, in some measure, to restore the balance. And this equality between private expenditures and private incomes tends ultimately to produce equality between the commercial exports and imports.[44]

The contrast between the subtlety of Thornton's position on the one hand, and that of Ricardo on the other is evident. While Ricardo argued that what he regarded as the symptoms of inflation automatically required contraction of the note issue, Thornton was prepared to argue that, especially in the face of an internal drain, the note issue should be expanded. He was also prepared to argue that gold lost abroad as a consequence of an unfavourable balance of payments could be expected to return without a need for contraction.[45]

Another moderate Bullionist William Blake clarified the role of the exchanges as a test of depreciation.[46] Blake distinguished between what he

called the Real and the Nominal exchange. The real exchange was determined by the supply of and demand for foreign bills. It thus reflected the
state of the balance of payments. The nominal exchange however reflected
the relative worth of different currencies. Thus if over issue had depreciated
English paper by 5 per cent then the exchange would stand 5 per cent against
England automatically, to compensate for the reduced value of English
currency in relation to foreign currency. The point of the distinction is this.
In the long run the real exchange is self-correcting. Only the nominal exchange can remain permanently depressed. Therefore if the computed
exchange (the actual rate) remains depressed over a long period it is virtually
certain that there has been paper inflation.[47]

All this was very important. The Bullionists, especially the moderate Bullionists, had provided an analysis of the main elements of the operation of
an inconvertible paper currency, including the role of liquidity preference,
which laid the foundations for modern monetary theory.

By contrast the anti-Bullionists, who accepted very little of the basic
analysis of the Bullionists, contributed relatively little. They attributed a
depressed exchange to foreign remittances and the generally admitted rise
of prices to real rather than monetary factors. But their main reliance was
placed upon the celebrated Real Bills doctrine. This stated that so long as
notes were issued in payment for bills of exchange which related to real
transactions in goods and services they could not be over-issued. This was
on the grounds that holding notes involved an interest charge (deducted by
the Bank when paying the bill, or charged for a loan) and that no one would
hold notes for which he had no immediate need. The idea in fact stemmed
from Adam Smith where we find it stated clearly.[48] In its most extreme form
the Real Bills doctrine implied a complete reversal of the normally accepted
connection between the quantity of circulating medium and the price level.[49]

But there were obvious difficulties in applying it in the form supplied by
Smith to the post-1797 situation. In the first place what was under consideration was an inconvertible currency, whereas Smith's discussion related
quite explicitly to a convertible currency. In the second place a lot of the
extra notes were not issued against real bills at all (if indeed the Bank of
England could distinguish such 'real' bills from others, which some of the
Bullionists certainly doubted) but as a result of extending credit to government.

But these points aside, there were fundamental flaws in the theoretical
position of the Real Bills doctrine which the Bullionists, especially Thornton, pointed out. Basically the point was this: real transactions had to take
place at some *absolute* price level, and this price level depended on the
money supply. If extra notes were issued then the price level would rise and
they would then be required to support the same number of transactions as
before. Moreover, it was not only money which had a velocity of circula-

tion; the same goods changed hands many times and could give rise to many bills.

Secondly, in so far as there was unemployment the extra money supply might give rise to extra income: the anti-Bullionists saw this, especially Torrens (who argued that economies of scale would offset the inflationary effect of increasing the money supply). But they did not see that imports were a function of income so that a rise in income would depress the exchange. Thirdly, the payment of interest on loans did not of itself prevent people borrowing if the rate of interest paid was less than the going rate of profit. In this connection Thornton essentially developed the Wicksellian distinction between the real and the nominal rate of interest. The rate of interest was actually limited by the Usury Laws to a maximum of 5 per cent and, as Thornton pointed out, there was unlikely to be a sufficient rise in income from increasing the money supply to exhaust investment opportunities so far as to lower the going rate of profit to 5 per cent.

In addition, there were, given the existence of inflation, six different rates of interest to take account off: the going rate of profit (Wicksell's real rate), Bank Rate and the market rate, and deflated versions of each of these. Quite apart then from any genuine profit arising from a discrepancy between e.g. the (deflated) money and the (deflated) real rates of interest, there were money profits to be made as prices rose and the true cost of borrowing was less than the nominal cost. Thornton saw this also.

But if the Bullionists offered acute analysis here, there were other points on which they proceeded less far. In particular both Thornton[50] and Ricardo blamed the Bank of England for all the over-issue. The argument was that the relative price level in the country would, if the country banks over-issued, rise *vis-à-vis* the London price level. This would result in a return to the country banks of their notes and a demand on them either for Bank of England notes or for bills on London, to purchase cheaper London goods. Both of these effects would run down their reserves which they kept in the form of either Bank of England notes or in balances with the London bankers. This in turn would force them to contract their note issue. Only Wheatley really saw clearly on this issue. He knew that by means of varying their reserve ratios the country banks could increase the notes issue significantly. He also saw that, through the agency of London houses, they were able to replenish their stock of notes at the Bank of England's expense in time of pressure by discounting country bills at the Bank of England. If the latter adhered to the Real Bills doctrine, as it seems often to have done, they would then produce an expansion of the Bank of England note issue.

In addition to this criticism it must be noted that some of the Bullionists, especially Ricardo, failed to recognize the vital role of the Bank of England as lender of last resort[51]—although this criticism cannot be levelled at Thornton.

Finally, all the Bullionists, intent on developing the theory of money under a regime of inconvertible paper, assumed that, given convertibility, its action in preventing over-issue was sufficient to ensure the safeguard (wartime conditions excepted) of its own continuance without the Bank of England ever being brought to a state of exhaustion of its gold reserves. On this they were wrong; and it was the development of theory to fill this gap which was the subject of the Bank Charter controversy to which we now turn.

## V. MONETARY CONTROL: THE BANK CHARTER DEBATE

The participants in the Bullion debate had been concerned with the problems of an inconvertible currency. It does not seem to have occurred to either the opponents or proponents of the return to convertibility that such a system, once established, could break down of its own accord. Convertibility, in other words, was its own safeguard. If a currency was convertible, then over-issued notes, which raised the price level, would be returned to the issuer in exchange for gold, in order to make purchases in countries where the price level had not risen. This loss of gold abroad would in turn lower the home price level back to an equilibrium one.

Although convertibility was soon accepted by all but a very few as a desirable state of affairs, following its resumption in 1819–21, it soon became clear that its own continuance under a system of currency only fractionally backed by gold was by no means a foregone conclusion. A series of monetary crises in the 1820s and 1830s focused attention on the possibility of the need for some monetary policy which would ensure the continuance of convertibility. To five authors belongs the credit of establishing the basic principle of 'metallic fluctuation' as the requisite for the maintenance of convertibility. These five were Thomas Joplin, Henry Drummond, Richard Page, James Pennington, and J. R. McCulloch.[52] Their proposition was that a convertible currency should fluctuate in amount as an identically circumstanced metallic currency would fluctuate. What they had in mind was clear enough. Convertibility of the note issue had been endangered because of the delay in contracting the volume of that note issue as gold was withdrawn from the Bank of England. If the note issue was reduced *pari passu* with the outflow of gold (rather than behind it), then a steady readjustment of the price level to equilibrium would follow. The theory (which implicitly assumed that the velocity of circulation of paper and of metal was the same) was then in accordance with the theory of the distribution of the precious metals and of relative international price levels advanced by Hume and his successors: and its policy recommendation was a straightforward deduction from the Ricardian definition of excess (although Ricardo himself had believed that convertibility was its own safeguard).

This approach quickly gained adherents within the Bank of England which, from about 1827 onwards, began to follow what became known as the 'Palmer Rule' after Horsley Palmer who was governor of the Bank in the years 1830–3, and who explained this rule before the Bank Charter hearings of 1832. The Bank, under this rule, aimed at having a bullion reserve equal to one-third of its total liabilities of notes and deposits when the exchanges were 'full', i.e. just on the point of becoming unfavourable. From this point on the securities were supposed to be kept fixed in amount while notes and deposits were varied as the bullion varied. It thus allowed a drain of gold to fall on deposits leaving the note circulation uncontracted. It was essentially defective unless deposits were *as important as* notes in their effect on prices because otherwise the Bank might be drained of gold while the exchanges (in disequilibrium because of disequilibrium relative international price levels) remained uncorrected. Unless deposits and securities were *both* kept even so that fluctuations in the bullion were reflected in fluctuations in the note issue the rule was not sufficient to protect convertibility; in addition constancy of both securities and deposits was virtually impossible for the central Bank, and attempts to contract the note circulation through open-market operations when the drain fell on deposits would, in any case, necessarily result in variations in the amount of securities. This last also applied to rationing of discounts.

All this applied to the rule on its own terms. But in addition to this the Bank found that, partly because of a series of special circumstances, it was unable to operate the rule anyway. The Bank's failure both to operate the rule and to avoid serious monetary crises in which convertibility was endangered led to the development of a critique of its policy by Robert Torrens, Lord Overstone (S. J. Loyd), and G. W. Norman (a Director of the Bank), who became grouped together as the leading members of the Currency School. Their programme, which was embodied in the Bank Charter Act of 1844, involved separating the Bank of England into two departments, of Issue and Banking respectively. A drain of gold could then no longer fall on deposits alone, because as deposits in the Banking Department were paid in notes not gold those same notes had to be presented at the Issue Department in order to obtain gold. The note circulation was thus reduced *pari passu* with the gold, with the aim of achieving 'metallic fluctuation'. Their proposals had two main aims. Firstly there was the maintenance of convertibility. This was necessary both on quasi-moral grounds (commutative justice) and also on the grounds that endangering convertibility disturbed the relationship between debtor and creditor, thus harming confidence and interfering with economic activity and growth. Their second main aim (and this is worth stressing, since it was sometimes alleged against them that they sacrificed everything to convertibility) was stabilization of the level of activity. They, and in particular Overstone, advanced a theory of an endogenous trade cycle. Monetary policy could then either act counter-cyclically, expanding the money supply as the level of activity fell and reducing it when activity increased so as to minimize fluctuations in activity; or it could act passively and adapt the money supply directly to changes in the level of activity. The Currency School insisted that the first course was following Currency principles; and that the second course was following Banking principles. Their proposal involved stablization because they believed that fluctuations in the level of activity in the 1820s and 1830s stemmed largely from sudden changes in the money supply which in turn resulted from the Bank of England delaying contraction of the note issue in the face of a drain until the last moment, and then being forced to take violent action. As Overstone put it:

There is an old Eastern proverb which says, you may stop with a bodkin a fountain, which if suffered to flow will sweep away whole cities in its course. An early and timely contraction, upon the very first indication of excess in the circulation, is the application of the bodkin to the fountain; commercial convulsion and ruin in consequence of delay, is the stream sweeping away whole cities in its course.[53]

In order to achieve such early contraction it was necessary that discretion should be removed from the Bank of England and an automatic system substituted. This is what the separation of departments was to achieve. There was to be no distinction between different kinds of drains. Conceptually there were three kinds: those originating in balance-of-payments deficit brought about by disequilibrium in relative international price levels; those brought about by balance-of-payments deficit originating in extraordinary causes such as harvest failure; and those classified as 'internal drains' which resulted from an increase in the desire to hold gold by the inhabitants of the country. Strictly speaking only the first of these required contraction, in the logic of the theory. But the Currency School took the view, firstly, that no single cause underlay a particular drain; secondly, that there were insufficient data to disentangle the causes of a drain; thirdly, that even if a drain originated in one cause others soon became intermingled; and fourthly, (perhaps the overriding reason) that allowing the Bank discretion was a recipe for late contraction and this *must* be avoided.

Control of the note issue was then all important. But the Bank of England was not the sole issuer. Now we have already seen that most of the writers in the Bullion Controversy believed the issues of the country banks to be under the control of the Bank of England; and at first Torrens adopted the same position during the Currency and Banking controversies. But Overstone was quick to point out that the theory of control through relative price levels in London and the country was defective in two important respects. Firstly, 'London' and 'the country' were not separate areas in which Bank of England and country bank-notes circulated independently. Secondly, whatever control was exercised through relative price levels in London and the country only operated after a lag—a lag sufficient to bring about a severe drain upon the Bank of England's gold reserves. It was then necessary that direct limitation of the issues of the country banks should become part of the Currency School's proposals; and accordingly, provision for this was incorporated in the Act of 1844.

Quite apart from this issue there was the further difficulty that any reasonable definition of the money supply includes deposits. The Currency School recognized their importance but insisted that they were not an independent variable but part of an inverted credit pyramid resting on a base of currency. This view implied a fixity of reserve ratios on the part of banks which did not in fact exist, although only Torrens seems to have recognized the need for such fixity explicitly. But even if the existence of such a ratio is conceded, there remains the problem that an outflow of gold resulting in a contraction of the currency supply will produce a *multiple* reduction in the total money supply through its effect on deposits. The final effect will depend not only upon reserve ratios but also upon the relative velocity of circulation of currency and deposits. Thus suppose a unit of currency is withdrawn. This will reduce the money stock by a multiple dependent on the reserve ratio. But the effect on the price level (in quantity-theory terms) will depend not only on this ratio but also on the relative velocity of currency and deposits. Thus if we take a reserve ratio of 10 per cent so that the ratio of currency to deposits is $1:10$ then, if the relative velocities of currency and deposits are the reciprocal of this ratio, viz. $10:1$, the effect of withdrawing the unit of currency will be twice its direct effect. The closer the velocity of deposits approaches that of currency the greater will be this factor.

Apart from the problem of deposits there is also that of bills of exchange. Again the Currency School conceived of these as being in the upper part of an inverted credit pyramid resting upon a currency base. But the actual method of control remained far from clear, particularly as figures collected by Newmarch indicated that the *number* of bills of exchange increased when the currency was contracted.[54]

Because of this difficulty, the Currency School (most especially Overstone) came to place more and more reliance upon what may be called the 'information-velocity of circulation' mechanism. To a considerable extent because of Overstone's insistence, the Act of 1844 required that the Bank should publish weekly returns of the state of its reserves. Overstone argued that the publication of these reserves had the effect of adjusting velocity of circulation through its effect on confidence and the precautionary motive for liquidity. This not only took care of the problem that notes in the hands of the public increased during times of pressure (which was strictly speaking, in any case, not a problem from the point of view of the Currency School because once notes were outside the Issue Department it did not matter whether they were in the hands of the public or in the Banking Department) but also had the important effect of reducing the 'effectiveness' (i.e. velocity) of deposits and near money such as bills of exchange.

But even supposing that all these difficulties were overcome there was still the problem of the actual mechanism of contraction and the lowering of the price level following a reduction in either the total money supply or its velocity. That this simply occurred was assumed from Hume onwards but the problem is still unsolved today.[55] In hearings before Committees Overstone did advance a number of different views of the way in which this contraction operated; yet none was wholly satisfactory.[56] But partly because of a certain lack of clarity on this score he came increasingly, together with other members of the School, to place reliance upon the rate of interest as generating short-term capital flows which corrected the exchange before price movements could have been completed.

There was also the problem of crises. These arose basically because both the Currency School and the Act refused to recognize the last-resort role of the Bank (though Norman did so reluctantly). Their refusal (or reluctance) to recognize it was consistent with a reliance upon the information—velocity mechanism, because if the Bank could always be relied upon as lender of last resort the precautionary motive would act much less strongly to reduce velocity. For the same reason they for long declined to recognize the necessity of a 'relaxing power' in the Act to deal with liquidity panics. Again the desire to avoid implanting in commercial minds the impression that the Bank could, in the end, be relied upon to offer last-resort facilities without limit was based upon the need to encourage operation of the precautionary motive. But their opposition led *inter alia* to the view, held immediately after the passing of the Act of 1844, that with the separation of departments the Banking Department could conduct its business like any other bank and compete with the rest of the market for discount business—which it did, and in doing so ran its reserves dangerously low. The Bank did not in any case carry large enough reserves in the Banking Department; because it was after all a private profit-making undertaking with duties to its shareholders. It is not then perhaps surprising that there *were* crises. The Act was suspended in 1847 and 1857 and again (though less seriously) in 1866. On at least the first two occasions there is no doubt that awareness of the limitations in the Act on the Bank's power to act as lender of last resort was crucial in engendering a liquidity panic.

A final problem of which the Currency School did not take sufficient notice was that of the money supply in a growing economy. Of course it is perfectly true that the price-specie-flow mechanism could be relied upon to produce additions to the money supply as productivity rose faster in one country than in another; but this meant that the money supply was rather inelastic and implies, in terms of conventional Keynesian apparatus, a rising rate of interest with increased demands for balances at higher levels of real income.

Of all these problems the Currency School's opponents, the Banking School, were able to make much. The members of this School, which crystallized around 1840, were Thomas Tooke, John Fullarton, James Wilson, and J. W. Gilbart. Their position contained the following propositions. Firstly, that over-issue of a convertible currency was impossible. This result they arrived at by applying the Real Bills Doctrine, which was discussed in the previous section, to the context of a convertible currency. Obviously they were at fault here because *temporary* over-issue, sufficient to produce an adverse exchange, and loss of gold, and to impose upon the Bank the need for severe contraction, is entirely compatible with the confining of discount to bills originating in transactions for real goods and services. Many of the arguments concerning the Real Bills doctrine (which in this period went under the name of the Doctrine of Reflux because of its stress on the return to the banks of notes issued in discounts as the bills of exchange matured) are applicable here and there is no need to repeat them. The important point to grasp is that the Banking School was simply resurrecting the old doctrine in a new context and failing to take account of the damage that short-run over-issue could produce. Linked with this was a tendency to disregard the Thornton analysis of the real and money rate of interest and to stress the importance of entrepreneurial expectations in determining the level of investment.

Their second proposition broke the link, vital in the Hume formulation, between the price level and metal flows, by arguing that the metal flows came from hoards of metal kept in central banks. To this the Currency School were able to argue that although, because of this institutional factor, a flow of metal did not automatically affect the price level, it had to be *made* to affect the price level or the flow would go on until the Bank's stock of metal was exhausted. The Banking School however argued that drains of metal originated from non-recurring causes affecting the balance of payments and they could thus be expected to come to an end automatically—or as they put it, drains were 'terminable'. This amounted to denying that the state of the exchanges and the balance of payments depended upon the price level.

The Banking School position was completed by arguing not only that the balance of payments did not depend upon the price level, but also that the price level did not depend upon the money supply. In this connection they reversed the normal quantity-theory causality. Their argument was that the supply of money depended upon the total of money incomes to which the Banking system responded passively. But of course the total of money incomes is the total of factor service prices. All that they were doing was to explain prices by prices.

In the light of their analysis they suggested that the Bank of England should hold a large reserve of £15–18 million in gold and that it should not start to contract the currency until that reserve had fallen to £10 or £12 million. This would take account of drains arising from non-recurring causes and would allow time for the correction of the exchanges by short-term capital flows generated by the rate of interest. This was in itself quite a sensible suggestion despite the fact, that as Overstone pointed out, exchange correction through interest rates could only be a palliative in the last resort, if relative international price levels were out of line.

There is no doubt that the Currency School had the better of the argument on a theoretical plane. Nevertheless the Banking School were correct to stress the difficulties of contraction and the vulnerability of the Banking Department as well as the importance of deposits and (after a while) the last-resort role of the Bank. Moreover they had the satisfaction that their warnings about the operation of the Act were borne out by events. The Banking reserve did prove too small, it had to be protected by frequent variations in Bank Rate (which they regarded as disruptive), and the Act had to be suspended in crises. But in the last resort their position was theoretically indefensible: and experience had demonstrated that convertibility was *not* its own safeguard—although their Reflux doctrine amounted to saying that it was. It simply was not possible to proceed as if relative international price levels were independent of the money supply. Their position was, it is true, in many ways more subtle than that of their opponents; but it was not thought through. It may be open to question whether fluctuations in the level of activity would have been greater or less if their system, rather than that of the Currency School, had been adopted; but there does seem relatively little doubt that convertibility would have been endangered under their proposals. Yet convertibility was a commonly agreed objective for both Schools; and the Currency School was able to point to the fact that after 1844 it was never in doubt.

## vi. A FUNDAMENTAL FLAW?

Having thus far discussed Classical monetary theory and seen the importance attached by Classical monetary theorists to changes in the quantity of money we now have to recognize that a serious charge has been levelled at such theory by several modern writers most especially Lange and Patinkin. (The accusation also covers neo-Classical writing but we are not concerned with the latter here.)

A feature of Classical economics was the widespread acceptance of what has become known as Say's Law. Although this originates in Book I, Ch. xv, of J. B. Say's *Treatise*,[57] the argument is perhaps put most strikingly by James Mill who has, in any case, a possible claim to have formulated this Law independently.

Demand and supply are terms related in a peculiar manner. A commodity which is supplied, is always, at the same time, a commodity which is the instrument of demand. A commodity which is the instrument of demand, is always, at the same time, a commodity added to the stock of supply. Every commodity is always, at one and the same time, matter of demand, and matter of supply. Of two men who perform an exchange, the one does not come with only a supply, the other with only a demand; each of them comes with both a demand and a supply. The supply, which he brings, is the instrument of his demand; and his demand and supply are of course exactly equal to one another.

But if the demand and supply of every individual are always equal to one another, the demand and supply of all the individuals in the nation, taken aggregately, must be equal. Whatever, therefore, be the amount of the annual produce, it can never exceed the amount of the annual demand. The whole of the annual produce is divided into a number of shares, equal to that of the people to whom it is distributed. The whole of the demand is equal to as much of the whole of the shares as the owners do not keep for their own consumption. But the whole of the shares is equal to the whole of the produce. The demonstration, therefore, is complete.[58]

Now what Mill and Say were stressing was the circularity of the economic system. Indeed the discovery of this circularity, although rooted in eighteenth-century French economics, involved a major analytical insight. Moreover, in so far as the proposition related to the impossibility of a failure of aggregate demand, it was a proposition directed against writers such as Malthus who were arguing that economic growth brought about a capital stock adjustment problem. (This will be dealt with in Chapter 8.) However, as interpreted by some modern monetary theorists, this statement is taken to imply firstly that people do not hold cash balances which yield them no utility; secondly, and following from this, that the absolute price level is indeterminate; and, thirdly, that money is 'neutral'—i.e. that it does not influence the level of activity.[59]

The argument is this. According to Mill's formulation the supply of goods to the market is a demand schedule for money. Similarly, the demand schedule for goods from the market is a supply schedule of money. But this money is not demanded to hold in balances but merely in order to purchase other commodities. At a supply-and-demand equilibrium there is zero net demand for money. The demand for money on the market is identically zero at any equilibrium set of *relative* prices, regardless of the *absolute* price level. This is said to make the price level indeterminate, and Classical economics is then supposed to have determined the price level by adding the quantity theory in which the demand for balances determines velocity of circulation and hence the absolute price level produced by a given money supply. So on the one hand, demand for commodities depends only on relative prices because money itself, in balance form, yields no utility; on the other, when it came to the determination of the absolute price level, the classicists are supposed suddenly to have recognized that money balances did yield utility—which in turn implies that the demand for commodities did not depend solely on relative prices.

The indeterminacy of the absolute price level is formally explained by the proposition that we have fewer independent equations than unknowns (although, mathematically, equality of equations and unknowns is neither necessary nor sufficient for equilibrium). Now $n$ goods involve $n$ demand-and-supply functions. It is a property of any set of simultaneous equations of this kind that only $n-1$ of them is independent. If one of the commodities is money we have $n-2$ demand and supply equations for commodities and one for money. We have $n-2$ commodity prices and a price of money (the absolute price level). So we have $n-1$ unknowns. But the excess demand for money is identically zero at any set of relative prices. The money equation is then not independent. So we have only $n-2$ independent equations and $n-1$ unknowns.

Now it is easy enough to establish that the Classical writers, in their discussion of the nature of money, did in fact recognize the utility of holding cash balances.[60] This should hardly surprise us since the monetary literature is replete with references to changes in velocity of circulation, as we have already seen. It may be true that for some neo-Classical writers velocity of circulation was determined by institutional considerations; but this defence cannot be applied to the Classical writers.

There are two ways out of this difficulty. One is to extend the demand-and-supply analysis in order to make demand for commodities depend upon real cash balances as well as on relative prices. Strictly this is not necessary because, as other modern theorists have shown, if we are only interested in comparing successive positions of long-run equilibrium, we can dispense with this real-balance effect.[61] But it is not desirable to do so because this real-balance effect is one which ensures stability of the price level. If prices rise the real value of balances held by individuals falls. In order to reconstitute them individuals will reduce their demand for commodities. This will cause prices to fall again and they will only stop falling at the point where the real value of the balances has been restored.

But if this criticism is to have any substance in relation to Classical economics it must be that it shows Classical economics to have treated money as neutral. Now it is quite clear, and indeed it should be from the preceding sections of this chapter, that Classical economics certainly did not regard money as neutral. The most striking case here is that of J. S. Mill since he wrote on both monetary and value theory whereas many of the writers we have considered earlier in this chapter wrote little or nothing on value theory and were largely or even exclusively monetary theorists. In Mill's *Essays on Some Unsettled Questions of Political Economy*, he distinguished clearly between, on the one hand, the literal interpretation of Say's Law, which could only be true in an economy where money was purely used for accounting purposes (what some commentators have called Say's Identity) and the proposition, applied as an equilibrium proposition only, in a monetary economy—now referred to as Say's Equality. Mill is certainly the clearest writer here. But he was not adopting a novel position. McCulloch expressed himself extremely distinctly upon the matter.[62]

All the same it has to be conceded, that by *modern* standards, the Classical economists were not sufficiently careful in distinguishing the Identity from the equilibrium proposition. Nevertheless it must be stressed that the real-balance effect, especially in the restricted form in which it is advanced by the critics of the Classicists, was by no means the only, or even the most important, aspect of the non-neutrality of money. We have seen in the previous section the importance of sharp shifts in the demand for cash balances brought about, not by changes in the price level, but by changes in expectations of the availability of lending facilities at the central bank. This aspect of the non-neutrality of money was of much greater importance in Classical monetary theory. In the final section of this chapter, we shall turn to another aspect of the non-neutrality of money to which the Classical writers paid considerable attention; and ironically enough we will find that, as a subsidiary part, it contains a real-balance effect.

## vii. INFLATION

An analysis of the effects of a change in the money stock on the level of income is to be found both within the Classical fold and outside it. Very few Classical writers indeed were prepared to argue that changes in the stock did not affect the level of activity, although there were several versions of the way in which money achieved its effects. The analysis had its roots in such pre-Classical writers as Potter and Law, and also in Cantillon's analysis of the different effects of changes in the money supply depending upon which sector of economic activity the new money entered (although it is true that Cantillon concentrated very largely on price changes and although his *Essai* was not published until three years after Hume's *Essays*).

The latter is undoubtedly the main source for the Classical analysis. The following quotations are from Hume's Essay 'Of Money'.

though the high price of commodities be a necessary consequence of the encrease of gold and silver yet ... some time is required before the money circulates through the whole state ... it is only in this interval ... that the encreasing quantity of gold and silver is favourable to industry. When any quantity of money is imported into a nation, it is not at first dispersed into many hands, but is confined to the coffers of a few persons, who immediately seek to employ it to advantage ... they are thereby enabled to employ more workmen than formerly, who never dream of demanding higher wages, but are glad of employment from such good paymasters. If workmen become scarce, the manufacturer gives higher wages, but at first requires an encrease of labour; and this is willingly submitted to by the artisan, who can now eat and drink better, to compensate his additional toil and fatigue. He carries his money to market, where he finds every thing at the same price as formerly, but returns with greater quantity and of better kinds, for the use of his family. The farmer and gardener, finding, that all their commodities are taken off, apply themselves with alacrity to the raising of more; and at the same time can afford to take better and more cloths from their tradesmen, whose price is the same as formerly, and their industry only whetted by so much new gain. It is easy to trace the money in its progress through the whole commonwealth; where we shall find, that it must first quicken the diligence of every individual, before it encreases the price of labour.

Accordingly we find, that, in every kingdom, into which money begins to flow in greater abundance than formerly, everythng takes a new face: labour and industry gain life; the merchant becomes more enterprising, the manufacturer more diligent and skilful, and even the farmer follows his plough with greater alacrity and attention.

A nation, whose money decreases, is actually, at that time, weaker and more miserable than another nation, which possesses no more money, but is on the encreasing hand ... the workman has not the same employment from the manufacturer and merchant; though he pays the same price for everything in the market. The farmer cannot dispose of his corn and cattle; though he must pay the same rent to his landlord. The poverty, and beggary, and sloth, which must ensue, are easily foreseen.[63]

Several points about this are noteworthy. Firstly, the effect works through cash balances. Secondly, the emphasis is on changes in output, not in prices. The price adjustment follows after a lag. Thirdly, there is apparently an assumption of unemployed resources. Fourthly, the effect is only transitional and does not continue once prices have adjusted to the new money supply. Finally, it should be noted that some emphasis is given to the role of incentives.

This analysis was inherited by the main Classical writers. They took from Hume not only the analysis of inflation but also a view that deflation had the reverse effect. However in their version the emphasis is placed upon 'forced saving'—the redistribution of income from fixed-income receivers to the capitalist entrepreneurs. Although Thornton was probably the first of them to make this clear the best developed Classical analysis is to be found in Malthus.[64] He stressed the operation of inflation as producing forced saving and the effect of this on accumulation as income was redistributed to the accumulating classes. He expected output to rise because of this through increased division of labour—a union of Hume and Smith which thus avoided assuming less than full employment at the beginning of the process. But Malthus was not an inflationist: he reminded his reader of Hume's capital-mobility thesis which has already been referred to in this chapter, stressed that the redistribution itself involved injustice, and put forward the view that there was a danger that inflation would encourage speculation rather than productive entrepreneurship. With the experience of the Assignats episode before him he also stressed the danger of hyperinflation.

Malthus was not then an inflationist: rather he was, like a number of the other Classical writers, especially Wheatley, using the analysis to warn of the dangers of deflation, given the prospect of resumption. But there were others less inhibited. McCulloch, less worried by the social injustice involved (though still conscious of the danger of capital flight) seems to have believed that a gradual steady depreciation, benefiting the industrious classes, was desirable. He was here thinking of forced saving; wages, he believed, adjusted quite quickly during inflation and it was only the fixed-income receivers who suffered. Although they lost, the community gained, not only through the redistribution to the industrious classes, but also through the effect on profit margins and thence on entrepreneurial incentives. Nevertheless, for him, as for others, avoidance of deflation was much more important than securing inflation—and until as late as 1852 he seems to have believed that there should have been devaluation prior to 1819.

Torrens, at least in his early anti-Bullionist phase, was even more impenitently inflationist: and the mechanism he relied on was the redistribution effect supporting increased division of labour and producing entrepreneurial confidence. Within the Classical school very few economists rejected the analysis. Ricardo, focusing as usual on successive periods of long-run equilibrium, denied the damage of deflation, and the stimulating effect of rising prices (he saw only harmful speculation ensuing which, given his assumptions of full employment and fixed technology, was hardly surprising), and resorted to his Corn Model to show that only a change in corn prices or wages could affect profits. He also asserted that any increase in saving would be offset by decreased saving by those who lost from the redistribution, and stressed the violation of cummutative justice involved.[65] But he found little support—James Mill was in the same camp but even J. S. Mill reluctantly recognized the mechanism, though he condemned inflation.[66]

For the later Classical writers the stimulating effect of an increase in the money supply on the level of activity involved price rises and redistribution. Nevertheless, none of the Classical writers was an out and out inflationist. The reason for this is clear enough. Without a continual increase in world gold production (of which however McCulloch was hopeful at one stage) inflation must, under a gold-standard system, soon be checked and indeed reversed. Since convertibility was a major objective for the Classical writers, as we have seen, this ruled out inflation. For Thomas Attwood and his followers however such was not the case. *Their* aim was quite simply full employment. To secure this Attwood suggested monetary 'pump priming' to raise the level of prices.[67] After full employment had been restored the additional currency could be *gradually* withdrawn. He suggested open-market purchases to increase the money supply; these could also be put into reverse if prices rose too quickly.[68] Rising prices in turn affected entrepreneurial expectations (to which he gave a key role). 'Restore the depreciated state of the currency, and you restore the reward of industry, you restore confidence, you restore production, you restore consumption, you restore everything that constitutes the commercial prosperity of the nation.'[69] Inflation was for Attwood a necessity—he did not pretend to justify freedom of note issue by a Real Bills doctrine. He did not *want* stable prices but full employment. The economic system was unstable in a downward direction—falling prices caused unloading of stocks producing depression of expectations and further unloading of stocks. There was a downward multiplier effect, the low turning-point of the cycle only being reached when stocks were exhausted and prices began to rise because of shortage.[70] The effect of this upon the unemployed labour was obviously cruel in the extreme. Because of the suffering caused, and also because of the hardship which deflation caused to the commercial classes, downward movements of prices should be avoided at all costs.[71]

Attwood was not a member of the Classical School. But his analysis came from them and ultimately his differences with them were over the fundamental objectives (full employment, or convertibility which they deemed necessary for growth as well as justice) rather than over analysis. They too were strongly opposed to deflation; they saw the hardship that this could produce and they saw too that increases in the money supply could offset this hardship and raise the level of activity. But they believed that Attwood's inflationism, containing within itself the dangers of hyper-inflation (of which, be it noted, there was a recent example to hand) had the potentiality of producing, through the destruction of not only convertibility but the currency itself, far more suffering even than was entailed in bouts of deflation under convertibility. Rather, as we have seen throughout this chapter, their approach was to try to make a convertible system work more gently.

## NOTES

1. See B. R. Mitchell with P. Deane, *Abstract of British Historical Statistics* (Cambridge, 1962), p. 471.
2. See Hume (ed. Rotwein), pp. 47–59, 'Of Interest'.
3. Ibid., p. 33.
4. *Wealth of Nations*, ed. Cannan, i. 417–19. See the whole of Smith's Bk. IV, Ch. I, on this issue.
5. Even Hume allowed the quantity of money significance here. See Hume (ed. Rotwein), pp. 40–6; see also Joseph Harris, *An Essay upon Money and Coins*, Pts. I and II (1757–8), repr. in J. R. McCulloch (ed.), *A Select Collection of Scarce and Valuable Tracts on Money* (London, 1856), pp. 339–512, p. 368.
6. Smith, op. cit, p. 24. These roles are also enumerated by Harris.
7. Smith, op. cit., p. 279.
8. Ibid., p. 25.
9. In his notes to Smith's *Lectures*, p. 186 n.
10. Smith, *Wealth of Nations*, i. 26.
11. Ibid., p. 272.

12. See e.g. Hume (ed. Rotwein), pp. 35–6.

13. Ibid., pp. 307–9. But Smith believed that paper money should be limited to large denominations thereby effectively confining it to inter-merchant transactions.

14. Ibid., pp. 274–6.

15. Ibid., pp. 277–8.

16. Cantillon, *Essai* (ed. Higgs), pp. 141–3, 299–305; Smith, op. cit., p. 276.

17. Smith, op. cit., pp. 280–3.

18. Ibid., p. 304.

19. Ibid., p. 307.

20. Ibid., p. 303.

21. See Overstone's striking letter to Torrens in D. P. O'Brien, *The Correspondence of Lord Overstone*, ii. 713–17.

22. *Studies*, p. 75.

23. Cantillon, *Essai*, pp. 127–9; Harris, *Essay*, pp. 391–2, 404–8.

24. Quoted in Viner, *Studies*, pp. 249 n.

25. Hume (ed. Rotwein), pp. 62–3. See also Harris, op. cit., pp. 404–9, 427–9; Cantillon, op. cit., pp. 105, 167–9.

26. Ricardo, *Works*, ed. Sraffa, i. 137. See also ibid., iii. 62, 94.

27. See Ricardo, i. 193, 195, 196, 283, 352.

28. Senior, *Three Lectures on the Value of Money* (dating from 1830, privately printed 1840) in N. W. Senior, *Selected Writings on Economics* (repr. A. M. Kelley, New York, 1966).

29. This dated from Cantillon and from Harris—op. cit., pp. 409–29. Expertise in this matter is not however apparent in Smith's work.

30. See especially *Wealth of Nations*, i. 274–5 where it is recognized that $M <$ PT and that $MV = PT$.

31. *Lectures*, p. 197.

32. *Wealth of Nations*, i. 276–7, 283–4.

33. See Hume (ed. Rotwein), pp. 34–5.

34. On this issue see the excellent article by J. M. Low, 'An Eighteenth Century Controversy in the Theory of Economic Progress', *Manchester School*, 20 (1952), 311–30.

35. On Ricardo's attitude to this problem see R. S. Sayers, 'Ricardo's Views on Monetary Questions', in T. S. Ashton and R. S. Sayers, *Papers in English Monetary History* (Oxford, 1953); on Wheatley and Ricardo see E. V. Morgan, *The Theory and Practice of Central Banking* (repr. London, 1965), pp. 58–62.

36. H. Thornton, *An Inquiry into the Nature and Effects of the Paper Credit of Great Britain* (1802), ed. F. A. Hayek (repr. London, 1939), p. 192.

37. Ibid., pp. 96–7.

38. Ibid., pp. 100, 205, 227–8, 268–70.

39. Ibid., p. 259. See also *ibid.*, pp. 142–3.

40. See especially ibid., pp. 91–2.

41. Ibid., p. 156.

42. Ibid., pp. 152–3, 259.

43. Ibid., pp. 118–19.

44. Ibid., pp. 142–3.

45. Ibid., Ch. 5.

46. W. Blake, *Observations on the Principles which Regulate the Course of the Exchange* (1810), repr. in J. R. McCulloch (ed.), *A Select Collection of Scarce and Valuable Tracts on Paper Currency and Banking* (London, 1857).

47. See also The Bullion Report repr. as *The Paper Pound of 1797–1821*, ed. E. Cannan (London, 1919), p. 29.

48. Smith, op. cit., i. 287.

49. See B. A. Corry, *Money Saving and Investment in English Economics 1800–1850* (London, 1962), p. 76.

50. Thornton, op. cit., p. 219.

51. See Sayers, op. cit.

52. Thomas Joplin, *Views on the Currency* (London, 1826); Henry Drummond, *Elementary Propositions on the Currency* (4th edn. London, 1826); Richard Page, *'Daniel Hardcastle' Letters to the Editor of 'The Times' Journal* (London, 1826); James Pennington's private memorandum to Huskisson repr. in R. S. Sayers (ed.), *The Economic Writings of James Pennington* (London, 1963); J. R. McCulloch, 'Fluctuations in the supply and Value of Money, Banking Systems of England', *Edinburgh Review*, 43 (Feb. 1826), 263–98, especially 278.

53. Overstone, *Tracts and Other Publications on Metallic and Paper Currency*, ed. J. R. McCulloch (1857), p. 23.

54. On this problem see D. P. O'Brien, *The Correspondence of Lord Overstone*, i. 123–4.

55. See F. H. Hahn, 'Professor Friedman's Views on Money', *Economica*, 38 (1971), 61–80.

56. See O'Brien, op. cit., pp. 100–2, 127.

57. J. B. Say, *Treatise*, Bk. I, Ch. XV, 'Of the Demand or Market for Products', pp. 132–40.

58. J. Mill, *Economic Writings*, ed. D. Winch, pp. 328–9.

59. The classic and standard reference is D. Patinkin, *Money, Interest and Prices* (2nd edn. New York, 1965).

60. See e.g. D. P. O'Brien, *J. R. McCulloch*, pp. 147–8, 155.

61. See G. C. Archibald and R. G. Lipsey, 'Value and Monetary Theory: temporary versus full equilibrium', repr. in R. W. Clower (ed.), *Monetary Theory* (London, 1969).

62. On both J. S. Mill and McCulloch see the classic article by G. S. Becker and W. J. Baumol, 'The Classical Monetary Theory', *Economica*, N.S. 19 (1952), 355–76.

63. See Hume (ed. Rotwein), pp. 37–8, 40.

64. T. R. Malthus, 'Depreciation of Paper Currency', *Edinburgh Review* 17 (1811), 339–72; 'Pamphlets on the Bullion Question', ibid., 18 (1811), 448–70; *The Grounds of an Opinion on the Policy of Restricting the Importation of Foreign Corn* (London, 1815).

65. Ricardo, *Works*, iii. 99–127, especially 122–3; ibid., iv. 36–7.

66. J. Mill, op. cit. (ed. Winch), pp. 294–5; J. S. Mill, *Principles* (ed. Ashley), Bk. III, Ch. XIII, pp. 542–55.

67. T. Attwood, *The Remedy: or Thoughts on the Present Distress* (London, 1816), p. 9.

68. Ibid., p. 53.

69. Ibid., p. 66.

70. Ibid., pp. 60–1.

71. T. Attwood, *A Letter to the Earl of Liverpool* (Birmingham, 1819), pp. 35–42.

# BIBLIOGRAPHY

This has been a long chapter, and the further reading is widely diffused. On the first section see the historical material in J. Viner, *Studies in the Theory of International Trade* (repr. London, 1964); in E. Wood, *English Theories of Central Banking Control* (Cambridge, Mass., 1939); in F. W. Fetter, *The Development of British Monetary Orthodoxy* (Cambridge, Mass., 1965); and in the book by Mitchell and Deane cited in Chapter I. Two other useful references are T. S. Ashton and R. S. Sayers, *Papers in English Monetary History* (Oxford, 1953) and J. R. T. Hughes, *Fluctuations in Trade, Industry and Finance* (Oxford, 1960).

For Section ii see the *Wealth of Nations*, Bk. I, Ch. iv, Bk. II Ch. ii, and Bk. IV, Ch. i; Smith's *Lectures*, Pt. II, pp. 182–9; J. S. Mill, *Principles*, Bk. III, Chs. vii, xi, and xii; and an important primary reference for this section, Joseph Harris's *Essay upon Money and Coins*, repr. in J. R. McCulloch (ed.), *A Select Collection of Scarce and Valuable Tracts on Money* (London, 1856). For secondary references see in particular O. St. Clair, Chs. 11 and 15; D. O'Brien, *J. R. McCulloch*, pp. 147–9; and the lecture by Senior on the Value of Money repr. in R. W. Clower (ed.), *Monetary Theory, Selected Readings* (London, 1969).

The basic reference with which to start Section iii is David Hume's Essay 'Of the Balance of Trade'; E. Rotwein's introduction to the economic writings cited is also very useful. See also Cantillon's *Essai*, Pt. I, Ch. xviii, Pt. II, Chs. iii–x, and Pt. III, Chs. ii–viii. Of the primary literature Senior is also particularly interesting here: see his *Three Lectures on the Transmission of the Precious Metals* (1828), *Three Lectures on the Cost of Obtaining Money* (1830), and *Three Lectures on the Value of Money* (1840).

A good place to start the secondary readings is the classic article by J. H. Hollander, 'The Development of the Theory of Money from Adam Smith to David Ricardo', *Quarterly Journal of Economics*, 25 (1911), 429–70. Another important reference, despite its unpromising title, is J. M. Low, 'An Eighteenth Century Controversy in the Theory of Economic Progress', *Manchester School*, 20 (1952), 311–30. This deals with Smith's failure to offer the price-specie-flow mechanism in the *Wealth of Nations*. On this same subject see F. Petrella, 'Adam Smith's rejection of Hume's price-specie-flow mechanism: a minor mystery resolved', *Southern Economic Journal*, 34 (1968), 365–74, and, for a contrary view, R. V. Eagly, 'Adam Smith and the Specie Flow Mechanism', *Scottish Journal of Political Economy*, 17 (1960), 61–8. See also St. Clair; and O'Brien, *J. R. McCulloch*, pp. 150–4.

Turning now to section iv, there are the books by Viner (Chs. iii and iv), Fetter (Ch. ii), and Wood, which contain, together with Lord Robbins's magisterial discussion in *Robert Torrens*, the definitive coverage of the period. These are treatments that repay repeated study. Other very useful references are E. V. Morgan's *The Theory and Practice of Central Banking* (Cambridge, 1943) Ch. iii, B. A. Corry, *Money, Saving and Investment in English Economics 1800–1850* (London, 1962); and L. W. Mints, *A History of Banking Theory* (Chicago, 1945), Ch. iv—this last is a classic which is no longer easy to obtain. See also the first of the two valuable essays by J. K. Horsefield in Ashton and Sayers, and the paper on Ricardo by Sayers in the same volume. The primary literature of the period makes particularly fascinating reading. Thornton's *Paper Credit* is available in a reprint edited by F. A. Hayek (see p. 166, note 36 above), and in J. R. McCulloch (ed.), *A Select Collection of Tracts on Paper Currency* (1857). This volume also contains the Bullion Report and Blake's pamphlet on the exchanges. See also the *Economic Writings of Francis Horner*, ed. F. W. Fetter (London, 1957) and John Wheatley, *An Essay on the Theory of Money and Principles of Commerce* (London, 1807–22)—unfortunately a very scarce work.

The reading for the next section really builds on all this. See especially Viner, Ch. v, and Lord Robbins, Ch. v. This last is especially good on the role of bank credit in the Currency School's theory. The discussion of Torrens may also be supplemented by D. O'Brien, 'The Transition in Torrens' Monetary Thought', *Economica*, 32 (1965), 269–301. See also D. O'Brien, *J. R. McCulloch*, pp. 167–88 and D. O'Brien (ed.), *The Correspondence of Lord Overstone*, 3 vols. (Cambridge, 1971), especially the introduction to Vol. i. On the origins of the Bank Charter Act see Sir J. Clapham's great history *The Bank of England* (London, 1944) and J. K. Horsefield's second essay in Ashton and Sayers. Much of the literature so far recommended concentrates on the Currency School: but no one should miss Sir T. E. Gregory's introduction to Tooke and Newmarch's *History of Prices* (London 1928). J. S. Mill was really a member of the Banking rather than the Currency School; and in this connection the article by L. C. Hunter, 'Mill and Cairnes on the Rate of Interest', *Oxford Economic Papers*, N.S. 11 (1959), 63–87 is particularly interesting as providing insights into the subtlety and complexity of the Banking School treatment.

Also most valuable is the essay introducing James Pennington in R. S. Sayers (ed.), *The Economic Writings of James Pennington* (London, 1963).

For Section vi the right place to start is undoubtedly the much misrepresented J. B. Say: see his *Treatise*, Bk. I, Ch. XV. See also J. S. Mill's *Essays on Some Unsettled Questions of Political Economy* (London, 1844, L.S.E. repr. London, 1948). The secondary literature is prolix and some of it is awful. But there is an excellent discussion in M. Blaug's *Economic Theory in Retrospect* as well as the classic treatments in Schumpeter's *History* (pp. 615–25) and G. S. Becker and W. J. Baumol, 'The Classical Monetary Theory: The Outcome of the Discussion', *Economica*, 19 (1952), 355–76. See also D. O'Brien, *J. R. McCulloch*, pp. 154–9. Two of the important modern contributions to the debate are reprinted in the volume edited by R. W. Clower: those by D. Patinkin, and by G. C. Archibald and R. G. Lipsey. Mill's own treatment of the problem is discussed in B. Balassa, 'John Stuart Mill and the Law of Markets', and L. Hunter, 'Mill and the Law of Markets: Comment', *Quarterly Journal of Economics*, 73 (1959), 263–74 and 74 (1960), 158–62.

Classical inflation theory is treated in the secondary literature especially by Rotwein (on Hume see pp. lxiii—lxxi), Lord Robbins (pp. 74–86), Viner (Ch. iv), Corry (pp. 81–95), O'Brien, *McCulloch* (pp. 159–67), and in an excellent unpublished thesis by E. McKinley (University of California, 1954).

See also the excellent survey by F. A. Hayek, 'A Note on the Development of the Doctrine of "Forced Saving" ', *Quarterly Journal of Economics*, 47 (1932), 123–33. But anyone who misses the original will be much the poorer. Start with David Hume's great Essay 'Of Money' and Cantillon's *Essai*, Pt. II, Chs. vi–viii. Then proceed to Malthus's two articles in the *Edinburgh Review* 17 (Feb. 1811), 339–72, and 18 (Aug. 1811), 448–70, and his *Grounds of an Opinion on the Policy of Restricting the Importation of Foreign Corn* (1815). Finally proceed to full inflationism in T. Attwood's *Economic Writings*, ed. F. W. Fetter (London, 1964). The first two pamphlets in this, *The Remedy* (1816), and *A Letter to the Earl of Liverpool* (1819), are particularly remarkable. After this heady stuff the position of J. S. Mill (*Principles*, Bk. III, Ch. xiii) seems tame indeed.

Finally, readers concerned to see where monetary theory and the theory of monetary policy have gone since the Classical era will find five references useful: H. G. Johnson, *Essays in Monetary Economics* (London, 1967) (esp. essays 1–3); A. D. Bain, *The Control of the Money Supply* (London, 1970); Miles Fleming, *Monetary Theory* (London, 1972); W. L. Smith, 'On Some Current Issues in Monetary Economics', *Journal of Economic Literature*, 8 (1970), 767–82; and D. Fisher, *Money and Banking* (Homewood, Illinois, 1971).

# 7. International Trade

## i. ABSOLUTE ADVANTAGE: TRADE AND GROWTH

The Classical theory of International Trade essentially grew out of the work of Adam Smith—from that *locus classicus* of the free-trade doctrine, the *Wealth of Nations*. Smith's work itself was not independent of what had gone before. In particular the Physiocrats popularized the idea of free trade. Even though they had very little original to say on the subject, and based their advocacy of freedom of trade largely on natural-law considerations, they were undoubtedly an influence in favour of the idea.[1] There were also earlier English writers like North[2] whose advocacy of freedom of trade was however of little influence until Smith had published his great *tour de force*. Having given all due weight to these earlier writers, there still seems no reason to doubt the verdict that Classical trade theory, and the modern trade theory which is essentially descended from it, stem directly from Adam Smith.

In essence what Smith put forward was a theory of the interaction of trade and economic growth. In the *Wealth of Nations* great stress is laid upon division of labour as the engine of economic development. But division of labour is limited by the extent of the market. What trade does is to widen this market, so increasing the scope for division of labour.

Such a view of trade leads on to two further considerations. Firstly, there is a parallel between inter-regional and international trade. They are in fact both forms of the same thing. But if they are, then this implies that factors are mobile internationally as well as between regions. Smith does seem to have made this assumption. But if factors are mobile internationally, then trade will be on the basis of *absolute* advantage. That is to say that commodities will be produced where their resource inputs are absolutely lowest, each country having particular absolute advantages in the production of particular commodities. The advantage of trade then lies in buying commodities cheaper abroad than at home.

It is the maxim of every prudent master of a family, never to attempt to make at home what it will cost him more to make than to buy ... All of them find it for their interest to employ their whole industry in a way in which they have some advantage over their neighbours, and to purchase with a part of its produce, ... whatever else they have occasion for.

What is prudence in the conduct of every private family, can scarce be folly in that of a great kingdom. If a foreign country can supply us with a commodity cheaper than we ourselves can make it, better buy it of them with some part of the produce of our own industry, employed in a way in which we have some advantage.[3]

The advantage of buying from the cheapest source was then one of the major advantages of trade; and with this was coupled the advantage of obtaining, through trade, commodities which were completely unobtainable by domestic production.

It should be stressed that it was not only Smith who saw trade in these terms. McCulloch, in particular, saw trade as resting upon absolute advantage, with the prices of internationally traded goods determined by their cost of production. He believed that there was a tendency towards international equalization of factor prices through factor mobility. For him, as for Smith, the basis of absolute advantage was in land and natural resource factor endowment. The other factors then migrated to co-operate with these endowments. There was, he believed, a complete parallel between international and inter-regional trade, and he argued, following Smith, that nations, like individuals, should seek the cheapest source of supply.[4]

The second consideration to which this view of trade led was that trade was essentially a means of disposing of surplus produce obtained by extending the division of labour beyond the scope which the domestic market would support.[5] This is the so-called 'vent for surplus' doctrine. The idea is important and it was propounded by both Smith and McCulloch[6] although J. S. Mill, who actually coined the term, dismissed it.[7] It has important implications which contrast it strongly with the 'comparative cost' approach to be dealt with in the next section. In particular it implies that international specialization is not reversible but part of the development process. Secondly, while the 'comparative cost' approach assumes given resources fully employed before trade opens, trade then reallocating resources more efficiently with new prices, the 'vent for surplus' approach assumes that there is actual or potential surplus-productive capacity before trade begins. This in turn implies inelastic domestic demand for exportables (or specificity of resources, an assumption that Smith did not make). As a view of the interaction between trade and growth it is not only perfectly reasonable but highly suggestive. In this view, random natural-resource endowment gives countries an imbalance between their production and consumption capacities.

But as a weapon in the argument for freedom of trade the 'vent for surplus' doctrine is something of a two-edged weapon. On the one hand it suggests that imports are more or less costless; but on the other it also suggests that, because of the non-reversibility of specialization, an exporting country is very vulnerable to a reduction in the demand for its products. The latter consideration was however neglected by Smith and his immediate successors. For them, the 'vent for surplus' doctrine merely confirmed that freedom of trade was necessary in order to achieve the onward-going process of growth. Smith also saw other advantages in trade. He saw it as moving commodities to where their utility was greatest[8] and as raising profits,[9] but these are not the essential parts of Smith's theory of trade and indeed the arguments he used in these connections were often confused and unsatisfactory. The core of Smith's theory was a doctrine of trade and growth—and as such it was capable of leading to some of the most interesting recent developments in trade theory such as those building on the idea of available commodities being exported,[10] and the transfer of technology through imitation after a country has originally established a trade advantage through technological leadership. This last idea is indeed implicit in some of the Classical writings, especially in McCulloch's attitude towards the export of machinery to France—he was happy about a ban on this if it would be effective. Indeed the range of considerations suggested by the Smithian analysis is much wider than that of the theory which later built upon the comparative cost approach. In particular for Smith, as for Hume who preceded him, and for McCulloch who followed him, the stimulation of wants involved in the development of trade was all-important as supplying the motive for further division of labour, further exertion, and technological change. Moreover in its stress upon the links between capital, division of labour, and trade, it foreshadowed the links suggested by modern writers between capital accumulation and technological advance and advantage.

All of this of course was productive of a classic case for freedom of trade. Trade increased income not only because it supported growth but because it meant that commodities could be imported from where their input requirements were lowest. This in turn minimized input requirements for any particular collection of goods and, provided that the extra output of particular kinds of goods could be disposed of through trade, maximized the income which could be obtained from particular resources. Freedom of trade also ensured that capital flowed to those employments where it would be most productive in increasing the division of labour. This was the message in the *Wealth of Nations*; and this message, and indeed the very phrases in which it was written, found constant repetition in the Classical works.

## ii. COMPARATIVE ADVANTAGE

The next stage in the development of the Classical theory of international trade is the emergence of the theory of comparative advantage. What is involved can be seen most clearly from Ricardo's example of England and Portugal.[11] He supposed that the man-years required to produce particular quantities of cloth and wine were as shown in Table 4:

TABLE 4

|  | Cloth | Wine |
|---|---|---|
| England | 100 | 120 |
| Portugal | 90 | 80 |

He then argued that it would be in Portugal's interest to import cloth in exchange for wine even though she could make cloth with a smaller resource input than England. The advantage lay in the fact that in order to obtain this given quantity of cloth she would have to employ ninety men for one year if she produced it internally, whereas if she produced wine and can then exchange this wine for the same quantity of cloth from England, she could get the same quantity of cloth for the labour of eighty men for one year.

Now, so far, all that Ricardo had explicitly done was to show that it might be advantageous for a country to import commodities in which it had an absolute advantage. But as is so often the case with Ricardo, there is much more implied here. The ratio of labour inputs in England implies that the relative price of cloth and wine will be $1:1\cdot2$. The corresponding figures for Portugal will be $1:0\cdot88$. Clearly this implies that it will be advantageous to Portugal to send wine to England where one unit of it will sell for $1\cdot2$ units of cloth. But the price does not have to be so high. As long as $0\cdot88$ of a unit of wine sells for more than one unit of cloth (neglecting transport costs) it will be advantageous for Portugal to obtain its cloth through trade. Similarly, England will gain if it has to give anything less than $1\cdot2$ units of cloth for every unit of wine. So that any relative price of cloth and wine between the limits $1:0\cdot88$ and $1:1\cdot2$ will offer a gain to both countries.

Ricardo did not spell all this out clearly. But he had gone far enough to establish a theory of the gain from trade which was clearly distinguished from that based upon absolute advantage. What was now being argued was that there was an advantage in trade even if one country was absolutely more efficient (used absolutely fewer inputs) for both commodities, just as long as it was relatively less efficient in the production of one commodity than of another. The distinction between absolute and comparative advantage may be put as it was by Haberler.[12]

Take two commodities $a$ and $b$ where subscripts 1 and 2 refer to production inputs in countries 1 and 2. Absolute advantage may then be denoted by $\frac{a_1}{a_2} < 1 < \frac{b_1}{b_2}$. Country 1 has an absolute advantage in $a$ $(a_1 < a_2)$ and 2 has an absolute advantage in $b$ $(b_2 < b_1)$. Comparative advantage may be denoted by $\frac{a_1}{a_2} < \frac{b_1}{b_2} < 1$. Country 1 has superiority in both goods but a greater superiority in good $a$. The consequence of such a theory was, as J. S. Mill put it: 'A thing may sometimes be sold cheapest, by being produced in some other place than that at which it can be produced with the smallest amount of labour and abstinence.'[13]

Now that such a state of affairs should exist at all, clearly involves an assumption which Smith did not make, but which Ricardo, Torrens, and other writers certainly did make: that labour and capital were immobile internationally. They were quite clear that it was this that made international trade distinct from inter-regional trade. As J. S. Mill put it:

> If the north bank of the Thames possessed an advantage over the south bank in the production of shoes, no shoes would be produced on the south side; the shoe-makers would remove themselves and their capitals to the north bank, or would have established themselves there originally; for being competitors in the same market with those on the north side, they could not compensate themselves for their disadvantage at the expense of the consumer: the amount of it would fall entirely on their profits; and they would not long content themselves with a smaller profit, when, by simply crossing a river, they could increase it. But between distant places, and especially between different countries, profits may continue different; because persons do not usually remove themselves or their capitals to a distant place without a very strong motive.[14]

It was this which gave international trade its very special character. As Ricardo put it:

> The same rule which regulates the relative value of commodities in one country, does not regulate the relative value of the commodities exchanged between two or more countries.
>    The quantity of wine which she [Portugal] shall give in exchange for the cloth of England, is not determined by the respective quantities of labour devoted to the production of each, as it would be, if both commodities were manufactured in England, or both in Portugal ... The labour of 100 Englishmen cannot be given for that of 80 Englishmen, but the produce of the labour of 100 Englishmen may be given for the produce of the labour of 80 Portuguese, 60 Russians, or 120 East Indians. The difference in this respect, between a single country and many, is easily accounted for, by considering the difficulty with which capital moves from one country to another, to seek a more profitable employment, and the activity with which it invariably passes from one province to another in the same country.[15]

All this involved a significant theoretical development. Before proceeding further it is perhaps as well to consider who was responsible for it. As early as 1701 the advantages of import from abroad had been stated in comparative cost terms.[16] But the author, as far as Classical economics was concerned, was clearly Robert Torrens who published the idea in 1815.[17] Ricardo's *Essay on Profits*, which was published the same day as Torrens's pamphlet[18] has nothing to say about this despite the fact that the message of the work is the necessity of a free trade in corn.[19] There seems little doubt about the correctness of Torrens's claim that Ricardo had borrowed the idea from him and his claim was, at least partially, accepted by J. S. Mill.[20] But having said that, three points should be made. First of all there seems no doubt that Ricardo was responsible for the appreciation and acceptance of the idea—despite his own presentation.[21] Secondly, the seeds of the idea are clearly to be found in the *Wealth of Nations*.[22] Thirdly, Torrens often relied upon absolute advantage examples in his writings on international trade.[23]

But whoever was responsible for the idea, certain fundamental questions remained to be answered. In particular, although the advantage from trade might consist in differences in the comparative resource uses involved in producing the commodities as between the two countries, such differences had to be reflected in *prices* before trade would actually take place. The vital point is this: absolute differences in money costs determine trade. The eighteenth-century writers, especially Adam Smith, assumed that these differences reflected absolute differences in input requirements—as indeed they would have done given international factor mobility. In this case there would have been only single sources of production for particular commodities—assuming constant costs. The contribution of Torrens and Ricardo was then to show that, even given lower inputs for both of any pair of commodities in any one country, trade was still advantageous to a country, if the international ratio of exchange between the commodities was better than the internal rate of exchange between them. But trade depends upon absolute money prices which depend in turn on money costs. Money costs in turn depend upon factor productivity and factor remuneration. The price-specie-flow mechanism however provided the Classical writers with a means whereby comparative advantage in real terms would be turned into absolute advantage in money terms and hence prices. Thus England in the example would run a balance-of-payments deficit with Portugal until absolute differences in money prices made it advantageous for trade to take place in a two-way direction. Ricardo was able to show this perfectly successfully. His analysis was not complete, as we shall see; for the exact point at which relative price and wage levels would settle would depend on the relative strength of demand of the two countries for each other's goods. This in turn would determine which goods in the chain of comparative advantage (once we step outside a two-good case) would be imported and which exported. We shall find that the point about demand was appreciated by the later Classical writers; but the interaction of this with the chain of comparative advantage was not really clarified until Edgeworth.

Ricardo gives an example[24] in which the relative prices of wine and cloth are as shown in Table 5.

TABLE 5

|          | Wine | Cloth |
|----------|------|-------|
| England  | £45  | £45   |
| Portugal | £45  | £50   |

The relative prices of wine and cloth in the two countries are shown in Fig. 14. From this diagram it is clear that there is an advantage to England

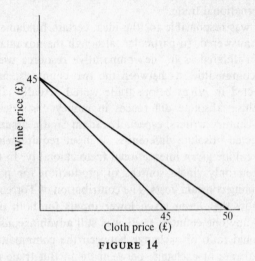

FIGURE 14

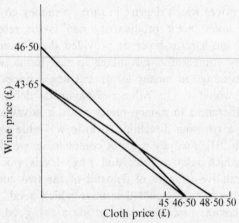

FIGURE 15

in trading cloth for wine at any better price than that represented by the slope of its internal price line, which will then no longer represent the boundary of a feasible region. Merchants will in fact buy cloth in England for £45 and sell it for £50 in Portugal. England is temporarily trading at

Portugal's price ratio. But they would make no profit from selling Portuguese wine in England at these prices, so the new situation does not represent trading equilibrium. Portugal will then run a balance-of-payments deficit with England. Metal flows of the type described in the previous

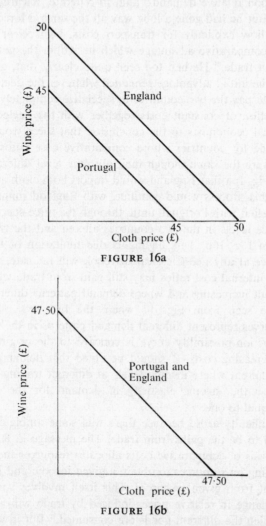

FIGURE 16a

FIGURE 16b

chapter will result, altering the relative price levels in the two countries. With the same relative resource inputs as before the price of cloth in Portugal will now fall. Let us suppose it falls to £48·50 and rises in England to £46·50. These new prices are shown in Fig. 15. The price of wine (Ricardo does not give the changes) will rise in England to £46·50 and fall in Portugal to £43·65. But different prices (neglecting transport costs) for the same good cannot persist. Given complete specialization (which constant costs do imply) the (international) price will settle at £43·65 for wine and £46·50 for cloth. This will be the terms of trade between England, the cloth exporter, and Portugal, the wine exporter. *Exactly* where the terms of trade will settle will depend upon relative demand: and, to reiterate, Ricardo did not get quite this far. But he had gone a long way all the same. Moreover although he does not allow explicitly for transport costs, he is clear enough that differences in comparative advantage which lie within the gold points will not bring about trade.[25] He had too seen quite clearly that, given constant costs, so that the initial advantage remained whatever the degree of specialization, it would pay the two countries to specialize completely.

The assumption of constant costs together with the neglect of demand led the Classical economists to the conclusion that there would be no advantage in trade for countries whose comparative cost ratios for different commodities were the same though their absolute level differed.[26] Thus we can see from Fig. 16a that England would import both cloth and wine from Portugal and this process would continue, with England running a balance of payments deficit with Portugal, until, through the price-specie-flow mechanism, the price levels in the two countries altered and the two price lines coincided as in Fig. 16b. This highlights one limitation of the approach. For, as a glance at any neo-Classical textbook will indicate, two countries with the same internal cost ratios may still gain from trade where costs are not constant but increasing and where demand patterns differ. What is involved can be seen from Fig. 17 where the two sets of community-indifference curves represent different demand patterns in the two countries and the production-possibility curve is concave to the origin representing the case of increasing costs. It should be noted that demand patterns are likely to be different where income levels in different trading countries are different, unless the income elasticity of demand for the goods traded is uniformly equal to one.

A further difficulty arose because there was some ambiguity over what were supposed to be the gains from trade. The message in Ricardo is that trade on the basis of comparative costs allocates resources more efficiently, thus economizing on resources to obtain a given income and increasing the possible output from given resources. This itself involves some ambiguity because the change in relative prices induced by trade will alter the combination in which the different goods are consumed.[27] But in any case there was more to trade than this, as Malthus, in the eighteenth-century tradition, insisted.[28] Following Smith he emphasized the importance of obtaining through trade commodities which were not obtainable at home at all, as well as the moving of commodities, by trade, from where their utility was low to where it was high. But, as Malthus argued, if the combination of goods consumed after trade was different from the combination consumed before trade (either because of price changes or newly available commodities) then, from a welfare point of view, serious problems of comparability arose.

There was also the problem of income distribution. If labour was heavily

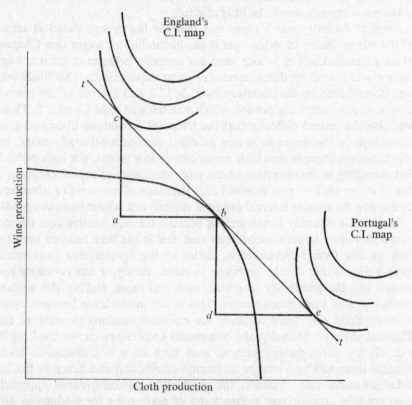

England exports *ab* of cloth in exchange for wine imports from Portugal of *ac*. Portugal exports *bd* of wine (= *ac*) in exchange for *de* of cloth (= *ab*). The international terms of trade are given by *tt*.

FIGURE 17

involved in the production of commodities produced relatively less efficiently at home, and was a heavy consumer of goods which would become an export staple, then it was likely to lose by the opening of trade. Of course, as the Classical economists tended to assume, it could move to the export industries. But it might still lose even then, if its marginal product declined fast in these industries. Of course it was true that if trade increases total available income the state can redistribute—but the Classical economists were silent on this issue except in so far as they recognized the transitional welfare problems of removing protection from a particular industry. Nevertheless there was an implied judgement: that the redistribution resulting from trade would in the main be automatically away from landlords and protection lobbyists. The former would lose rent and the latter would lose the high profits which went with market power. Wages, tending towards subsistence anyway, would be little affected.

Another difficulty which arose was that the theory was stated in terms of the labour theory of value—yet if the hierarchies of wages (see Chapter 5) for different kinds of labour were not common between countries, wage costs would not reflect different relative input requirements. This likelihood was strengthened by the discovery by J. S. Mill and Cairnes of the phenomenon of non-competing groups, which was referred to in Chapter 5. There was also the related difficulty that the Classical economists dismissed generally high or low wages as having no effect on comparative advantage, on the Ricardian grounds that high wages caused low profits, not high prices.[29] But according to the operation of the wage/durability of capital theorem, a rise of wages *vis-à-vis* profits would alter the range of comparative advantage by altering the relative internal prices of capital- and labour-intensive goods.

In fact this difficulty is not serious because the comparative cost theory, as stated, clearly implies opportunity cost, and it has been restated successfully in this form.[30] Nevertheless, critics of the restatements have made three points which should be borne in mind. Firstly, a labour-theory approach has the possibility of a link with real costs, making the welfare implications of trade much clearer. This is not insignificant because, apart from anything else, there certainly are real-cost elements in some of the Classical writers.[31] Secondly, the community-indifference curves used (as in Fig. 17) are unsatisfactory because each time there is a change in trade patterns there will be a change in income distribution and hence in the indifference-curve map. Thirdly, the production-possibility-curve approach does not take account very satisfactorily of preferences for working in different industries, or of the choice between income and leisure. But having said all that it should be emphasized that the reformulation of comparative-cost theory in terms of opportunity cost has enabled the essence of the theory to be preserved.

As developed by Ricardo (and also as explained in the typical neo-Classical textbook today) the theory did not really go beyond the two-country and two-commodity case. Ricardo however did hint at the extension of the theory to the multi-commodity case, indicating that metal flows between countries would alter the range of exports and imports.[32] Later writers amongst the Classical economists, notably Longfield and Senior, did however attempt to develop the argument further. Longfield saw that relative money wages determined which of the commodities in the scale of comparative advantage would be exported and which imported.[33] Just what he was driving at (though he did not reach his destination) can be seen from Table 6.[34] Taking Portugal as the standard (i.e. 1) we have the ratio of man-years required to produce a range of commodities A–J in the two countries.

TABLE 6

|          | A   | B   | C   | D   | E   | F   | G   | H   | I   | J   |
|----------|-----|-----|-----|-----|-----|-----|-----|-----|-----|-----|
| Portugal | 1   | 1   | 1   | 1   | 1   | 1   | 1   | 1   | 1   | 1   |
| England  | 2·0 | 1·8 | 1·6 | 1·4 | 1·2 | 1·0 | 0·8 | 0·6 | 0·4 | 0·2 |

If the wage rates are the same in the two countries then England will import A–E and export G–J. If Portuguese wages are 1·2 times English wages then England will only import A–D and will export F–J. Longfield saw that the relative wages depended on relative labour productivities in the two countries, and only failed to complete the analysis as far as was possible at that stage because he talked in terms of *average* labour productivities in the two countries—an approach which did not afford sufficient weight to differences in productivity in the production of *traded* commodities.

Before leaving the subject of comparative advantage one final, but absolutely central, point remains to be discussed. This is the question of the *origin* of differences in comparative advantage, a question which has led to heated theoretical and empirical controversy in our own day. From Ricardo's original example it seems clear enough that differences in technology are involved.[35] Now in our own day different endowments of capital and labour—the so-called Heckscher–Ohlin theory—has been developed to establish that, even with uniform technology, different factor endowments will produce different slopes for the production possibility curves and hence differences of comparative advantage. This involves a particularly restricted view of capital; and only when the theory, in its modern form, seemed to be contradicted by empirical testing did some writers suggest that the problem had been mis-specified and that 'capital' should have included human capital. But of course this involves the difficulty that, in any case, differences in human capital are likely to give rise to differences in technology—always assumed away in the modern version of Heckscher–Ohlin.

In fact the Classical writers were nothing like so blinkered in their view of the origin of comparative advantage. Thus for instance we find Torrens seeing comparative advantage as deriving from natural resource endowment and geographical position, different stages of economic development, and a technological superiority itself based upon natural-resource endowment.[36] Some of the Classical writings will certainly bear a Heckscher–Ohlin interpretation—at least if we are talking of the original (and much more elastic) formulation of the theory.[37] Certainly this is true of Cairnes;[38] and it is true to some extent of Longfield.[39] But the latter's range was very much wider than that of the modern theory. He saw comparative advantage as arising from 'integrity, intelligence, industry, perseverance, and the general good conduct, among the labourers'; from liberty and security leading to optimal resource allocation; from abundance of capital leading to low profits and export of capital-intensive goods; from cheap fertile land; and from differences of soil and climate. His formulation was probably much nearer to Heckscher–Ohlin than anything else in the Classical literature yet it is still much wider. He has non-homogeneous factors, and, in particular, some stress on the importance of natural resources. This is particularly interesting as some of the work since Leontief suggests that part of the difficulty with his famous results from testing the theory lay in his neglect of natural resources.[40] The essential characteristic of the Classical approach however was its elasticity. The Classical economists would never have made the assumption of uniform technology—an assumption which has arguably retarded the development of trade theory during much of this century. For, as Professor Johnson has pointed out, the extent to which a particular economy makes use of available knowledge will vary with the degree of development of that economy. The same author's suggestion that 'capital' should be thought of as including natural resources, while it will give rise to considerable difficulties over testing, is very much in the spirit of the Classical formulation.[41]

iii. RECIPROCAL DEMAND

We have noted that the formulation by Ricardo of the way in which comparative advantage was translated into money prices which gave rise to trade left unsolved the actual determination of the terms of trade and of relative price levels. There were in fact several early attempts to solve this problem. Ricardo simply made the arbitrary assumption of an equal split of the advantage from trade[42] while James Mill made the mistake (in the first two editions of his *Elements*) of attributing *all* the gain to *both* parties.[43] Longfield seems to have recognized the fact that the location of the equilibrium terms of trade depended upon reciprocal demand[44] and Torrens's recognition of the importance of demand dated from the fourth (1827) edition of his *External Corn Trade*.[45] Indeed Torrens has some claim to priority in this field as the following quotation from his *Letters on Commercial Policy* of 1832–3 indicates.

The existence of a greater difference in the *relative* cost of producing commodities in one country, than that which exists in the *relative* cost of producing them in other countries; the different degrees in which countries demand the productions of each other; and the amount required to pay carriage and merchant's profit. The operation of these several circumstances, in determining the value, in relation to each other, of commodities produced in different countries, I have endeavoured to explain, at length, in my Essay on the Corn Trade.

A country possessing superiority in the production of articles extensively demanded in the countries of the mines becomes the *entrepôt* of the precious metals, and has a higher scale of prices than those other countries to which she distributes the metals:—the limit to the higher scale of prices maintainable by the country which has become the *entrepôt*, is determined by the comparative difference in the cost of production in different countries; by the different degrees of intensity with which countries demand the products of each other; and by the cost of importing the last articles with which the balance of payments is adjusted:—superiority in the production of articles extensively demanded in other countries, and having great value in a small compass, compelling other countries to purchase their portion of the metals with bulky commodities, on which the expense of carriage is considerable, removes to a greater distance the limit to the higher scale of prices maintainable by the country which has become the *entrepôt*.[46]

Another notable effort was that by Senior who explained that relative price levels (and thus the terms of trade) depended upon the relative productivity of labour in export industries. The argument was quite simple. If the labour of 100 men in England produced commodities which sold for 100 ounces of gold in the precious-metal-producing countries, and if it took the labour of 200 men in France to produce the same amount of exports as were produced by 100 men in England then, according to Senior, wage levels in England would be twice as high as in France.[47] This was not unreasonable as far as it went; but to make the productivity of labour in the export industries the determinant of the level of money wages encountered the very real difficulty that *which* industries from the possible range were actually exporters depended upon the relative level of money wages. The analysis was then incomplete.

The correct solution was really provided by two writers, James Pennington and J. S. Mill. It was Pennington who made clear what had not been clear in other writers though it was certainly implied, viz. that the terms of trade must settle between the different comparative cost ratios.[48] But it was J. S. Mill who, in one of the greatest performances in the history of economics,[49] showed that where the terms of trade settled depended upon the reciprocal demand of each country for the products of the other. He did this in his *Essays on Some Unsettled Questions of Political Economy* written in the years 1829–30, although not published until 1844, and in his *Principles* of 1848.[50] He was able to do this because he, most clearly of all the Classical writers, thought in terms of schedules when discussing supply and demand, and he extended the idea of an equilibrium equation of supply and demand from the internal to the international market.[51]

... the Equation of International Demand ... may be concisely stated as follows. The produce of a country exchanges for the produce of other countries, at such values as are required in order that the whole of her exports may exactly pay for the whole of her imports. This law of International Values is but an extension of the more general law of Value, which we called the Equation of Supply and Demand. We have seen that the value of a commodity always so adjusts itself as to bring the demand to the exact level of the supply. But all trade, either between nations or individuals, is an interchange of commodities, in which the things that they respectively have to sell constitute also their means of purchase: the supply brought by the one constitues his demand for what is brought by the other. So that supply and demand are but another expression for reciprocal demand: and to say that value will adjust itself so as to equalise demand with supply, is in fact to say that it will adjust itself so as to equalise the demand on one side with the demand on the other.[52]

What Mill had in mind can clearly be seen in Fig. 18. Fig. 18a is one way of explaining what Mill had in mind and it has the advantage that domestic supply conditions are explicitly taken account of. It is in some ways a fair representation of what Mill was getting at, although the use of a rising supply schedule is arguably dubious in this connection and, as Viner pointed out, the use of partial curves is hard to defend because changes in the amounts of exports and imports and movements in metal will alter the positions of the curves.[53] Fig. 18b is familiar to students of neo-Classical textbooks and dates from Marshall. This shows quite clearly the determination of the equilibrium terms of trade, in barter terms, by the intersection of the two-offer curves. The curves as drawn differ from those in the textbooks because they move towards intersection only beyond the point on the original internal price ratios at which consumption would have taken place in the absence of trade. The elasticity of the curves in Fig. 18 is greater than one up to the point where the English offer curve becomes vertical and the German horizontal.[54] Although he drew no such curves, an understanding of the elasticity characteristics of the curves enables us to appreciate that Mill was perfectly in command of their properties, as the following quotation shows.

If, therefore, it be asked what country draws to itself the greatest share of the advantage of any trade it carries on, the answer is, the country for whose productions there is in other countries the greatest demand, and a demand the most susceptible of increase from additional cheapness. In so far as the productions of any country possessed this property, the country obtains all foreign commodities at less cost. It gets its imports cheaper, the greater the intensity of the demand in foreign countries for its exports. It also gets its imports cheaper the less the extent and intensity of its own demand for them. The market is cheapest to those whose demand is small. A country which desires few foreign productions, and only a limited quantity of them, while its own commodities are in great request in foreign countries, will obtain its limited imports at extremely small cost, that is, in exchange for the produce of a very small quantity of its labour and capital.[55]

The possibilities considered in the first half of the quotation are illustrated in Fig. 19a where with greater and more elastic German demand for British goods the terms of trade move steadily in favour of Britain; and Fig. 19b relates to the second half of the quotation where the terms of trade are obviously better where the British demand is smaller along the offer curve E2.

Mill's treatment was comprehensive. He extended the analysis to more

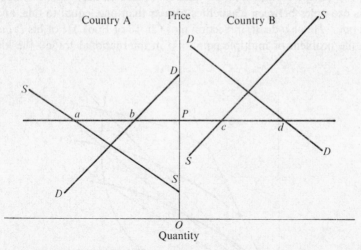

The international price settles at *O.P.* Exports of country A (*ab*) equal imports of country B(*cd*).

FIGURE 18a

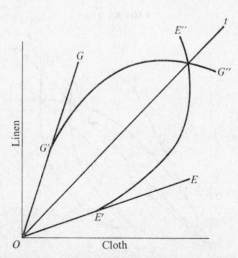

*OG* represents Germany's internal opportunity cost ratio before trade.
*OE* represents England's internal ratio.
*G′* and *E′* represent the combinations that the countries would consume without trade.
*OG″* and *OE″* are the two trade-offer curves, and *Ot* the equilibrium terms of trade.

FIGURE 18b

than two countries, and to more than two commodities,[56] and distinguished in his examples between elasticities greater than one, equal to one, and less than one.[57] He also dealt, in Section 6 of Ch. 18 of Book III of his *Principles* with the problem of multiple equilibria in international trade—the kind of

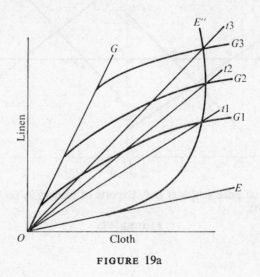

FIGURE 19a

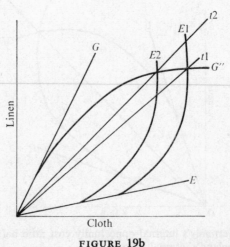

FIGURE 19b

problem illustrated in Fig. 20.[58] Mill was also able to offer an answer to the question of what determined the force of competition between two countries in a third market.[59] One country will be able to undersell another in a third market to the extent of monopolizing that market only if reciprocal demand ensures that the terms of trade between that country and the market in the third country are better from the point of view of the third country than the maximum advantage that could be given by the second country trading at its own internal cost ratio. Mill also explored the effects of improvements in production on the terms of trade. Assuming trade between England and Germany, Mill makes England the cloth producer and Germany the linen producer. He then assumes that reciprocal demands are such as to establish equilibrium at 10 cloth for 17 linen. An improvement in production of linen

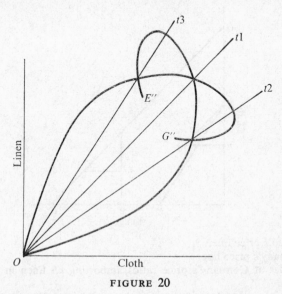

FIGURE 20

in Germany then cuts the cost per unit of linen by one-third. This causes Germany to offer 50 per cent more linen than before for particular amounts of cloth. He then concludes correctly that if the English demand for linen has unit elasticity the new equilibrium terms of trade will be 10 cloth for $25\frac{1}{2}$ linen and that if elasticity of demand is less than one the terms of trade for Germany will be worse than this while, if elasticity of demand is greater than one the terms of trade for Germany will be better than this.[60] As Edgeworth later pointed out, this treatment neglects the gain to the improving country if the commodity in question is also consumed at home.[61] But it was a considerable achievement none the less.

It is also important to recognize, particularly as some later critics had apparently not read Mill's *Principles*, that Mill faced and solved the problem of trade between countries whose demands were of disparate size, in which case the international price might well settle at the internal price ratio of the country with the larger demand, that country being incompletely specialized.[62] The kind of possibility is illustrated in Fig. 21. The point is that after one country has specialized completely there is still some

excess demand for the commodity and the international terms of trade
cannot change beyond the limits set by the internal comparative cost ratios.
Any unsatisfied demand will then have to be met by production in the larger
country which will not be completely specialized. In fact Mill went beyond
the reasoning in this diagram to argue that if there was still unsatisfied demand in one country for the product of the other then it was very likely that

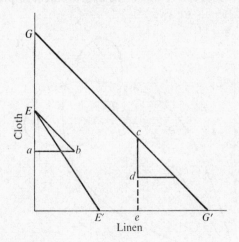

*EE'* is England's price line.
*GG'* is Germany's price line.
England trades at Germany's price ratios, importing *ab* linen in exchange for
*aE* cloth.
Germany however, supplements its cloth imports *cd* (=*aE*) with home produc-
tion of *de*.
England specializes completely, Germany does not.

FIGURE 21

the producer of the product in demand would transfer extra resources into
that product by adding to its range of imports and thus freeing resources
for exports. But if this happened it was no longer necessary that the terms
of trade should settle at the limiting ratio of the country with larger demand
as the extra (freed) resources might be more than enough to satisfy the
previously unsatisfied demand at those terms of trade and so the extra
supply of the export commodity would move the terms of trade back against
the smaller country.

Mill also faced, though he did not solve, the problem of the relationship
between reciprocal demand, and internal demand and production conditions.[63] This was only clarified roughly a century later by Meade as a result
of criticism by F. D. Graham.[64] Mill made his effort in Section 7 of his
chapter which was entitled 'International values depend not solely on the

quantities demanded, but also on the means of production available in each country for the supply of foreign markets'. Although it is possible to interpret his Section 7 as an exercise in non-linear programming, as has been done in a brilliant article by J. S. Chipman, the judgement of Edgeworth, that this last part of the chapter adds very little to the argument, seems to be essentially correct[65] as regards this section. For Mill found it necessary to make assumptions about demand in the section which are so stringent that they robbed the conclusions of interest.

One final matter may be dealt with in this part of the discussion: the exact concept of the terms of trade which the Classical economists used. Now there are of course very many concepts of the terms of trade, and these have been clarified by such writers as Taussig and Viner. The two which are found most commonly in the Classical writings are the gross barter terms of trade and the single factoral. The former may be written

$\frac{Qx_1}{Qm_1} : \frac{Qx_0}{Qm_0}$. These simply relate the quantity of exports and imports in period 0 and period 1. The single factoral terms of trade represent the rate of exchange between a country's factor services and imported goods. As written by Viner,[66] who was clarifying the Classical literature, they are

$$Tc, f = \frac{\dfrac{eP_1}{eP_0}}{\dfrac{iP_1}{iP_0}} \cdot \frac{eF_0}{eF_1}$$

where $e$ represents exports, $i$ represents imports, $P$ represents prices, subscripts 1 and 0 refer to years 1 and 0, and $\frac{eF_0}{eF_1}$ represents the reciprocal of the index of factor cost per unit of exports. $Tc, f$ thus represents the index of the physical amounts of foreign goods obtained per unit of factor cost. These were not the only concepts of the terms of trade which the Classical economists used. They also used the double factoral terms of trade (in which the exchange of factor services in both countries is taken into account) and sometimes tended to equate these with the gross barter terms—which, as Viner pointed out, would only be correct under conditions of constant costs and historically stable costs.[67]

## iv. TRADE POLICY

The *Wealth of Nations* was, as already noted, the *locus classicus* of the free-trade case. There can indeed be no doubt that the Classical economists took their cue from this, and that they were basically free traders.[68] In the *Wealth of Nations* the pursuit of self (and hence community) interest implied the removal of import duties to allow purchases to be made in the cheapest market. The knowledge of individuals of self (and community) interest might be imperfect but the State's knowledge was even more imperfect. Protection was either useless or distorting; it removed the dynamic stimulation of trade, and it greatly increased economic fluctuations especially those stemming from over-investment and over-entry. It was also productive of smuggling and corruption. It distorted the allocation of resources in the interests of particular lobbies who had political power. The spinners, who were poor, did not obtain protection; while the rich weavers were able to obtain protection. The costs of transport provided a sufficient natural protection without there being any necessity of adding to this through import duties. The Classical economists condemned not only import duties but also bounties, as distortions of the pattern of trade.[69] This was the Classical heritage; and its impact can clearly be seen in the writings of major neo-Classical writers such as Marshall and Edgeworth.[70]

It is true that the Classical writers did recognize a number of exceptions to the free-trade case. Import duties levied for defensive purposes were allowed, and drawbacks were entirely satisfactory—indeed if they were not allowed there would be distortion of the price mechanism. The exceptions which the Classical writers were prepared to allow beyond these however varied somewhat. In the case of McCulloch, import duties of 12, 15, or even 25 per cent were permissible when imposed for revenue purposes—he recognized, like Smith, that the protective and revenue effects of duties were maximized at different levels.[71] The protective effect should be balanced by the levying of excise duties at home. Disproportionate taxation of any branch of industry at home provided a case for protection, and over-enthusiastic removal of import duties involved reliance upon duties on basic foodstuffs as a source of revenue, thus having a regressive effect. McCulloch was also prepared to allow the levying of export duties as admissible if there was no competing source of supply. But some other Classical writers were not prepared to go so far. Thus J. S. Mill did not agree that it was permissible to levy revenue tariffs to any marked extent; and he objected to export duties that their incidence was uncertain when account was taken of elasticities, and objected also that they offended international morality.[72] However both Mill and McCulloch grudgingly, and somewhat erratically, conceded that there might sometimes be some sense in the infant-industry argument—although Smith had made the point that even if the infant industry ultimately grew up, the gain from this might still not be sufficient to offset the loss of growth of the capital stock during the protected interim.[73]

But with these few exceptions the Classical economists were free traders: and they believed that free trade should be adopted on a unilateral basis. They were opposed to commercial treaties which, they argued, involved distorting preferences which injured the country and constrained it unnecessarily, and they expressed opposition to the Methuen treaty with Portugal from the time of Smith onwards.[74] They felt able to do this because, neglectful in this context of terms of trade considerations, they were able to advance a series of reasons why trade automatically balanced. The reasons they gave included the price-specie-flow mechanism, as well as a supposed institutional peculiarity of trade whereby exporters spent the proceeds of their sales in a foreign country bringing back their purchases as imports, and an implied demand transfer—an increase in the imports of one country involved payment to the exporting country, which involved in turn an increase in the exporting country's ability to command imports. McCulloch in particular used all these arguments.[75] They believed that protective measures were likely to provoke retaliation; that tariffs would rebound. In general they accepted Adam Smith's view that a posture of demanding reciprocity in freedom of trade could only be justified if there was a *good* chance of persuading other countries of the wisdom of lowering their duties.[76]

It is against this background that Robert Torrens's trenchantly proclaimed belief that, because of the effects on the terms of trade, free trade should only be adopted on the basis of reciprocity, has to be seen—particularly as Torrens was himself a former opponent of reciprocity.[77]

The roots of Torrens's case go back to Chs. 7 and 25 of Ricardo's *Principles*. In these Ricardo had shown how taxes or bounties altered the distribution of the precious metals thus affecting the relative price levels in different countries.[78]

As finally presented by Torrens, the argument involved the following propositions.

*First*,—When commercial countries receive the productions of each other duty free, then (the efficacy of labour being the same in each) the precious metals will be distributed amongst them in equal proportions, and the general scale of prices will be the same in each.

*Second*,—When any particular country imposes import duties upon the productions of other countries, while those other countries continue to receive her products duty free, then such particular country draws to herself a larger proportion of the precious metals, maintains a higher rate of general prices than her neighbours, and obtains, in exchange for the produce of a given quantity of her labour, the produce of a greater quantity of foreign labour.

*Third*,—When any country is deprived of that command ever [*sic*] the precious metals which is due to the efficacy of her labour in producing articles for the foreign market, by the hostile tariffs of other countries, she may recover her due command over the metals, by imposing retaliatory and equivalent duties upon the importation of the productions of the countries by which the hostile tariffs are maintained.

*Fourth*,—When, from foreign rivalry and hostile tariffs, a country begins to lose a portion of her former command over the precious metals, and to experience a contraction of the currency, a fall in prices, in profits, and in wages, and a falling off in the revenue, then, the lowering of import duties upon the productions of countries retaining their hostile tariffs, instead of affording relief, would aggravate the general distress, by occasioning a more rapid abstraction of the metals, and a deeper decline in prices, in profits, in wages, and in the revenue, accompanied not by a diminution but by an increase in the real extent of taxation.[79]

Torrens was not advocating wholesale imposition of import duties; they should not be levied on raw materials or wage goods because this would raise the cost of production and affect a country's comparative advantage, thus cancelling out to some extent the increased command over the precious metals from the imposition of duties.[80] But on other products Torrens was advocating the imposition of duties with the aim of creating an Imperial Zollverein.

By extending our colonial system, and opening new and expanding markets in our trans-marine dependencies, coupled with the rigid enforcement of the principle of reciprocity, we may arm ourselves with accumulating force to break down hostile tariffs, and to establish free trade throughout the world.[81]

Now in fact Torrens's thesis, that by the imposition of import duties the terms of trade could be turned in our favour (and that the unilateral removal of such duties turned the terms of trade against us) has three different facets. Firstly, the presentation can be regarded in purely barter terms— as Overstone put it, 'Import duties by A diminish demand for produce of B—therefore lower its price. Retaliatory duties by B diminish the supply of B's produce to A, and therefore restore the prices.'[82] Now in fact Torrens did put the argument this way in one of its main statements[83] and what is involved may be seen from Fig. 22. The imposition of an import duty by Cuba shifts the Cuban offer curve to $OC''$ and worsens the terms of trade for England from $OT$ to $OT'$. The tariff shown here is an *ad valorem* tariff levied in terms of sugar and amounting to $A\ B$ at the new equilibrium terms of trade.

But the same argument can be put in money terms: and this is how Torrens, almost certainly following Ricardo, originally put it.[84] The imposition of a duty by one country causes it to run a balance-of-payments surplus resulting in a metal inflow which produces a higher level of general prices in that country. Its exports are now relatively more expensive, having risen with the general price level, in relation to its imports which have fallen in value because of the outflow of metal from the country on whose produce the duty is imposed.

But this in turn has an aspect which is very important, and it is one which should never be forgotten given Torrens's original background as an anti-Bullionist and inflationist. The loss of precious metal involved deflation in the country discriminated against, and this deflation would increase the weight of fixed burdens. Such a process would, Torrens argued, cause severe economic depression.

*Previous* to the contraction of existing pecuniary engagements, it would have been of little or no consequence at what point the value of money might have settled—a more abundant supply of gold and silver would have rendered prices higher, and a less abundant supply would have rendered them lower; but, in either case, the same quantity of other commodities would have been produced and exchanged, and the real reward of producers and dealers would have remained unaltered. But to infer from this, that *after liabilities have been con-*

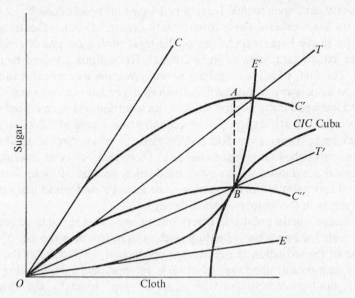

Cuba levies a tariff of 100 per cent on English cloth. The tariff is paid in sugar.
The Cuban offer curve then moves from *OC'* to *OC''*.
The terms of trade move from *OT* to *OT'*, against England, and *AB* is the amount of the tariff.
The 100 per cent tariff is optimal in this case; for the community indifference curve for Cuba is the highest that can be reached.

FIGURE 22

*tracted, and while they continue to be pending,* changes in the distribution and the value of the precious metals are of little practical importance, would be to fall into an error of the most dangerous tendency. A slight examination is sufficient to show that, in any industrious community, burthened with debt, a rise in the value of money is one of the greatest evils which can occur.

Even in these branches of manufacture and trade, in which the process of bringing commodities to market is the shortest, and the returns the quickest, a rise in the value of money, during the period between the first production and the final sale, may diminish profit or perhaps occasion loss. When the process of production is a protracted one, an intermediate fall of price is proportionably more injurious. In agriculture, in which there are annual and rotation crops, and leases running for a term of years, a continuous fall in the markets, occasioned by a rise in the value of money, is destructive, not only of profit but of capital. The ruin which such a fall in prices has wrought in the agricultural districts is unfortunately too generally known to require illustration.[85]

Given the background noted at the beginning of this section, it was not surprising that the Classical economists should react pretty sharply at what was argued by Torrens. Criticism came from Peronnet Thompson and from Herman Merivale. But neither was particularly damaging, although the latter did begin to show some of the limitations of the two country two commodity case upon which Torrens had based his conclusions.[86]

But the main critique came from Nassau Senior.[87] It was a theatrical performance in the highest traditions of the legal profession and it reads like a rather extravagant submission by counsel. His critique involved two main points. The first, which was entirely wrong given the theoretical framework which he held, was that international values depended not upon supply and demand but upon costs of production[88]—an assertion which could only have been accepted at the expense of abandoning the whole of Classical international trade theory from Ricardo onwards to which Senior, unlike McCulloch, subscribed. Torrens was able to show that prices in international trade could not depend upon cost of production because of factor immobility;[89] and this point is worth stressing since Senior's contention has surfaced subsequently in the history of trade theory.[90]

But Senior's main point was a very telling one—that the gain of precious metals from the imposition of a duty might well be less than the loss of metal because of the reduction in the average productivity of factors in the home country, consequent upon the reduction in international specialization.[91] For Torrens (and practically everyone else) accepted basically the thesis of Senior's *Lectures on the Cost of Obtaining Money* that command over the precious metals depended on the productivity of resources. As Torrens himself put it,

in England the labour and abstinence of 200 produce 300 bales of manufactured goods, which, in the markets of the world, exchange for 300 ounces of gold; in Cuba, the labour and abstinence of 300, raises 300 casks of tropical produce, which also command 300 ounces of gold in the markets of the world.[92]

Now in terms of Torrens's 'two country two commodity' model this was not a serious problem, because *both* countries lost by the reduction in specialization. But in the wider context, where one country imposed a duty on the products of another, but both obtained metal from other (mining) countries and from trade with the rest of the world, it was a perfectly valid point. Perhaps this is why Torrens carefully evaded the issue in his rather astringent reply to Senior, by concentrating on his own admission that raw materials should not be dutied, and on the Whigs' failure to repeal the Corn Laws.[93] He had earlier avoided this issue by using examples which concentrated on large differences in absolute advantage and so did not involve changes in the sources of supply of the traded goods after the imposition of the duty.[94] But, as Senior pointed out, the loss of efficiency by the dutying country would put it at a disadvantage compared with the other country in third markets.[95]

Senior also made other points. He attempted to use his cost-of-production theory of the *value* of the precious metals[96] to refute Torrens's use of the Ricardian theory of the *distribution* of the metals.[97] Obviously this was invalid. He also argued that in a multi-commodity case the terms of trade would turn much less than supposed by Torrens because of a switch to other exports than the one discriminated against.[98] These other exports would then be sold in third markets. This was a perfectly fair point; but Senior seemed to think that, by showing that the possibility of a change in the trading pattern existed, he had banished the adverse effect on the terms of trade instead of merely minimizing it. Torrens in his reply was thus able to show, with some glee, that a worsening of the terms of trade was involved in this readjustment, and to avoid the issue of the extent of this worsening.

Other writers were also critical of Torrens. J. S. Mill, while he accepted the reasoning of Torrens's case, made the points firstly that retaliation to duties was likely, secondly that the behaviour of a country which imposed a duty in order to obtain a terms of trade advantage was unjust, and thirdly that there was a loss involved in such conduct to the whole world and that the gain of one country was not greater than the concomitant loss.[99]

But perhaps the most telling critique came from George Warde Norman, a critique developed in consultation with Overstone.[100] Unfortunately Norman was too diffident to publish his main attack[101] for many years. But it was a comprehensive and damaging critique. He pointed out that Torrens had assumed constant outlay (i.e. an elasticity of demand equal to one) in the two countries in his hypothetical example. Norman showed that if this assumption was relaxed then it was quite likely that the terms of trade would turn only partially in the direction indicated by Torrens, and part of the burden of the duty would be borne by the consumer in the country imposing that duty.[102] Norman's analysis is particularly noteworthy here since it was written before J. S. Mill published his analysis of reciprocal demand. He also dwelt at some length on the illegitimacy of assuming only two countries, England and 'Cuba', the latter being taken by Torrens to represent all the other countries with which England traded.[103] It was impossible to assume that all the other countries in the world would combine against England as required by Torrens's example. Taking an alternative example of England and Germany, where each represented only part of world trade, he concluded that the loss of the dutying country in third markets, following the initial metal flow to it, would be greater than the loss of the country whose exports had originally been the subject of duty.

*Pari passu* and in exact proportion to the discouragement of importation from the country whose goods are exposed to the increased tax, will be the discouragement of exportation to all countries whatever. The precious metals will flow out as long as and as fast as they flow in, the eflux will only cease with the influx. No permanent rise of general prices will occur, and the final result of the change will be a state of things exhibiting the great and most important truth, that it is not fiscal regulations, but the real efficiency of their respective industry, which ever has, and always must regulate the interchange of commodities between nation and nation, and between each nation and the world.[104]

Norman also made the important point that the larger part of our imports were of raw materials and semi-manufactures.[105] It was not possible to obtain these cheaper by turning the terms of trade in our favour through the levying of duties on luxuries, because of the relative important of the two categories. Moreover the luxuries came from colonies[106] with which Torrens thought we should in any case have free trade in order to achieve the goal of the Imperial Zollverein. In addition Norman was able to argue that dutying such articles as sugar and tea would have a regressive effect and injure the working classes,[107] about whose welfare Torrens professed to be concerned—he had argued that their wages had been depressed by the unilateral remission of duties. Norman himself was very doubtful indeed that there was evidence either from historical experience or contemporary England for the truth of this assertion; and he argued that, since all the evidence pointed in the opposite direction, the onus was upon Torrens to substantiate his belief.[108] He was able to point too to a very considerable ambiguity in Torrens's attitude towards the levying of duties upon imported wage goods.[109] This was not unimportant not only from the point of view of the labourer's welfare but also because of the effect on a country's competitive position of raising the cost of wage goods. (The implication of the Ricardian inverse movement of wages and profits for trading patterns has been discussed above.)

Apart from all these difficulties Norman was able to point to other and more practical difficulties. He pointed out that the logic of Torrens's case was that we should levy not equal duties but higher duties than those levied by other countries, in order to turn the terms of trade in our favour.[110] But this in turn intensified the very real danger lying behind adoption of Torrens's proposals that a tariff war would result, from which all countries would suffer.[111] There was also the fact that many items in the balance of payments came under the heading of invisibles and could not be subject to duties.[112] There was a practical limit to the duties which could be levied on imported commodities before smuggling became a real problem.[113] Finally there was the point, which today appears minor but which to nineteenth-century writers was not insignificant, that protection imposed or retained by the wealthiest country in the world would mislead other countries as to the source of our wealth and thus hinder the adoption of international freedom of trade.[114]

In addition there were a number of other criticisms which could have been made. Thus for instance the concept of the optimum tariff enables us to see that, even if the whole framework of Torrens's analysis is accepted, there is a limit to the gains to be made from improving the terms of trade. We can see this referring back to Fig. 22—although it should be emphasized again that use of the community indifference curves does involve the difficulty that a change in the terms of trade will change income distribution and hence the community indifference map—and, since Pearce has shown that the Samuelson–Stolper theorem is a special case,[115] the change in the direction of income distribution is unpredictable. The idea of an optimum tariff is none the less perfectly valid; but the exact form of the relationship is very far from clear; and thus the whole relationship between the terms of trade and welfare is hardly unambiguous, even though Torrens clearly implied that it was. Other Classical writers were much more reluctant to make such clear presumptions.

Another point neglected by Torrens is that of secondary (multiplier) income effects. Torrens simply assumed that money income varied directly with changes in the stock of metal. However, expansion on a multiplier basis in the country receiving metal might have raised demand for the exports of the country losing metal, and so have offset to some extent the deterioration in the terms of trade of the country which was losing metal.

Yet for all this Torrens may be said to have had the last laugh. For trade negotiations are now uniformly conducted on the basis of reciprocity, even if this owes more to the modern counterpart of Torrens's fear of metallic deflation—the need to deflate under a regime of fixed exchange rates to maintain payments balance—than it does to considerations of the terms of trade and welfare.

## V. THE TRANSFER PROBLEM

One final problem which received quite a lot of attention in the Classical literature it is necessary to explore here, particularly as the extent of the Classical contribution has been seriously underestimated until relatively recent times. This is the 'transfer problem'—the analysis of the mechanism by which unilateral payments, outside the normal run of trade payments, are made from one country to another.

The problem is quite simply this. In order for such a payment to be made, the payer has to generate an export surplus so that the money payment is transformed into a payment in real resources. Now there are basically three mechanisms by which such a transfer can be made and a surplus generated. The first is the price mechanism. Under a gold-standard system this will involve metal flowing from the country which is making the payment to the country which is receiving it. This will raise prices in the latter and lower them in the former. This makes exports from the payer to the receiver more attractive and increases their amount. The price mechanism of transfer will also operate under a paper-standard system where the exchange rate is free;

making of the transfer payment will involve sale of the currency (or bills of exchange) of the paying country in the foreign exchange market thus depressing the exchange rate of that country; as the free rate moves downwards the attractiveness of the country's exports increases.

The second mechanism by which a transfer may be made in real terms is through a transfer of demand. What we find now in a typical neo-Classical textbook is this. The payment by one country to another increases the purchasing power in the recipient country and lowers it in the paying country by the amount of the transfer. In the two-country case the transfer will be effected in this way if the sum of the marginal propensities to import for the two countries is equal to one. Thus suppose that a transfer of £100 million is made from country $A$ to country $B$. If country $B$ has a marginal propensity to import of 0·5 then its imports will rise by £50 million. If country $A$ also has a marginal propensity to import of 0·5 its imports will *fall* by £50 million. The total change in the trade balance will then just be equal to the amount of the transfer.

In fact, as writers in the 1920s and 1930s established, this is a very simplified view of demand transfer. As Viner argued in *Canada's Balance*[116] there is not only the question of how far the receipts by $B$ of the transfer from $A$ are spent upon imports from $A$ but also the question of how far those receipts are spent upon country $B$'s exportables, thereby lowering $B$'s exports. He later recognized that even where some of the transfer is spent on domestic commodities this, in the full employment case, would help to make the transfer by withdrawing resources from export industries. In addition Taussig pointed out that this rise in the price of resources and in the price of domestic commodities will increase the attractiveness of imports so increasing their amount.[117] Taking all these elements together it is clear that the demand mechanism will be a powerful one in making the transfer even though, when we move outside the two country model, we have to recognize that an increase in demand for imports will be spread over many countries so that, at least in the short run, some price effect is also likely to be necessary and the terms of trade will have to turn against the paying country.

The third mechanism in the making of a transfer is the income adjustment. This is an extension of the demand transfer where we allow income in the paying and the receiving countries to change by more than the amount of the transfer. Thus if we write[118]

$$B_A = M_B - M_A$$

we are saying that the balance of trade of the paying country $A$ is equal to the difference between her exports ($B$'s imports) and her own imports. If we then write $Y_A$, $Y_B$ for disposable income in the two countries we can write the change in the trade balance of country $A$ as

$$dB_A = \frac{dM_B}{dY_B}\frac{dY_B}{dT}dT - \frac{dM_A}{dY_A}\frac{dY_A}{dT}dT$$

From this we can see that the demand transfer where the sum of the marginal propensities was equal to one was a special case of this formulation where

$$\frac{dY_B}{dT} = 1 \text{ and } \frac{dY_A}{dT} = -1$$

for if that is the case then the requirement becomes

$$dB_A = \left(\frac{dM_B}{dY_B} + \frac{dM_A}{dY_A}\right)dT = (MPM_A + MPM_B)dT$$

so that if

$$MPM_A + MPM_B = 1$$

then

$$dB_A = dT$$

and so the paying country generates an export surplus sufficient to make the transfer. Obviously if

$$\frac{dY_B}{dT} > 1, \frac{dY_A}{dT} < -1$$

it will not be necessary that the sum of the marginal propensities is equal to one.[119] Again however the caveat must be entered that we are dealing here with a two-country case and that, in the short term at least, the transfer is less likely to be effected in a multi-country case.

Having examined the three main mechanisms by which a transfer is effected, we can now look at the Classical literature. What we in fact discover is that all these three mechanisms are to be found therein. Both forms of the first method are present. Malthus and Thornton offer a version of the price-specie-flow mechanism. In their case a transfer payment will necessitate an outflow of gold which, via the quantity theory, will alter relative price levels and so generate an export surplus for the paying country.[120] (Ricardo avoided the central problem of a transfer—the generation of an export surplus. We find him advancing the slightly curious 'redundancy of currency' argument, in the case of harvest failure. His thesis was that following harvest failure there would be fewer goods but the same amount of currency some of which would therefore be redundant. Some gold would then be exported. This was not a very happy argument; it neglected the effect on the demand for money of the rise in corn prices following harvest failure, and it treated commodities as a stock rather than a flow. The Thornton–Malthus mechanism was different from this, as Viner has pointed out.[121] The Ricardian view was of gold leaving the country to restore international price levels to their original relationship while the other view saw the metal flow as altering relative price levels to generate an export surplus—Ricardo remaining vague on this last point.)[122] But at least there can be no dispute that Classical economics did contain the price mechanism, in its gold-standard form, for the making of a transfer.

It is interesting to find that it also contained the price mechanism in its free-exchange-rate form. This is to be found in the work of William Blake whose concept of the self-correcting real exchange has already been noted in Chapter 6. This mechanism was also recognized by McCulloch.[123]

The idea of demand transfer is also to be found in the Classical writers. It is present in the work of McCulloch in his treatment of the problem of Irish absenteeism,[124] and it is in this latter connection that most of the Classical demand-transfer analysis was developed. It stems from the writings of J. L. Foster and of Sir Henry Parnell.[125] The way in which these writers approached the problem was to satisfy themselves that there was not sufficient specie in Ireland to make remittances of rent to absentee landlords, so that the gold-standard form of price transfer could not operate; while, with the exchange rate fixed in terms of gold, the free-exchange-rate form of the price transfer could not operate either. There must, therefore, they argued, be a transfer of demand, which enabled Ireland to generate a sufficient export surplus to make the transfer in real terms.

Because the Classical writers lacked the multiplier concept, treatment of the income-adjustment mechanism of transfer is not always easy to distinguish in the Classical literature from straightforward transfer of demand. But it is arguably present in the work of Wheatley[126] and a good case can certainly be made out for Longfield having recognized this mechanism[127]—although it should be emphasized that, because he did not confine himself to a two-country case, Longfield was sceptical about the power of demand and income adjustments to make a transfer without assistance from the terms of trade.

vi. CONCLUSION

It is to be hoped that this survey of Classical international-trade theory will have done something towards showing the reader the extent and complexity of the theory. The achievement of the Classical economists in this field was an enormous one, and this should be recognized; for the international-trade theory which today's student learns is drawn almost in its entirety from this Classical literature. But perusal of this chapter should suggest a lesson in this connection. For there are many elements in Classical trade theory, particularly in its interconnection with its growth and development, which have been almost entirely neglected in the modern treatments of that theory. Concentration upon the results of static reasoning, upon theorems which lend themselves to neat geometrical exposition, has led to the neglect of much that was valuable in the Classical literature. It has been left to recent writers to rediscover paths which could have been followed directly from the Classical heritage had not parts of that heritage been neglected.

## NOTES

1. See the article by Bloomfield referred to in the bibliography to this chapter.
2. Sir Dudley North, *Discourses upon Trade* (1691).
3. *Wealth of Nations*, ed. Cannan, i. 422.
4. See D. P. O'Brien, *J. R. McCulloch*, pp. 191–6.
5. *Wealth of Nations*, i. 341, 345, 352–3, 413.
6. See O'Brien, op. cit., pp. 197–204.
7. *Principles*, ed. Ashley, p. 577.
8. This was also true of McCulloch. See O'Brien, op. cit., p. 197—without diminishing marginal utility the argument was unsatisfactory.
9. Smith believed that a high rate of profit in foreign trade raised general profit, a contention which Ricardo (*Principles*, Ch. VII) later rejected on the basis of the corn model. Smith also has a rather curious argument about the respective effects on the level of domestic activity of the home and foreign trade (op. cit., i. 348, 419–20).
10. See I. Kravis, 'Availability and other influences on the commodity composition of trade', *Journal of Political Economy*, 64 (1956), 143–55.
11. Ricardo, *Principles, Works*, ed. Sraffa, i. 135–6.
12. G. Harberler, *Theory of International Trade* (London, 1936), p. 129.
13. J. S. Mill, *Principles*, p. 574.
14. Ibid., p. 575.
15. Ricardo, *Principles*, pp. 133, 134–5, 135–6.
16. Viner, *Studies*, p. 440.
17. Robert Torrens, *An Essay on the External Corn Trade* (1st edn. London, 1815), pp. 263–5.
18. This is pointed out by J. S. Chipman in the article cited in the bibliography to this chapter, p. 480.
19. Torrens's development of the idea is traced in Lord Robbins, *Robert Torrens*, pp. 21–35.
20. Mill, *Principles*, p. 576.
21. In this connection the contrast between the treatment in the 1st edn. of Torrens's *Essay* and that in the 5th (1829) edn., pp. 401–7, is striking. The latter is far clearer.
22. i. 422, second paragraph.
23. e.g. *The Budget* (London, 1844), p. 48.
24. *Principles*, p. 138.
25. Ibid., pp. 139–40.
26. e.g. J. S. Mill, *Principles*, p. 577; see also the passage from Torrens's *Essay* (4th edn.), pp. 402–3, cited in Lord Robbins, *Torrens*, p. 24.
27. See the excellent diagram in R. Findlay, *Trade and Specialisation* (London, 1970), p. 110.
28. On the differences between them see the discussion in Viner, *Studies*, Ch. IX.
29. See e.g. J. S. Mill, *Principles*, pp. 684–5.
30. Haberler, op. cit., Ch. IX; W. Leontief, 'The Use of Indifference Curves in the Analysis of Foreign Trade', *Quarterly Journal of Economics*, 47 (1933), 493–503.
31. See O'Brien, *J. R. McCulloch*, Ch. viii.
32. *Principles*, p. 141.
33. M. Longfield, *Lectures on Commerce and Absenteeism*, repr. in *Economic Writings*, ed. R. D. C. Black, pp. 50–6, 63–4, 69–70.
34. The table in this form derives from that in the book by B. Sodersten cited in the bibliography, p. 20. But the original treatment was by Edgeworth—*Collected Economics Papers*, ii. 52–8, and this was further developed by Viner, *Studies*, pp.

458–62. The treatment can be extended to trade between more than two countries—ibid., pp. 462–7.

35. Cf. H. G. Johnson's 1968 Wicksell Lectures cited in the bibliography to this chapter, p. 8.

36. See especially his *Letters on Commercial Policy* of 1832–3, pp. 36–8, 40–1, 42.

37. Cf. Johnson, op. cit., pp. 8–9 who refers to 'The more ambitious contemporary Heckscher–Ohlin model (not to be identified with Ohlin's original *Theory of Inter-regional and International Trade*)'.

38. *Leading Principles* (1874), pp. 119–20. See also Viner, *Studies*, pp. 500–7.

39. *Lectures on Commerce and Absenteeism*, pp. 57 ff.

40. See especially J. Vanek, *The Natural Resource Content of United States Foreign Trade 1870–1955* (Cambridge, Mass., 1963).

41. Johnson, op. cit., pp. 21, 25–7.

42. There is strictly some ambiguity in the meaning of such an equal division—see Chipman, op. cit., p. 482.

43. He corrected this in the 3rd edn. References on the debate which resulted in correction of the error are given in Viner, *Studies*, pp. 444–6.

44. Op. cit., pp. 99–100.

45. See the discussion in Lord Robbins, *Torrens*, pp. 27–30.

46. *Letters on Commercial Policy*, pp. 17, 26.

47. N. W. Senior, *Three Lectures on the Cost of Obtaining Money* (London, 1830), Lecture I, pp. 1–35.

48. J. Pennington, *A Letter to Kirkman Findlay*, (London, 1840), pp. 32–41. But J. S. Mill had arrived at the same idea independently though he did not publish it till later. See his *Essays*, p. 12, and his *Principles*, p. 587, which quotes from the *Essays*.

49. This seems an indisputable judgement. See Edgeworth, op. cit., ii. 7, 10, 20, and Viner, *Studies*, p. 535.

50. *Essay* I, *Principles*, Bk. III, Ch. xviii.

51. *Principles*, pp. 448, 592.

52. Ibid., pp. 592–3.

53. See Viner, *Studies*, pp. 589–90, for criticism of this approach which stems from Cunynghame and Barone.

54. At this point total outlay becomes constant. See M. Blaug, *Economic Theory in Retrospect*, 1st edn., pp. 189–90, for an excellent formal treatment of the elasticity of the offer curves. It should be noted in relation to Fig. 18a that where offer curves are parallel so that *at given outlays* they have the same slope the outer curve will have the greater elasticity.

55. Mill, *Principles*, p. 591.

56. Ibid., especially pp. 590–3.

57. Ibid., pp. 593–6.

58. This Section 6, pp. 596–7 of Mill's chapter, was for long underrated even by Edgeworth.

59. Ibid., p. 679.

60. Ibid., pp. 593–6. *Studies*. See Viner, pp. 537–41, and Blaug, *Economic Theory in Retrospect*, p. 190 for alternative diagrammatic treatments of the argument.

61. Edgeworth, op. cit., ii. 10.

62. Mill, *Principles*, p. 601 n.

63. Ibid., pp. 597–604.

64. Graham's criticism is to be found in 'The Theory of International Values Re-examined' and 'The Theory of International Values', *Quarterly Journal of Economics*, 38 and 46 (1923 and 1932), 54–86, 581–616. It was subjected to stern criticism by Viner, *Studies*, pp. 548–55. Meade's solution appeared in his *Geometry of International Trade* (London, 1952), Ch. ii, and it has now been incorporated into the neo-Classical textbooks.

65. Chipman, op. cit., pp. 483–91; Edgeworth, op. cit., ii. 22.

66. *Studies*, p. 559.

67. See the discussion, ibid., pp. 558–64.

68. See especially *Wealth of Nations*, Bk. IV, Chs. iii, iv, and viii. See also Ricardo, *Principles*, Ch. 22.

69. See O'Brien, *J. R. McCulloch*, pp. 217–23.

70. See especially Edgeworth, op. cit., ii. 18.

71. See O'Brien, op. cit., pp. 223–7. See also Smith, op. cit., i. 427, 429, 436, and Bk. IV, Ch. iv, *passim*.

72. Mill, *Principles*, pp. 850–3, 921–2.

73. Ibid., p. 922, Smith, op. cit., i. 422–3, O'Brien, *J. R. McCulloch*, p. 221.

74. Smith, op. cit., Bk. IV, Ch. vi.

75. See O'Brien, *J. R. McCulloch*, pp. 204–8.

76. See op. cit., i. 431–3; O'Brien, op. cit., p. 219.

77. R. Torrens, *An Essay on the Production of Wealth* (London, 1821), pp. 268–72. The tone of this work is undeniably a free-trade one. But by the time of the *Letters on Commercial Policy* (1832–3) Torrens was even prepared to pour scorn, when it suited him, on the whole idea of international specialization (ibid., pp. 50–5).

78. See in particular Ricardo's *Principles*, pp. 141–2, 341–2. See also Letter X of Torrens's *The Budget*, pp. 336–8, for acknowledgment of Ricardo's influence.

79. *The Budget*, pp. 28–9. See also *Letters on Comercial Policy*, p. 6.

80. *Letters*, p. 24.

81. *The Budget*, p. 66.

82. D. P. O'Brien, *The Correspondence of Lord Overstone*, i. 346.

83. Torrens, *Postscript* to Letter IX of *The Budget*, pp. 333 ff.

84. *Letters on Commercial Policy* and *The Budget*, Letters II, III, and X, *passim*.

85. *Letters on Commercial Policy*, pp. 28–9. See also *The Budget*, Letter II, pp. 39–42, and Letter X, p. 388.

86. Their criticisms are discussed in Lord Robbins, op. cit., pp. 207–11.

87. 'Free Trade and Retaliation', *Edinburgh Review*, 88. (July 1843), 1–47.

88. Ibid., pp. 36–7.

89. *The Budget*, Letter X, pp. 346–7.

90. F. D. Graham, *The Theory of International Values* (Princeton, 1948).

91. Senior, op. cit., pp. 12–15, 29–35.

92. *The Budget*, Letter X, p. 352.

93. Ibid., pp. 363–7, 375–93. As Norman was to point out (see below), Torrens's position on the dutying of raw materials was not unambiguous.

94. *The Budget*, Letter II, pp. 37–8.

95. Senior, op. cit., p. 32.

96. See Ch. vi. above.

97. Senior, op. cit., pp. 16–28; Torrens, *The Budget*, Letter X, 335–6.

98. Senior, op. cit., pp. 15–16.

99. See J. S. Mill, *Principles*, pp. 853–4, 856, 919, 925–6.

100. See D. P. O'Brien, *Overstone*, i. 335–6, 345–6.

101. Norman did attack Torrens anonymously in the *Spectator*—see O'Brien, *Overstone*, p. 335 n. But his main assault, a pamphlet entitled *Remarks on the Incidence of Import Duties*, was never published, and not even privately printed until 1860.

102. Ibid., pp. 12–19.

103. Ibid., pp. 19, 20–5, 29–30, 33, 68.

104. Ibid., p. 33.

105. Ibid., pp. 34–6.

106. Ibid., p. 37.

107. Ibid., pp. 37–8.

108. Ibid., pp. 51–7, 58–65.

109. Ibid., pp. 8, 38–9, 39–41, 67.

110. Ibid., p. 28.

111. Ibid., p. 8.

112. Ibid., pp. 43–6.

113. Ibid., pp. 27, 46.

114. Ibid., p. 31.

115. I. F. Pearce, *International Trade* (London, 1970), Ch. 14.
116. *Canada's Balance of International Indebtedness* (Cambridge, Mass., 1924), pp. 204–6; see also *Studies*, pp. 305–6.
117. Viner, p. 305. Viner, who was of course close to Taussig, makes the point more clearly than the latter. See F. Taussig, 'International Freights and Prices', *Quarterly Journal of Economics*, 32 (1918), 410–14.
118. The notation here follows C. E. Staley, *International Economics* (Englewood Cliffs, 1970), pp. 263–5.
119. See the models developed by H. G. Johnson in 'The Transfer Problem and Exchange Stability', *Journal of Political Economy* 64 (1956), 212–25, especially 217–21 and reproduced in *International Trade and Economic Growth* (London, 1958), Ch. vii, and in Staley, op. cit., pp. 266–7.
120. Thornton, *Paper Credit* (McCulloch's edn.), pp. 220–1; Malthus, 'Depreciation of Paper Currency', *Edinburgh Review*, 17 (1811), 339–72, 342–5.
121. Viner, *Canada's Balance*, pp. 195–6; Ricardo, *High Price of Bullion*, in *Works*, iii. 106.
122. See the article by Mason, 'Ricardo and the Transfer Mechanism', cited in the bibliography to this chapter.
123. W. Blake, *Observations on the Effects Produced by the Expenditure Of Government* (London, 1823), pp. 30–32. See O'Brien, op. cit., pp. 208–17, for McCulloch's treatment of the transfer problem.
124. See ibid., pp. 213–14 for McCulloch's treatment of the demand transfer.
125. J. L. Foster, *An Essay on the Principles of Commercial Exchange* (London, 1804); Sir H. Parnell (Baron Congleton), *Principles of Currency and Exchange* (4th edn. London, 1805).
126. J. Wheatley, *An Essay on the Theory of Money*, Part I (London, 1807), pp. 180–1, 219–20, 238.
127. *Lectures on Commerce and Absenteeism*, pp. 84–6 and 110, 'Banking and Currency', pp. 20–1 (both repr. in *Economic Writings*, ed. R. D. C. Black).

# BIBLIOGRAHPY

The great source of eighteenth-century trade theory is Smith's *Wealth of Nations* where the vital links between trade and economic growth are spelt out in an unforgetable manner. See Bk. II, Ch. v, and Bk. IV, Chs. i–viii. See also Malthus's *Principles* (2nd edn., pp. 382–98) where the fundamental link between trade and growth is also stressed. Secondary references which sufficiently recognize this are few: but there is a classic article by H. Myint, 'The "Classical Theory" of International Trade and the Underdeveloped Countries', *Economic Journal*, 68 (1958), 317–37. For McCulloch's treatment of trade in terms of absolute advantage see D. P. O'Brien, *J. R. McCulloch*, pp. 191–7. On the development of the free-trade case prior to Smith see Viner, Ch. 2, and A. I. Bloomfield, 'The Foreign-Trade Doctrines of the Physiocrats', *American Economic Review*, 28 (1938), 716–35.

The literature on comprehensive advantage is, by contrast, massive. Expositions of basic ideas are to be found in G. Haberler's elderly but still-valuable text book *The Theory of International Trade*, trans. A. W. Stonier and F. Benham (London, 1936), and in such excellent neo-Classical textbooks as C. P. Kindleberger, *International Economics* (Homewood, Ill., 1963), R. H. Heller, *International Trade* (London, 1968), C. E. Staley, *International Economics* (London, 1970), and B. Södersten, *International Economics* (London, 1971). See also the excellent Penguin by R. Findlay, *Trade and Specialisation* (1970). But these modern discussions have greatly narrowed and aridified the original Classical conception of comparative advantage. For some indication of what can be gained by returning to the older approach see H. G. Johnson's brilliant 1968 Wicksell Lectures, *Comparative Cost and Commercial Policy Theory for a Developing World Economy* (Stockholm, 1968). There are two superb surveys of the literature on the subject: Chs. VIII and IX of Viner, *Studies*, and John S. Chipman,

'A Survey of the Theory of International Trade: Pt. 1, The Classical Theory', *Econometrica*, 33 (1965), 477–519. The great source for comparative cost in the Classical literature is Ch. VII of Ricardo's *Principles*. The logical implications for international balance of Ricardo's chapter are spelled out in K. Kojima, 'Ricardo's Theory of International Balance of Payments Equilibrium', *Annals of the Hitotsubashi Academy*, 2 (1951), 76–92. But for the *origin* of the doctrine see the debate between Seligman and J. H. Hollander (references are in Viner, *Studies*, pp. 441–4) and the balanced evaluation in Lord Robbins, *Robert Torrens*, pp. 31–5.

The later treatments of comparative advantage can best be studied through the writings of J. S. Mill, whose work in any case is essential reading for its treatment of reciprocal demand. See the first of his *Essays on Some Unsettled Questions of Political Economy* written in 1829–30, and first published in 1844. This, together with Bk. III, Chs. 2, 17, 18 (this especially) 20, 21, 22, and 25 of his *Principles* should banish any doubts about the contribution of J. S. Mill to economic theory. See also M. Longfield's *Lectures on Commerce and Absenteeism* in *Economic Writings*, ed. R. D. C. Black. Longfield came closer to appreciating the importance of demand in international trade than anyone except Mill and Torrens: yet there is an enormous gap between his exposition and that of Mill. Torrens came much closer however: and the 4th edn. of his *Essay on the External Corn Trade* shows that he stands almost with Mill. Their arguments are however much better appreciated in terms of offer curves which they did not use: these are to be found in any of the neo-Classical texts cited above, but Edgeworth's treatment in his *Papers Relating to Political Economy* (London, 1925), ii. 3–60, is sometimes illuminating both in relation to this and to other matters discussed in the chapter. See also M. Blaug, *Economic Theory in Retrospect*, pp. 189–90 for an excellent demonstration of the elasticity of the offer curve.

The best way to approach Classical trade-policy theory, *given* digestion of the material in the *Wealth of Nations* already referred to, is to start with Chs. 7 and 22 of Ricardo's *Principles*. Then proceed through Torrens's *Essay on the Production of Wealth*, pp. 251–88, following that with the same author's *Letters on Commercial Policy*, and Letters II, III, and IX (Postscript only) of *The Budget*. *Then* read Senior's *Edinburgh Review* attack ('Free Trade and Retaliation' Vol. 88, 1843) before moving on to Torrens's reply to Senior in Letter X of *The Budget*: and follow that with G. W. Norman's *Remarks on the Incidence of Import Duties*. Unfortunately this last work is very rare, never having been published but having been privately printed in 1860, long after it was written. See also J. S. Mill's *Principles*, Bk. V, Ch. 4 (S6) and Ch. 10. All this may however prove a little indigestible to the non-specialist: and there is a splendid account of the debate in Lord Robbins, *Robert Torrens*, Ch. VII. See also D. P. O'Brien, *J. R. McCulloch*, pp. 217–26 and M. E. A. Bowley, *Nassau Senior*, Ch. 6. The latter contains a more sympathetic account of Senior's role in the controversy.

The primary literature on the transfer problem is scattered indeed. This is because the Classical economists addressed themselves not to the analytical problem in the abstract, but to concrete problems such as Irish absenteeism, harvest failure, and foreign wars. Fortunately there are some excellent surveys. See in particular Viner, *Studies*, Ch. VI, and W. E. Mason's articles 'Ricardo's Transfer-Mechanism Theory' *Quarterly Journal of Economics*, 71 (1957), 107–115; 'The Stereotypes of Classical Transfer Theory', *Journal of Political Economy*, 64 (1956), 492–506; and 'Some Neglected Contributions to the Theory of International Transfers', ibid., 63 (1955), 529–35. Irish absenteeism particularly concerned McCulloch: on his treatment of the transfer problem see D. P. O'Brien, *J. R. McCulloch*, pp. 208–17.

# 8. The Classical Theory of Growth and Development

We now turn to the Classical theory of growth. What follows will be necessarily a limited treatment. The long-run trends of the distributive shares were dealt with in Chapter 5, money was dealt with in Chapter 6, and taxation will be dealt with in Chapter 9. Despite this we shall find that there is plenty of material to discuss; for in this kind of growth theory far more is endogenous than in later economic writings.

We shall start with Adam Smith. But it should be emphasized that he was writing against a background of eighteenth-century discussions of the problem of economic growth. We find in Hume and other eighteenth-century writers such features as an importance attached to the capital-accumulating class and to frugality as a source of capital, as well as to luxury as an incentive to effort and to accumulation. The division of economic growth into ordered stages, the role of commerce in growth, the benefits of growth, and the importance of incentives (in particular the importance of not having *too* favourable a climate and fertile land, or idleness would result)—these are all to be found in Hume and the other eighteenth-century writers; while Smith's particular emphasis on the importance of the agricultural sector derives from the Physiocrats.

## i. THE SMITHIAN GROWTH PROCESS

Adam Smith was a writer centrally concerned with the problem of economic growth. This is apparent not only from the *Wealth of Nations* but also from the *Lectures*. Unlike the mercantilist writers Smith was interested in G.N.P. per head rather than the total wealth of a state; and, instead of concentrating upon the circular flow of income as the Physiocrats had done, he advanced a view of an economy moving in an upward spiral of growth. This spiral was produced by two elements: the existence of basic economic phenomena, the interrelationship between which is capable of being stated, very approximately, in the form of a functionally related model: and a set of institutional requirements.

The latter can be disposed of first. Perhaps the most important was security of property[1] which was necessary for both the supply of effort and of capital. Also necessary was control over primogeniture and the entailing of estates upon a particular line of succession,[2] both of which were harmful to agriculture—the large estates they produced were not fully cultivated and great proprietors were seldom great improvers—which was given a central place in Smith's view of development. In addition the metayer system (whereby the landlord received half the crop in return for advancing working capital) should be removed and security of tenure should be introduced.[3] Freedom of trade both internal and external was necessary if the productive powers of resources were to be utilized. Finally, it was important that an infrastructure should be provided—this was an important function of the State.

Within this framework the basic determinants of wealth, given whatever condition of soil and climate there was, were two. Firstly there was the effectiveness with which labour was applied; and secondly there was the proportion of the labour force which was employed in productive work. Smith judged the first of these as the more important on the grounds that in the poorest societies almost all work. He devoted Book I to this topic, showing that the effectiveness of labour depended upon the degree to which the division of labour had developed. The amount of productive labour depended (in all societies but the poorest) upon the amount of capital and the different sectors in which it was employed. This was the subject matter of Book II. Productive labour was, in Smith's view, that which was employed in processes which produced something that ensured the continuity of production—usually something tangible. The point will be examined in more detail in Section iv of this chapter.

From these basic determinants we can see what the narrower economic relationships were. They involved the accumulation of capital, which supported the division of labour, which in turn increased the size of the total product through increasing productivity. This increased the scope for further capital accumulation. As capital was accumulated, wages were bid up. Population increase ensued, ensuring increased demand for the final product. This in turn stimulated further division of labour. We will have to return to this basic model; but first we need to look more closely at the elements in it.

Firstly let us look at capital. Adam Smith called the production of previous periods 'stock'—the accumulated wealth of society at any moment of time. This was divided into three parts: that for the immediate consumption of the holders of stock (food, clothes, housing, and furniture); circulating capital (in which Smith included money, stocks of provisions, raw materials, stocks of finished goods); and fixed capital (machinery, productive buildings, land improvements, and useful or acquired abilities). According to Smith, fixed capital was of no use without the co-operation of circulating capital[4] and, writing at the beginning of the Industrial Revolution, he placed relatively little emphasis upon it. Capital formation was produced by directing stock into categories 2 and 3. It was increased by parsimony and diminished by prodigality and misconduct. However, although Smith brought all his Scottish severity to bear upon the latter, he did express the view that it was normally less important and more intermittent than the desire to better our condition which led to parsimony.[5]

The capital that was accumulated could be employed in one of four different ways, and Smith ranked each of these in order of their importance.[6] Capital employed in agriculture was the most beneficial to the community. Nature laboured along with man in this employment—it is clear that Smith meant that capital employed in agriculture set into motion the most productive of productive labour rather than, as he was apparently arguing, that it set into motion the greatest quantity of productive labour. Ranked below agriculture was manufacturing. The capital of the manufacturer employed his workmen and also replaced the capital of the farmers and miners who supplied him with raw materials. According to Smith this meant that manufacturing employed a greater quantity of productive labour than the next category, trading. The merchant's capital employed only sailors and carriers. (In this connection Smith distinguished between the capital of a merchant employed in the home carrying trade and that of one engaged in foreign trade. He asserted that capital in the former employment replaced two home capitals on the grounds that a merchant would buy one lot of goods produced at home, sell them, and with the proceeds purchase another. Capital in the foreign carrying trade however replaced only one home and one foreign capital.) Finally there was distribution. The capital of the retailer employed only himself. If particular countries did not have enough capital for all their needs then the greater the proportion which was employed in agriculture, the greater would be the quantity (according to Smith) of productive labour and the greater the annual produce.

At first sight this is an awful muddle. There are several points to be made about it. Firstly the whole argument about the sectoral ranking of investment seems to derive from the influence of the Physiocrats with their emphasis on the singular importance of agriculture; yet their vision of the circular flow of payments could have helped Smith to untangle this peculiar argument which he advances. But although he did not accept the unique position which they afforded to agriculture, he attached a great deal of weight to the primacy of agriculture and thus did not approach the problem in a frame of mind which would have helped him to disentangle the sense from the nonsense. Secondly, the tangle became even worse when Smith argued that there was a further advantage to employing capital in the home trade—the quick return compared with its employment in the foreign trade; as Cannan pointed out[7] the emphasis on quick return was perfectly capable of upsetting the argument about agricultural supremacy. Thirdly the whole argument about the greater benefit from capital employed in the home trade sat very oddly in a book which contained as a fundamental message the idea that purchases from abroad led in turn to exports.

But Smith was not a fool; and what he was really concerned to do was to make an attack upon the forcing of capital into channels which it would not have entered, given an undistorted choice for the owners of that capital. This is his main concern—he does in fact draw attention to this—and it is rather unfortunate that he should have advanced a perfectly reasonable argument in terms which were not reasonable. But he was noticeably concerned about the Colbertist policy of artificial encouragement of manufacturing at the expense of agriculture; and he was concerned too at the forcing of capital into the carrying trade.[8] It was both of these tendencies that he was trying to attack. This was not only because of the need to allocate capital in accordance with undistorted profit opportunities but also because of the need, fundamental as we shall see to Smith's view of the stages of growth, for the development of an agricultural surplus as a prior base for the development of manufactures.

Now let us turn to division of labour.[9] This is given an enormously important role in the *Wealth of Nations* and it is operative in all four employments of capital. Its extent is limited by the size of the capital stock which is to support it. It takes its origin from an innate propensity in man to truck and barter. Specialization (and division of labour) and exchange then go hand in hand. It is *the* great cause of increases in productivity. It raises productivity in three ways: firstly, through improved dexterity; secondly, through a saving of time in passing from one task to another; and thirdly, because it gives rise to invention of machinery. It also leads to the development of natural and acquired talents. Smith was enormously impressed with its potential, relating how output per head in pin manufacture had been raised from twenty to 4,800 pins per day by the division of labour. It operated both within and between occupations. Ironically enough in view of the argument about agricultural superiority, it is agriculture which Smith singles out as the sector in which, because of the seasonality of many tasks, division of labour is limited so that productivity rises less fast than in other sectors.

Division of labour is also limited by the extent of the market. Although we have neatly linked the size of the market with population and the income level in our encapsulated version of Smith, it is necessary to say that Smith himself was not so clear and unambiguous, perhaps with reason as we shall see. In particular, the extent of the market for him depended on the stage of economic development. It depended upon the growth of towns, and of transport. Water carriage widened a market and thus it was that industry developed along rivers and that technology was developed where there was water transport.

The operation of division of labour in development has another aspect which we should mention here. There is some dispute amongst scholars as to whether Smith had an ambivalent attitude towards this process. On the one hand it is true that there is a distinction between the optimistic view of it in

Book I and the tendency to stress its harmful effects, in producing monotony
and dulling intelligence, in Book V. It is certainly true too that Smith did
emphasize the need for education to offset these harmful effects.[10] It is quite
possible to accept this but to argue that there was at least no contradiction
in Smith's view of the growth process. For though invention was supposed
to spring from division of labour, and though dulling of the inventive faculty
by repetitiveness would slow that faculty, it can be argued that, parallel
with the dulling, comes the development of invention as a specialism rather
than as something due to the operatives themselves. The modal intelligence
is higher at early stages of development, but the dispersion is smaller while
the reverse is the case at later stages. Nevertheless, though there is no contradiction, Smith's view of growth was very wide, and he remained concerned
about harmful effects which made the transition from G.N.P. per head to
welfare less easy.

   The *order* of development in economic growth was something to which
Adam Smith, as a member of the Scottish Historical School, paid some
attention.[11] He seems to have had two views of the stages of historical
development. Firstly there was what might be called the 'natural' order
of development. This involved the growth of an agricultural surplus which
itself arose from division of labour in the countryside and the improvement
of agricultural technology. On the basis of the surplus, towns then grew up,
affording a ready market for that surplus, and pursuing the specialized
division of labour involved in manufacturing, the products of which were
exchanged for the surplus. However, partly it seems influenced by Hume,
Smith felt that historically another process had been more in evidence.
Towns had been artificially built up by kings as allies against the feudal lords.
This gave the towns themselves security, and thus capital accumulated. They
acted as entrepôts, importing manufactures in exchange for the produce of
the countryside. In time they imitated these manufactures themselves; but
what was more important about their introduction was that by introducing
manufactures they destroyed the power of the feudal lords who, with the
proceeds of the agricultural surplus, bought manufactured luxuries instead of
the services of retainers, dismissed their supernumerary tenants and gave the
remaining ones long leases. But whichever process of development was followed, the towns benefited the countryside, growing in mutual interdependence with the country, buying land in the country and improving it, and
introducing order and government.

   But there was no infinite horizon in the growth process. All economies
would in the end reach a stationary state.[12] With the progress of growth,
investment opportunities were steadily exhausted and wages bid up until
profits reached a minimum. The process might be extended, and the stationary state postponed, by the acquisition of new territories and new branches
of trade, but it was inevitable in the end. The point at which a country

arrived at the stationary state depended in part upon its laws and institutions: so that a country which opposed trade and reduced the range of investment opportunities would reach its stationary state earlier—as Smith believed China to have done. Where there was lack of security of property the stationary state would also be reached sooner, because the minimum level of profits necessary to ensure net investment would be that much higher. But where an advanced and stable country was approaching the stationary state—Smith had, like the other Classical economists, Holland in mind here —only the very richest could afford to live on interest payments, and many more had to live on the wages of management by going into business to employ their own capital.

The discussion so far of Smith's growth theory should enable us to appreciate two things. Firstly, there is a central core of functional relationships in Smith's theory: secondly, there is much more to his view of growth than this, and we confine ourselves to the functional relationships at the cost of missing much that is of fundamental importance. The basic functional relationships are set out in Figs. 23–7.

We start with a particular capital stock $K_1$. This produces a demand for labour $D_1$ through Fig. 27; this in turn produces in Fig. 23 a wage rate $W_1$ with a population $L_1$ on the long-run supply of labour schedule. It also gives an output $O_1$ in Fig. 24 where the gap between the two increasing linear functions is due to division of labour (technology). Effective demand from Fig. 23 (Wage Rate × Population) with output from Fig. 24 combine to give profits $P_1$ in Fig. 25. These profits give us capital accumulation $k_1$ in Fig. 26 which raises capital stock to $K_2$ in Fig. 27. This produces a demand for labour $D_2$. This fed into Fig. 23 at first raises wages to $W_1^*$ along the short-run labour-supply schedule. But population expands to a new equilibrium $L_2$ at wage $W_2$. This raises effective demand in Fig. 25 to $W_2 \times L_2$ and the rise in capital stock to $K_2$ also raises output in Fig. 23 to $O_2$. The cumulative process continues upwards along this path.

But the preceding discussion should show that this omits much. Specifically, the 'extent of the market' is a much more complex idea than is shown here. It depends not just on aggregate demand as normally conceived, but on such processes as the development of towns, the location of economic activity near water, transport development, colonies, foreign trade, and the removal of obstacles to competition, as well as the enrichment of the internal market—indeed Adam Smith stresses this aspect relatively little. Moreover we have not included non-wage income in aggregate demand. Secondly the divergence between the two lines in Fig. 24 has to represent the whole relationship of technical progress, economic growth, education, and division of labour. Thirdly, the importance which Smith attached to restrictions on free development cannot be incorporated very easily into these diagrams—indeed this is true of all the institutional requirements.

Natural liberty simply cannot be incorporated. Fourthly, there is no exhaustion of investment opportunities and no stationary state in the model as here presented. Fifthly, the population/wage relationship in the diagrams

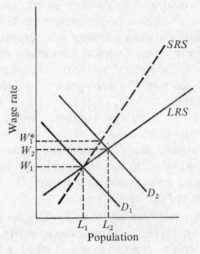

FIGURE 23

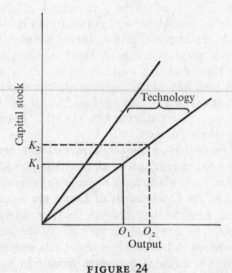

FIGURE 24

is arguably oversimplified—Smith does not offer a rigid relationship between population and wages. Sixthly, the motive force for, and means of, capital accumulation, as envisaged by Smith, offers no clear relationship between profits and the rate of capital accumulation—hence all the stress on parsimony. Seventhly, it is not clear to what extent Smith thought that machinery always complemented labour; and we have not distinguished fixed and circulating capital. Eighthly, there is no explicit role in the diagrams for the

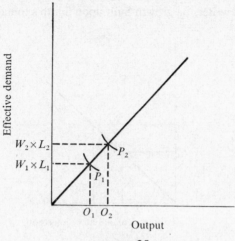

FIGURE 25

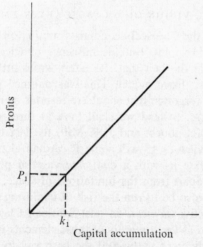

FIGURE 26

distinction between productive and unproductive labour; indeed all labour which is demanded is employed herein. Ninthly, the sectoral ranking of investment opportunities to which we devoted some space above, does not appear here.

Nevertheless the central functional relationships as herein depicted should provide a framework. The diagrammatic treatment is designed to enable the reader to grasp something fairly solid amidst the rich profusion of Smith's treatment of growth and it should be useful for this reason. But if the *Wealth of Nations* had contained only the model and not the rich profusion it is doubtful whether it would have had the influence which it did. As it was all the later Classical writers on growth built upon Smith's foundations.

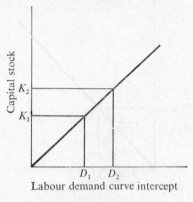

FIGURE 27

## ii. THE CLASSICAL VISION OF GROWTH AFTER SMITH

After Adam Smith the Classical economists writing on growth all took his work as their starting-point. But the influence of Ricardo was not unimportant also, despite the fact that the latter wrote little on growth, apart from formulating his basic model. This was outlined in Chapter II: and the reader who has forgotten that should refresh his memory, because it will not be repeated here. Instead we shall look at three other post-Smithian writers, Malthus, McCulloch, and J. S. Mill, the last two of whom incorporated into their view of growth some Ricardian elements. Such a treatment will not provide us with a *complete* view of post-Smithian growth theory: but, quite apart from the limitations of space, to be exhaustive in this context would also be to run the risk of confusing the reader. It is not so much the distinctive *elements* in post-Smithian Classical growth theory which are important as the *assembly* of those elements into a whole, and the stress laid on the different parts; and the best way to deal with this is to look at three separate Classical writers.

### 1. Malthus

Malthus, like Smith, and much more than his contemporary and friend Ricardo, was above all a growth economist.[13] The basic elements that he used are very similar to Smith's. We find the stress on the necessity of security of property,[14] the importance of accumulation (economic growth could only come from saving and Lauderdale had gone too far in deprecating parsimony)[15] the role of natural resources,[16] and the importance of incentives —like many Classical writers Malthus generalized from Humboldt's evidence about the deleterious effects of a freely available supply of bananas to argue that over-fertile land was inimical both to incentives and to the development of agricultural technology.[17] We also find considerable stress on the import-ance of invention[18] although, like the fertility of the soil, this only affected productive potential, and was of no use unless there was demand. Malthus also followed Smith in emphasizing the importance of trade in stimulating the demand for manufactures.[19]

Where the treatment differs from Smith, however, is in the explicit stress on the role of population both as responding to high wages and as a stimulus to development (although that this was part of his position was not always clear to his contemporaries)[20] and in the stress on distribution as vital in extending the market.[21] The derivation from Smith is clear enough; but, be-cause of Malthus's preoccupation with the maintenance of a sufficiently high level of aggregate demand, the emphasis is much greater. Indeed it is the role afforded to demand for the products of industry which perhaps most of all distinguishes Malthus's treatment from that of Smith. Firstly, Malthus argued, under the influence of Lauderdale, that in order to produce a demand pattern suitable for development, division of landed property was necessary[22] —though he was satisfied with the degree of division in the Britain of his time, arguing that too great a division of property interfered with division of labour and that the remaining large fortunes had an incentive effect. Secondly, internal and external commerce were necessary in order to achieve a sufficiently high level of demand. The third constituent necessary for this was the maintenance of an adequate proportion of society employed as unproductive labourers i.e. in personal services. Economic development was impossible without the stimulation of demand; the importation of capital into Ireland would be futile unless measures were first taken to raise demand.[23]

## 2. J. R. McCulloch

McCulloch's writings on growth were, in some ways, even more distinctively Smithian.[24] In them we find the basic process of growth seen in terms of Smith's apparatus. Growth rested on the accumulation of capital and the division of labour. A vital role was assigned to capital which was, strictly, that part of the produce of labour which was saved from immediate con-sumption and employed in maintaining productive industry or in facilitating production. But McCulloch's view was that the Smithian distinction between capital and revenue was rather hard and fast. The role of capital was to increase the productivity of labour, with both fixed and circulating capital being necessary, the latter lengthening the period of production. Capital enabled commodities requiring time or machinery to be produced and saved labour both directly and through the creation of an infrastructure. But, pointing to the fact that 'revenue' had supported Watt and Arkwright he was disinclined to give quite the pre-eminence to capital, as narrowly defined, that Smith had done.

The supply of capital arose, as it had done for Smith, through the desire of betterment—at times (and inconsistently with his final value theory) McCulloch implied a zero supply price of saving although he agreed, especially in his later writings, that high profits strengthened the motive to save as well as the ability to save.

McCulloch's treatment of the division of labour followed Smith very closely in arguing that capital was a prerequisite for the process and that it increased productivity through dexterity, time-saving, and inventions, although McCulloch made the extension of the analysis to intellectual occupations much clearer, and laid more emphasis than had Smith upon the use of particular talents being facilitated by division of labour. The growth of mechanization was part of the continuing process of division of labour and to this McCulloch did not object. Unlike Smith, J. S. Mill, and others, he did not believe that the factory system dulled intelligence. What he did dislike about it were its distributional consequences as we shall see.

In McCulloch's treatment of growth we find too the Smithian institutional requirements, but developed even further and with even greater emphasis. Having lived through the events leading up to 1830 and 1848 McCulloch (whose correspondence shows fear of revolution) stressed even more than Smith the need for security of property. With enlightened government and internal freedom of trade this was the great *sine qua non* of economic growth, and it was vital to effort, accumulation, and invention. Ireland and India provided strong evidence of what occurred when there was not security of property and where two other fundamental requirements for growth were also lacking—religious tolerance and equality of public burdens. McCulloch also attached importance to internal freedom of trade, which gave scope to competition and to pursuit of self-interest; though it is perhaps as well to stress that, in spite of hardy misconceptions on this point, McCulloch was not a *laissez-faire* dogmatist—he believed that the phrase had been abused as a slogan and that freedom was only valuable in so far as it achieved public prosperity and happiness. Like Smith he emphasized the role of government in development, notably in relation to communications, contracts, security, food quality, fisheries, building regulation, shipping regulation, the Post Office, liability for accidents, child labour, and public utilities, although he believed that price fixing by government, except in the last context, was undesirable, as was interference with either trade unions or manufacturing. He also believed, like Hume, that moderate taxation could have a stimulating effect on entrepreneurs.

He also emphasized, as had Smith, but perhaps, as the author of a grand *Geographical Dictionary*, even more clearly, the importance of geographical position, a moderately unfavourable climate (the 'banana' argument pops up again), and the availability of inputs, especially coal, as well as the creation of an infrastructure. The latter was important because communications increased specialization, turned over capital quicker, and increased factor mobility. A banking system was also important both as providing security and in aiding allocation. McCulloch saw the stages of growth very much in the same terms as Smith had done, that is in terms of the interaction of towns and the countryside, with the growth of towns (which were competitive and stimulating and attracted the inventive and enterprising) providing both markets and stimulation for the countryside.

McCulloch's treatment of agriculture however differed somewhat from Smith's. Although he stressed the importance of abundant cheap and fertile land, he did not accept Smith's belief in the prime importance of the agricultural sector, preferring to draw attention to the interdependence between the different economic sectors, with growth in one stimulating the others through demand. Moreover, he was a far more outspoken opponent of the subdivision of agricultural holdings than Smith, and an advocate of primogeniture, unlike Smith who had opposed it.

More distinctively perhaps McCulloch was one of the earliest writers to emphasize the importance of investment in human capital through education, and the stimulating effect of this on invention. He agreed with Smith that the stock of investment in education was part of the national capital, but took the argument much further, advancing the idea that the spread of popular education would increase invention, and laid much more emphasis than his contemporaries on the role of the diffusion of knowledge in increasing growth both by raising the level of invention and by preventing a few people from engrossing its results.

All of this allows us to notice three significant features of McCulloch's analysis of growth. Firstly, he was very close to Smith—indeed what he advanced in his voluminous writings was the Smithian tradition writ large, at least in terms of the institutional requirements. Secondly, although McCulloch was a growth economist who believed that onward-going growth was the desirable state and who wanted to avoid the stationary state, he was far from blind to the fact that economic growth was not solely productive of benefit for all. There certainly were benefits. Wealth provided scope for the development of our higher and nobler faculties; and, after criticism from Malthus that McCulloch had not excluded production of immaterials from productive activity, the latter broadened his definition of wealth to include anything which involved human industry in its production and was possessed of exchangeable value. The desirable state of society was, as for Smith, one in which high profits ensured the continuation of the growth process and the accumulation of wealth. But there was another side to all this.

For it was necessary to 'manage' growth to some extent to maintain a balance between the different sectors. The manufacturing sector was peculiarly subject to demand fluctuations in both the home and export markets; and McCulloch began to feel that manufacturing should have been limited in size because the economic system was for this reason becoming basically unstable. The existence of the Poor Law was indeed the only reason that the instability had not led to more trouble.

But, most of all perhaps, the system had distributional consequences which were nothing short of disastrous.

It is impossible at this moment to cast the horoscope of this [the manufacturing] system ... [but] It appears to be, of its essence, that most sorts of employments should be conducted on a large and continually increasing scale ... providing, in this way, for the exhaltation of a few individuals by the irremediable helotism of the great majority ... though there has been a vast increase ... of wealth and comforts among the upper classes ... the condition of the workpeople ... has certainly not been in any degree improved, but has rather, we incline to think, been sensibly deteriorated.[25]

The third and last point to note about McCulloch's treatment of growth is that it for long incorporated Ricardian elements, especially the declining rate of profit due to declining agricultural productivity and the rising cost of wage-good procurement. But, as the present author has shown elsewhere,[26] these elements were all ultimately rejected by McCulloch. He seems to have come to doubt whether the rate of profit was declining, and to believe that the apparent decline of profits in Holland was due to the running down of investment opportunities; that the Corn Laws were unimportant in their effect on wage goods, and that agricultural improvements could permanently offset diminishing returns in agriculture. McCulloch also rejected the Malthusian population mechanism so that a rise in productivity did not mean that an increase in population would ensue and that cultivation would have to be extended to an even more distant margin. His whole stress on movable psychological subsistence broke the Ricardian link between population, wages, and the margin. He also believed that falling non-agricultural wage good prices could offset any rise in the cost of 'corn', and even ultimately rejected the inverse movement of wages and profits on the grounds that a rise in wages would stimulate the entrepreneur to extra effort and ingenuity.

## 3. J. S. Mill

The third writer we deal with in this section is the great figure of J. S. Mill. His aim, in producing his *Principles*, was to write a work on economic growth which covered the whole range of factors affecting a country's growth performance. His book was then rather relativist in its approach—

it was necessary to have knowledge of a country's circumstances and it was not possible simply to transplant conclusions from one country to another. Mill's *Principles* was basically the result of an attempt at producing a *Wealth of Nations* after the Industrial Revolution had manifested itself far more fully than it had done in Smith's time. His treatment was influenced by four major sources apart from Smith (who of course provided the bulk of his foundations). The first of these was Compte. Nothing more will be added to what was said in Chapter II about his influence. The second was Charles Babbage, Lucasian Professor of Mathematics at Cambridge; the third was John Rae, eccentric Scottish inventor and writer; and the fourth was Ricardo.

Babbage produced a monumental work *On the Economy of Machinery and Manufactures*,[27] which has never received its due recognition from later generations of economists. In this he built upon one particular part of the *Wealth of Nations*—that dealing with the technology of industrial advance. To Smith's pin making he added numerous other instances of the operation of the division of labour and of the way in whch an advanced society organized its economic activity. It was a very considerable performance by a man distinguished in natural science, applying, like Smith, the Baconian method to economic and social phenomena. Mill acknowledged the work's importance and drew numerous examples from it. But he was really relying upon it being available in its entirety to his readers—which was reasonable since within two months of publication 3,000 copies had been sold. Its influence was notably strong on Mill's treatment of scale and organization.[28] The latter laid great importance on economies of scale (though these were of course still dependent on the extent of the market). They were easiest to achieve when capital was increasing fast and when it was concentrated in a few hands, as well as when business confidence was high. The trend towards large scale would weaken competition (though Mill, despite his enthusiasm for competition, was unsure about the welfare implications of any resulting redistribution).[29] Mill made some play with the advantages of joint-stock organization[30] which gave access to capital and made the realization of economies of scale easier. He agreed that the owner-manager was more vigilant and had more drive, but believed that large concerns had the power of attracting management of good quality and that the organization had the capability of building in incentives for managers. All this was very much in contrast wth Adam Smith who had a poor opinion of joint-stock organization, and in contrast also to the outright opposition of McCulloch and Overstone to limited liability. Babbage's influence is also apparent in Mill's treatment of the elements in industrial development which made for increasing productivity, as well as on such matters as industrial fraud.[31]

Mill's attention was drawn to John Rae by Nassau Senior. Rae's book influenced Mill in three directions. First and most importantly Rae provided a treatment of the motivation to accumulate capital.[32] This involved provision for the future. Knowledge was very important in determining the power to make provision for the future; but so also was motivation, and the level of motivation varied widely between countries and peoples.[33] Rae offered an analysis which Mill did not reproduce in its entirety but which lay behind some of his thinking even where he did not spell out precisely what he meant. Rae's position was that all capital instruments have three characteristics: that they can supply future wants; that before their capacity to supply wants is exhausted they yield a return; and that this process takes time. Rae proceeded from this point to argue that every instrument could be arranged in some part of a series.[34] Its ranking in this series was determined by the period of time which had to elapse before it had returned its cost of production multiplied by a factor of two. Capital instruments of the first order, $A$, returned this amount in one year. Those of order $Z$ returned this amount in 26 years. Those of order $a$ returned this amount in 27 years and so on. Now every extention of accumulation meant making instruments of a lower rank than previously. How far members then accumulated would depend on their time preference—how long they considered it worth while waiting to get double the present sacrifice—as well as how *certain* they were of the receipt of the return. Time preference, the ease with which we could be pursuaded to sacrifice now, depended on affection for others and habits of prudence. The amount of investment could also be affected by the rate of wages (a fall of which lowered the cost of production of capital goods so that a greater amount of investment could be made for a given expenditure) and by invention, which had a similar effect except that it, unlike reductions in wages, had no assignable limit.

All this was important. It contained a theory of a determination of the amount of investment through the interaction of time preference and the marginal productivity of investment which leads straight forward to neo-Classical economics. It certainly influenced Mill's own treatment of capital although it had to take its place beside the influence of Smith and Ricardo. Mill saw capital as a stock of previously accumulated products of labour affording a means to future production.[35] Industry was limited by capital but not all of capital was necessarily employed at any one time. Nevertheless there was an impossibility of overproduction and exhaustion of investment opportunities. Capital, the result of saving, was demand for labour. Demand for commodities, as we saw in Chapter 5, was not demand for labour. How much capital was saved depended upon the amount of the fund from which savings could be made (which was the whole of total product minus subsistence wages) and the strength of the disposition to save.[36] It is in Mill's treatment of this that the influence of Rae is clear. He leant heavily on Rae, referring to the general state of social conditions, time preference, and affection for others.

Mill was probably also influenced by Rae's treatment of invention[37]—

certainly he lays more stress than virtually any writer except McCulloch on this aspect of things. Finally Mill was also influenced by the treatment given by Rae (and also by E. G. Wakefield) of division of labour. He followed Rae in arguing that the division of labour meant that capital equipment could be utilized more fully and so its returns would be gathered more quickly, and he accepted that division of labour was to some extent a result of invention and capital accumulation rather than a cause.[38] He followed Wakefield in calling division of labour 'co-operation' and in distinguishing simple co-operation (within a particular employment) and complex co-operation (separate employments). Like Lauderdale and Rae, Mill thought that the process was a numbing one which did not always increase invention.[39] Apart from these influences Mill followed Smith and Babbage in discussing the way in which division of labour actually operated.[40]

The Ricardian influence is clear enough in Mill's treatment of agricultural progress. Two chapters on the increase of labour and capital were followed by one on the increase of the *produce* of land.[41] The limited quantity of land and its limited productiveness were the real limits to the increase of production. There was an inevitability about the emergence of diminishing returns in agriculture, though these might be delayed by the advances in agricultural technology which went with economic growth as well as by advances in the technology of other industries which led to cheaper agricultural implements, better communications, and falling prices for non-agricultural wage goods. Indeed, despite the Ricardian genuflections, Mill recognized that the price of corn had *fallen* through agricultural improvements since about 1830.[42]

Yet for all this he felt able to insist upon the inevitability of, and the approach to, the stationary state.[43] This would occur when the marginal profitability of investment fell to equality with the marginal rate of time preference, and net investment became zero. There was a minimum rate of profit necessary to induce savings as already noted. There was also, Mill recognized, a precautionary motive for saving in addition to the 'ordinary' motive; but he argued that this would not lead to net saving because it would be matched by capital consumption by those who were forced to draw on their precautionary savings. The reason for the decline in profits to the minimum which halted accumulation was the Ricardian mechanism. Despite the evidence of advances in agricultural technology Mill felt that these could only stave off the stationary state. Yet interestingly enough, although Mill rejected the Smithian explanation for falling profit, that of exhaustion of investment opportunities, on the grounds originally put forward by Sir Edward West that not everything could fall in value in relation to everything else and thus depress profit margins, he still appeared to accept the Wakefield thesis, which in fact derived from Smith, that investment opportunities were limited by land and by foreign demand for manufactured products.[44] But he still managed to put a Ricardian gloss on the argument. Mill anticipated the imminent arrival of this stationary state in England, which he estimated would occur at a 1 per cent rate of interest—social conditions in England, especially puritanism, ensured that the stationary state would occur at a much lower rate of interest than in most countries. However, it had been staved off for the time being by the following circumstances: capital export (which also helped to develop overseas sources of wage goods); capital consumption in the form of unproductive consumption and business failures—this last was a fruitful source of postponement because a low rate of interest and abundance of capital encouraged people to invest in risky enterprises; new investment opportunities because of inventions; improvements in production which cheapened wage goods; falling luxury goods prices which gave to the rich surplus purchasing power and increased their willingness to save; and imported wage goods.[45]

But if Mill insisted upon the inevitability of the stationary state, the end product was still distinctly non-Ricardian. Firstly, while Ricardo had assumed that the stationary state was to be avoided—indeed the whole object of his system was to show that such a state should be pushed away into the future by repeal of the Corn Laws—Mill saw it as an approach to Nirvana.[46] This was despite the fact that he was clear enough about the benefits of growth.[47] He saw it as productive of a rapid advance of pure and applied science and of an increase in security, including security from arbitrary government, of an improvement in the business capacity of the general mass of mankind, and of improved transport facilities which improved market transparency and thus reduced market fluctuations. But *if* moral restraint were exercised the stationary state need not be uncomfortable.[48] (Mill did not want too crowded a population on the grounds of amenity, quite apart from considerations of income per head.)[49] He believed that such a growth of moral restraint could be expected with the emancipation in a stationary state of the working class and of women of all classes.[50] Redistribution of property would be necessary in the stationary state[51] but, given that, the state would be comfortable, and machinery could be used, as it had not so far been, to lighten drudgery. He saw a likely replacement of capitalism by partnership in the stationary state[52] —this despite the fact that he ended his discussion with a spirited defence of competition against socialist denunciations.[53]

For Mill then the stationary state would not be unhappy. In addition to this, while Ricardo had been as opposed to capital consumption and prodigality as Smith, Mill adopted a very different attitude. Capital was of course important. But as an economy approached the stationary state capital became relatively less and less scarce, and prodigality by governments did little harm.[54]

The declining relative importance of capital did not mean however that Mill was satisfied with the distribution of either income or property, as existing or as likely to exist (without further interference) in the stationary state.

His concern on this question was far from unique amongst the Classical economists, but he was almost alone amongst the major writers in calling for substantial redistribution from the prevailing state. Yet for fear of subverting the motivation to the supply of effort, he stopped short, as had McCulloch, of recommending wholesale redistribution of income through the tax system. Instead he argued very strongly (despite some misgivings about the reaction of population to redistribution)[55] for redistribution of property (and hence of the income from its ownership) through a punitive system of death duties. He believed there should be an upper limit to the permissible amount of inheritance and, in sharp contrast to McCulloch, he was strongly opposed to primogeniture.[56]

The concern with distribution seems in fact to have influenced Mill's treatment of scale in agriculture which was unusual amongst the Classical economists. Against such writers as Arthur Young, McCulloch, and Richard Jones, Mill stood out as the defender of peasant agriculture. He offers an entire chapter in praise of peasant proprietorship; and then follows it with another![57] There was hardly a moral virtue he did not attribute to it. Temperance, self control, self-education; all these resulted from peasant proprietorship.[58] Perhaps a further clue to all this elevation of peasant agriculture, apart from the concern with distribution, lies in Mill's belief that it would lead to another virtue; moral restraint. He even found virtues, though in a lesser degree, in the metayer system (a further chapter dealt with this)[59] which virtually every writer from Smith onwards had condemned. Only cottier tenancies (where the landless competed for land by offering rents they could not pay) did he find lacking.[60] Though he had laid great emphasis on the advantages of economies of scale in other spheres of economic activity, he considered them of much less importance in agriculture.[61] Peasant farming was deficient only in skill and knowledge, and this was counterbalanced by the greater supply of effort; given satisfactory tenure the peasant farmer obtained at least some of the fruits of increasing his effort. Mill buttressed his beliefs with copious references to empirical studies. He believed that other writers had relied too much on the case of pre-Revolutionary France, especially as observed by Arthur Young.

Yet all of this was within a basically Smithian framework and the treatment of the stages of growth and of the need for security of property was entirely within Smith's mould. The same was true of Mill's treatment of productivity as depending upon capital, natural advantages, natural resources, and 'the regular energy of labour'—though Mill's Victorian sureness of the superiority of the English labourer as a race is not to be found in Smith, and indeed Mill himself became less sure of it with successive editions.[62] The treatment is garnished with material about advancing technology which comes from Babbage; but its roots in the *Wealth of Nations* are clear enough.

iii. MACHINERY AND GLUTS

Now we turn to a very central question which arose in the Classical debates
on growth: whether the process was hitchless or whether there might arise
periodic crises (apart from those associated with monetary causes or with the
kind of endogenous trade cycle which we saw in Chapter 6 was envisaged
by Overstone). The question really comes in two parts: the narrower question about the effects of the introduction of machinery on wages and employment; and the much broader one of the possibility of a general (non-
monetary) glut.

*1. The Machinery Question*

Adam Smith seems rather to have taken it for granted that machinery and
labour were complementary. Machinery would be erected out of new capital
accumulation as part of the process of extending further and further the
division of labour. This general presumption was for long accepted. Perhaps
the writer who first seriously upset it was John Barton. In a pamphlet
published in 1817[63] Barton offered the following numerical example.

A manufacturer has a capital of £1,000. He employs 20 weavers at £50 per
annum. His capital is suddenly doubled to £2,000. He invests £1,500 of this
in a machine which raises labour productivity fourfold and now employs
only 5 men. If (as assumed by Barton) the machine lasts 15 years then (on
straight line depreciation) average annual expenditure by a manufacturer on
machines is £100. So the manufacturer will, at a wage of £50, keep two of
the men employed as machine makers. Another man is assumed to be
employed in maintenance and repairs. But the employer's capital has increased from £1,000 to £2,000 assuming profits at 10 per cent and an annual
wage of £50 (and note that all this is done without any reference to the
price and output of the final product); and so he will be able to employ two
more servants. Total employment was previously:

20 weavers and it is now 5 weavers

2 machine makers
1 maintenance man
2 extra servants

20 (plus an unspecified  10 (plus the original servants)
number of servants)

Barton triumphantly concludes: 'With half the capital, and half the revenue,
just double the number of hands were set in motion.'

Three points should be noted about this example. Firstly there was no
role assigned to the demand for the final product so no scope was given to
extra employment arising from extra sales, themselves arising from lowered

production costs due to the installation of the machine. Secondly there was no account taken of possible employment of displaced labour in the production of other commodities on which consumers might spend purchasing power released by a fall in the price of the original article due to installation of the machinery. Thirdly the machine is installed (partly) by conversion of circulating into fixed capital.

Ricardo then followed Barton with an example which contained this last assumption and a further one. It was that the entrepreneur was prepared to invest in machinery to earn the *same* income as before and to produce a smaller output. As Ricardo put it, an increase in net income (that is net of depreciation, including replacement of circulating capital) did not necessarily involve an increase of gross income (which included circulating capital). Ricardo's example was as follows.

A capitalist has a capital of £20,000. £7,000 is fixed capital (implicitly assumed by Ricardo to have an infinite life since he makes no provision for amortization) and £13,000 is circulating capital. Profits at 10 per cent are £2,000. Each year output of the enterprise (which is both farming and manufacturing) is £15,000. Of this £13,000 amortizes the circulating capital and £2,000 is the profit income. But the capitalist decides to employ half his men during one year in the construction of a machine. At the end of the year he will have output worth £7,500 and a machine worth £7,500. So with his original £7,000 of fixed capital (which is not apparently rendered redundant by the new machine) he has a maintained capital of £20,000 plus £2,000 in profits. But after deducting this £2,000 from the output he has only £5,500 circulating capital to advance for next year's production so he can employ only $\frac{5,500}{13,000} = 42 \cdot 3$ per cent of the labour he employed before and gross produce has fallen from £13,000 to £7,500 while profits remain unchanged. Price is assumed to fall as a result of the reduced cost of operating the machine compared with the old process; output falls also but demand falls *pari passu* with the displacement of labour so that the reduction in output will not raise price.

Ricardo did add (rather unusually for him) a number of qualifications to the basic argument.[64] He recognized that the discovery and introduction of machinery was gradual and that it was likely to affect the employment of *new* capital rather than involve the conversion of existing circulating capital; that as new capital was accumulated it would be spent on machinery in advanced countries because of rising wages and wage-good prices; and that saving would rise (thus increasing the stock of circulating capital which demanded labour) as the purchasing power of consumers increased as a result of the fall in price of the articles made by the machines. Moreover he argued that the introduction of machinery could not be safely discouraged otherwise capital would be exported and there would be even less demand for labour; and he also argued that there would be a precious-metal flow to other countries if they employed machinery and we did not, and that thus the double-factoral terms of trade (the rate at which the services of factors of production exchanged internationally) would be turned against ourselves.

But let us ignore the qualifications and look at the core of the argument. There are three main points to be made at this juncture. Firstly, the particular assumptions made were only part of a larger set. As Hicks has pointed out,[65] there are in fact three possible sets of assumptions *even about the relative labour input of machine making and the old and new processes*. Both may require lower labour inputs; or the labour input in making the machine may be higher than in providing whatever fixed capital was provided before but the labour input in operating the machine may be low enough to compensate for this: or the labour input in using the machine may be higher than under the old process but the labour input in constructing the machine may be sufficiently lower to compensate. Ricardo was dealing (at most) with only the second case; and even this is not clear because the old fixed capital apparently (since profits are inputed to it in the example) continues in operation. In addition to all this the assumption that machinery was created by turning circulating capital into fixed was fairly important; Barton's example also involved this in part. If this did not occur then, given that circulating capital was demand for labour, labour rendered unemployed by the introduction of machinery installed with *new* capital in one employment would find employment somewhere else as the circulating capital, displaced by the fixed capital, found new employment somewhere else.

Secondly, as Wicksell effectively pointed out, Ricardo's argument depended on his scaling up a single enterprise to represent an entire sector. If we do not do this then the fall in wages brought about by the initial displacement of labour will prevent other entrepreneurs installing machines. Indeed the argument that gross produce will fall is, according to Wicksell, untenable, because falling wage rates increase the profitability of the old method and so output, by the old method, will be increased.[66]

Thirdly, the argument neglects the income leverage (multiplier) effects of the investment in machinery. It is wrong to argue that Ricardo is neglecting the income leverage of a *new* flow of investment, as some authors have implied, because he is specifically dealing with the case of a conversion of part of the capital stock from one form to another. But there is no prima facie reason for expecting that the employment multiplier of one kind of investment will be different from the employment multiplier effects of the other kind of investment.

Fourthly, the assumption that an entrepreneur is prepared to invest in specific fixed capital in order to make the same profits as before and sell a smaller output does not seem a very reasonable one, given that risk is associated with the specific nature of fixed capital. (Ricardo is of course relying here on the fall in demand *pari passu* with the displacement of labour so that the fall in output does not result in higher prices and profits and extra investment.)

The Barton–Ricardo argument was then a special (though not impossible) case. The argument (which also received some support from the Swiss economist Sismondi) was however taken sufficiently seriously for three of the major Classical writers, Malthus, McCulloch, and J. S. Mill to consider it at some length. Malthus,[67] impressed (as was virtually every Classical economist) by the recent history of the cotton industry was reluctant to accept the Ricardian case, refused to be classed with Sismondi, and argued that, for commodities in elastic demand, the end result of the introduction of machinery was likely to be an increase in employment. However, he agreed that for commodities in inelastic demand this was not necessarily the case; and also argued that even if the investment was made out of new capital rather than through the conversion of circulating capital, unemployment might well result while the circulating capital was finding new employment elsewhere.

McCulloch[68] got involved in some difficulties over this because, in answering such writers as Barton and Sismondi, he kept switching between capital as demand for labour and consumption demand as demand for labour. Starting from the position that machinery was necessary in order to emerge from barbarism, he still accepted that displacement of labour was likely to be an *impact* effect of the introduction of machinery. At first he also accepted Barton's invalid argument that fixed capital had to displace a greater quantity of circulating capital to make its installation worthwhile (the argument was invalid because the fixed capital might have resulted in a greater output and thus increased entrepreneurial income that way). He later accepted Ricardo's basic case as logically possible. But he insisted that machinery had not historically diminished the total product; that capitalists did not accept the risks of specific fixed capital without any compensating increase in output and income; that machinery only caused frictional unemployment; and that a shortage of capital, frictions, and patents, would all slow the introduction of machinery.

These were his general arguments. More specifically he argued that some of the displaced labour would be employed in making machinery, that any displaced circulating capital would employ labour elsewhere, and that the fall in the price of nonagricultural wage goods from the introduction of machinery would increase profitability, capital accumulation, and demand for labour. Switching then from capital as demand for labour to demand for commodities as demand for labour he argued that if elasticity of demand was greater than 1 then the price fall resultant upon the introduction of machinery might mop up some of the displaced labour. This argument was somewhat inconclusive because price could be expected to fall only in proportion to the reduction in costs. Proportionately more labour would be displaced than costs would be reduced through the very process of replacing circulating capital with fixed. There was then no guarantee that, even if elasticity of demand was greater than 1, all the displaced labour would be reemployed. McCulloch also considered the case in which elasticity of demand was less than 1 and here argued that the extra purchasing power which consumers were given by the fall in price of the original article but which they did not choose to spend upon that article would result in extra demand for other articles and the mopping up of the displaced labour in that way. Again this was inconclusive since there was no guarantee that sufficient purchasing power would be freed, that demand for such products would increase sufficiently, and that the process of their manufacture would be sufficiently labour intensive, to take up the extra labour. Indeed it seems *prima facie* unlikely. The trouble with both McCulloch's and indeed Malthus's treatment here is that they allowed themselves to reason largely in terms of the static examples of Ricardo and Barton instead of treating the installation of machinery in terms of an economy which was growing steadily over time.

J. S. Mill's view[69] was that, in so far as installation of machinery involved the conversion of circulating into fixed capital which did not wear out every year, this was prejudicial to the interests of the labourer. He noticed that extra demand for commodities might arise but dismissed this on the ground that demand for commodities was not demand for labour. He also noticed the point about extra purchasing power; this was dismissed upon the same grounds, and it was not until late in his treatment that he noticed Ricardo's point that this might lead to greater accumulation.[70] But having said all that, Mill took the view that, historically, improvements had been introduced gradually, using *new* capital, so that they hardly ever did harm. Historically in fact both circulating and fixed capital had increased together. Machinery was only introduced when there was security of property, considerable economic activity, and a high level of desire to accumulate. These were characteristics of a country in which both kinds of capital were increasing rapidly. But the conclusive answer to objections against machinery was, in Mill's view, that it postponed the stationary state by raising the productivity of investment[71]—this despite his optimistic view of the stationary state.

His final conclusion was that new capital was overflowing, so that machinery would not affect the wage fund; but that if, at any time, the evil effects envisaged by Barton and Ricardo should arise, then government should be prepared to intervene to slow up the process of mechanization.

This is not an issue which is dead. The controversy has continued into the twentieth century. The essential question is whether income (or the voluntary and widespread taking of leisure) grows as fast as the growth of productivity.

## 2. Capital Accumulation and Gluts

We now turn to the even more fundamental question as to whether economic growth can continue without crises or whether general gluts will arise. Now on this score there were a number of critics of Classical economics such as William Spence, John Rooke, John Barton, and John Fullarton, who had interesting things to say: and there were some more clearly within the Classical main stream who were concerned about this matter. Such writers as Scrope, De Quincey, Blake, and Chalmers were in particular concerned about this problem. There were also some relatively little-known figures such as John Lalor, General Sleeman, and Captain Pettman, whose work has only been rediscovered in our own time.[72]

Most of these writers tended to stress three things: the possibility of a money-induced glut, the existence of a trade cycle (these have both been dealt with—the latter only briefly—in Chapter 6), and the problem of optimal adjustment of the capital stock to the level of income. It is this last point which is really of interest here: and for the sake of space the discussion will be confined to the two major writers who dealt with this problem, Lauderdale and Malthus.

Lauderdale's analysis of the problem involved the following points. Firstly, for him, as for virtually all these writers except Lalor,[73] saving and investment were the same act. There was no possibility of a Keynesian disequilibrium arising between plans to save and plans to invest. The problem was that the plans to save and invest were realized. This in turn raised the capital/labour ratio beyond its optimal point. The essence of his position seems to have been that, with a given technology, there was an optimal aggregate capital/labour combination, and that if more saving was undertaken the result would be a negative marginal productivity of investment. If there were a change in circumstances, such as a new invention or the acquisition of new territory, then more capital would be required.[74] He was essentially arguing for the existence of a series of plateaux on the way to the stationary state. Over-saving not only created more capital than was required but reduced the demand for consumption goods and thus lowered investment opportunities.[75] Reversing Smith's dictum he asserted that it was fortunate that prodigality counteracted over-saving.[76] However there were two ways in which demand could be kept at a sufficiently high level. Firstly, government expenditure could counteract the over-saving, and government prodigality could lower the savings/income ratio, adding to demand so as to offset the profit-depressing effects of investment. Secondly, distribution of property was of fundamental importance in maintaining demand. Demand in turn dictated the pattern of industrialization, and demand itself depended also upon the pattern of wealth distribution.[77] England was, in his view, the only country with a sufficient diffusion of wealth. Substantial inequality of fortune was the great impediment to economic growth.

Prior to Keynes the work of Malthus on the problem of aggregate demand attracted little attention although it occupies nearly one-third of Malthus's *Principles* and is the main theme of the Ricardo–Malthus correspondence.[78] Nevertheless the first and fundamental point to grasp is that it is not a Keynesian model with which Malthus is dealing. It is not a case of savers being unable to find an outlet for their savings so that *ex ante* saving is greater than *ex ante* investment. Saving is realized—it is not mere hoarding[79] —but this is what causes the trouble. What we have here is in fact a *post-Keynesian* model—a capital-stock-adjustment model. Now the essential features of such a model are, as R. C. O. Mathews puts it, that

In order that full employment should be maintained, it is necessary not merely that *ex ante* investment should be equal to *ex ante* savings at a high enough level, but also that the current level of investment should not be such as to cause the stock of capital to increase so rapidly that a decline in its marginal efficiency occurs.[80]

Now this is surely what Malthus was trying to get at. The same author continues

The dilemma is, then, that a rate of investment high enough to give full employment leads to excessive capital accumulation and is not maintainable; whereas if investment were kept steady at a level intermediate betwen boom and slump, there would not be full employment, although there might be a fair chance that this moderate pace of investment would preserve the marginal efficiency of capital roughly constant and so not be inconsistent with stability.[81]

The policy prescription is to fill the gap with something else—either to raise the consumption function and/or to add government spending. Now in fact Malthus advocated both of these as we shall see.

But *why* should the marginal productivity of investment fall in this way? Now in Malthus's case the answer is given by the apparent necessity of confining production to a narrow range of goods.[82] Saving, which turns domestic servants into producers of these goods, will result in the production of goods for which there is not demand at cost covering prices.

The argument is essentially this. The saver does not add to the demand for goods. He was already paying his servants wages. But by effectively converting these servants into productive labourers he is producing extra goods for which there is not a demand at cost covering prices. But this in turn raises the question *why* should saving rise so fast as to exhaust investment opportunities in this way. Ricardo's answer to such a suggestion was of course that the fall in the marginal productivity of investment would choke off excessive capital accumulation. The same answer was given by other Classical writers like J. S. Mill, also relying, in this context, on Say's Identity.[83] In a wider context Mill relied, as we saw in Chapter 6, on a complex and subtle monetary analysis to explain aggregate demand failures; while Ricardo relied on 'Sudden Changes in the Channels of Trade.'[84] He also cited Say as an answer to Malthus;[85] and at times his treatment seems a little crude. It is not possible to refute the idea that investment opportunities will be exhausted by reference to Say's Identity: this merely implies that *if* exhaustion *has taken place* then there will not be further investment *because* the rate of profit is low.

In any case such an approach was really evading the issue. There could perfectly well be a glut if savings responded too quickly to a high marginal productivity of investment as Malthus seems sometimes to have envisaged.[86] Ricardo was really talking about long-run equilibrium (as usual): it was only as a glut emerged that the fall in profits would signal the capitalist to cease accumulating, and thus cause investment to be cut back. In addition to this Malthus was concerned about savings which were not motivated by the rate of return, hence his stress on relying on self-interest as the criterion of a desirable level of saving.[87]

Malthus was satisfied that over-saving crises had occurred, and he cited conversion operations (whereby holders of National Debt were forced to accept a lower rate of interest) as indicative of the difficulties encountered in employing capital at various times. He therefore sought remedies in two ways. Firstly, demand had to be kept up through 'unproductive consumption'.[88] This meant demanding personal services to ensure that a high level of demand for goods was maintained without adding to the supply of goods. Secondly, the market should be widened as far as possible by development of the channels of distribution.[89] Both these remedies can be seen as stemming from the *Wealth of Nations*, the former from Smith's view of the process of development out of feudalism. But in addition Malthus recommended another measure: the use of Public Works in order to maintain demand. At first he seems to have doubted their efficacy. A letter unearthed by Mr. Sraffa and published in 1955 shows how Malthus at first believed that public works would be paid for out of 'revenue' and not impinge upon saving at all.[90] But he subsequently changed his mind: his *Principles* is quite unequivocal on the subject.

It is also of importance to know that, in our endeavours to assist the working classes in a period like the present, it is desirable to employ them in those kinds of labour, the results of which do not come for sale into the market, such as roads and public works. The objection to employing a large sum in this way, raised by taxes, would not be its tendency to diminish the capital employed in productive labour [Ricardo's objection]; because this, to a certain extent, is exactly what is wanted; but it might, perhaps, have the effect of concealing too much the failure of the national demand for labour, and prevent the population from gradually accommodating itself to a reduced demand. This however might be, in a considerable degree, corrected by the wages given. And altogether I should say, that the employment of the poor in roads and public works, and a tendency among landlords and persons of property to build, to improve and beautify their grounds, and to employ workmen and menial servants, are the means most within our power and the most directly calculated to remedy the evils arising from that disturbance in the balance of produce and consumption, which has been occasioned by the sudden conversion of soldiers, sailors, and various other classes which the war employed, into productive labourers.[91]

Of course it is possible to be critical of Malthus's handling of all this. His neglect of the multiplier effects of the investment spending is important. But he had latched on to an intellectual problem of some size. It really was a capital stock adjustment problem which concerned him—his constant references to 'proportionality' between productive and unproductive activity, and between consumption and investment, show this very clearly—and if we need post-Keynesian economics to understand what he was after, this is not entirely his fault.

iv. PRODUCTIVE AND UNPRODUCTIVE LABOUR

The distinction between productive and unproductive labour is singled out for special treatment here because it permeates Classical growth theory and the Classical economists were sharply divided between those who accepted and those who did not accept the distinction.

The Physiocrats had distinguished productive and unproductive labour on the basis that only labour employed in agriculture should be classed as productive—all other occupations giving rise to no net product and being classified as 'sterile'. Adam Smith rejected this and made instead the distinction between labour which added to the value of an object on which it was bestowed *and/or* resulted in a tangible and storable commodity on the one hand, and labour which produced only intangibles and did not directly add value on the other. 'There is one sort of labour which adds to the value of the subject upon which it is bestowed: there is another which has no such effect. The former, as it produces a value, may be called productive; the latter, unproductive labour.' Productive labour 'fixes and realizes itself in some particular subject or vendible commodity, which lasts for some time at least after that labour is past. It is, as it were, a certain quantity of labour stocked and stored up to be employed, if necessary, upon some other occasion.' Unproductive labour 'on the contrary, does not fix or realize itself in any particular subject or vendible commodity. His services generally perish in the very instant of their performance, and seldom leave any trace or value behind them, for which an equal quantity of service could afterwards be procured.'[92] Smith was not arguing that unproductive labour was always unimportant;

In the same class must be ranked, some both of the gravest and most important, and some of the most frivolous professions: churchmen, lawyers, physicians, men of letters of all kinds; players, buffoons, musicians, opera-singers, opera-dancers, &c.

But he was arguing that their labour was different in kind from the labour which he classified as productive. Thus of officers of government he wrote :

Their service, how honourable, how useful, or how necessary soever, produces nothing for which an equal quantity of service can afterwards be procured. [value criterion]. The protection, security, and defence of the commonwealth, the effect of their labour this year, will not purchase its protection, security, and defence for the year to come. [storage criterion].[93]

The importance of the distinction was in relation to growth. In Smith's view of economic progress it was the proportion of the produce of previous years which was employed in maintaining productive labour during the current year which determined the amount of that year's produce. According to Smith, part of the annual produce replaces capital and part constitutes profit and rent. The former employs only productive hands. The latter may or may not employ productive labour; and their share in total income helped to determine the size of the unproductive sector and to determine whether the inhabitants (and here Smith contrasted Edinburgh unfavourably with Glasgow) were industrious or idle.

Now all of this seems rather unhappy. If expenditure on defence, for instance, increases security, then, given the rest of Smith's analysis, annual produce was likely to increase with expenditure on defence. If the employment of lawyers increased the security of contracts then, in the same way, annual produce was likely to increase. But there are two points to be made. Firstly, Smith, with his historical picture of the development out of feudalism in mind, and the replacement of retainers by productive labourers, was on fairly firm ground in insisting that the annual produce would be increased by increasing either the productivity of labour (through division of labour) or the number of productive labourers. Where one must dissent from Smith is in his *confining* the epithet 'productive' in the way already indicated. Secondly, any reader of the *Wealth of Nations* will be well aware that Smith saw economic progress as depending upon parsimony, i.e. capital accumulation, and being interfered with by prodigality. It was *public* prodigality and imprudence which he feared rather than the private variety which was constrained by the limitations of private property. He was thus concerned to advance an argument against the extension of public spending. There is also the implication that whatever the *average* productivity of state employees, the state faced no sanctions similar to those which faced the private business man if he increased the number of employees to a point where their *marginal* productivity fell to negative levels.

Classical writers after Smith divide into two camps on this issue. On the one hand there are those who rejected outright the distinction—notably Say, Lauderdale, and McCulloch. Say's view was that all labour was productive which produced *utility*; there was no point in distinguishing various kinds of labour[94]. Now from a neo-Classical point of view this was a perfectly defensible argument; it is reasonable if we confine ourselves to what are now conventionally conceived of as welfare questions. But in the context of the growth-orientation of Classical economics it was a rather unsatisfactory position.

Lauderdale's rejection links up with his treatment of the capital-stock-adjustment problem which we have already dealt with—he was not concerned about the need to maximize parsimony. Like Say he argued that anything which created utility was productive.[95]

McCulloch's rejection was based on a different and rather more subtle ground.[96] This was that even such labour as that of musicians had an *incentive* effect in stimulating those who wished to be able to employ the musicians' services; and it was therefore productive. He was not then rejecting the distinction on utility grounds, as might appear to be the case from his inclusion of musicians, but on the grounds that Smith had unduly narrowed the category of labour which produced economic growth. He also rejected the 'storage' version as inconsistent with his recognition of the importance of investment in human capital.

In contrast to these writers we find both Malthus and J. S. Mill stoutly defending Smith's distinction. Malthus used both a value and a storage version in distinguishing labour which was productive of wealth. His main aim was to separate productive labour from that involved in supplying personal services—the aim of this will be clear from the previous section. The distinction was a necessary one : capital was the source of profits and was necessary to division of labour, and so it was important to distinguish labour which maintained and replaced capital (productive labour) and that which did not. Productive labour was 'that labour which is so directly productive of material wealth as to be capable of estimation in the quantity or value of the object produced, which object is capable of being transferred without the presence of the producer'.[97] There is a subtle point here then; Malthus was not distinguishing the kinds of labour which conduced to growth so much as the kinds of labour which related to his analysis of the capital-stock-adjustment problem. We find him defining unproductive labour as

that kind of labour or industry, which however highly useful and important some of it may be, and however much it may conduce *indirectly* to the production and security of material wealth, does not realise itself on any object which can be valued and transferred without the presence of the person performing such service. and cannot therefore be made to enter into an estimate of national wealth.[98]

Yet Malthus's treatment was not really consistent; for although he argued that only labour engaged in producing something which was transferable without the presence of the producer was productive, he still felt able to classify labour engaged in education as productive.[99]

J. S. Mill devoted some time to clarifying this matter at an early stage in his career. In his *Essays*[100] Mill distinguished not only between productive and unproductive labour, but also between productive and unproductive capital and expenditure. He distinguished that labour, capital, and consumption which made a country better off by adding to wealth and that which did not. Labour which *directly* afforded enjoyment (such as that of a musician) was unproductive; and whatever was consumed by such a performer was unproductive consumption. Nevertheless Mill felt able to argue that the making of musical instruments was productive (here we have the storage version again) and so was the labour of the musician in acquiring his skill. Labour involved in maintaining law and order was not however productive. In his *Principles*[101] Mill set out to continue in this path. Labour produced three kinds of utilities—those in material products, those embodied in human beings (as a result of the activities of teachers and governments) and services (as rendered by actors and others). In his *Essay* Mill had classified as productive anything which created a permanent utility; in the *Principles* he attempted to narrow this by confining the concept to material wealth. Yet he still included the acquisition of skill as productive labour (the material element being supplied by the embodiment of the skill in human beings!) while vacillating considerably over classification of the activities of soldiers, policemen, and judges.[102]

This distinction between productive and unproductive activities has now passed out of economics. Yet ironically enough it tends to reappear during wartime and under authoritarian regimes, when it is put to uses that (at least in the latter case) would have horrified the essentially liberal-minded Classical economists. As J. S. Mill put it, freedom was preferable to efficiency.[103]

V. CONCLUSION

We have now finished our survey of Classical growth and development theory. It should be apparent that it contained a great deal that is still of interest today: and it should be apparent also that there are real lessons to be learnt from this kind of approach to the subject. Today we find growth theorists who delight in playing with models. But, in the words of a recent survey of the subject:

Nothing is easier than to ring the changes on more and more complicated models, without bringing in any really new ideas and without bringing the theory any nearer to casting light on the causes of the wealth of nations. The problems posed may well have intellectual fascination. But it is essentially a frivolous occupation to take a chain with links of very uneven strength and devote one's energies to strengthening and polishing the links that are already relatively strong.[104]

We find also development economists who really have something interesting and useful to say about economic development; and their approach is wholly in the line of descent from Classical economics.

## NOTES

1. *Wealth of Nations*, ed. Cannan, i. 267.
2. Ibid., pp. 360–70.
3. Ibid., pp. 366–8.
4. Ibid., pp. 265–6.
5. Ibid., pp. 321–5.
6. Ibid., pp. 340–54.
7. Ibid., p. 348.
8. Ibid., pp. 351–2.
9. Ibid., pp. 5–14.
10. Ibid., ii. 267–73.
11. Ibid., i. 355–94.
12. Ibid., i. 89–100.
13. Malthus, *Principles* (2nd edn. 1836), Bk. II, Ch. 1, pp. 309–437.
14. Ibid., pp. 309–10.
15. Ibid., p. 314.
16. Ibid., pp. 332–3.
17. Ibid., pp. 334–9.
18. Ibid., pp. 351–60.
19. Ibid., p. 357.
20. Ibid., pp. 311–14; see also O'Brien, *J. R. McCulloch*, p. 318, and the references therein.
21. Malthus, op. cit., pp. 361–71, 382–90.
22. Ibid., pp. 342, 372–82.
23. Ibid., pp. 348–9.
24. For a full discussion of McCulloch's view of the growth process see O'Brien, *J. R. McCulloch*, Ch. XII.
25. McCulloch, *Treatise on Taxation* (1st edn. 1845), p. 110.
26. *J. R. McCulloch*, pp. 291–9.
27. London, 1832.
28. Mill, *Principles* (ed. Ashley), Bk. I, Ch. 9.
29. If it simply resulted in increased profits the community might still gain since the shareholders were part of it (see ibid., pp. 142–3).
30. Ibid., pp. 134, 137–42.
31. Ibid., Bk. I, Ch. 7, pp. 101–15.
32. John Rae, *Statement of Some New Principles on the Subject of Political Economy* (Boston, 1834, repr. A. M. Kelley, New York, 1964), Bk. II, pp. 78–357.
33. Ibid., Bk. II, Ch. 7, pp. 130–63.
34. Ibid., Bk. II, Ch. 4, pp. 100–8.
35. Mill, op. cit., pp. 54–62.
36. Ibid., pp. 163–75.
37. Rae, op. cit., Bk. I, Ch. 10, pp. 208–64.
38. Mill, op. cit., pp. 116–31; Rae, op. cit., pp. 164–97.
39. Mill, op. cit., p. 128; Rae, p. 356; Lord Lauderdale, *An Inquiry into the Nature and Origin of Public Wealth* (Edinburgh, 1804, repr. A. M. Kelley, New York, 1962), pp. 293–5.
40. However he doubted the second ground for division of labour—increasing productivity through time saved in changing jobs.
41. Mill, op. cit., pp. 176–88.
42. Ibid., pp. 193, 704.
43. Ibid., pp. 172, 725–39.
44. Ibid., pp. 725–8.
45. Ibid., pp. 731–9.
46. Ibid., pp. 746–51.
47. Ibid., pp. 695–9.

48. Ibid., pp. 747–8.
49. Ibid., pp. 750–1.
50. Ibid., pp. 759–60.
51. Ibid., pp. 749–50, 752.
52. Ibid., pp. 763–4, 764–72.
53. Ibid., pp. 791–4.
54. Ibid., pp. 76–7, 740.
55. Ibid., p. 191.
56. Ibid., pp. 219 ff.
57. Ibid., pp. 256–82, 283–301.
58. Only late in the book (pp. 762–3) did he recognize some of the other aspects of peasant proprietorship such as patriarchal despotism.
59. Ibid., pp. 302–17.
60. Ibid., pp. 318–42.
61. Ibid., pp. 144–54.
62. Ibid., p. 105 n.
63. See the bibliography to this chapter. The quotation in the text below is from p. 16 of Barton's pamphlet.
64. Ricardo, *Principles*, ed. Sraffa, pp. 395–7. Ricardo's numerical example is pp. 388–91.
65. See the bibliography to this chapter.
66. K. Wicksell, *Lectures on Political Economy* (repr. London, 1934), i. 134–5.
67. *Principles*, 2nd edn., p. 352.
68. See O'Brien, *J. R. McCulloch*, pp. 302–6.
69. See *Principles*, ed. Ashley, pp. 94–100, 135, 742–5.
70. Ibid., p. 98.
71. Ibid., pp. 98–9.
72. See the bibliography to this chapter.
73. Lalor's work is discussed in Corry, *Money, Savings and Investment*, pp. 145–51.
74. Lauderdale, op. cit., pp. 214–15, 227–8.
75. Ibid., pp. 220–2.
76. Ibid., pp. 228–9.
77. Ibid., pp. 304–14.
78. This is pointed out in the article by Corry on Malthus and Keynes which is cited in the bibliography to this chapter.
79. Malthus, *Principles*, pp. 38–9.
80. R. C. O. Mathews in K. Kurihara (ed.), *Post-Keynesian Economics* (London, 1955), p. 173.
81. Ibid., pp. 173–4.
82. Malthus, *Principles*, pp. 315, 317, 318, 319, 320, 322.
83. Mill, *Principles*, ed. Ashley, pp. 556–63.
84. *Principles* (ed. Sraffa), pp. 263–72.
85. Ibid., pp. 289–90.
86. Malthus, *Principles*, pp. 398, 400.
87. Ibid., p. 434.
88. Ibid., pp. 398–413. Here he does seem to be considering overproduction of *all* goods: but the range of these is finite and the *un*satisfied demand is for services.
89. Ibid., pp. 382–97.
90. *Economic Journal*, 65 (1955), 543–4.
91. Malthus, *Principles*, pp. 429–30.
92. *Wealth of Nations*, ed. Cannan, i. 313–14.
93. Ibid., p. 314.
94. Say, *Treatise*, trans. Prinsep, pp. 119–27. At the same time Say was quite clear that this offered no justification for the existence of an unnecessarily complicated legal system which merely provided employment for lawyers.
95. Lauderdale, *Inquiry*, pp. 148–52.
96. See D. P. O'Brien, *J. R. McCulloch*, pp. 299–302.

97. Malthus, *Principles*, p. 35.
98. Ibid.
99. Ibid., p. 37.
100. J. S. Mill, *Essays*, pp. 75–89, Essay III 'On the Words Productive and Un-productive'.
101. J. S. Mill, *Principles*, ed. Ashley, pp. 44–53.
102. Cf. ibid., pp. 37, 46–7, 48–9.
103. See the quotation from Mill's Essay *On Liberty* in Lord Robbins, *Theory of Economic Development*, p. 169.
104. F. H. Hahn and R. C. O. Mathews, 'The Theory of Economic Growth: A Survey', *Economic Journal*, 74 (1964), 779–902, especially p. 890.

## BIBLIOGRAPHY

For a general discussion of Classical growth theory Lord Robbins's magisterial *Theory of Economic Development in the History of Economic Thought* (London, 1968), can be strongly recommended; and the reader will find that it covers such topics as money and population which were not included in this chapter. A useful additional reference is E. McKinley's survey of Classical growth theory contained in B. F. Hoselitz (ed.), *Theories of Economic Growth* (New York, 1960), and the same author's 'The Problem of "Underdevelopment" in the English Classical School', *Quarterly Journal of Economics*, 69 (1955), 235–52. Valuable discussions of the eighteenth-century background will be found in E. A. J. Johnson, *The Predecessors of Adam Smith*, and in E. Rotwein's introduction to Hume, both of which have been cited earlier.

There is *no* substitute for reading the *Wealth of Nations*—see especially Bk. I, Chs. 1–3 and 9, Bk. II, Chs. 1 and 3–5, and Bk. III, Chs. 1–4. There is a wealth of secondary discussion: probably the most immediately useful references are A. Lowe, 'The Classical Theory of Economic Growth', *Social Research*, 21 (1954), 127–58; a diagrammatic treatment inspired by this (alternative to the one given in the text above) in W. O. Thweatt's article in *Social Research*, 24 (1957), 227–30; and the massive treatment (in part a critique of the preceeding two references) by J. Spengler, Pts. I and II of which appeared in *Southern Economic Journal*, 25 (1959), 397–415 and 26 (1959), 1–12. Another diagrammatic treatment may be found in H. Barkhai, 'A Formal Outline of a Smithian Growth Model', *Quarterly Journal of Economics*, 83 (1969), 396–414. See also the discussion by Letiche in the Hoselitz volume cited above. For the discussion of Adam Smith's view (or views) of division of labour see E. G. West, 'Adam Smith's Two Views on the Division of Labour', *Economica*, N.S. 31 (1964), 23–32, and N. Rosenberg, 'Adam Smith on the Division of Labour: Two Views or One', *Economica*, 32 (1965), 127–39. For those who wish to pursue further the Classical concept of capital there is Cannan, *Production and Distribution*, Chs. 1 and 4, and Iriving Fisher, 'What is Capital?', *Economic Journal*, 6 (1896), 509–34. On the general question of the declining rate of profit see B. A. Corry, 'Progress and Profits', *Economica*, N.S. 28 (1961), 203–11.

On the general Malthusian theory of growth there is no substitute for Malthus's *Principles*: there are as many secondary interpretations as authors. McCulloch's writings on growth on the other hand are extremely diffuse and any small sample is likely to be misleading. See D. P. O'Brien, *J. R. McCulloch*, Ch. 12. Mill's *Principles* by contrast gives a good picture of his position: see Bks. I and II, Ch. 14 of Bk. III, and Bk. IV. There is an excellent discussion of Mill by J. Spengler in the Hoselitz volume cited above. Spengler has also produced a valuable article 'John Rae on Economic Development', *Quarterly Journal of Economics*, 73 (1959), 393–406. This is recommended reading even for those brave enough to tackle Rae's prolix but fascinating book *Statement of Some New Principles on the Subject of Political Economy* (Boston, 1834), of which there is fortunately a reprint (A. M. Kelly, New York, 1964). See also R. H. and J. S. Deans, 'John Rae and the Problems of Economic Development', *Review of Social Economy*, 30 (1972), 97–111. Babbage's book *On the Economy of Machinery and Manufactures* (London, 1832) (which Babbage had difficulty in publishing because of material about restrictive practices in publishing!), should not be missed.

On the machinery question see Barton's *Observations on the Circumstances which Influence the Condition of the Labouring Classes of Society* (London, 1817), repr. in G. Sotiroff (ed.), *Economic Writings*, i (Regina, Sask., 1962); Ricardo, *Principles,* Ch. 31; O'Brien, *J. R. McCulloch*, pp. 302–6, and a recent and very interesting exchange in the *Economic Journal*, 81 (1971), 916–25 between Professor E. F. Beach and Sir John Hicks. The former's contribution contains useful references to the literature in the continuing debate on the subject. On the wider  question of capital-stock adjustment there is a voluminous literature. The classic statement of the idea is to be found in R. C. O. Mathew's contribution to K. Kurihara, *Post-Keynesian Economics* (London, 1955). The critics are arrayed in an article by B. J. Gordon, 'Say's Law, Effective Demand, and the Contemporary British Reviews', *Economica*, 32 (1965), 438–46 and in *Non-Ricardian Political Economy* (Baker Library, Boston, 1967); by R. D. C. Black, 'Parson Malthus, the General [Sleeman] and the Captain [Pettman]', *Economic Journal*, 77 (1967), 59–74; and B. A. Corry, *Money, Saving and Investment in English Economics* (London, 1962). See also the latter's very useful articles 'The Theory of the Economic Effects of Government Expenditure in English Classical Political Economy', *Economica*, 25 (1958), 34–48, and 'Malthus and Keynes—A Reconsideration', *Economic Journal*, 69 (1959), 717–24. A good corrective to an over-facile view of Say's Law is to be found in A Skinner, 'Say's Law: origins and content', *Economica*, N.S. 34 (1967), 153–66. But, as Professor Black points out in the article cited above, this is an area in which virtually every shade of opinion is to be encountered: see as examples of this articles by Vatter, *Canadian Journal*, 25 (1959), 60–4, Sowell, *Oxford Economic Papers*, 15 (1963), 193–203, Hollander, *History of Political Economy*, 1 (1969), 306–35, and Lambert, *Annals of Public and Co-operative Economy*, 37 (1966), 3–23, and the books by M. Paglin, *Malthus and Lauderdale* (New York, 1961), and T. Sowell, *Say's Law* (Princeton, 1972), as well as the treatment of Malthus's demand for services in J. J. Spengler, 'Today's circumstances and yesterday's theories: Malthus on "Services"', *Kyklos*, 18 (1965), 601–13. There is also R. G. Link's *English Theories of Economic Fluctuations* (New York, 1959), which has a particularly interesting discussion of Malthus and also covers Thomas Attwood, Thomas Joplin, James Wilson, Thomas Tooke, and J. S. Mill, which makes it relevant to Ch. VI as well. But, to repeat, comparison of these works will show that there is an enormous range of interpretation of the primary sources. For this reason, if for no other, there is no substitute for reading Malthus's *Principles*, Bk. II, and Lord Lauderdale's *Inquiry into the Nature and Origin of Public Wealth*, 2nd edn. 1819 (repr. A. M. Kelley, New York, 1962).

On productive and unproductive labour the classic secondary references are H. Myint, 'The Welfare Significance of Productive Labour', *Review of Economic Studies*, 11 ,1943), 20–30 and Ch. V of the same author's *Theories of Welfare Economics* (London, 1948). See also D. P. O'Brien, *J. R. McCulloch*, pp. 299–302, and V. W. Bladen, 'Adam Smith on Productive and Unproductive Labour: a theory of full development', *Canadian Journal*, 26 (1960), 625–30. The key primary references are Smith, Bk. II, Ch. 3; Malthus, Bk. I, Ch. 2 §2; and J. S. Mill, *Essays* (Essay III 'On the Words Productive and Unproductive') and *Principles*, Bk. I, Ch. 3.

The Classical economists were of course concerned with particular underdeveloped areas. The full range of their thinking can be seen in the classic study by R. D. C. Black, *Economic Thought and the Irish Question* (London, 1960).

Finally those who wish to see what development economics has to offer and how close are its links with Classical economics should read W. Elkan's splendid little book, *An Introduction to Development Economics* (London, 1973). Juxtaposition of this with Lord Robbins's book prompts some interesting questions about progress in economic thought.

# 9. Classical Public Finance

The Classical treatment of Public Finance started from the position that there were four main sources of revenue for the State—taxation, debt creation, State property (mainly land) ownership, and State enterprise. We can dismiss the last two quickly. There was fairly widespread agreement that State ownership of property was unlikely to yield much revenue—Smith had argued persuasively that the land languished under State ownership.[1] James Mill, it is true, favoured State ownership of land in new countries with revenue being raised through auctioning of the ground rents. But he received little support—McCulloch for instance believed that private property in land was necessary to encourage investment in improvements, and Ricardo pointed out that, since there would not be a shortage of land in a new country, prospective revenue receipts were hardly encouraging.[2]

Nor was there much enthusiasm for State enterprise as a source of revenue with the exception of Jeremy Bentham who suggested that the State could raise funds by taking over business from the Friendly Societies, by operating deposit banking on behalf of such large customers as the East India Company, and by the issue of paper money as a substitute for borrowing from the Bank of England and the market.[3]

Debt finance was obviously an important possibility: but equally obviously (for, apart from the problems of unlimited growth of debt, existing debt had to be serviced) it could not constitute a major source of revenue except in emergency situations such as wartime. However the Classical economists paid a lot of attention to public debt; and it will be dealt with in the third section of this chapter.

Tax finance had then clearly to be the major source of public revenue. Now virtually all the Classical treatments of tax finance start from Adam Smith's classic four maxims of taxation—equality, certainty, convenience, and economy of collection.[4] Even where the later writers such as Say and Mill set out to provide their own maxims the derivation from Smith was obvious.[5]

The first of the maxims, as formulated by Smith, contained however a fundamental ambiguity. According to Smith:

The subjects of every state ought to contribute towards the support of the government, as nearly as possible, in proportion to their respective abilities; that is, in proportion to the revenue which they respectively enjoy under the protection of the state. The expence of government to the individuals of a great nation, is like the expence of management to the joint tenants of a great estate, who are all obliged to contribute in proportion to their respective interests in the estate.[6]

Now this maxim contained elements of two contrasting approaches to taxation—the benefit approach and the 'ability to pay' approach—and attempted to combine them. Yet they are quite distinct. The hallmark of the benefit approach is that it is a *quid pro quo* approach—the taxpayer pays for the benefit he receives from state protection and other state services. Such an approach takes the distribution of income as given and has its roots in the idea of a social contract.

The 'ability to pay' approach on the other hand separates revenue-raising from expenditure and denies the possibility of imputing benefit shares to individuals. Instead it attempts to apportion taxes between individuals on the basis of some kind of equity. Its roots lie in sixteenth-century writers such as Bodin, although it can be traced back as far as the Middle Ages.[7]

Smith was probably not consciously attempting to combine these two elements; rather, it seems probable that eighteenth-century and earlier writers were not clearly aware of the distinction. The seventeenth-century writer Sir William Petty for instance is a notable forerunner of Smith in his approach.[8]

The later Classical writers did however divide into two separate camps. Among the benefit writers we find Hume and also Bentham. The approach was espoused by a number of minor figures, notably Thiers, who narrowed it so far as to equate taxation with insurance premiums for state protection, and also by one major figure, J. B. Say.[9]

In the 'ability to pay' group the most important writers were McCulloch and J. S. Mill. 'Equality' was the aim for them and indeed for all of the writers in this group in dealing with the question of the distribution of the tax load. But there were important differences between members of the group, not least between these two writers in particular. On the one hand McCulloch's position was to contend that the benefit approach was impracticable. The important thing, taking the State's revenue requirement as given,[10] was not complete equality of taxation between individuals but equality between sectors so that taxation interfered as little as possible with growth. The criteria of ability to pay in this sense were closely bound up with Smith's last three maxims—the more a tax conformed with these the more satisfactory it was from a growth point of view.[11] J. S. Mill's reason for rejecting the benefit approach and his concept of ability to pay were both however rather different. On the one hand he believed that property was not a good measure of benefit received or of expenses incurred by the State; moreover he believed that, in the last resort, the poor needed more protection than the rich and so the benefit approach would lead to regressive taxation which he regarded as unacceptable. On the other, he believed that the correct way to approach the problem was in terms of attempting to achieve equal sacrifices (of utility) by different taxpayers.[12] Now there were ambiguities involved in this which were not clear to Mill and were not in fact resolved until such later writers as Cohen-Stuart and Edgeworth. For there are three possible concepts of equal sacrifice: equal absolute sacrifice, equal proportional sacrifice, and equal marginal sacrifice. Writing $U$ for utility, $Y$ for income, and $T$ for tax, these three concepts may be written:[13]

Equal Absolute Sacrifice: $U(Y) - U(Y - T)$ equal for all taxpayers

Equal Proportional Sacrifice: $\dfrac{U(Y) - U(Y - T)}{U(Y)}$ equal for all taxpayers

Equal Marginal Sacrifice: $\dfrac{d\,U(Y - T)}{d(Y - T)}$ equal for all taxpayers

Even with *known* and *identical* income-utility schedules (propositions which Mill would have been too sensible to grant) the tax treatment involved is far from clear as we shall see, although granted these *and* diminishing marginal utility of income—and Mill was even doubtful about the hypothesis of diminishing marginal utility of income for higher income levels[14]—Mill's requirement of least aggregate sacrifice[15] involved equal marginal sacrifice, which in turn involved levelling all incomes down from the top. It is, to put it mildly, very doubtful whether Mill would have supported such a tax system, as we shall see.

The 'ability to pay' approach links up naturally with the idea of a nation's taxable capacity. The view of taxable capacity to be found in Classical economics stems mainly from Hume and the Physiocrats. The latter had recommended a single tax on land proportioned to its net produce as the only constituent of net national income.[16] Surprisingly perhaps the influence of this is less clear in the case of Smith (who tended to stress *gross* national income) than in the case of the later writers, especially Ricardo who, in the chapter on Gross and Net Revenue in his *Principles*, distinguished profits and rent as the only long-run sources of taxation, although it could fall on capital (stock) in the short run. Other writers, as we shall see, were prepared to allow that wages could be a source of tax revenue where these were above physical subsistence. There was however fairly general agreement that there was no one single index of taxable capacity and that measurement was impossible.[17]

The element stemming from Hume was the notion of 'tax stimulation'. The idea was that the imposition of a tax increased the supply of effort, ingenuity, and enterprise (and, in some cases, saving), so that income rose to compensate at least partially for the tax. Ricardo made no use of the idea, and Say rejected it on the grounds that output was limited by capital.[18] But this argument, which was linked to the argument we encountered in dealing with economic growth, that too favourable a climate discouraged effort, was enthusiastically adopted by McCulloch in particular, who saw taxation as stimulating saving as well as the other factors.[19] He even argued that national income could be increased through over-reaction to the imposition of taxation. Nevertheless it was recognized that this was not an unlimited resource; taxation could pass beyond the point of stimulation to one where it gave a shock to these same sources of economic advance, and there was also the danger of its leading to capital export.[20]

There was general agreement that what taxes were levied had to be levied in money terms, not in kind. Otherwise there were difficulties of collection, price fluctuations in the markets for the commodities concerned as they were released from storehouses for the purposes of raising revenue, and the widely accepted inefficiency of Corvée, as well as the total immorality of impressment (conscription) which was strenuously condemned by such writers as McCulloch.[21]

But, even when levied in money, taxes could still do considerable harm to the level of activity if they were set at too high a level in relation to taxable capacity.[22] The case of Holland was frequently cited as exemplifying a country which had been pushed into economic decline by taxes which were so high that they fell not upon net national income but upon capital stock, or at least fell upon that part of net national income which would otherwise have been saved. In a curious episode in the history of economic thought, Say argued that taxation reduced demand and therefore production, while Ricardo used what we now call Say's Identity in an attempt to combat this idea. Ricardo was prepared to concede that taxes could affect the size of the capital stock; but he was not prepared to concede the importance of taxation in relation to aggregate demand.[23]

But, whatever harm was done by taxation, most Classical writers felt that such harm was greatly magnified by tax-farming, although McCulloch was not opposed to it in principle.[24] Smith however, in particular, argued that tax-farming increased the total tax bill, because the tax-farmer's profit had to be met. At first sight this is a dubious argument since the need for such a profit would only arise if the 'farmer' first advanced the expected tax proceeds to government; and if he did not do this then government would have to borrow in the market anyway and meet an interest charge. But what Smith was getting at was that tax-farming was not open to competition because of barriers to entry into the profession, produced by the need for access to large quantities of capital and by the need for knowledge of the tax system. The profits referred to were then, to some extent, monopoly profits.[25]

Amongst both benefit and 'ability to pay' theorists there was some opposition to local taxation. On the one hand Say, as a benefit theorist, judged that local taxes were only suitable for paying for such local services as schools and libraries;[26] on the other hand J. S. Mill, an 'ability to pay' theorist, agreed that local taxation should be limited because it was much less open to discussion and public control than national taxation.[27]

There was widespread (though not universal) agreement that the tax base should be wide. Thus Hume argued that it was necessary to have many sources of revenue if a state was to be strong,[28] and this view was endorsed by McCulloch (although in fact in the latter's *Treatise on Taxation* very few duties actually passed his inspection as satisfactory). In particular Mc-Culloch strongly opposed Gladstone's narrowing of the tax base, as needlessly sacrificing revenue (a point which was of considerable importance both in relation to the possible abolition of the income tax and to the reduction of the National Debt). McCulloch also argued that concentration of taxation on a few duties at a high level led to intensification of the regressive characteristics of indirect taxation, which in turn was productive of the danger of social discontent. Moreover he believed that a strong revenue was necessary as a deterrent to the French, that the broader the base the less that taxation was felt, and that the narrower the base the greater the distortions in the allocative mechanism.[29] Say also argued that a wide spread of taxes would help to reduce the regressive character of indirect taxes and to minimize distortion.[30] But Adam Smith believed that the range of customs duties could be narrowed with advantage[31] (though given the *very* wide range of duties in his day such a position is not entirely inconsistent with the preceding one) while J. S. Mill was a believer in a narrow tax base, though there was a need to avoid sharp inequalities and this limited the narrowness to some extent.[32]

One final point should be made before we pass on to the details of tax finance. In the Classical treatments of public finance there is a sharp distinction to be made between two kinds of approach. On the one hand there were those who addressed themselves to a real tax system. Smith is the leading figure here, but McCulloch was fundamentally concerned with fiscal policy in relation to the maintenance of growth, and there was the outstanding case of Sir Henry Parnell who devoted a great deal of effort to devising plans for a complete overhaul of the tax system in the light of Smith's four maxims, especially the last three.[33]

On the other hand there were those—Ricardo above all, but also James Mill—who wrote more or less completely divorced from the tax system of their day.[34] The income tax, introduced in 1799, was a subject of hot debate during Ricardo's lifetime—yet he hardly considered it anywhere. About the only tax (apart, of course, from the duty on imported corn) to which these two writers addressed themselves was the Poor Rate.[35] J. S. Mill was influenced by his father and Ricardo to some extent; but he did not succeed in divorcing himself from the real tax system to anything like the extent that they achieved.

ii. TAX FINANCE

Taxes can be divided (though there was not agreement amongst the Classical economists as to where the dividing line should be drawn)[36] into direct and indirect taxes, and there are a number of discussions of the merits of the two kinds of taxation to be found in the Classical writings. Several writers had a strong preference for indirect taxes. Thus Hume regarded direct taxes as a regrettable necessity to be used only when there was a shortfall of revenue from indirect taxes.[37] Adam Smith was also in general favourable to indirect taxation, at least at moderate levels, although he did recognize that indirect taxes did not reach absentees, and believed that they offended against the economy maxim, led to vexatious investigation and smuggling, and distorted the allocation of resources.[38] J. B. Say, although he was, as we shall see later on, an advocate of progressive taxation, was nevertheless favourably disposed towards indirect taxes.[39] They were paid almost unconsciously and according to the means of the tax payer at that time, and they were reliable and, potentially at least, economical. They contained incentives to fraud but this was not a serious problem if the tax levels were moderate. McCulloch, who offered probably the fullest discussion of this topic, expressed a strong preference for indirect taxation.[40] This was however more because of the serious defects which he believed to exist in direct taxation than out of positive enthusiasm for indirect taxes. The latter were, it was true, 'convenient' in Smith's sense, they did not involve investigation of personal details, they had a useful sumptuary role, they encouraged accumulation (and hence demand for labour), and they stimulated effort, ingenuity, and saving, whereas direct taxes stimulated only saving. But he conceded that indirect taxes were regressive and that they altered relative prices. They encouraged smuggling (and fraud where drawbacks were allowed) and raised prices by more than the amount of the tax if the producer were required to advance the tax, for he would require interest on his advance. But these were defects which McCulloch regarded as tolerable, so long as the taxes were kept at a fairly low level. His attitude towards defects in direct taxation was however much more severe. Assessment of an income tax posed, he believed, insoluble problems. On the one hand, as we shall see later on, McCulloch believed that, to be just, an income tax should be levied according to the present value of an income stream (which would vary, *inter alia*, with life expectancy); on the other hand there was the difficulty that amortization of investment in education should be allowed. This however was very difficult and some tax payers were in a position to make themselves unofficial allowances while others (including civil servants like McCulloch) were not. Direct taxes were liable to lead to fraud and evasion. They were either attacks on honesty or they necessitated giving undesirable and 'inquisatorial' powers to the tax authorities. Moreover they were likely to become progressive—and, as we shall see, McCulloch was firmly opposed to this.

Ricardo on the other hand was in favour of direct taxation. He regarded the customs and excise as 'those great sources of the demoralization [i.e. corruption] of the people' and he wanted them got rid of.[41] He believed that a tax on wage goods (which, according to his analysis, would be passed on and come out of profits) together with a tax on rent and on income from government securities would provide the best revenue base.[42]

J. S. Mill as usual managed to come between these two extremes. On the one hand he thought the English dislike of direct taxes to be 'puerile'. On the other hand, he believed that too great a reliance on direct taxation would create a strong climate of opinion opposed to necessary government expenditure on education and other services.[43] Indirect taxes were convenient, while it was impossible fairly to assess direct taxes. Nevertheless a house tax and a land tax, together with a tax on increments in rental values and a punitive tax on inheritance, were all acceptable. But this must be the limit of direct taxation; an income tax should only be used in emergencies. Nevertheless Mill was concerned about the regressive effects of substantial reliance on indirect taxation, and he considered various methods for making indirect taxes progressive.

A number of writers (including Ricardo) saw indirect taxes as having the advantage of being 'optional'.[44] The taxpayer could avoid them by not buying the good in question. Amongst the major writers only J. S. Mill saw the fallacy, pointing out that this was simply ignoring the income effects of indirect taxation.[45] Even Mill however did not see through another fallacy; the common Classical argument that while indirect taxes distorted choice direct taxes did not—an argument which obviously ignores the income/leisure choice distortion involved in direct taxation.[46] All however conceded that indirect taxes could raise prices if producers were required to advance the tax before selling the good; in such a case they would require interest upon the advance. However the amounts involved were generally agreed to be very small after the keen cutting edge of Ricardo's mind had shown that Sismondi's attempts (starting from a suggestion by Say)[47] to attribute *large* increases in price to this source involved assuming that producers earned *annual* rates of interest for the period of the advance however short.[48]

## 1. Direct Taxes

The Classical literature covers a wide range of direct taxes; but almost all the Classical writers discussed wage taxation. One group of writers including both Smith and Ricardo believed that such taxes must be passed on. Adam Smith relied for this on the subsistence wage mechanism—if wages were at subsistence then they could not be depressed and so a tax on wages must be passed on.[49] Smith however condemned taxes on wages as 'absurd and destructive'[50] (though apparently on the grounds that the resulting rise in wages would raise manufacturing costs and interfere with growth). Any rise in wages produced by taxation would, in Smith's view, work through to the 'liberal professions' in order to maintain wage differentials. Exactly how this was to come about was not clear; and Ricardo simply passed over this difficulty.[51]

Ricardo made some confused, and at times fairly disastrous, attempts to meet the criticism that the long run was being telescoped into the short run[52] in the argument that a wage tax was passed on, but really only one of these is worthy of notice. He offered the argument that if government raised taxes on wages it could demand labour with the proceeds: private demand for labour would be unchanged and the government's demand would then be added to it, raising wages by the amount of the tax (assuming zero elasticity of labour supply).[53] Various writers, especially McCulloch, pointed out to Ricardo that government was unlikely to spend all the proceeds in demanding extra labour, and both Ricardo and James Mill conceded that, in this case, wages would not adjust in the short run.[54]

McCulloch was amongst the group of writers, which also included Hume,[55] that did not accept that wage taxes were automatically shifted. Thus he argued that taxes on the wages of piece-rate earners could be offset by increased effort but that otherwise (except in the special case of domestic servants) taxes on wages would fall on wage earners depressing their (psychological) subsistence level, an effect which could spill over into the long run. Moreover wages were prevented from rising by the freely available supply of child labour and by immigration from Ireland. Even James Mill conceded that if wages were not actually at *physical* subsistence a tax would fall on the wage earner[56] and, switching briefly from capital as demand for labour to demand for commodities as demand for labour, he argued that the reduced purchasing power of labour (as a result of the tax) could reduce demand for labour and hence wages.[57] But otherwise he followed Smith and Ricardo, telescoping the long run and short run together and arguing that a tax on wages at physical subsistence would be passed on via the Malthusian population mechanism. His son made a similar concession concerning wages above physical subsistence and also argued that a tax could fall on professional earnings.[58] With the exception of Ricardo wage taxes were condemned by the Classical economists.[59]

If such taxes were shifted however there was the effect on the general price level to consider. Smith believed that a rise in manufacturing wages would shift the tax to the consumer but that a rise in agricultural wages would be recouped by the farmer from rent.[60] The latter point will be dealt with below in discussing the effects of a tax on agricultural profits. The former point came in for some strong criticism from the later Classical economists who argued that if wages were raised by a tax this would not raise the general price level but depress profits. The arguments which were employed were basically three. Firstly there was the simple argument that not everything could rise in price in terms of everything else.[61] Secondly there was the argument which invoked the price-specie-flow mechanism— Ricardo used this a great deal, although what was clearly at the back of his mind was another argument in terms of the invariable measure of value.[62] If all prices did rise as a result of a wage tax then the money stock would be reduced (through gold flowing abroad) and the price level lowered again. If real wages were unaffected after these vicissitudes then the tax must fall on profits. Thirdly there was an argument used by Ricardo (in criticism of Adam Smith) that there was no limit to a price rise generated in this way if one should occur, and that therefore one could not occur! Whewell was able to show that in fact the successive rises in price as a result of cost increases working their way through the system were progressively smaller and that the series summed to a finite value. Ricardo's lack of formal mathematical training had let him down here.[63] However there was general agreement on another of his arguments, that if wages rose because of taxation, and profits were depressed, then relative values would be altered via the wage/ durability-of-capital theorem which we discussed in Chapter 4.

Taxes on profits were also considered. Adam Smith was opposed to them not only because they were 'interfering' and arbitrary but because he considered that the various constituents of profit were not suitable for taxation. Profits, according to Smith, were interest, wages of management, and compensation for risk. The last was not, in his view, suitable for taxation because it was part of the necessary supply price of capital to any particular occupation. Wages of management were subject to the general analysis of taxes on wages—and we have seen that Smith was opposed to these. Interest was not suitable for taxation for three reasons. Firstly there was the difficulty of knowing the amount received by any individual—this necessitated 'inquisitorial behaviour'; secondly there was a danger of capital migrating abroad if interest was taxed and this would interfere with growth; thirdly when a profits tax was not proportioned to actual sales it favoured the large firms. They would have market power bestowed upon them if the small firms were eliminated, and they could use this to restore their profit levels.[64]

It became conventional amongst the Classical economists to follow Ricardo's treatment in distinguishing between a general profits tax and a tax on the profits of a particular occupation.[65] It was generally agreed that a universal tax on profits would depress profits. If the return on capital invested in mining was excluded from this the money stock would increase, the price level would rise, and profits would be restored in money terms but would still have fallen in real terms. If profits did fall this would bring the stationary state closer and thus affect both the landlord (since the final rental share would be reduced as the margin was not extended so far) and the wage earner (since wages would have less tendency to be bid above subsistence). J. S. Mill also argued that if a profits tax were imposed when the economy was already at the stationary state then capital would emigrate.[66] He believed that a profits tax was undesirable in any case because it encouraged risk-taking by diminishing safe gains.

McCulloch however lost patience with this particular piece of conventional Ricardianism and came to argue that the whole analysis was irrelevant: a universal profits tax was impossible.[67]

There was general agreement too that a tax on the profits of a particular occupation would raise the price of the product. It is perhaps as well to explain what was involved here. Employments of capital in a competitive economy were normally assumed to yield only normal profits, adjusted for risk and inconvenience. A tax on the profits of a particular occupation would then lower the return on capital in that occupation below returns in other fields. Capital would, as a result, leave this particular employment, reducing the supply of the goods involved and raising their price to a level sufficient to restore the profits to equality with those in other employments of capital. This 'profit-equalization mechanism' as we shall call it is to be found in Classical economics from Smith onwards and for the Classical economists it constituted a major tool in the analysis of tax incidence. The argument was essentially a long-run one and it was put to some highly improper uses, not only through a more or less universal telescoping of the long and short run in the Classical discussions but also through the ignoring of the requirements for competition and free entry. (However Smith did make the point that free entry was not universal and he regarded monopoly profits as a most proper source of taxation.)[68] Moreover all the Classical writers ignored the possibility that a tax might cover a sufficiently large segment of the economy that migration of capital to the tax-free sector could sink the rate of profit there.[69]

Two of them however, McCulloch and J. S. Mill, did recognize that this piece of conventional Ricardianism was rather too limited by its static assumptions. McCulloch argued that a partial profits tax might not raise price if it were offset by tax stimulation; that the imperfect mobility of capital made the profit-equalization mechanism itself somewhat imperfect and thus that it might not succeed in adjusting prices in the way envisaged; and that competition from imported supplies might prevent the price rising. J. S. Mill was less critical; but he did recognize that invention and innovation could offset the tendency of price to rise.[70]

Ricardo[71] also considered the case of a profits tax which covered all sectors except agriculture. In such a case the price of corn would not rise and money and corn rents would be unchanged but the price of manufactured goods would rise and so the landlords would be worse off. If the tax was then extended to agriculture the price of corn would rise by the amount of the tax, money rent would rise, and so the landlord would gain through restored purchasing power over manufactures though his corn rent (the amount of corn which his money rent would buy) remained unchanged.

Ricardo and J. Mill also considered the case of a particular tax on agricultural output which will initially affect profits. Smith had believed that such a tax would fall on the landlord in the form of a reduction of rent. He believed that this would happen because the demand for agricultural land would fall as the profitability of employing capital in agriculture fell. Ricardo, making the quite explicit assumption that elasticity of demand for agricultural output was zero, was able to show that in these circumstances the price of corn would rise to a level which would restore profits to their old level *without* any reduction of output. In such a case demand for agricultural land would not be reduced and the tax would not fall on the landlord in the form of a reduction of rent.[72]

The Classical economists also considered the possibility of taxing rent. They normally distinguished between gross rent (which included return on capital invested in improvements) and net rent (which was the pure economic surplus).[73] Taxes on the latter were very proper in principle, as falling on a surplus reward, although in practice it was very difficult to distinguish gross from net rent. Thus Ricardo thought that the Poor Rate, though theoretically a tax on net rent, was actually a tax on gross rent which raised the price of agricultural produce by taxing part of the return on capital invested in agricultural improvement,[74] thus acting (in part) as a tax on the profits of a particular occupation. James Mill was the main enthusiast amongst the Classical economists for taxing rent, and in dealing with Indian revenue he went much further than any of his contemporaries in his suggestions for making land rental the basis of the revenue system.[75] In a more general context he was enthusiastic about the idea of taxing increments of rental value. His argument was that existing rents determined the price paid for land but that any further increments in rent were a pure bonus to the land owner. The argument was fallacious because in a growing economy a growing future income stream should be reflected in price, as the younger Mill was prepared to admit.[76] The elder Mill was particularly anxious that any legislative measure which increased the value of land should give rise to taxation of the resulting surplus. Ricardo objected to this on the grounds that it was impossible to tell how much of an increase in rent was due to legislation and how much to investment in improvements, and that such a tax would give rise to gambling in land, in that land would become a major source of revenue, its price would fluctuate with prospects of peace and war (since war required extra revenue), and speculation would ensue. McCulloch objected to the argument, that it was as open to the legislature to increase the reward of capital (an argument which Mill rejected essentially on the grounds that capital's reward contained no rental element), but he later came to stress other objections; the discouragement of investment in improvements through the tax falling on gross rental, and the violation of his requirement of inter-sectoral justice through taxation of only one kind of property.[77] (This last despite the fact that he was happy with a tax on houses which his analysis led him to believe—as we shall see—fell partly on the landlord. The source of his position here is to be found in Adam Smith's belief that ground rents were an even more proper subject for taxation than ordinary land rents because the problem about capital invested in improvements did not arise and ground rents owed their existence largely to good government.)[78]

Closely linked with this was the discussion of a land tax. The British land tax had been approved of by Smith.[79] It operated on the basis of a fixed valu-ation. Although this infringed the first (equality) maxim as relative land values changed over time it complied with the remaining maxims and, because it was fixed, it did not obstruct improvements. Smith recognized that a fixed land tax could, as Say was later to argue,[80] be very harmful if land values fell; but the British historical experience was of rising land values with a fixed tax which therefore did little harm to economic activity. In Smith's view a land tax varying with value would be more equal, but it might be less certain and less economical. However he believed that the difficulties might be got round by the registration of rents and the payment to informers of penalties exacted from those who had misinformed the authorities about the size of the rents.[81]

Approval of the British land tax was fairly widespread amongst the Classi-cal economists.[82] However Ricardo and James Mill addressed themselves to the rather different problem of a fixed tax per acre. They concluded that such a tax would raise the cost of production on inferior lands, thus increas-ing marginal costs and, given their demand assumption, raising price. However price would not rise by the full amount of the tax because, as a result of the tax, there would be a re-equation of the extensive and intensive margins. But the extra use of the intensive margin would involve some increase in cost which would be reflected in an increase in price. Such a tax would leave corn rents unaffected but raise money rents.[83]

A general income tax had been introduced in 1799 and although peace time permitted its abolition in 1816 it was reintroduced by Peel (despite opposition from Gladstone) in 1842.[84] It found little enthusiastic support amongst the Classical economists; although it was conceded that its use in a financial emergency, such as confronted Peel at that time, was defensible, there was also general agreement that it should only be used in such circum-stances.[85] There was general agreement too that, where such a tax was used, a subsistence minimum should be exempted from taxation. The idea goes back to the Mercantilists and has a steady line of support stretching from Bentham to J. S. Mill.[86]

Such an allowance however introduces a degree of progression into the income tax. This is then perhaps the moment to raise the question of whether it was generally accepted by the Classical economists that an income tax, when used, should be progressive. It seems clear that majority opinion was opposed to such an idea. Ricardo simply ignored the whole problem. But McCulloch, who devoted a good deal of attention to it, believed that progression would be subversive of the motives to growth; that once strict proportionality had been departed from there was *no* rule whatever to follow; and that income redistribution was not part of the government's role (this despite his concern with distribution noted in Chapter 8).[87] J. S. Mill, who also devoted a considerable amount of attention to the problem, took a similar view. Despite his normally radical attitudes and his support for steeply progressive death duties, Mill accepted that redistribution of income was not the concern of the State. There is indeed a very interesting contrast between his attitude towards the work ethic, and towards capital accumulation elsewhere in his *Principles*, and his forcefully expressed opposition to progression.[88] He believed that the State should try to diminish inequality of opportunity but not of earned income. He also rejected very strongly the idea of a progressive tax on unearned income as unfair to the recipients who were typically, he believed, not wealthy.[89]

There is a further paradox here because the principle of least aggregate sacrifice which Mill favoured implied equal marginal sacrifice, as Edgeworth and Pigou later pointed out.[90] With *known* and *identical* utility schedules this in fact involved levelling down from the top which Mill certainly did not want, given his opposition to progression. In fact there are complications here which even Mill never reached. For, given these same utility schedules, equal absolute sacrifice (see Section i of this chapter) involves proportionality if the marginal utility of income declines as fast as income increases, but regression if marginal utility declines less fast, and progression if it declines faster. Equal proportional sacrifice involves proportional taxation if marginal utility falls at the same rate as the average utility of income. If marginal utility of income falls faster than average utility then progression is required but if the reverse is the case then regression is required.[91]

These complications did not disturb the advocates of progression either. Indeed while such writers as McCulloch and J. S. Mill devoted some attention to the question of progression, the writers who favoured it dealt with it only briefly. Say and Smith who favoured progression dealt with the matter very briefly;[92] and the main advocates of progression were minor figures outside the main Classical group.[93]

There was also another hotly disputed question in relation to the income tax : whether it should be levied at the same rates on permanent and temporary incomes. There were four basic arguments used by the proponents of differentiation. Firstly they argued that the capitalized values of permanent and temporary incomes were not the same and that these incomes should therefore be taxed at different rates according to their capitalized values. This was valid if the income tax was to be only temporary; otherwise it was correct to answer that a temporary income paid tax temporarily and a permanent income paid permanently. If the tax were permanent then taxing the two at the same rate would give a difference in present values of the stream of tax payments equivalent to the difference in the present values of the two incomes. McCulloch however used the capitalized value of income argument, with justification since income tax was always supposed (virtually to the end of his life) to be a temporary tax.[94] But J. S. Mill, perhaps sensing the permanency of the tax, was unhappy about the argument.[95] If it were valid however it became a strong argument against the use of the tax which ran into severe assessment problems, firstly because the various life tables available at the time gave different life expectancies and hence different present values for temporary income, and secondly because of the problem of separation of the permanent and temporary elements in entrepreneurial income. McCulloch in fact used the argument in this way, i.e. as an argument against the use of an income tax at all.

J. S. Mill's argument for different treatment of permanent and temporary incomes relied upon the necessity to exempt the savings of the temporary income recipient from taxation so that he could make provision for old age and for his successors in order to put himself on the same footing as the recipient of a permanent income.[96] McCulloch also came to use this argument. However it bothered Mill because there was regression implied by this and so he wanted to limit savings allowances to professional savings, in order to avoid benefiting the wealthy residual saver.[97]

Mill buttressed this argument for differentiation with the wholly fallacious argument that unless the saver was exempted from taxation he was taxed twice on his savings: once on the income from which he saved and once on the income produced by his investment.[98] It was wholly fallacious because the latter was a new and separate income. Nevertheless Mill stuck to his guns and suggested that temporary income should be taxed at only three-quarters of the rate of permanent income, and that wages of management should be treated in this way, as should a return on capital which was greater than the rate of interest.[99] (The presumption here was that any such return, in a competitive environment, was a reward for risk; but, on the one hand, this was not necessarily the case and, on the other, if it were, then such a reward would require *extra* special treatment because the income was not only temporary but uncertain.)

A fourth argument used by the advocates of differentiation was that there was a difference in kind between income received by incurring disutility and income received from ownership of assets. Hubbard (of the Bank of England) who was a leading campaigner for differentiation offered this argument and suggested a two-thirds rate on earned income, as one-third was the estimate of the Average Propensity to Save by the statisticians W. Farr and G. R. Porter.[100]

Closely allied to the discussion of income taxation was that of property taxation. In general the attitude towards this was fairly hostile. Thus Mc-Culloch argued that there were enormous difficulties of valuation unless industrial property was excluded; but such an exclusion would violate inter-sectoral justice. In addition there was the problem that some recipients of high incomes owned no property (he had bishops in mind here), there was no clear limit at which the tax should stop, forced liquidation of capital with a low yield might be necessary, and there was the danger of capital emi-gration.[101] In general he believed that it could not provide much revenue without interfering with growth.

But one particular kind of property that it was agreed could properly be taxed was houses. Smith had approved of such a tax as a compromise be-tween direct and indirect taxation and McCulloch pointed to its advantages in terms of valuation and difficulty of evasion, and was quite happy with it—at least on a proportional basis. It did run into a difficulty in dealing with 'Baronial Halls' which would command a negative rent on the market; but both McCulloch and J. S. Mill were prepared to have the tax assessed on building costs in such cases.[102] Mill was satisfied that housing was in general a good representation of income. He dismissed the argument that it favoured misers, on the grounds that if it exempted saving this was satis-factory (taken in conjunction with his previous arguments he must have had only professional-class misers in mind!) and he did not accept as valid the argument against the use of the tax that needy people with large families were more likely to buy large houses and that the tax would then be regres-sive, on the grounds that in such a case a house tax would act as a sumptuary tax on procreation (thus encouraging moral restraint). However he was pre-pared to allow the exemption of a subsistence minimum in dealing with house taxes; and even McCulloch, who did not go this far, recommended that on the lowest grade of houses the tax should be collected from the landlord. But there was also general agreement that such a tax could not be pushed too far, and Mill in particular was afraid of overcrowding.[103]

Smith had been uncertain as to the incidence of such a tax and Ricardo agreed with him in this.[104] However McCulloch attempted to resolve this question. He believed that a tax on the rent of houses would fall on the owner in the short run but that, in the long run, through the profit-equal-ization mechanism, it would be shifted to the occupier and the ground land-lord in the proportion that the building rent and ground rent were of total rent. J. S. Mill partially followed this. Actually Smith's instinct had been right; the distribution of the burden, as Edgeworth later showed, is indeter-minate although if demand for houses is of zero elasticity the occupier would normally bear all the tax. (Ironically McCulloch believed that a house tax would not interfere with the allocation of resources—which was only true if elasticity of demand *was* zero.[105]

Although there was general approval of the house tax, window taxes were widely condemned as unhealthy and regressive—a London house had few windows.[106]

There was, as already noted, fairly broad agreement about the need to make income tax, and indeed most direct taxes, proportional. There was however sharp disagreement over the scale to be properly applied to inheritance, though there was no disagreement on the proposition that it was a proper subject for taxation. On the one hand there were those, notably Bentham and J. S. Mill, who advocated steeply progressive rates of duty, and even appropriation by the State of estates not directly succeeded to.[107] On the other hand there were those like McCulloch who favoured proportional legacy duties.[108] There was however general agreement that such a duty fell upon the receiver of the legacy and that it fell upon capital—J. S. Mill being the only one who was not concerned about this, because of his belief in capital abundance.[109] Other direct taxes discussed included poll taxes[110] (which were inexpensive but regressive, might raise wages, were arbitrary, and, in the case of slaves, a tax on agricultural profits, as well as being without limit), the Poor Rates[111] (which were partly taxes on profits, partly taxes on houses and partly taxes on rent, and subject to the analysis of these three forms of taxation) and even the possibility of a general expenditure tax—dismissed by J. S. Mill on the grounds that the difficulties of information were virtually insuperable.[112]

## 2. Indirect Taxes

The Classical treatment of indirect taxes may be divided into three parts: that dealing with those on domestically supplied and consumed commodities; that dealing with those on imported or exported commodities; and that dealing with those on a wide range of miscellaneous services. Those in the first two categories were also divided by the Classical economists into taxes on luxuries and taxes on necessaries, as we shall see. In either case it was necessary to keep a balance between taxes on home and taxes on imported supplies to avoid distortion.[113] Indirect taxes balanced in this way were capable of providing a good revenue, especially if broadly based and hence at low levels on particular commodities. Low levels had the advantage, firstly, of avoiding smuggling, and, secondly, of minimizing the distorting and protective effects of duties. High duties, especially on imports, were held to be counterproductive, and Swift's statement that in the arithmetic of the customs 'two and two do not always make four, but sometimes only one' was widely quoted in the Classical literature.[114] The expense and inconvenience of customs duties could be minimized by warehousing, as writers from Smith onwards pointed out.[115] They were easy and cheap to collect, and did little harm so long as they were at revenue-maximizing rather than protection-maximizing levels.[116] For most writers their incidence was a matter of some uncertainty. McCulloch was satisfied that they fell on the home consumer—which was a perfectly defensible position assuming constant costs and international factor mobility so that prices in international trade depended on costs. They did not however depend upon costs in Ricardo's model of international trade; and J. S. Mill's analysis of demand in international trade indicated that the incidence was indeterminate.[117]

It was generally accepted that excise and other home duties raised the price of the taxed product. Since, as we saw in Chapter 4, most of Classical value theory assumed constant costs for the production of most commodities, it was normally expected that a tax raised the price of the commodity by the amount of the tax. However Say, whom we have already seen had a different value theory, went rather further than this, arguing that price might not rise by the full amount of the tax and that the extent to which the tax resulted in a price rise depended upon the elasticity of supply of inputs and elasticity of demand.[118] But this was exceptional. Most of the Classical writers used the profit-equalization mechanism to argue that a tax must be passed on.[119] However J. S. Mill went further than this and argued that taxes on particular commodities might raise their price by *more* than the tax.[120] This was partly because of the necessity of imposing restrictive regulations to check evasion—these were expensive in themselves and interfered with the use of optimal production methods; partly because of capital advanced in paying the tax before the goods on which it was charged had been sold; partly because this in turn meant that producers had to have larger capitals which in turn constituted a barrier to entry, giving existing producers market power to raise prices and reducing incentives to cost reduction; and partly because the rise in price produced by the tax would narrow the market and remove the incentive to technical improvements.

All this related to particular taxes on commodities. There was also some treatment of the idea of a general *ad valorem* tax. James Mill argued that such a tax could raise the general price level through increased velocity of circulation—which was possible in the short run but would presumably be corrected by loss of metal in the longer run.[121] Say also advanced (though not in terms of such an explicitly general tax) the argument that taxation could raise the price level through reducing national output in relation to the money stock.[122] Again this would presumably be corrected in the longer term by loss of metal.

The Classical treatments in dealing with indirect taxes invariably distinguished between taxes on luxuries and taxes on necessaries. Generally there was agreement that taxes on necessaries should be avoided. Smith condemned them on the grounds that raising the price of wage goods would raise wages, which in turn would raise prices (by more than the tax because of interest on the capital advanced to pay the tax prior to sale)—and in his model these effects raised the general price level and narrowed the market thus interfering with growth.[123] Smith also argued that raw materials should not be taxed either since this raised costs.[124] After the appearance of the Ricardian model however the argument was generally stated in terms of taxes on necessaries raising the level of subsistence wages, lowering profits, and thus hastening the onset of the stationary state.[125]

Taxes on luxuries on the other hand were considered an excellent idea by all the Classical economists—just so long as the luxuries concerned were sufficiently widely consumed to make them a firm tax base, and not one that would melt away as had been the case when hair powder was taxed. Hume, Smith, Ricardo, Say, McCulloch, and J. S. Mill all warmly recommended such taxes. The sort of luxuries that they usually had in mind were tobacco, tea, beer, and even sometimes sugar; and in addition to their revenue-raising capacity these taxes had a sumptuary role which was not undesirable.[126]

Far more attention was however paid to taxes on necessaries, especially to taxes on raw produce. According to Ricardo, price would rise by the full amount of the tax; because demand elasticity was zero, such a tax would affect the cost of supplying all units of output including those produced at the margin, and agricultural profits had to be as high as profits in other employments of capital. Money rent in such a situation would be unchanged because the intra-marginal surplus would be the same but the price of corn would rise and so the corn rent would fall. The incidence of such a tax was different from that of one on agricultural profits, because in the latter case the landlord was unaffected by the tax which left him with the same (rather than a smaller) corn rent and an increased money rent.[127]

From the analysis of a tax on raw produce, and the analysis of taxing agricultural profits, the Classical economists developed an analysis of the incidence of tithes. Smith thought that they fell on the landlord in the form of a reduction of rent—which would have been true if there had been any reduction in the demand for land, which presupposed a reduction in the demand for the output of land. Ricardo did not make this presupposition, and he believed that tithes raised the price of raw produce and fell on the consumer in the same way as in the analysis above. McCulloch however pointed out that the assumption of zero elasticity of demand was a special one, and that without it there would be some reduction in corn output. In addition he pointed out that the argument assumed that all land was tithed (otherwise there would be a reshuffling of the tithed and untithed margins so that price would rise by less than the amount of tax), and that there was an assumption that there were no imports otherwise price was not necessarily free to rise by the amount of the tax.[128]

However the Classical economists were united in their condemnation of tithes. Smith condemned them as discouraging improvements.[129] Ricardo, pointing out that they were proportioned to gross rather than to net output, saw them as an ever-growing burden on the way to the stationary state;[130] and J. S. Mill used the Ricardian model to show that tithes raised the price of raw produce, raising wages, thus lowering profits, and made the stationary state arrive earlier. He was perhaps less worried about this than some of his colleagues, as he believed that the main loser by premature arrival of the stationary state was the landlord.[131] Such a conclusion depended upon the analysis of the trend of long-run shares which we examined in Chapter 4.

The miscellaneous taxes on services discussed by the Classical economists included those on insurance (to which they were hostile)[132] and postage. They were divided on the latter; McCulloch favoured a tax upon postage, but J. S. Mill did not think that it was a good base but rather an obstruction to commerce, like tolls.[133] There was however fairly general condemnation of taxes on law proceedings; and the Classical economists endorsed Bentham's view that such taxes fell on the suitors, and constituted a premium on injustice.[134] They also discussed stamp duties, most of which, they held, fell upon the consumers of the commodities (such as cards, dice, and newspapers) on which they were levied.[135] Generally there was little opposition to those which fell on commodities (though J. S. Mill did not like those on newspapers as interfering with the spread of mental exercise and information);[136] nor was there any great objection to stamp duties on borrowing money which were generally thought to fall on the borrower (there was an implied assumption of infinite elasticity of supply here).[137] There was however rather more hostility towards stamp duties on leases,[138] and very considerable hostility to taxes on the transfer of property. These were held to interfere with the free circulation of resources and thus their optimal allocation; and, quite frequently in the Classical discussions, there is an implied assumption of zero elasticity of supply so that they fell on the seller at a time of 'necessity'.[139]

Lotteries also came in for rough handling[140]—with good reason, considering their history especially during the late eighteenth and early nineteenth centuries. They also condemned tolls; J. S. Mill was however prepared to concede that these could be used to pay for roads and bridges, although once the investment had been amortized transit should be free.[141]

Their attitude towards licences was rather more favourable. Say stressed their effects in distorting the allocation of resources[142] but McCulloch was happy enough with them at moderate levels[143] and Jeremy Bentham was in favour of widespread sale of licences to engage in commercial activities, and of granting monopolies (which could then be taxed) in certain occupations such as banking and stockbroking—he did not consider these would suffer from monopolization.[144] However, from Adam Smith onwards, the proposal of a mercantilist writer, Sir Mathew Decker, for consumption licences as a general substitute for taxes on commodities, met with an unfavourable reception; they were, it was held, not in proportion to consumption and therefore unequal; they were less convenient than piecemeal payments; they had a less sumptuary effect than normal indirect taxes; and they were regressive.[145] But there was no objection to taxes on servants.[146]

In general, indirect taxation was thought of by the Classical economists as providing the main source of revenue. This it had in fact done historically, with any shortfall being met either by income tax or debt creation. From Peel's income tax of 1842 the income tax became the important method of filling the gap, and the National Debt ceased to be a problem for more than seventy years. But prior to that the Debt had been a very real problem, and it was one which exercised all the Classical economists. It is to their views on this that we now turn.

### iii. NATIONAL DEBT

The old mercantilist view of National Debt, which was similar to the neo-Keynesian 'New Orthodoxy' was that such debt was no problem but merely something owed by one part of the community to another and of no more significance than a debt owed by the right hand to the left.[147] The Classical economists, faced with a doubling of the size of the British debt in the years 1800 to 1816 and with the annual charge on the debt amounting to £31·4 million out of a gross tax revenue of £57·6 million, rejected this view. Amongst the Classical writers only Lord Lauderdale held the old view. With the annual charges for servicing the debt amounting to between 8 and 10 per cent of national income this was perhaps hardly surprising.[148] The change of mind really started however with Hume, who contended that public finances should be operated on the same basis as private finances, because otherwise there was a danger of taxation rising to a harmful level and tax sources being exhausted. There was a danger that the community in general would be sacrificed to the interests of the rentier class which would be difficult to tax because of the power it would have acquired.[149]

The full Classical position involved the belief that debt creation relieved present generations by transferring a burden forward to future generations. The mercantilists (like the New Orthodoxy) argued that any burden in debt creation occurs at the moment of debt creation through the command which it gives to government over resources (except in the case of external debt). But the Classicists offered two grounds for believing that the debt constituted a burden in the *future*. The first ground was that debt creation involved capital consumption by government which reduced the level of private investment, resulting in a lower national income in the future so that future generations were less well off than they would have been had the debt not been created. Secondly taxation in order to service the debt (i.e. pay the interest upon it) was also held to involve a burden. The latter was ignored by the mercantilists on 'right hand–left hand' grounds. The Classical economists however stressed other aspects of the interest payment—those subsequently relegated by the New Orthodoxy to secondary effects under the heading of 'tax friction'. Firstly, all except Ricardo agreed that output could be depressed by taxation. It is noteworthy in this respect that 'everyone' included J. B. Say.[150] Thus, for instance, McCulloch believed that taxation to service the debt would pass the point of stimulation and reach the point of shock.[151] It is clear that there was sense in what the Classicists were arguing: receipt of interest by the bond holders is not likely, on its own, to offset the adverse incentive and allocational effects of raising the taxes. Secondly all the Classical economists, including Ricardo, who otherwise agreed with the mercantilist view of interest payments on debt, accepted that taxation to service the debt could cause capital emigration which would in turn be harmful to growth.[152] It was generally agreed that debt had advantages from the point of view of banking and insurance (though by the same token it might displace some metallic money through providing near-money)[153] but these were not sufficient to compensate for the harm which it did.

The possibility of reaching the limit of taxable capacity in raising taxes to service the debt was considered seriously, particularly by Hume, and Adam Smith. Hume forecast bankruptcy in the light of past European experience and seems to have favoured repudiation of the debt:[154] 'either the nation must destroy public credit, or public credit will destroy the nation'.[155] Nor did Hume think that such an occurrence would do long-run harm. 'So great dupes are the generality of mankind, that, notwithstanding such a violent shock to public credit, as a voluntary bankruptcy in England would occasion, it would not probably be long ere credit would again revive in as flourishing a condition as before.'[156] Smith seems to have taken a somewhat similar view of the inevitability of bankruptcy.[157] Say however was very much less sanguine about such a prospect, foreseeing possible disastrous social and economic consequences resulting from repudiating the debt, with a downward spiral in the level of activity ensuing because of the ruin of the bond holders.[158]

Hume (with other eighteenth-century writers) was also concerned about externalities associated with the growth of the debt, especially the growth of London and of the rentier class associated with it.[159]

But the capital consumption involved in the debt creation was held to be the most serious burden of the debt, and this was a view generally accepted by the Classical economists.[160] Such capital consumption could, in their view, occur in two ways. Firstly it could involve investment of existing circulating capital (which would otherwise have continued as circulating capital *or* been wholly or in part invested in fixed capital) in government securities, the proceeds being spent unproductively by government. Secondly it could involve diversion of the flow of new savings from productive investment to government expenditure. Of course this was not necessarily correct. If the supply of new savings is of zero-interest elasticity then it is true that government borrowing will replace private capital formation; but should the private-investment demand schedule be of zero-interest elasticity then the government borrowing will fall entirely on private consumption. Between these two extremes we can see that the government's funds are likely to come partly from private capital formation and partly from consumption. But all that was necessary for the Classical case was, firstly, that a not insignificant part of the funds should come from private capital formation and, secondly, that under tax finance a larger proportion of the funds would have come from private consumption. If this were the case then national income would be lower in the future and a burden would be imposed upon future generations.

This part of the general Classical view of debt was not however accepted by J. S. Mill. Mill held that in a capital-abundant economy (which he believed himself to be in) it was unlikely that government borrowing did harm; it was more likely that it simply drew upon funds which otherwise would have flowed abroad or been wasted. There was even positive benefit in this because government was demanding soldiers and other functionaries with funds which would otherwise have overflowed abroad rather than demanded labour for productive purposes. But the test of whether government did harm was the rate of interest. If the rate of interest rose then government was impinging upon private investment; if it did not then the funds borrowed would otherwise have flowed abroad.[161]

In the case of a rise in the interest rate Mill went much further than the other Classical economists in arguing that the debt was a burden. For he followed Malthus's disciple, the Revd. Thomas Chalmers, in arguing that the debt constituted a burden at the time of its creation, similar to the burden which taxation would have imposed, through the resource command transferred to the State: debt however was worse than taxation because the capital absorbed was withdrawn from the wage fund, wages were depressed, and the burden was felt by the working class, while the whole community was left with debt-service taxes to pay in future.[162] Mill was then, given that he believed the stationary state was fast approaching, not concerned like the other Classical writers, with the problem of lower national income in the future, if borrowing impinged on capital, but with the immediate effects of a smaller wage fund, together with the long-run effects of interest payments.

It followed from the main Classical position that external (foreign-held) debt was no more harmful than domestically held debt. It left on future generations a service charge to be paid abroad (which therefore reduced net national income) but this payment was to be made out of an income that was higher by the amount of the debt accumulated at compound interest since the time that it was raised, because home consumption of capital had been avoided. If therefore it were cheaper to borrow abroad than at home there was an advantage to be had from doing so. McCulloch in fact argued this to be the case;[163] and J. S. Mill was also in agreement with the idea of borrowing what he considered to be the overflowings of world accumulation.[164] Some of the earlier Classical writers however were rather less happy about this; both Hume and Smith were uneasy about foreign holdings of debt on vaguely nationalistic (indeed quasi-mercantilist) grounds,[165]

But all these considerations were relevant only if debt was to be created at all. The Classical economists clearly perceived that borrowing allows government to increase its activities without voters being forced to consider the limits to government activity which they would prefer.[166] As a peacetime expedient it was then, except in very special circumstances such as 1688, to be deplored,[167] apart from the special case of borrowing for investment in infrastructure.[168]

The wartime case was different. Hume had advocated the amassing of pre-war surpluses. These could be used to finance war; there was indeed a danger that their existence would lead to warlike behaviour, but Hume considered this a less serious risk than the danger of borrowing.[169] Moreover the spending of the surpluses during wartime would, he argued, help to raise the level of activity and offset the economic damage of war. Smith however explained that the possibility of surplus accumulation was removed by historical evolution.[170] When expensive luxuries were unknown, persons with large revenues were likely to hoard their savings, so that the ancient sovereigns of Europe amassed treasure. When however luxuries were introduced the Sovereign's expenditure rose to equal his revenue in peacetime. History showed that the accumulation of treasure then became rare and that, in times of war, governments got into debt. But the same economic growth which produced the luxuries produced the merchant and manufacturing classes which could lend. Some of the later Classical writers were no more enthusiastic than Smith about the idea of surpluses. Say believed that the existence of treasure invited attack, and that the treasure itself was likely to be wasted; while McCulloch argued that the amassing of treasure involved withdrawing of capital from productive purposes, thus reducing national income and weakening the country.[171]

Most Classical writers then accepted that borrowing in wartime was both inevitable and necessary—surpluses were ruled out, and if taxation were relied on alone it would pass beyond the point where it might stimulate activity to a level which depressed it. Tax finance should be pushed as far as possible, but not to the point where it did harm.[172]

There was however one major exception to this as indeed to most of the Classical reasoning on debt. Ricardo[173] held that tax finance was preferable to debt creation even in wartime. He believed that it would help to discourage wars and that, if tax finance were used, the capital consumption involved in debt creation could be avoided.[174] He recognized that, since property would bear a larger proportion of the tax burden than income, the professions would benefit, but argued that this did not matter—by a startling telescoping of the long and short run he asserted that exit or entry into the professions would restore the relative position of their post-tax income in relation to the post-tax income of the property owner.[175] Tax finance of war would mean a lower peacetime tax level because there was no need to service the debt, which in turn would reduce peacetime distortion of the allocation of resources through taxation. It would make possible the abolition of a great deal of the revenue machinery, the Bank of England charges for management of the debt, and the customs and excise. If individuals were unable to meet their individual tax payments they could borrow to do so.[176] However McCulloch and other critics pointed out that this borrowing would be on worse terms than those obtained by governments, since individual credit was worse than that of government, and thus the total interest bill would be increased.[177]

Consistently with his position Ricardo, almost alone amongst the Classical economists, held that the burden of debt was not shifted forward but existed from the time that the debt was created. He argued this, not however on the mercantilist grounds or those considered by J. S. Mill, but on the grounds that individuals wrote down the capitalized value of their income streams to allow for future payments of debt service taxes.[178] Of course this was not really a legitimate argument. As a modern critic has pointed out,[179] the individual who owns no assets is not really in a position to capitalize the future burden of tax payments. He will capitalize only as far as his death and, since human life is short, much of the debt burden remains uncapitalized. In any case some individuals who do own assets may not plan to submit them intact to their heirs, and there is also the problem of individual irrationality.

But Ricardo was at least in agreement that debt was a burden (though he vacillated on even this).[180] He therefore proposed a capital levy to pay off the debt.[181] The idea was not new, and it in fact stemmed from an early-eighteenth-century writer Archibald Hutcheson. It had been criticized by Hume[182] as unjust, because much property could be concealed and it would thus fall only on visible property, and also because it would not fall on the professional classes. McCulloch and others initially supported a different idea—that of unilateral reductions of debt interest, on the grounds that post-war deflation had both given a windfall to the bond-holders and increased the burden of service taxes. However the calculations of one Robert Mushet convinced McCulloch that, because the bond-holders had often received interest in depreciated currency, they had lost as much during the war as they had gained afterwards by deflation. McCulloch then supported Ricardo's scheme for a time but in turn rejected this and accepted Hume's criticisms of the earlier proposal for a capital levy.[183] J. S. Mill also disapproved of the capital-levy scheme.[184] Though he agreed that taxes to service the debt were vexatious and distorting, a capital levy could not be operated justly. Indeed it would fall only on property, while property was not the only source of service taxes, so that the switch from taxation to the levy would benefit the non-property-owning classes; that property was not the ony benefit inherited from previous generations (there were, for instance, roads and other public goods which the community as a whole had inherited and these had to be set on the opposite side of the ledger against the inherited debt); and that a capital levy would involve individuals borrowing and paying higher rates of interest than government.

The Classical consensus came to be in favour of the accumulation of budget surpluses as the preferable way of paying off the debt. Bad taxes it was agreed should be removed; but there was general agreement with Smith's view that there were sufficient good tax bases to provide a high enough level of revenue gradually to pay off the debt.[185]

There was general agreement too, following the detailed work of a writer called Robert Hamilton on whom McCulloch, Ricardo, and indeed all the Classical economists leant, that the Sinking Fund was a sham which had *increased* the size of the debt, because the State had borrowed extra sums during wartime to keep up payments into the Fund.[186] Most writers felt that the Sinking Fund should be abolished, and that its existence actually encouraged the creation of debt; and Say argued,[187] in addition to this, that if the Fund improved public credit then the price of government securities rose and debt took longer to pay off—so that if a Sinking Fund really was successful in paying off the debt it would make life difficult for itself! Only Ricardo seems to have had any qualms about abolishing the Fund;[188] and in the end he too recommended its abolition.[189]

Hamilton had also argued that borrowing in the French wars had been very ill conducted because the State had varied principal rather than interest, borrowing in the 3 per cents rather than the 5 per cents. The 3 per cents rose to par after the war, and the State found itself faced with repayment of funds it had never borrowed. The argument was accepted as valid by Parnell and McCulloch amongst others, although Ricardo correctly pointed out that the extra difficulty of placing the 5 per cents (because of the risk of conversion operations to reduce the interest after the war was over) meant that proportionately *more* debt would have to be created to borrow in 5 per cents as compared with 3 per cents.[190]

Amidst the general condemnation of debt one voice stood out almost alone. Malthus approved of debt as involving interest payments to the unproductive classes thus keeping the level of unproductive consumption high; and at the same time the creation of debt achieved the capital consumption which he wanted. All this accords closely with his view of the capital-stock-adjustment problem discussed in Chapter 8 and there is no need to pursue it further here. Malthus did recognize some other disadvantages of debt however, notably the effects of *raising* the service taxation, the danger of public bankruptcy, and the aggravation of the evils arising from changes in the value of money. For these reasons even he was unhappy about unlimited growth of debt, and was prepared indeed to see some diminution of the debt.[191]

## iv. CONCLUSION

We have now completed our survey of the Classical theory of public finance. It is undeniable that, by comparison with the sophistication of the neoClassical analysis much of the treatment was analytically underdeveloped and a great many important questions ignored. Yet its very diffuseness, together with the willingness of the majority of Classical writers to tackle the very real problems of public finance with which the country was faced, make the literature on the subject interesting. For some reason texts in the history of economic thought usually omit discussions of the public finance writings of the Classicists. If this chapter has at least shown that there is much in the literature that is worthy of attention, despite the latter's manifest imperfections, it will have achieved its aim.

## NOTES

1. *Wealth of Nations*, ed. Cannan, ii. 302–9.
2. See J. Mill, *Economic Writings*, ed. Winch, pp. 338 n. D. P. O'Brien, *J. R. McCulloch*, p. 252.
3. See Bentham, *Economic Writings*, ed. Stark, ii. *passim*; see also Smith, op. cit., pp. 302–3.
4. Smith, op. cit., ii. 310–12. For their wide acceptance see F. Shebab, *Progressive Taxation*, p. 70. See also J. S. Mill, *Principles*, ed. Ashley, pp. 802–3; Ricardo, *Works*, ed. Sraffa, i. 181–2.
5. J. Mill, op. cit., pp. 412–14; Say *Treatise*, trans. Prinsep, pp. 449–50. McCulloch rejected the first maxim because of the benefit elements it contained but accepted the other three.
6. Smith, op. cit., ii. 310.
7. See the brilliant discussion of the two approaches in R. A. Musgrave, *Theory of Public Finance*, Chs. 4 and 5.
8. Shehab, p. 10. An eighteenth-century unawareness of the distinction is the only explanation that can be adduced for the range of other examples of attempts to combine the two approaches given in E. R. A. Seligman, *Progressive Taxation in Theory and Practice*, especially pp. 242–3.
9. Seligman, op. cit., pp. 170–6; Say, *Treatise*, p. 444.
10. D. P. O'Brien, *J. R. McCulloch*, p. 233.
11. Ibid., McCulloch's requirement of inter-sectoral equality (ibid., pp. 234–5) was also accepted by Babbage and Ricardo but rejected by Say—see Say, op. cit., pp. 468–9 and Shehab, op. cit., pp. 104–5. For Ricardo see p. 269 n, 175, below.
12. Mill, op. cit., pp. 804–5.
13. This follows Musgrave, op. cit., p. 96.
14. Mill, op. cit., p. 807.
15. Ibid., p. 804.
16. Turgot and the elder Mirabeau linked this explicitly with benefit—see Seligman, op. cit., p. 162. Hume rejected the idea (*Economic Writings*, ed. Rotwein, pp. 86–7).

17. See especially McCulloch, *Treatise on Taxation* (3rd edn. 1863), Pt. II, Ch. 12.
18. See Say, op. cit., p. 447: see however ibid., p. 473.
19. Hume, op. cit., p. 83; see also E. A. J. Johnson, *Predecessors of Adam Smith*, p. 175.
20. See D. P. O'Brien, *J. R. McCulloch*, p. 238.
21. Say, op. cit., pp. 453, 473–6; Smith, op. cit., ii. 313–14; McCulloch, *Treatise*, pp. 39–40.
22. O'Brien, op. cit., pp. 235–6.
23. See Say, op. cit., p. 452 n; Ricardo, op. cit., pp. 236–8; see also Smith, op. cit., ii. 423–4.
24. McCulloch, *Treatise*, pp. 32–3.
25. Smith, op. cit., ii. 386.
26. Say, op cit., pp. 444–5. Say also believed that such a limitation would lead to efficient administration (ibid., p. 446).
27. J. S. Mill, op. cit., p. 862.
28. See E. A. J. Johnson, op. cit., pp. 175–6.
29. O'Brien, op. cit., p. 263; McCulloch, *Treatise*, Pt. II, Chs. 9 and 10.
30. Say, op. cit., pp. 463, 464–5.
31. Smith, op. cit., ii. 366–7.
32. J. S. Mill, op. cit., pp. 870–2.
33. Sir H. Parnell, *On Financial Reform*—see the bibliography to this chapter.
34. See C. Shoup, *Ricardo on Taxation*, Ch. XV.
35. Ricardo, *Works*, i. 257–62; J. Mill, op. cit., pp. 357–8.
36. Thus McCulloch (*Treatise*, pp. 279–89) included the 'assessed' taxes—land tax, servants tax and so on—under the heading of indirect taxes: J. S. Mill (op. cit., p. 823) included them under the heading of direct taxes.
37. Hume, op. cit., p. 85.
38. Smith, op. cit., ii. 378 ff.
39. Say, op. cit., pp. 463–4.
40. McCulloch, *Treatise*, Pt. II, Ch. 1.
41. Ricardo, *Works*, iv. 190.
42. Ibid., i. 159–61; see also Shoup, op. cit., p. 67.
43. J. S. Mill, op. cit., pp. 864–72.
44. e.g. Hume, op. cit., p. 85; Smith, op. cit., ii. 378; Ricardo, *Works*, i. 241; Say, op. cit., p. 463.
45. J. S. Mill, op. cit., p. 866.
46. See Musgrave, op. cit., pp. 232–56 for a discussion of this problem.
47. Say, op. cit., 470.
48. Ricardo, op. cit., i. 379–80; Shoup, op. cit., pp. 198–200.
49. Smith, op. cit., ii. 349.
50. Ibid., pp. 350, 423–4.
51. Shoup, op. cit., p. 66.
52. Ricardo, op. cit., i. 160–6, 226–7.
53. Ibid., pp. 220–1.
54. Ibid., p. 221; J. Mill, op. cit., p. 344. The argument was also rejected by J. S. Mill (pp. 827–8).
55. Hume, op. cit., p. 87; O'Brien, op. cit., pp. 253–4.
56. J. Mill, op. cit., p. 344.
57. Ibid., pp. 347–8.
58. J. S. Mill, op. cit., pp. 827–9.
59. See e.g. J. S. Mill, pp. 828–9.
60. Smith, op. cit., ii. 350.
61. J. S. Mill, op. cit., p. 828. The argument here seems to be derived from West: however it should be stressed that there are a variety of possible interpretations for the inverse relationship of wages and profits in J. S. Mill.
62. Ricardo, op. cit., i. 227–33. For the invariable measure of value see Ch. IV above.

63. Smith, op. cit., ii. 356–7; Ricardo, op. cit., i. 222–6; Shoup, op. cit., Appendix A.
64. Smith, op. cit., ii. 331–42.
65. Ricardo, op. cit., i. 205–14; J. S. Mill, op. cit., pp. 824–5. Smith had made such a distinction but it was Ricardo's which was followed.
66. J. S. Mill, op. cit., pp. 825–6.
67. O'Brien, op. cit., p. 254.
68. Smith, op. cit., ii. 377.
69. This point is made by Shoup, op. cit., p. 104.
70. O'Brien, op. cit., loc. cit.; J. S. Mill, op. cit., p. 825.
71. Ricardo, op. cit., i. 210–11.
72. J. Mill, op. cit., pp. 356–7; Smith, op. cit., ii. 340; see also the excellent discussion in Shoup, op. cit., Ch. IV. For Ricardo's explicit assumption about elasticity see *Works*, i. 193.
73. See Ricardo, op. cit., i. 173–5; J .S. Mill, op. cit., pp. 823–4.
74. Ricardo, op. cit., i. 258.
75. J. Mill, op. cit., pp. 391–5. See also Winch's comments ibid., pp. 197–202.
76. J. S. Mill, op. cit., pp. 818–19.
77. O'Brien, *J. R. McCulloch*, pp. 251–3; for Ricardo see Winch's note in J. Mill, op. cit., p. 338.
78. Smith, op. cit., ii. 328–9; and compare Ricardo, op. cit., i. 203–4, and J. S. Mill, op. cit., pp. 823–4.
79. Smith, op. cit., ii. 312.
80. Say, op. cit., pp. 476–7.
81. Smith, op. cit., ii. 314–17. Smith also recommended levying heavier taxes on objectionable leases such as those specifying a method of cultivation or requiring payment of the lease in kind.
82. See e.g. J. S. Mill, op. cit., p. 862 and McCulloch, *Treatise*, pp. 57–8.
83. J. Mill, op. cit., pp. 358–60; Ricardo, op. cit., i. 181–2; see also Shoup, op. cit., Ch. 7; J. S. Mill, op. cit., p. 842.
84. Shoup, op. cit., Ch. 15; see also Shehab, op. cit., *passim*, for details of the history of the tax.
85. See J. S. Mill, op. cit., pp. 829–30; O'Brien, *J. R. McCulloch*, p. 249.
86. Seligman, *Progressive Taxation*, p. 183; J. S. Mill, op. cit., pp. 806, 829–32.
87. O'Brien, op. cit., pp. 249–50.
88. J. S. Mill, op. cit., pp. 807 ff. especially p. 808; and compare pp. 808–9 and pp. 821–2, where he argued that it did not matter if a tax fell on capital because it only delayed the arrival of the stationary state.
89. Ibid., pp. 808–10.
90. Musgrave, op. cit., p. 98.
91. For a brilliant discussion of these questions see Musgrave, op. cit., pp. 95–102.
92. Say, op. cit., pp. 454–5; Smith, op. cit., ii. 326–7.
93. For a survey of them see Seligman, op. cit., pp. 238–90, esp. 256–61; Shehab, op. cit., pp. 38–41, 91–2.
94. Thus Gladstone, becoming Chancellor of the Exchequer in 1852, pledged himself to its abolition by 1860—Shehab, op. cit., p. 115. McCulloch died in 1864.
95. J. S. Mill, op. cit., pp. 810–17.
96. Ibid., p. 812. The argument was foreshadowed by his father—J. Mill, op. cit., pp. 350–1.
97. See the citations of J. S. Mill's Select Committee evidence in F. Shehab, op. cit., pp. 147–55.
98. J. S. Mill, op. cit., pp. 813–14.
99. Ibid., p. 814.
100. See Shehab, op. cit., pp. 123, 139.
101. See O'Brien, op. cit., pp. 250–1.
102. Ibid.; and J. S. Mill, op. cit., pp. 835–6.
103. Ibid., pp. 834–5, 867.
104. Smith, op. cit., ii. 324–31, esp. 325–6; Ricardo, op. cit., i. 203.

105. For references see O'Brien, op. cit., pp. 252–3. See alse J. S. Mill, op. cit., p. 833.

106. e.g. Smith, op. cit., ii. 330–1; J. S. Mill, op. cit., p. 835.

107. Bentham, *Economic Writings*, i. 61–2; J. S. Mill, op. cit., p. 809.

108. O'Brien, op. cit., p. 249.

109. Smith, op. cit., ii. 342, 346; Say, op. cit., p. 455; Ricardo, op. cit., p. 153; J. Mill, op. cit., p. 360; J. S. Mill, op. cit., pp. 821–2.

110. Hume, op. cit., p. 86; Smith, op. cit., ii. 341, 351–4.

111. e.g. J. Mill, op. cit., p. 357; Ricardo, op. cit. i, Ch. 18.

112. J. S. Mill, op. cit., p. 831.

113. e.g. Ricardo, i. 179–80, 187–8, 314; see also Shoup, op. cit., pp. 172, 179. McCulloch was at first sceptical about the idea (Ricardo, *Works*, viii. 353) but later accepted it—it underpins his *Treatise*).

114. Smith, op. cit., ii. 365. Cannan points out that the same remark was quoted by Hume and Lord Kames. See also McCulloch, *Treatise*, p. 338 (from which the actual quotation comes) and pp. 338–87 *passim*.

115. Smith, op. cit., ii. 368, 370; McCulloch, *Treatise*, pp. 24–6; J. S. Mill, op. cit., pp. 866–7.

116. Smith, op. cit., ii. 367; J. S. Mill, op. cit., pp. 847–50, 868–9; O'Brien, *J. R. McCulloch*, p. 225.

117. J. S. Mill, op. cit., pp. 850–6. See also Ch. 7 above.

118. Say, op. cit., pp. 465, 467–8.

119. e.g. Ricardo, op. cit., i. 243. This is really the *locus classicus* of the argument.

120. J. S. Mill, op. cit., pp. 838–9.

121. J. Mill, op. cit., pp. 352–5.

122. Say, op. cit., p. 472.

123. Smith, op. cit., ii. 355, 422–4.

124. Ibid., pp. 369, 390.

125. Ricardo, op. cit., i. 159; J. S. Mill, op. cit., pp. 868–9.

126. Hume, op. cit., p. 85; Smith, op. cit., i. 355–6, 370–2; Ricardo, op. cit., i. 241; Say, op. cit., p. 457; McCulloch, *Treatise*, pp. 172–82; J. S. Mill, op. cit., pp. 807, 869–72. On hair powder see McCulloch, *Treatise*, p. 283.

127. See J. Mill, op. cit., pp. 355–7. If the case is not intuitively obvious see the numerical examples in Ricardo, op. cit., i. 158, 162, and Shoup, op. cit., pp. 64–5.

128. See O'Brien, *J. R. McCulloch*, pp. 261–2.

129. Smith, op. cit., i. 322.

130. Ricardo, op. cit., i. 177–8.

131. J. S. Mill, op. cit., pp. 842–50.

132. e.g. ibid., p. 859.

133. McCulloch, *Treatise*, Pt. II, Ch. 7; J. S. Mill, op. cit., p. 860.

134. Say, op. cit., pp. 456–7; J. Mill, op. cit., pp. 360–1; J. S. Mill, op. cit., pp. 861–2; Ricardo, op. cit., i. 153–4.

135. Smith, op. cit., ii. 343, 348; McCulloch, *Treatise*, p. 298.

136. J. S. Mill, op. cit., p. 860. Mill also opposed the duty on advertisements as slowing the turnover of stocks of goods.

137. e.g. Smith, op. cit., ii. 346; Ricardo, op. cit., i. 153–4.

138. J. S. Mill in particular condemned stamp duties on leases because the leases themselves were necessary for good agriculture.

139. Smith, op. cit., i. 346–7; J. B. Say (less hostile than some other writers), op. cit., p. 456; Ricardo, op. cit., i. 153–5; J. Mill, op. cit., p. 300; J. S. Mill, op. cit., p. 859.

140. Shoup, op. cit., p. 200; McCulloch, *Treatise*, pp. 333–7.

141. e.g. Smith, op. cit, ii. 377; J. S. Mill, op. cit., pp. 862–3.

142. Say, op. cit., p. 457.

143. McCulloch, *Treatise*, p. 312.

144. Bentham, *Economic Writings*, i. 73–4.

145. Smith, op. cit., ii. 360–1 (see however ibid., 422); McCulloch, *Treatise*, pp. 313–14.

146. Smith, op. cit., ii. 341–2; McCulloch, *Treatise*, pp. 282–3.
147. See J. M. Buchanan, *Public Principles of Public Debt* (Homewood, Illinois, 1958).
148. See Shehab, op. cit., pp. 70–1. On Lauderdale see Sowell, *Say's Law*, p. 85.
149. Hume, op. cit., pp. 91, 96–9; see also Smith, op. cit., ii. 412.
150. Say, op. cit., p. 472.
151. O'Brien, *J. R. McCulloch*, pp. 264, 266. Smith held a somewhat similar view— op. cit., ii. 412.
152. Ricardo, op. cit., i. 244, 247–8.
153. They would add to the general stock of means of payment, raising the general price level and displacing metal via the price-specie-flow mechanism—see Hume, op. cit., pp. 93–5.
154. Ibid., pp. 103–4. See also Rotwein's introduction, pp. lxxxv–lxxxvii.
155. Ibib., p. 102.
156. Ibid., p. 104.
157. Smith, op. cit., ii. 415–18.
158. Say, op. cit., pp. 486–7.
159. Hume, op. cit., pp. 94–6; Rotwein's introduction, pp. lxxxiv–lxxxv.
160. e.g. Ricardo, *Works*, i. 244, 247, iv. 187–8; Smith, op. cit., ii. 410–11.
161. J. S. Mill, op. cit., pp. 874–6.
162. Ibid., pp. 77–8, 873–4.
163. See O'Brien, *J. R. McCulloch*, p. 264.
164. J. S. Mill, op. cit., p. 874.
165. Hume, op cit., p. 96; Smith, op. cit., ii. 412.
166. e.g. Smith, op. cit., ii. 405.
167. Ibid., pp. 397–400; Hume, op. cit., p. 92; Ricardo, op. cit., i. 247.
168. e.g. Say, op. cit., p. 481.
169. Hume, op. cit., pp. 90–2.
170. Smith, op. cit., ii. 392–6.
171. Say, op. cit., p. 487; McCulloch, *Treatise*, p. 422; O'Brien, *J. R. McCulloch*, p. 263 n.
172. Ibid., p. 264; J. S. Mill, p. 876.
173. Ricardo, op. cit., i. 244–5.
174. Ibid., i. 247, iv. 185–8. This may also have been Smith's view—op. cit., ii. 411. But his words are ambiguous.
175. Ricardo, op. cit., iv. 188–9.
176. Ibid., i. 245.
177. See O'Brien, *J. R. McCulloch*, p. 264.
178. Ricardo, op. cit., i. 247–8; iv. 185–6.
179. J. M. Buchanan, op. cit., p. 45.
180. Thus in op. cit., i. 244, 246 Ricardo appeared to accept the left-hand–right-hand argument: and contrast this with ibid., p. 242—material inserted at the instance of McCulloch.
181. Ibid., i. 247–8; iv. 197.
182. Hume, op. cit., p. 102.
183. For references see O'Brien, *J. R. McCulloch*, pp. 266–8.
184. J. S. Mill, op. cit., pp. 876–8.
185. Ibid., pp. 878–80; Smith, op. cit., ii. 419–31.
186. Ricardo, op. cit., i. 248–9; ibid., iv. 145, 148; McCulloch, *Treatise*, Pt. III; Say, op. cit., p. 485.
187. Ibid., p. 484.
188. Ricardo, op. cit., iv. 171–2.
189. Ibid., pp. 197–200.
190. Ricardo, iv. 184–5; see O'Brien, *J. R. McCulloch*, pp. 264–5 for further references.
191. Malthus, *Principles*, 2nd edn., pp. 411–12.

# BIBLIOGRAPHY

A general discussion of the Classical tax literature can be found in E. R. A. Seligman, *Progressive Taxation in Theory and Practice* (2nd edn. Princeton, 1908). Despite its age the book is still valuable for its coverage which extends far beyond the Classical writers both in time and space. But the reader should take care: although Seligman's erudition was staggering he was only human; and classing McCulloch as a benefit theorist as he did, was undoubtedly a slip. E. A. J. Johnson's *Predecessors of Adam Smith* is also a useful reference—the roots of most of the Classical ideas on public finance can be found here. There is also an excellent survey by F. Shehab, *Progressive Taxation* (Oxford, 1953). This book is particularly valuable because of the attention it pays to the evidence before Parliamentary Committees on taxation.

Of commentaries on particular writers which deal with taxation at any length there are few. See however C. Shoup's generally excellent *Ricardo on Taxation* (New York, 1960). Rotwein's introduction to Hume's economic writings contains a short but interesting section on taxation (pp. lxxxi–lxxxviii) and the present author's *J. R. McCulloch* contains a discussion of public finance (pp. 229–70). (There is also at the time of writing, an edn. of McCulloch's *Treatise on Taxation* in the press, with a full analytical introduction.)

The Classical literature on public finance is, as so often with other subjects best started by reading Hume—the two essays 'Of Taxes' and 'Of Public Credit' (Rotwein edn., pp. 83–9, 90–107). Smith's great treatment of taxation and debt is to be found in Bk. V of the *Wealth of Nations*, Chs. 2 and 3 (Cannan's edn., 11. 302–433). The four maxims of taxation are on pp. 310–12. Say was greatly influenced by Smith's treatment—see his *Treatise* (trans. Prinsep), Bk. III, Chs. 7–9 (pp. 444–88).

Ricardo's tax chapters occupy a significant place in his *Principles*—about a third of the pages. See Chs. 8–18 and 29 as well as 26 on Gross and Net (National) Revenue. See also Ricardo's article 'Funding System' written for the Supplement to the 6th edn. of *Encyclopaedia Britannica* and repr. in *Works*, iv. 149–200.

As a pure theorist his lack of mathematical training occasionally led him astray— and there is illuminating criticism of some of his treatments by the great Cambridge polymath William Whewell, recently reprinted as *On the Mathematical Exposition of Some Doctrines of Political Economy* (Gregg, 1970). The roots of Marshall's work are probably to be found therein. (Shoup's book also has an appendix on Whewell.)

James Mill followed Ricardo's tax treatment deliberately, providing the essence of it in his *Elements*: and on the whole the condensation is well done. Fortunately it is now possible to read not only the *Elements* but also Mill's treatment of problems of Indian land revenue in Winch's excellent edition. Mill was deeply influenced by Ricardo's reasoning but went much further than Ricardo or indeed any of the Classical economists in his proposals for land nationalization and rent taxation.

His son's treatment of taxation and debt is much more diffuse but also much more interesting. See Bk. V of his *Principles*, Chs. 2–7 (Ashley edn., pp. 802–80). These chapters show the ambivalence of J. S. Mill's attitude towards capital accumulation, and indeed towards the whole Ricardian model, very clearly.

Bentham was one of the great influences on J. S. Mill and although his own writings are chaotic and eccentric there can never be any doubt of his influence on the whole of nineteenth-century thought. His *Economic Writings*, ii contain his principal plans for augmenting state revenue: and fortunately Professor Stark's introduction provides a way through the maze. Also interesting, though in a very different way, was Sir Henry Parnell. His *On Financial Reform* (4th edn., London, 1832) was an extremely thorough exercise in putting the public finance details of his day under a microscope and applying to the resulting minutiae the light of Smith's maxims. The book was highly influential; indeed it is probably a major source of the Gladstonian financial orthodoxy.

The need for financial reform was of course widely acknowledged: and in particular the uses and abuses of the Sinking Fund became something of a *cause célèbre*. Place in particular had agitated against it and sent Ricardo a collection of pamphlets when the latter began to write his article 'Funding System'. A good deal of the relevant material is repr. in McCulloch's *Select Collection of Tracts on the National Debt and the Sinking Fund,* which has recently been repr. (A. M. Kelley, New York). The most influential writer on National Debt was undoubtedly Robert Hamilton: and his contribution (borrowed from extensively by, *inter alia,* Ricardo, Parnell, and McCulloch) is repr. in McCulloch's *Select Collection.*

Modern treatments of public finance are of course numerous. The uncontested leader in this field is however undoubtedly R. A. Musgrave's modern classic *The Theory of Public Finance* (New York, 1959, Tokyo 1961): and the reader will find Chs. 4, 5, 16, and 23 singularly illuminating. An excellent text is J. F. Due, *Government Finance: Economics of the Public Sector* (4th edn. Homewood, Illinois, 1968). Chapter 11 on debt is particularly good. There is also a valuable survey by J. Burkhead, 'The Balanced Budget' in A. Smithies and J. K. Butters (eds.), *Readings in Fiscal Policy* (A. E. A., London, 1955). But no one should fail to read J. M. Buchanan's *Public Principles of Public Debt* (Homewood, Illinois, 1958). Whatever the ultimate verdict the book bubbles like champagne. Finally there is a very interesting article, now old, by P. Leroy Beaulieu 'On Taxation in General', repr. in R. A. Musgrave and A. T. Peacock (eds.), *Classics in the Theory of Public Finance* (London, 1958), which deals in particular with the Hume–McCulloch concept of tax stimulation.

# 10. The Policy Prescriptions of Classical Economics

## i. THE LEGITIMATE ROLE OF GOVERNMENT

The caricature of the Classical economists as the die-hard defenders of extreme *laissez-faire* is one which has proved extremely persistent.[1] This is partly because some commentators have wished to sustain this view for their own purposes; but mainly because of the identification of *laissez-faire* with free trade and the activities of the Manchester School and the Anti-Corn Law League which are often confused with those of the Classical economists.[2] Examination of the Classical writings on the role of government quickly reveals the misleading nature of the caricature, as we shall see.

The first thing to recognize is that while the Classical writers were the earliest fully to appreciate the allocative mechanism of the market and the power, subtlety, and efficiency of this mechanism, they were perfectly clear that it could only operate within a framework of restrictions. Such restrictions were partly legal and partly religious, moral, and conventional, and they were designed to ensure the coincidence of self and community interest.[3] The exact framework required was to be revealed by experience, as defects in the operation of the system were discovered. Now this is very important because it begets an entirely pragmatic attitude towards legislation: and, as we shall see, this is exactly what the Classical economists exhibited. Their attitude towards *laissez-faire* was of a very relativist and conditional kind. As J. S. Mill put it:

the admitted functions of government embrace a much wider field than can easily be included within the ring-fence of any restrictive definition, and ... it is hardly possible to find any ground of justification common to them all, except the comprehensive one of general expediency.[4]

McCulloch was typically more forthright:

The principle of *laisser-faire* may be safely trusted to in some things but in many more it is wholly inapplicable; and to appeal to it on all occasions savours more of the policy of a parrot than of a statesman or a philosopher.[5]

In a letter to a friend he put the matter even more strongly:

Too much is sometimes made of principles—What is all the legislation about money and about the poor but an invasion of the freedom of action? The question is not whether any regulation interferes with the freedom of industry, but whether its operation is on the whole advantageous or otherwise—A vast deal of arrant nonsense is talked under the cloak of principle.[6]

The Classical economists in general *were* concerned—and this is especially true of J. S. Mill—about the accretion of power to the State involving dangers to individual liberty. There was a danger in a democracy that every-one would try to increase the power of the State and use it to their own advantage. Moreover progress depended upon a variety of different methods and philosophies competing—the Classical championship of the market depended not on considerations of static optimization but on dynamic ones —and activity by the State could well result in a single-method monolith. Even if the State were highly efficient there were still grounds for treating its activities with reserve because of the danger of creating a passive popula-tion.[7] But this did not rule out intervention by the State where such interven-tion could be justified on the grounds of utility.[8] They did not see the natural order as flawless—indeed an extensive list of flaws can be found in the *Wealth of Nations*[9]—and in the last resort their test of the desirability of intervention was expediency.[10]

The limit of state activity varied between countries and stages of develop-ment. Bentham (followed by J. S. Mill) distinguished between *Agenda* (where the State should act) *Sponte acta* (phenomena developed naturally by society), and *non-Agenda* (areas of government inaction).

The distribution of the imaginable stock of institutions will in a very consider-able degree differ according to the different circumstances of the several political communities ... In England abundance of useful things are done by individuals, which in other countries are done either by governments or not at all ... In Russia, under Peter the Great, the list of *sponte acta* being a blank, that of *agenda* was proportionately abundant.[11]

J. S. Mill's view was that

In the particular circumstances of a given age or nation, there is scarcely any-thing really important to the general interest, which it may be desirable or even necessary, that the government should take upon itself, not because private in-dividuals cannot effectually perform it, but because they will not. At some times and places there will be no roads, docks, harbours, canals, works of irrigation, hospitals, schools, colleges, printing-presses, unless the government establishes them; the public being either too poor to command the necessary resources, or too little advanced in intelligence to appreciate the ends, or not sufficiently prac-ticed in joint action to be capable of the means.[12]

Classical economics stems in large measure, as we have seen throughout this book, from the *Wealth of Nations*: and the *Wealth of Nations* was a fundamental blast against mercantilism which Smith saw as the regulation of economic activity by the State in the interests of the merchant classes.[13] This accounts for the negative character of much of the Classical writing on government activity. Such intervention was not only evil: it was crude and clumsy as well[14] and it is the Classical economists' attacks upon mercantilism which have helped to create the impression of their being totally opposed to state activity, which they were not. What they were mainly criticizing was the use of government power in the interests of a small minority to create for themselves privileged conditions. It was this same opposition to the creation of special privilege which made them strongly in favour of competition and opposed to monopoly.[15]

Their opposition to mercantilism must not then be allowed to conceal from us the extent of state activity which they approved. Of course there was not total unanimity. They were men of widely diverse political views—Tories at one extreme, Philosophical Radicals at the other[16]—but men with a common interest in reform of the corrupt government interference associated with mercantilism—and corrupt it was indeed.[17] They were not revolutionaries; but they were reformers, critical of middle-class influence on legislation and convinced that the condition of society was that of the majority of the ordinary people.[18] Though they were undoubtedly misguided on some issues, as we shall see, they were concerned about the condition of the ordinary people. In particular they were, in striking contrast to the mercantilist writers, strongly in favour of all measures which could reasonably be expected to raise real wages.[19]

We began our examination of the *Agenda* with a piquant example of the prevalence of caricature. In a (deservedly) best-selling modern textbook we find the following:

The history of 19th and early 20th century banking on both sides of the Atlantic is replete with examples of banks ruined by monetary runs on their cash and gold reserves. When this happened, the bank's depositors and the holders of its notes would find themselves holding worthless pieces of paper. Future social historians may wonder how it was possible, in the face of such a system, that early economists could have believed that free-market capitalism provided evidence that the hidden hand of perfection was guiding the economic affairs of mankind.[20]

To the reader who knows anything about nineteenth-century monetary thought and controversy there is clearly something wrong here. The great debates, culminating in that major piece of framework construction the 1844 Bank Act, were hardly conducted on such a basis. The strict limits in that Act on the powers of the country banks to issue notes were hardly conceived on such a basis. Nor did any such adherence to *laissez-faire* dogma prevent government intervention in the years when the framework proved inadequate in times of crisis—1847, 1857, 1866. But the words of Adam Smith on the subject of banking regulations are perhaps the most striking:

To restrain private people, it may be said, from receiving in payment the promissory notes of a banker, for any sum whether great or small, when they themselves are willing to receive them; or to restrain a banker from issuing such notes, when all his neighbours are willing to accept of them, is a manifest violation of that natural liberty which it is the proper business of law, not to infringe but to support. Such regulations may, no doubt, be considered as in some respect a violation of natural liberty. But those exertions of the natural liberty of a few individuals, which might endanger the security of the whole society, are, and ought to be, restrained by the laws of all governments ... The obligation of building party walls, in order to prevent the communication of fire, is a violation of natural liberty, exactly of the same kind with the regulations of the banking trade which are here proposed.[21]

We might also note that Ricardo proposed the substitution of a National Bank run by the State for the Bank of England.[22]

The basic role assigned to the State by the Classical economists from Smith onwards were defence,[23] justice[24] (including such matters as enforcement of contracts and security of property as well as stamps of metallic purity and linen and cloth certificates—they did not believe in *caveat emptor*,[25] and the provision of basic infrastructure in the form of roads, canals, harbours, lighthouses, and other requirements such as coinage and the Post Office, as well as providing for such matters as the regulation of mortgages and the levying of taxes designed to discourage undesirable leases.[26]

Smith also defended the mercantilist Navigation Acts which attempted to ensure a reservoir of seamen by forcing goods into British ships;[27] and he defended the Usury Laws—which fixed the maximum rate of interest—on the grounds that this prevented 'prodigals' from bidding sums away from productive investors.[28] For this he was however severely criticized by later Classical writers from Bentham onwards. Thus we find J. S. Mill arguing that, given a rising supply schedule of loanable funds, a maximum rate of interest reduces the available supply and prevents the attainment of equilibrium in the market for loanable funds. At the same time the prodigals would very likely be supplied illegally at rates of interest even higher than those at which the market would have been cleared.[29] However there were few qualms about interfering, as Smith suggested, with consumer choice through the imposition of sumptuary taxes.[30]

Smith (and the later Classical economists) also considered public-health regulation a function of government. Indeed later writers, faced with the great growth of towns, laid very considerable emphasis on the need for public-health regulation and for regulations against the adulteration of food, while Senior even envisaged public provision for medical treatment.[31]

Coupled with this was the need, as they saw it, for building regulations to combat the development of the nineteenth-century industrial slums.[32]

Some writers went a good deal further. McCulloch in particular favoured making employers liable for accidents so as to make the interest of the employer coincide with that of society. He also favoured regulation of shipping; insurance protected owners and merchants but not the unfortunate sailors.[33] He was, additionally, one of a number of writers (J. S. Mill was also prominent here) who believed that the State should regulate public-utility charges, limit the dividends, and levy a charge on the concern in order to finance public acquisition of its stock. Profits beyond twenty-five years were not part of the supply price of risk capital.[34]

There were also a number of other areas which we shall look at in more detail later on where the Classical economists recognized the need for intervention. These included child labour,[35] education,[36] and pauperism—although their views were not always very helpful in this respect, as we shall see.

Before we go on to more detailed consideration of these areas however there are four points which should be made to retain a balanced picture. Firstly, there were in the Classical economists' view, a number of areas where state intervention was definitely undesirable—notably in price fixing and the regulation of industrial processes (except for safety or similar purposes). Such interference would probably check inventions.[37] Protection also came into this category[38] as did usury laws (after Smith), food-price regulations, establishment of monopolies, and the taxing of basic foodstuffs.[39] McCulloch was also opposed to public works.[40]

Secondly, although they approved action in many areas, as we have noted, it is of considerable importance to see how *far* they thought it was legitimate to go. This we shall see in the next section of the chapter.

Thirdly, we have to recognize that, during the very long period covered in this study, social conditions changed, legislation was initiated, Select Committees uncovered horrible things about factories and ships—in short political and economic history and social inquiry went forward together. We have to ask ourselves how far the Classical prescriptions made the running, and how far they were merely pragmatically accepting the proposals of others. Even if the latter proves to be the case however there is an important lesson to be learnt. For no *laissez-faire* dogmatism prevented them from accepting the legislative proposals and evidence brought forward by others.

Finally there is the question of socialism and the social order. However pragmatic the Classical economists were they, by and large, accepted a regime of private property—though here it must be stressed that for them the basis of property right lay in public utility, not natural law. Property and security of property were vital parts of the incentive to economic growth as well as safeguards against arbitrary government. Only Bentham and J. S. Mill really had plans even for the reform of property and inheritance.[41] McCulloch considered inequality of fortune an important stimulus to effort (and hence growth).[42] He and Malthus also approved of primogeniture although Smith and J. S. Mill did not. Only the latter showed any real sympathy for socialism. The attitude of the majority of the Classical writers was probably well expressed by Cairnes when he wrote 'Thus economic ignorance, when it has conceived, brings forth socialism, and socialism breeds despotism, and despotism, when it is finished, issues in war, misery, and ruin'.[43]

J. S. Mill's attitude towards socialism is interesting, and unfortunately we can only deal with it briefly.[44] Initially he was highly sceptical about innovation, incentives, distribution, and the likely course of population under a socialist system. In particular he feared that it would remove the motives to 'prudential restraint'. Then, under the influence of Mrs. Harriet Taylor (who became his wife) Mill made changes in the third edition of his *Principles* which display a much more favourable attitude.[45] Though he was still a little concerned about the problem of personal liberty, and believed too that the regime of private property had not yet had a fair trial because the existing system was a distortion of it, he was now happy that prudential restraint could prevail under socialism, and believed that individual incentives could be replaced by social ones. Finally however, after the death of his wife, he published his *Autobiography* which showed a much less sympathetic attitude: and after his own death his step-daughter published some chapters on socialism which showed an even greater retreat. But through all these vicissitudes one point remains entirely clear: the socialism which Mill had in mind was that of Fourier and St. Simon, and of Robert Owen —decentralized socialism with competition between producing co-operatives. This explained his strong defence of competition against socialist denunciations even while he was at his most sympathetic towards socialism.[46] Totalitarian socialism made no impression on him at all. Indeed he presciently forecast the effects of forced collectivization.[47] If he believed in socialism he did not believe in centralization; and he attributed the triumph of Napoleon III (which he deplored) to excessive French centralization.[48]

## ii. DETAILED TREATMENTS OF INTERVENTION—THE DOMESTIC ECONOMY

### 1. The Factory Acts

The attitude of the Classical economists towards the Factory Acts epitomizes two aspects of their thought on policy; their pragmatism and the extent to which external events influenced them, rather than the other way round. All of them from Malthus onwards were, it is true, in favour of the regulation of child labour.[49] But such regulation had been introduced by the elder Peel's Act of 1802—and in general they were following, not making the running. At the same time this Act had been ineffective: and if they had not favoured regulation of child labour it would have been much harder for legislators to remedy this. Their concern was perfectly sincere. When McCulloch wrote to Lord Shaftesbury about the latter's proposals for the regulation of child labour

> I hope your Factory Bill will prosper and I am glad it is in such good hands. Had I a seat in the House it should assuredly have my vote. A notion is entertained that political economists are, in all cases, enemies to all sorts of interference, but I assure you I am not one of those who entertain such an opinion. I would not interfere between adults and masters; but it is absurd to contend that children have the power to judge for themselves as to such a matter ... if your Bill has any defect it is not by the too great limitation, but by the too great extension of the hours of labour.[50]

there is no doubt that he meant it. He meant too to oppose the parroting of *laissez-faire* in the name of scientific economics by the politically and the financially interested.

The economists' attitude towards the regulation of women's work was a good deal more variable. McCulloch was dubious about such regulation and J. S. Mill, who at one time favoured it, later decided (under the influence of Mrs. Taylor) that it was insulting to women and grouped them with children. The answer to their problems lay in the reform of the property and marriage laws.[51]

In general they opposed regulation of the hours of work of men. Torrens and Senior in particular are famous for their opposition to the legal introduction of the ten-hour day. Torrens argued that lower wages would have to be paid if the working day was reduced, or else costs per unit would rise leading to a loss of export markets—which implied an outflow of specie and consequent reduction in home wages and prices. Senior, assuming a constant productivity per hour whatever the length of the working day argued that the margin of profitability was extremely sensitive to the length of the working day, initial output going to cover costs.[52] Moreover although he was in favour of factory-safety legislation he believed that the damage to the health of operatives resulting from long hours in bad conditions had been exaggerated. This last view was based upon a singularly incomplete appreciation of conditions, especially in Lancashire. McCulloch was less dogmatic. Although he believed that long hours were the result of market forces he was not certain of the case against factory legislation. Though he regarded Torrens's pamphlet as the best against the Ten Hour Bill he also recognized the arguments of Lord Ashley in its favour and believed that a balanced appraisal of the two sides had not been produced.[53] Even J. S. Mill, who produced the strong argument in favour of legislation that one man was unable to shorten his working hours unless he was sure that his colleagues would do the same, was not in favour of such legislation at the time that he wrote.[54]

The strongest opponents of legislation however were to be found amongst those who considered such measures a device for avoiding repeal of the

Corn Laws which would, these parties believed, do much more for the mass of the people.[55] The Classical economists were themselves often less sure on both counts; and they were in addition strong opponents of the payment of wages in kind—the truck system. Ricardo seems to be the only exception here.[56]

## 2. Mechanization

In Chapter 8 we discussed the problem of machinery and so we can be brief here. Whatever the long term outcome all the Classical economists recognized the impact effect of machinery on the employment of labour. Accordingly Bentham recommended that care should be taken to provide immediate employment for those displaced by mechanization,[57] while according to Torrens,

Humanity and justice demand, that those who thus suffer for the public good should be relieved at the public expense. Whenever a new application of mechanical power throws a particular class of operatives out of employment, a national fund should be provided, to aid them in betaking themselves to other occupations. It is a disgrace to the Legislature and to the country, that the numerous body of hand-loom weavers should have been left so long in misery and destitution, and toiling to the death in hopeless competition with the power loom. A comprehensive plan for their relief should be one of the earliest measures of the reformed Parliament.[58]

J. S. Mill suggested that, if necessary, the pace of mechanization should be slowed.

If the sinking or fixing of capital in machinery or useful works were ever to proceed at such a pace as to impair materially the funds for the maintenance of labour, it would be incumbent on legislators to take measures for moderating its rapidity: and since improvements which do not diminish employment on the whole, almost always throw some particular class of labourers out of it, there cannot be a more legitimate object of the legislator's care than the interests of those who are thus sacrificed to the gains of their fellow-citizens and of posterity.[59]

However the one detailed treatment of the problem of mechanization to be found in the Classical writings went a good deal less far. This was the report of the Commissioners appointed to investigate the condition of the hand-loom weavers. The Commissioners were Senior, Overstone, and two non-economists, and the report was written by Senior. While the report takes for granted the provision of finance for the weavers through the Poor Law (of which in any case Senior was the author) and while there was no lack of appreciation of the hardships of the weavers—

We do not believe that anyone who has not mixed with the working classes, we do not believe that we ourselves, can adequately estimate how much mental and bodily suffering, how much anxiety and pain, how much despondency and disease are implied in the vague terms 'a fall of wages' or a 'slack demand for labour.[60]

—there was no disposition to recommend any extraordinary intervention. It is certainly true however that if the Commissioners had been convinced of the effectiveness of a particular remedy they would not have turned it down on the grounds of non-interference.

They considered the problem basically from an allocational point of view.[61] With the introduction of the power loom the hand-loom weavers experienced great difficulties. The Commissioners analysed the demand for weavers and found that high wages at times of high demand attracted too many new entrants into the occupation. Mobility of labour out of the industry was the only solution, but this was difficult to achieve both because the weavers themselves preferred independence to factory employment (and they also found employment of their own children at home profitable, though this was very harmful to the children) and also because trades unions resisted the entry of the weavers into other occupations. Increasing demand would be a useful short-term palliative but, because of the likely flood of new entrants if high demand was sustained, this was not a long-term solution. The Commission examined the possibility of taxing power looms—which would, they believed, only injure consumers and power weavers, driving the latter into hand-loom weaving and encouraging foreign competition, thus reducing demand again. They also considered the possibility of a tax on imports of fabric—but they believed that this would result in a reduction of exports in turn and produce no net gain. They did however see some hope from improvements of patterns and suggested the establishment of schools of design and lengthened copyright for designs. They rejected minimum wages as reducing demand for the final product (through cost increases), as encouraging new entrants, and as inappropriate to varying regions and circumstances, as well as being impossible to enforce. Ultimately then they relied upon occupational mobility, to increase which they suggested curbs on trades unions and education of the weavers, together with measures to improve the housing conditions of the weavers which they regarded as intolerable.

All this was distinctly unimaginative (and in the case of the argument about an import duty, faulty as well). But because the Commissioners failed to find a solution one should not conclude that they were opposed to any intervention on *laissez-faire* grounds. Rather they simply showed little imagination in dealing with a problem—the declining industry problem—which has proved exceptionally intractable in our own time.

### 3. Pauperism

During much of the era of Classical economics pauperism was a fairly considerable problem.[62] In dealing with it we find a great diversity of attitudes amongst the Classical economists. There is no proper discussion of the problem in the *Wealth of Nations*. But later writers divided into three groups.

Firstly there were Malthus and Ricardo. They favoured the gradual but complete abolition of the Poor Law on fairly straightforward Malthusian grounds.[63] They believed that it encouraged population growth by guaranteeing the means of subsistence, that as a result of the continued growth of population the whole net rental of the country would in time be absorbed by poor relief, and that the poor should be taught self reliance—by not being paid poor relief.

This was all really rather crude. A second group regarded abolition as impracticable and favoured a drastic reform of the system. Senior was the leading member of this group and it was his view which resulted in the 1834 Poor Law. This was based on confining relief to the workhouse, and not giving 'outdoor relief', and on the so-called principle of 'less eligibility'. The latter involved the idea that no one receiving poor relief should be as well off as somebody working. The standard of relief should therefore be below the level of wages.[64] A third group, of whom McCulloch (after a dramatic change of mind from endorsement of Malthus's view)[65] was the most important, favoured the retention of the old Poor Law with the continuation of outdoor (that is out of the workhouse) relief and without rigid insistence upon 'less eligibility'.[66] It was in the self-interest of the landlords and the large tenant farmers to take measures against cottage building, and they would thus check population. There was then no built-in population stimulus in the old Poor Law. They believed that the Commissioners appointed to investigate the workings of the old Poor Law had selected their evidence so as to produce a distorted picture. G. P. Scrope was also in this group.[67] He believed that the Poor Law was entirely necessary when the majority of the population were day labourers—it was necessary on the grounds of justice, charity, peace, and security. It was objected by various writers, including Senior, that this general view was over-sanguine. They argued that the landlords were ineffective in checking population, that those who paid the Poor Rates were not those who administered them, and that the subsidization of wages under the old system gave the farmers an interest in its continuance because it provided them with cheap labour and made them careless about the level of expenditure on relief.

The response of the defenders of the old Poor Law was to blame the so-called Speenhamland system for the evils which they acknowledged had existed under the old law—this was a system which allowed the Poor Law authorities to supplement wages according to the price of bread— and they believed that a return to the straightforward system of outdoor relief under the old Poor Law for those who were not earning wages was what was required. The allowance system depressed wages and was for the advantage of employers of labour; the ending of wage supplementation would cause wages to rise.

In fact they were probably too pessimistic in their appraisal of the Speenhamland system. Relief does seem to have been at a higher level in those counties which adopted it. But the fluctuations in the level of relief in the non-Speenhamland counties exactly mirrored the fluctuations in the Speenhamland counties so that the system was not of itself creating a problem. It is not even clear that it had the effect of depressing wages.[68] Moreover, as indeed McCulloch pointed out, population growth had been as great in Scotland and Ireland as in England although the old Poor Law did not apply in those countries.[69]

In the end events proved this last group to be basically in the right. The system of the 1834 Poor Law had to be relaxed and it was not possible to adopt a system of indoor relief exclusively.

All this related to relief of the able bodied poor. There was little argument that the blind and the crippled must be provided for—although Malthus in the first edition of his *Essay on Population* called for gradual removal of the whole system without distinguishing those who were not able to provide for themselves.[70] However there was some disagreement as to whether provision should be made for relief of the elderly; Senior in particular opposed this although Longfield was in favour of it. Senior's opposition was on the grounds that old age was entirely foreseeable and that people should be encouraged to make provision for it, a point of view which hardly took account of wages which left no margin for such provision.[71]

## 4. Education

A major weapon in the improvement of the people to which the Classical economists looked was the development of education. From Smith onwards the Classical economists advocated state provision of education on the lines of parochial education in Scotland. Smith and McCulloch believed that the teachers should however depend for a good part of their remuneration on fees, as complete state endowment was a sure method of developing sinecures, idleness, and useless subjects.[72] Senior and J. S. Mill believed in having a system of free or nearly free education and this was true also of J. B. Say.[73] There was a significant divide here between the two groups of economists. In making the income of teachers depend upon fees the first group were arguing for the market test applied to education. J. S. Mill and Senior were on the other hand arguing that education was a case of market failure as uneducated parents were not qualified to select educational sources for their children.[74]

But though there was this difference between the two groups it should be made very clear that neither was advocating a policy of total *laissez-*

*faire*. The following quotation from McCulloch, who as a member of the first group was more likely to be the object of such an accusation, makes this perfectly clear. He was contemptuous of the *laissez-faire* argument applied to education.

This is the cant of mere pretenders to sciences; and it is about the least tolerable of all cants. The fact is, that there are no absolute principles with respect to this or any other subject of politics ... there cannot be the shadow of a doubt that, were governments to interfere so far as to cause a public school to be established in every parish in England, where the fees should be moderate, and where really useful instruction should be communicated to the scholars, its interference would be in the highest degree beneficial.[75]

They recognized that education was in part a consumption good but regarded this as applying only to the upper classes who did not need to invest in their education.[76] Their main treatment of education was as an investment good. They saw it both as an individual investment giving rise to differences in earnings[77] and as a social investment which would increase economic growth through investment in human capital. Smith was the pioneer here and he was followed in particular by McCulloch[78] who laid great stress on the interdependence of education and technology. In addition, education provided an adaptable labour force and also learning skills. J. S. Mill saw it as supplying management for enterprise and he was, in addition, concerned to encourage it in order to erode the rents earned by those possessed of clerical skills.[79]

Looking at the problem more broadly it was also argued (by Smith) that education was desirable to maintain a martial spirit and, more importantly, to enable people to see through demagogues[80]—thus ensuring the stability and security of property so vital to economic growth. In addition it would help to improve the condition of the people and to ensure their participation in the benefits of growth through raising the psychological subsistence level, inculcating moral restraint, and thus raising wages through checking population, while at the same time overcoming the harmful dulling effects of the division of labour.[81]

There are two points which should be made before leaving this section. Firstly it is largely true that the Classical economists were talking about elementary education—hardly surprisingly, given the state of development of the country at the time. Yet at a late stage in his life J. S. Mill went so far as to advocate financial assistance up to university education.[82] Moreover his father was instrumental in the foundation of London University, and university education was something which many of them were concerned about. Secondly, although all of them were concerned about the establishment of a public educational system there was fairly general agreement that a state *monopoly* was undesirable as giving too much power to the State.[83]

## 5. *Trade Unions*

The defence of the trade-union movement by the Classical economists, and their part in the repeal in 1824 of the Combination Laws which had previously prevented trade-union activity is one of the areas of their thought which the caricaturists find it hardest to digest.[84] The usual solution is to assert that the Classical approval of trade unions was motivated by their adherence to the aim of removal of all legislative restrictions on allocation. Since, as we have seen, they had no such aim but were concerned to provide the correct legislative framework to produce coincidence of individual and social interests, such an explanation is hardly likely to be convincing. In fact the Classical economists offered three reasons for their hostility to the Combination Laws which J. S. Mill described as a 'kind of government interference, in which the end and the means are alike odious'.[85]

Firstly, and most importantly, although equilibrium wages might be achieved in the long run they would not be achieved in the short run without the exercise of trade-union power—without this power they could remain depressed below equilibrium for a long period, thus altering the distribution of income in favour of employers. Not only was this unjust but low wages depressed productivity.[86] Secondly, trade unions enabled workers to raise wages during periods of high profits and thus share in the high profits.[87] The Classical economists, as already noted, were (with the possible exception of Senior) in favour of high wages. Thus McCulloch argued that, given a rising supply schedule of labour, high wages meant more effort, that in any case the labourers were the majority of the population and their welfare was that of the community, that the higher were wages the higher was productivity, and the higher were wages, the more secure property and hence the motives to growth.[88] Thirdly, trade unions were a way of rectifying the balance between employers and employees—the former being free to combine, as well as constituting the magistrate class which enforced the Combination Laws against the would-be trade unionists. The employers were fewer in number, better educated, had greater reserves to fall back on during conflict, and were treated indulgently by the law.[89] Justice therefore demanded that the workers should be allowed to redress the balance, and it was thus necessary that the Combination Laws should be repealed. Moreover it should be stressed that the Classical economists certainly did not, as they have been accused of doing, use the idea of the wage fund (see Chapter 5) as an argument against trade-union activity.[90]

But to present a balanced picture it should be emphasized that not *all* the Classicists were in favour of trade unions, and that those who were favoured them only if they were peaceful. It was largely on the grounds that they were, in practice, anything but peaceful that Senior bitterly opposed them. He submitted legislative proposals to the Melbourne Government which would have resulted in the imposition of very severe laws against unions. The Hand Loom Weavers Report is very critical of the way in which unions impeded mobility of labour and in particular of the way in which the attempts of the weavers to move into other occupations were blocked. But above all it was the violence which troubled Senior. The details, drawn from the evidence before a Select Committee of 1838, are truly horrible and repulsive: and anyone indulging in the instinctive (and conventional) reaction that Senior was an old reactionary blackguard will find this evidence very salutary indeed, even if it does not, in the last resort, change his mind.[91]

### iii. POLICY FOR IRELAND

The situation which confronted successive British governments and their advisers in Ireland was an extremely daunting one. A population of more than 8,000,000 (before the Famine)[92] was largely composed of landless peasants living on a level of physical subsistence that was so low that there was no margin to ward off starvation should things take a turn for the worse—and things could be expected to do just that when the main dietary item was the potato. The landlords of this hapless population were at least one-third absentees, and their agents were simply required to squeeze the maximum rents from the luckless tenants who (except in Ulster which was an exception to most of these generalizations) received no compensation for improvements.

The Classical economists saw much of the problem—and were trenchant in their denunciations of the landlords,[93] of subdivision (which they saw as giving the landlords extra political power through their influence on the votes of their tenants—there was no secret ballot of course) of Irish tithes and of the position of the Irish church—Senior recommended that its revenues should be made over in large measure to the Catholic church as the religion of the vast majority of the population. McCulloch argued that the denial of human rights to the bulk of the population had the effect of lowering the psychological subsistence level, thus, in turn, increasing population; and he pressed for government reform, a reform of and reduction of taxation, the removal of British laws against Irish trade and manufactures, and justice for small tenants. He also urged Catholic emancipation, tithe reform, reduction of the Irish church establishment, abolition of the corrupt Irish executive, reform of the magistracy, and an extension of education.[94]

On a lot of these issues the demands of the economists were met.[95] Thus Catholic emancipation was achieved and legislation was introduced to deal with the laws against Irish manufactures and subdivision by landlords. But on some larger issues their analysis was less than satisfactory and relatively little was achieved.

At the root of the problem lay the land question.[96] The Classical economists saw clearly enough that landless peasants without capital were bidding rents far above their economic level in order to survive.[97] But many of them saw the introduction of English large-scale capitalist farming (and, if possible, large scale improving English landlords) into Ireland as the solution. This would produce commercial morality and security of property which in turn would produce a capital inflow into Ireland. Torrens, Ricardo, Senior, and McCulloch all took this view. In fact however attempts at consolidation of holdings only worsened relations between landlords and tenants, as the latter had no desire to become labourers. Other economists however, notably J. S. Mill (whose sympathy for peasant agriculture we have already noted) and G. P. Scrope, were strongly in favour of the substitution of peasant proprietorship for the landlord–tenant relationship, at least for parts of the island. J. S. Mill in his *England and Ireland* argued that Ireland was more like every other European country than England and therefore that only conversion of the peasant occupiers into peasant proprietors could solve the problem. Because of the imbalance of bargaining power he advocated legal control of rents rather than reliance on market forces. In England the charging of excessive rents would simply mean that the capitalist farmers would look to other landlords for their land. In Ireland the capital-less peasants had no such choice.[98]

Writers in the former group tended to favour emigration as a solution to Ireland's problems.[99] Population had outrun both capital and subsistence. Those in the latter group also favoured emigration; yet J. S. Mill in particular regarded this as a very Second Best solution.[100] In the third edition of his *Principles* Mill wrote:

Self-supporting emigration ... has, for the present, reduced the population down to the number for which the existing agricultural system can find employment and support ... Those who think that the land of a country exists for the sake of a few thousand landowners, and that as long as rents are paid, society and government have fulfilled their function, may see in this consummation a happy end to Irish difficulties.

But this is not a time, nor is the human mind now in a condition, in which such insolent pretensions can be maintained. The land of Ireland, the land of every country, belongs to the people of that country ... To the owners of the rent it may be very convenient that the bulk of the inhabitants, despairing of justice in the country where they and their ancestors have lived and suffered, should seek on another continent that property in land which is denied to them at home. But the legislature of the empire ought to regard with other eyes the forced expatriation of millions of people ... justice requires that the actual cultivators should be enabled to become in Ireland what they will become in America—proprietors of the soil which they cultivate.[101]

With regard to the effects of landlord absenteeism many of the Classical economists simply missed the point. In their treatment they concentrated on the long-run problem of the transfer (see Chapter 7) and assumed an adaptability of the Irish economy to the resource allocation required to make the transfer which simply did not exist. They recognized some social effects of absenteeism but on the whole tended to take the view that if the landlords were so bad there was no great advantage in having them in the country.[102]

Education, especially with regard to its effects on population and stability, was favoured as a policy measure for Ireland—again this did nothing about the short run problems—and there was general agreement on the need to do something to limit the potato though little agreement on how this should be limited.[103]

On the question of the introduction of a Poor Law into Ireland the economists were sharply divided. McCulloch and Scrope were strongly in favour of such a measure, believing that it was desirable to introduce the *old* English Poor Law into Ireland.[104] It would force landlords to take an interest in their tenants and limit subdivision. It would increase investment in Ireland because of the resulting increase in security. Both Scrope and McCulloch were anti-Malthusian and were able to take a less mechanistic view of the Irish problem than some of their colleagues; but other economists may have come round to their view, helped by the popular fear of the effects of Irish migration into England.[105] Ricardo, Senior, and Torrens were all however opposed to the introduction of the Poor Law into Ireland both on general Malthusian grounds and on the ground that the principle of 'less eligibility' could not be applied in a country where there was nothing 'less eligible' than a normal working income.[106] Longfield—who as an Irishman should have known better—supported the introduction of the *new* type of Poor Law—the 1834 model—into Ireland despite this problem.[107] But the issue was fairly clear; either you accepted the reasoning behind the 1834 Poor Law (McCulloch did not) or else you were able to support consistently the introduction of the Poor Law into Ireland.

Although Senior did not support the introduction of the Poor Law into Ireland he did advocate the need for a large-scale programme of public works in Ireland especially the building of roads, railways, harbours, docks, and canals, and the draining of bogs and the reclaiming of waste land. This was mainly with a view to producing economic growth rather than employment but he did accept the use of public works for famine relief as well. J. S. Mill and Scrope also supported public works.[108]

On balance the Classical economists did not do very well with the problem of Ireland. But it was not a simple problem. As Jacob Viner has remarked:

If, as I gather, the problem of extreme poverty has been largely solved in Ireland, political independence and land reform have, no doubt, made large contributions. But an unplanned reduction of population, without parallel anywhere else in the western world, or perhaps in the world at large, and attained by a combination of famine, of wholesale emigration, and of the practice of Malthusian 'moral restraint' to a degree far exceeding Malthus' most optimistic expectations, seems to have been largely responsible. Aware as I am of how grievously astray modern experts, equipped with a full set of newly invented forecasting techniques, have gone in predicting modern population trends, I find it difficult to criticize the statesmen and economists of the mid-nineteenth century for failing to foresee what Providence had in store for Ireland. It would be a nice problem to set before modern experts on economic development, with the advantage of all the information [now] made available to them ... to design a model reform programme for the Ireland of the 1840's and 1850's which the statesmen of the time could conceivably have adopted, and which would have worked successfully for the Ireland of the next century.[109]

## iv. COLONIES AND COLONIAL POLICY

Classical thought on colonies moved through two fairly distinct phases. In the first—roughly from Adam Smith until the mid 1820s—they were hostile to colonies and, helped by acceptance of the free trade case and the growth of England to commercial dominance, they largely managed to carry public opinion with them. It was not so much the foundation of colonies to which they objected as the retention of control. Smith (followed by McCulloch) was fond of contrasting the history of the Greek and Roman colonies— the former had been freed from control by the mother country and prospered, while the latter, remaining under control, had not. Colonies prospered when they were left free to pursue their own devices. They could then be pleasant places with cheap land, well cared for children, high wages, and labour in short supply with the desirable consequence, as Smith put it that:

In other countries, rent and profit eat up wages, and the two superior orders of people oppress the inferior one. But in new colonies, the interest of the two superior orders obliges them to treat the inferior one with more generosity and humanity.[110]

If control were retained the colonies cost a great deal to the mother country in defence expenditure and were productive of wars abroad and corruption at home.[111] They would not produce a surplus for the mother country. Indeed they would not even cover their costs. Although Smith considered the possibility of integrating colonies with the mother country and giving them Parliamentary representation, as the only way in which they could be persuaded to tax themselves to a sufficient extent to meet their expenses, this was probably an exercise in showing how stringent the conditions for solvency were, rather than a serious proposal.[112] Even India was of no benefit —indeed the monopoly of the East India Company and the attempts of His Majesty's Government to regulate the Company had produced a totally indefensible combination of exploitation and corruption, and the existence of a continued surplus from even Indian operations was highly doubtful.[113]

The monopoly of the colonial trade was of no benefit to the mother country—as McCulloch put it, it was either pernicious (if it forced high-cost sources of supply on either the colonists or the mother country) or unnecessary (if the protected source were the cheapest one anyway). In Smith's view it was a prime example of mercantilist policy—policy for the benefit of merchants at the cost of the rest of the community:

To found a great empire for the sole purpose of raising up a people of customers, may at first sight appear a project fit only for a nation of shopkeepers. It is however, a project altogether unfit for a nation of shopkeepers; but extremely fit for a nation whose government is influenced by shopkeepers. Such statesmen, and such statesmen only, are capable of fancying that they will find some advantage in employing the blood and treasure of their fellow-citizens, to found and maintain such an empire.[114]

Ricardo, it is true, was later able to show that the colonial monopoly turned the terms of trade in favour of the mother country; but this was not regarded as an argument for the monopoly but as demonstrating a simple welfare transfer with no net gain.[115]

The monopoly, Smith argued, distorted the allocation of capital. It raised profits in the colonial trade, thus attracting capital from other employments. Moreover it attracted capital into a protected carrying trade which ranked fairly low on Smith's scale of investment priorities because of the slowness of the turnover of the capital.[116] Smith did not consider the chances of precious metal discovery a worthwhile reason for colonial adventures —such enterprises were a lottery which was likely to be highly wasteful of resources. However McCulloch, who on most colonial matters followed Smith closely, believed as a result of his endorsement of the Hume inflationary mechanism, that this was an advantage of colonies.[117] However Smith was prepared to concede one major advantage to colonies—at least to their foundation. This was the widening of the market and vent-for-surplus argument which we have already considered in dealing with his theory of international trade; and it was coupled with the stimulus given to trade by the new products originating from colonial sources. But this did *not* constitute an argument for a continuation of the restrictive control system. The mother country should either wholly integrate the colonies into the United Kingdom or emancipate them.[118]

Later writers, imbued with the static Ricardian theory of international trade and the doctrine that industry is limited by capital rather than by the size of the market, rejected even this doctrine—Bentham and James Mill are examples of this latter trend.

But with the growth of concern over the problem of population came a new belief in the benefit of colonies as an outlet for surplus population, a belief to which many of the Classical economists came to subscribe.

This development of thought went through three phases. In the first a number of economists were canvassed by the energetic proponent of colonization schemes Sir R. J. Wilmot Horton, and expressed their support for state-financed schemes of emigration, the finance to come from the Poor Rates in one way or another. McCulloch, Torrens, and Senior all favoured this, though the first of these saw it only as an argument for the *establishment* of colonies not for retaining control of them, and he favoured financing emigration—to the extent of an expenditure of £10 million to £15 million—*anywhere* including South America.[119] But for the other two writers (and Torrens must be given some credit indeed for advancing his schemes before being approached by Wilmot Horton)[120] this provided a bridgehead to other and more ambitious schemes of colonization, as we shall see.

Not all the Classical economists were very enthusiastic about Horton's schemes however. Malthus and Ricardo both objected that the 'vacuum' (as they put it) created in the population by emigration would speedily be refilled by population increase and migration from Ireland—they believed that the expense of financing emigration would be incurred for no purpose. James Mill was also worried that the expenditure of capital in the scheme would result in a consumption of capital which would leave the population/capital ratio—and hence, in this very simplified train of reasoning, wages—in the same position as before.[121]

This view was however met by the argument that even in this case labour was being transferred from a margin of low to a margin of high productivity thus enabling capital accumulation to proceed quickly and repair the loss—both Torrens (in private communication with Horton) and J. S. Mill made use of this argument.[122]

However much more support was obtained by the considerably more ambitious—and indeed highly successful—schemes of Edward Gibbon Wakefield. Amongst the list of his converts were Torrens, Senior, J. S. Mill, Scrope, and the aged Jeremy Bentham[123]—a one-time scourge of colonialism. Malthus however remained sceptical.[124] He believed that the young couples whom Wakefield wished to emigrate were those least likely to feel in need of emigration, and he was also sceptical about another aspect of Wakefield's scheme—the concentration of population—to which we shall come in a moment.

Wakefield's schemes involved charging a price for colonial land. Both Smith and McCulloch had been opposed to the engrossing of large areas of colonial land, free of charge. Smith approved British colonial policy in restraining the engrossing of uncultivated land while McCulloch, Wakefield's most heavyweight opponent, proposed an initial grant to each settler of 100 acres and a charge of 3d. per acre for subsequent acres.[125] Wakefield, by contrast, had in mind a price of £2 per acre for all land.

Charging a price for colonial land had three dimensions. Firstly, the proceeds could be used to finance emigration of selected couples from the U.K.—it was a scheme of self-supporting colonization. It was this aspect which was particularly attractive to some of Wakefield's supporters.[126]

Secondly, it produced a degree of concentration of settlement in which services and the progress of economic development could flourish.[127] Concentration of activities produced external economies—diffusion of technical knowledge, stimulation of competition, supplies of labour, and economies of scale in services. This was in fact a straightforward development of the idea of the role of towns in economic growth expounded in the *Wealth of Nations*. However Wakefield and his supporters believed that government compulsion was necessary to achieve a suitable degree of concentration— as J. S. Mill put it, it was not in the interest of one man to abstain from engrossing land unless he could be sure that others would do the same. The price charged for the land was to be the form of compulsion. In concentrating population a large-scale capitalist agriculture would be produced, rather than the peasant agriculture which would arise if land were free. (Ironically Wakefield's most distinguished supporter proved to be the most outspoken defender of peasant agriculture amongst the Classical economists —J. S. Mill.) Wakefield himself attached great importance to this concentration, though some of the Classical economists were more sceptical. Torrens pointed out that if, as Wakefield envisaged, it would only be necessary for a new immigrant to be an employee for three years before accumulating enough to buy land himself, the number of immigrants would need to increase in geometric progression to keep supplied with labour.[128] It was the self-financing aspect of the scheme which attracted them much more.

But there is an important analytical dimension as well. According to Say, James Mill, and Ricardo, investment opportunities at home were limited only by the productivity of agricultural labour—the basic Ricardian thesis over gluts and the stationary state which we have seen in earlier chapters. Now we have also observed earlier that Smith envisaged the arrival of a stationary state by a simple exhaustion of investment opportunities—the idea of the 'competition of capitals' which the later Classical writers rejected on Say–Ricardo lines.

But Smith's position here was endorsed by Wakefield, who used as an argument for the establishment of colonies the notion of an imminent exhaustion of investment opportunities at home, and argued that hoarding and wasteful speculation were evidence of this. Now the vital question arises as to whether the later Classical economists also accepted the Smith– Wakefield position—which would contrast strangely with their general acceptance of the Say–Ricardo position. This is really an unanswered question, and the reader will be referred to references taking both points of view in the bibliography.[129] The difficulty of interpretation arises from two things. Firstly, although none of them was using the invariable measure, yet they still reasoned in terms of agricultural productivity, and apparently gave a Ricardian twist to the argument. Secondly, the writings of the principal exponents—Torrens and J. S. Mill—are rather elusive on this matter of acceptance of Wakefield. On balance it seems to be the case that Torrens probably did go most of the way with Wakefield on this particular issue: but it is much harder to be sure about the case of J. S. Mill, who continued to put a Ricardian gloss on the argument. How far this was conscious it is impossible to say.

v. CONCLUSION

We have now surveyed the Classical theory of policy. The record of the Classical economists in matters of policy is, we can now see with the benefit of hindsight, far from unblemished. No one could argue that they were always right: and on such matters as Factory Legislation and the Poor Law it would be hard to sustain a case that they were always reasonable. But having said that it should be clear that they were neither bigoted by *laissez-faire* preconceptions nor blinded by class prejudice. They were pragmatic in matters of policy: knowledge of the framework of legal and non-legal constraints which it was desirable to erect in order to produce coincidence of individual and social interest could only be gained by experience. As Cairnes put it, *laissez-faire* was 'above all, a rule which must never for a moment be allowed to stand in the way of the candid consideration of any promising proposal of social or industrial reform'.[130] It was this pragmatism which gave their policy recommendations their appearance of lagging behind the tide of social reform: and it was the same pragmatism which made Classical economics so flexible in matters of economic policy and helped to account for its extraordinarily long survival. Its proponents lived in an era of enormous growth of central government activity. In the years 1833 to 1853 sixteen central government agencies were created in the field of welfare alone, with powers to supervise both local authority and private philanthropic institutions.[131] True *laissez-faire* was not their creed; it was to be found in journals like *The Economist*, to some extent in the works of popular writers like Harriet Martineau, more so in the free-trade utterances of the Manchester School,[132] but above all in the mouths of politicians in Parliament defending a particular interest. The Classical economists were concerned with genuine scientific inquiry, not propaganda; and although they certainly made a mess of some of their inquiries they managed extraordinarily well to adapt the technical apparatus which they had.

NOTES

1. On the prevalence of this see A. W. Coats, *The Classical Economists and Economic Policy*, p. 144.
2. Ibid., p. 202; see also the items by Grampp cited in the bibliography to this chapter.
3. On this see Coats, op. cit., pp. 9–10.
4. Mill, *Principles*, p. 800; see also ibid., pp. 797–8, 941–79.

5. McCulloch, *Treatise on the Succession to Property Vacant by Death* (London, 1848), p. 156, quoted in Lord Robbins, *Theory of Economic Policy*, p. 43.

6. See D. P. O'Brien's, *J. R. McCulloch*, pp. 285–6. See also McCulloch's *Principles of Political Economy* (4th edn. London, 1849), pp. 308–9; Coats, op. cit., p. 17.

7. See P. Schwartz, *The New Political Economy of J. S. Mill*, pp. 119–21.

8. See ibid., pp. 108 and 105–52 *passim*.

9. See Jacob Viner, 'Adam Smith and Laisser Faire', in *The Long View and the Short*, p. 228 for an extensive list of flaws in the unregulated order, to be found in the *Wealth of Nations*.

10. Mill, *Principles*, p. 800; see also M. Bowley, *Nassau Senior*, pp. 265–7; Schwartz, op. cit., p. 116; Lord Robbins, op. cit., p. 45.

11. Bentham quoted in Lord Robbins, op. cit., pp. 39–40; see also ibid., p. 2.

12. J. S. Mill, *Principles*, p. 978; see also Viner, op. cit., pp. 318–19 and Schwartz, op. cit., pp. 128–9.

13. Viner, op. cit., p. 324; Lord Robbins, op. cit., pp. 3, 21–2, 115.

14. See the quotation from the *Moral Sentiments*, ibid., p. 117; and see also ibid., pp. 17–18.

15. e.g. *Wealth of Nations*, i. 130. See also ibid., p. 250 and Viner, op. cit., p. 243.

16. Lauderdale was in later life a Tory: the two Mills, Ricardo, and Bentham could all fairly be described as Philosophical Radicals.

17. On J. S. Mill's association with the Northcote–Trevelyan reforms see Schwartz, op. cit., p. 124. See also Scott Gordon in Coats, op. cit., p. 183.

18. Smith, i. 80; Handloom Weavers Report quoted in Lord Robbins, op. cit., pp. 89–90. See also ibid., pp. 169–70.

19. Ibid., pp. 70–88; on the mercantilists see S. Hollander, *The Economics of Adam Smith*, pp. 248–9; see also O'Brien, *J. R. M. McCulloch*, p. 365.

20. R. G. Lipsey, *An Introduction to Positive Economics* (3rd edn. London, 1971), pp. 546–7.

21. Smith, i. 307.

22. *Works*, ed. Sraffa, iv. 271–300.

23. Smith, ii. 186–202; Mill, *Principles*, pp. 881–3.

24. Smith, ii. 202–14.

25. See Viner, op. cit., p. 237; O'Brien, *J. R. McCulloch*, pp. 286–7.

26. Smith, ii. 214–99; O'Brien, op. cit., p. 286; Viner, op. cit., pp. 239–42.

27. Smith, i. 427–9; see also Hollander, op. cit., p. 264; Viner, op. cit., p. 236.

28. Smith, i. 338.

29. J. S. Mill, *Principles*, pp. 926–30.

30. See O'Brien, *J. R. McCulloch*, p. 256; Viner, op. cit., p. 243.

31. For references see Bowley, *Senior*, pp. 244, 261–2, 275; O'Brien, *J. R. McCulloch*, p. 287; Viner, op. cit., pp. 241, 308–9; Scott Gordon, op. cit., pp. 184–5.

32. Bowley, *Senior*, pp. 261–2, 266–7, 275; O'Brien, *J. R. McCulloch*, p. 287; Lord Robbins, op. cit., pp. 47, 89–90.

33. O'Brien, loc. cit.

34. Ibid., p. 288. See also J. S. Mill, *Principles*, pp. 960–3; Blaug, *Ricardian Economics*, p. 195; Lord Robbins, op. cit., pp. 43, 58.

35. D. L. Losman, 'J. S. Mill on Alternative Economic Systems', *American Journal of Economics and Sociology*, 30 (1971), 85–104, 100; Lord Robbins, op. cit., pp. 100–3; Bowley, *Senior*, p. 257.

36. Losmon, op. cit., p. 100; Robbins, op. cit., pp. 47, 90–3; Bowley, *Senior*, p. 268.

37. See J. S. Mill, *Principles*, pp. 950–3, on the tyranny associated with Colbertisme.

38. e.g. J. S. Mill, *Principles*, pp. 916–26; see however p. 922 for limited recognition of the infant–industry argument.

39. Ibid., pp. 930–3.

40. O'Brien, *J. R. McCulloch*, p. 290.

41. Mill, *Principles*, pp. 218–37, 889–915.

42. O'Brien, *J. R. McCulloch*, pp. 288–9.

43. J. E. Cairnes, *Essays in Political Economy*, p. 264. On other writers see Lord

Robbins, op. cit., pp. 111–41; Schwartz, op. cit., p. 165; and O'Brien, *J. R. McCulloch*, p. 321.

44. There are splendid discussions in Lord Robbins, op. cit., pp. 142–68, Schwartz, op. cit., pp. 153–92; Losman, op. cit.

45. *Principles*, pp. 199–237.

46. Ibid., pp. 792–4.

47. Losman, op. cit., p. 102.

48. See Schwartz, op. cit., p. 147.

49. Ibid., pp. 132–3; Bowley, *Senior*, p. 257; Mill, *Principles*, pp. 956–9; Lord Robbins, *Robert Torrens*, p. 294; Blaug, *Ricardian Economics*, p. 196; O'Brien, *J. R. McCulloch*, pp. 286, 371.

50. Quoted in Lord Robbins, *Policy*, pp. 101–2.

51. O'Brien, *J. R. McCulloch*, pp. 371–2; Mill, *Principles*, p. 959; Schwartz, op. cit., pp. 108, 132–3.

52. For Torrens see Lord Robbins, *Robert Torrens*, pp. 323–4. According to Senior: 'Now, the following analysis will show that in a mill so worked, the whole net profit is derived *from the last hour*. I will suppose a manufacturer to invest 100,000 l.: — 80,000 l. in his mill and machinery, and 20,000 l. in raw material and wages. The annual return of that mill, supposing the capital to be turned once a year, and gross profits to be fifteen per cent., ought to be goods worth 115,000 l., produced by the constant conversion and reconversion of the 20,000 l. circulating capital, from money into goods and from goods into money, in periods of rather more than two months. Of this 115,000 l. each of the twenty-three half hours of work produces 5–115ths, or one twenty-third. Of these 23–23ds, (constituting the whole 115,000 l.) twenty, that is to say, 100,000 l. out of the 115,000 l., simply replace the capital—one twenty-third (or 5,000 l. out of the 115,000 l.), makes up for the deterioration of the mill and machinery. The remaining 2–23ds., that is, the last two of the twenty-three half hours of every day, produce the net profit of ten per cent. If, therefore, (prices remaining the same), the factory could be kept at work thirteen hours instead of eleven and a half, by an addition of about 2,600 l. to the circulating capital, the net profit would be more than doubled. On the other hand, if the hours of working were reduced by one hour per day (prices remaining the same), net profit would be destroyed—if they were reduced by an hour and a half, even gross profit would be destroyed. The circulating capital would be replaced, but there would be no fund to compensate the progressive deterioration of the fixed capital.' *Letters on the Factory Acts*, pp. 12–13. The argument is well analysed in Bowley, *Senior*, pp. 255–7.

53. O'Brien, *J. R. McCulloch*, pp. 371–2 n.

54. Mill, *Principles*, pp. 963–6.

55. See M. Blaug, 'The Classical Economists and the Factory Acts', *Quarterly Journal of Economics*, 72 (1958), 215.

56. O'Brien, *J. R. McCulloch*, pp. 286, 372; Lord Robbins, *Policy*, pp. 100–3.

57. Ibid., p. 104; see also Viner, op. cit., p. 318.

58. Quoted in Lord Robbins, *Robert Torrens*, p. 250 n. 3.

59. Mill, *Principles*, p. 99.

60. Quoted in Bowley, *Senior*, p. 261.

61. On their report see ibid., pp. 261–3 and G. J. Stigler, *Five Lectures on Economic Problems* (London, 1949).

62. See M. Blaug, 'The Myth of the Old Poor Law', *Journal of Economic History*, 23 (1963), 157.

63. Blaug, *Ricardian Economics*, p. 198.

64. Mill, *Principles*, pp. 365–8, 966–9; Bowley, *Senior*, pp. 282–334.

65. O'Brien, *J. R. McCulloch*, pp. 319–24.

66. Ibid., pp. 324–31.

67. Scrope, *Principles*, pp. 293–339. Scrope's argument that the labourer, when reduced to the status of a day-labourer, had a *right* to relief is also to be found in Samuel Read's *Political Economy*, p. 364. The right is seen there as an essential condition of the right of property.

68. This all is strongly argued in the article by Blaug cited above.

69. O'Brien, *J. R. McCulloch*, p. 325 n.

70. Blaug, *Ricardian Economics*, p. 197.

71. For references see Bowley, *Senior*, pp. 244–5, 295–6; Lord Robbins, *Policy*, p. 96; O'Brien, *J. R. McCulloch*, p. 329. For Longfield see his *Economic Writings*, ed. R. D. C. Black, and the editor's introduction pp. 22–5.

72. Smith, ii. 250–66, 269–70; O'Brien, *J. R. McCulloch*, pp. 344–7; McCulloch's Note XXII to his edition of *Wealth of Nations* (Edinburgh, 1863).

73. Say *Treatise*, p. 436; Bowley, *Senior*, pp. 261–2, 268, 330–1; Schwartz, op. cit., p. 132; Lord Robbins, *Policy*, pp. 92–3; Mill, *Principles*, pp. 953–6.

74. On this issue see the article by E. G. West, 'Private vs. Public Education', cited in the bibliography to this chapter.

75. Quoted in O'Brien, *J. R. McCulloch*, pp. 345–6 n.

76. Senior, *Outline of Political Economy* (repr. London, 1939), pp. 205–6.

77. See especially *Wealth of Nations*, i. 103. See also the article by Tu cited in the bibliography to this chapter, pp. 693–4, and the article by Kiker cited therein also.

78. For references see O'Brien, *J. R. McCulloch*, pp. 274, 277, 280, as well as Tu, op. cit., pp. 699–700.

79. Mill, *Principles*, pp. 108–9, 393–4; see also Hollander, op. cit., pp. 258–64, and the article by Miller cited in the bibliography to this chapter, especially pp. 298–9. By 'learning skills' I mean Smith's suggestion that the rudiments of geometry and mechanics should be taught.

80. Smith, ii. 271–3.

81. Ibid., ii. 267.

82. I am indebted for this reference to an as yet unpublished paper by Professor M. Blaug cited in the bibliography to this chapter. The reference is in v. 627–8 of the Toronto edition of Mill's collected works.

83. e.g. J. S. Mill, *Principles*, pp. 953–6.

84. A striking example of this indigestion may be found in B. Inglis, *Poverty and the Industrial Revolution*, pp. 190–1.

85. Mill, *Principles*, p. 933.

86. Ibid., p. 937; and O'Brien, *J. R. McCulloch*, pp. 368–9.

87. See Schwartz, op. cit., p. 87.

88. See O'Brien, *J. R. McCulloch*, p. 365. For Senior see Coats, op. cit. p. 161.

89. O'Brien, *J. R. McCulloch*, p. 368.

90. F. Taussig, *Wages and Capital*, pp. 211–12, 238–9.

91. See N. W. Senior, *Historical and Philosophical Essays* (London, 1865), ii. 116–172, 'Combinations and Strikes'. See also Schwartz, op. cit., p. 86; Lord Robbins, *Policy*, pp. 108–9; Bowley, *Senior*, pp. 277–81.

92. The correct figure may have been 9,000,000 or more—see C. Woodham Smith, *The Great Hunger* (London, 1962), p. 31.

93. See R. D. C. Black, *Economic Thought and the Irish Question*, *passim*, especially pp. 21–2, 149.

94. Ibid.; Bowley, *Senior*, p. 249; O'Brien, *J. R. McCulloch*, pp. 347–9.

95. See J. E. Cairnes, *Political Essays* (London, 1873), p. 142.

96. For references see the exhaustive discussion in Black, op. cit., Ch. 2.

97. See O'Brien, *J. R. McCulloch*, pp. 348–9.

98. Black, op. cit., pp. 53–5, 61; J. S. Mill, *Principles*, pp. 330–42.

99. Black, op. cit., Ch. 7, pp. 130, 138, and Bowley, *Senior*, p. 247; O'Brien, *J. R. McCulloch*, pp. 349–50.

100. Scrope, *Principles*, pp. 336–7; Mill, *Principles*, pp. 330–1.

101. Ibid.

102. See the discussion in Black, op. cit., Ch. 3.

103. O'Brien, *J. R. McCulloch*, pp. 351–2; see also Black, op. cit., pp. 7, 10, 88, 135, 147, 204.

104. O'Brien, *J. R. McCulloch*, p. 350; Black, op. cit., p. 120, and Ch. 4, *passim*; Scrope, *Principles*, Ch. 12.

105. Black, op. cit., pp. 92–7, 104.
106. Ibid., pp. 91–3, 111; Bowley, *Senior*, pp. 246, 294.
107. Black, Introduction to *Longfield*, pp. 22–4.
108. Black, *Economic Thought and the Irish Question*, pp. 93, 111–13, 161, 166, 176; Bowley, *Senior*, pp. 247–8.
109. Viner, Introduction to Black, op. cit., p. vii.
110. Smith, ii. 67; see also ibid., pp. 58, 67–73; O'Brien, *J. R. McCulloch*, p. 337; Donald Winch, *Classical Political Economy and Colonies*, pp. 6–24.
111. Smith, ii. 115. For James Mill see Winch, op. cit., p. 44.
112. This possibility is advanced by Winch, pp. 16–17.
113. Ibid., pp. 44–5; Smith, ii. 137–8, 238–44; D. P. O'Brien, 'McCulloch and India', *Manchester School*, 33 (1965), 313–17.
114. Smith, ii. 114. See also ibid., p. 85.
115. Winch, op. cit., pp. 39–41; James Mill, *Economic Writings*, pp. 317–22.
116. Smith, ii. 96–7, 101, 103, 105.
117. Ibid., pp. 64–5; O'Brien, *J. R. McCulloch*, p. 336. On inflationism see Ch. 6 above.
118. Smith, ii. 92–109, 116–21; O'Brien, *J. R. McCulloch*, pp. 331–4.
119. Ibid.; Winch, op. cit., pp. 51–72.
120. Lord Robbins, *Robert Torrens*, pp. 149–50.
121. Malthus, *Essay on Population* (1826 edn.), ii. 49; Ricardo, *Works*, i. 99–100; R. Black, op. cit., p. 205.
122. D. P. O'Brien, 'Torrens on Wages and Emigration', *Economica*, 33 (1966), 336–40; Mill, *Principles*, pp. 740–2, 969–75. See also Lord Robbins, *Torrens*, pp. 175–6.
123. See Winch, op. cit., pp. 25–38 and Chs. 6–9; Mill, *Principles*, pp. 382, 969–75; Lord Robbins, *Torrens*, pp. 167–8.
124. See the article by Ghosh in *Economica* 1963, cited in the bibliography to this chapter, pp. 57–60.
125. Smith, ii. 73; O'Brien, *J. R. McCulloch*, p. 343; Winch, op. cit., p. 125.
126. For endorsement of this see Mill, *Principles*, pp. 381–4.
127. Ibid., p. 121.
128. See Lord Robbins, *Robert Torrens*, p. 172.
129. On this issue see Winch, op. cit., Ch. 6, pp. 73–89, and Ch. 9, esp. pp. 138–9; Lord Robbins, *Torrens*, pp. 149–50, 178–80; Mill, *Principles*, pp. 725–8, 740–2; and the articles by Kittrell cited in the bibliography to this chapter.
130. Cairnes, *Essays in Political Economy*, p. 251.
131. Scott Gordon in Coats, op. cit., p. 187. See also the works by Burn and by Roberts cited in the bibliography to this chapter.
132. See the references in the bibliography to the 1955 article by Scott Gordon and the books by Grampp. See also Blaug, *Ricardian Economics*, pp. 129–39, 202–9.

# BIBLIOGRAPHY

The reference which *must* be a starting-point for this chapter is Lord Robbins's delightful and scholarly *The Theory of Economic Policy in English Classical Political Economy* (London, 1952) and this can be supplemented by Warren Sammuels, *The Classical Theory of Economic Policy* (Cleveland, Ohio, 1966)—the style is tortuous but the content is interesting. There is also a valuable collection of essays, *The Classical Economists and Economic Policy*, ed. A. W. Coats (London, 1971); the editor's introduction and Scott Gordon's contribution are particularly valuable on the general question of intervention.

There is a considerable literature dealing with the broad question of Classical liberalism. See in particular D. H. MacGregor, *Economic Thought and Policy* (London, 1949), W. D. Grampp, *The Manchester School of Economics* (London, 1960) and the same author's *Economic Liberalism*, 2 vols. (New York, 1965), especially Vol. ii. On *laissez-faire* see Scott Gordon's 'Laisser Faire' in the *International Encyclopaedia of the Social Sciences*, Vol. 8, pp. 546–9; and on the role of *The Economist* in its promotion see the same author's 'The London *Economist* and the High Tide of Laisser Faire', *Journal of Political Economy*, 63 (1955), 461–88. On the meaning of *laissez-faire* as applied to this period see R. L. Crouch 'Laisser-Faire in nineteenth century Britain: myth or reality', *Manchester School*, 35 (1967), 199–215. Other references are Blaug, *Ricardian Economics*, pp. 129–39 and 193–212 and Jacob Viner's 'The Intellectual History of Laisser Faire', *Journal of Law and Economics*, 3 (1960), 45–69, which deals with the origins of the concept. Two of the references which indicate how little *laissez-faire* constrained social legislation are W. L. Burn, *The Age of Equipoise* (London, 1964), and D. Roberts, *Victorian Origins of the British Welfare State* (New Haven, 1960). Amidst all this S. G. Checkland, 'The Prescriptions of Classical Economics', *Economica*, 20 (1953), 61–72, sounds a somewhat discordant note.

But the reader should decide for himself. The key primary references are *Wealth of Nations*, Bk. V, Ch. 1; Mill, *Principles*, Bk. II, Chs. 1, 2, 12, 13, Bk. IV, Chs. 2, 7, Bk. V, Chs. 1, 8–11; Say, *Treatise*, Bk. III, Ch. 6; and the essays, 'Political Economy and Laisser-Faire' and 'Bastiat' in J. E. Cairnes, *Essays in Political Economy* (London, 1873, repr. A. M. Kelley, New York, 1965).

Smith has received a good deal of examination in this context. See in particular Jacob Viner 'Adam Smith and Laisser Faire', in *The Long View and the Short*, and S. Hollander, *The Economics of Adam Smith* (London, 1973), Ch. 8. For a full discussion of Senior see M. Bowley, *Nassau Senior*, Pt. II, pp. 237–339; for McCulloch see D. O'Brien, *J. R. McCulloch*, pp. 285–91; for J. S. Mill see Viner's essay on Bentham and J. S. Mill in *The Long View and the Short* and P. Schwartz, *The New Political Economy of J. S. Mill*, Ch. 6. Mill's interest in socialism has also received a good deal of discussion; three references which may be recommended strongly are Lord Robbins's *Theory of Policy*, pp. 142–68, Schwartz, Ch. 7, and D. L. Losman, 'J. S. Mill on Alternative Economic Systems', *American Journal of Economics and Sociology*, 30 (1971), 85–104.

On the Factory Acts see M. Blaug, 'The Classical Economists and the Factory Acts—A Re-Examination', *Quarterly Journal of Economics*, 72 (1958), 211–26; this is a rather severe view and less harsh ones will be found in Lord Robbins, in D. O'Brien, *J. R. McCulloch*, pp. 370–3, in M. Bowley, *Nassau Senior*, Pt. II, Ch. 1, and in the authors whom Blaug is, by implication, criticizing, such as Sorenson and Walker. But it is difficult not to be rather depressed at least by Senior's attitude—see his *Letters on the Factory Acts*, repr. in *Selected Writings on Economics*. On mechanization see Bowley, loc. cit., and the illuminating (and generous) interpretation of the Hand Loom Weavers Report by G. J. Stigler in *Five Lectures on Economic Problems* (London, 1949).

The Poor Law and its history have generated an enormous literature. Three references however will suffice to lead into this: O'Brien, *J. R. McCulloch*, pp. 314–31, Bowley, Pt. II, Ch. 2, and (a splendid example of economic history written by an economist) M. Blaug, 'The Myth of the Old Poor Law', *Journal of Economic History*, 23 (1963), 151–84—a well-timed corrective to over-facile acceptance of the Poor Law Commissioners' views. These references contain directions to the primary sources of which Scrope (already referred to in the text) and Samuel Read are particularly interesting examples.

For discussions of the Classical economists and Trade Unions and wages see Robbins, and F. W. Taussig, *Wages and Capital* (London, 1896), especially Ch. 10, as well as Schwartz, Ch. 5, O'Brien, pp. 355–70, and the essay by A. W. Coats, 'The Classical Economists and the Labourer', in his volume cited above. On the role of the Classical economists in the repeal of the Combination Laws see G. Wallas, *Life of Francis Place* (London, 1918). Reading on the Classical economists and education can well start with P. N. V. Tu, 'The Classical Economists and Education', *Kyklos*, 22 (1969), 691–716. There is also an excellent article by W. L. Miller, 'The Economics of Education in English Classical Economics', *Southern Economic Journal*, 32 (1966), 294–309. See also B. F. Kiker, 'The Historical Roots of the Concept of Human Capital', *Journal of Political Economy*, 74 (1966), 481–99. There is an excellent (though highly critical) survey by M. Blaug of the primary and secondary literature on the subject, as yet unpublished—it is to appear in a volume of essays to celebrate the bicentenary of the *Wealth of Nations*. The discussion was given very considerable momentum by the publication of E. G. West's 'Private versus Public Education, A Classical Economic Dispute', *Journal of Political Economy*, 72 (1964), 465–75. See also O'Brien, *J. R. McCulloch*, pp. 344–7.

On Ireland we can be mercifully brief. There is one great study, R. D. C. Black, *Economic Thought and the Irish Question* (London, 1960), which, complete with exhaustive bibliography, covers all the literature.

The attitude of the Classical economists towards colonies is analysed in a book which has the great merit of distinguishing the main currents in a balanced and sensible way—Donald Winch, *Classical Political Economy and Colonies* (London, 1965). Contrast K. E. Knorr, *British Colonial Theories* (Toronto, 1944), which is however valuable because of its enormous coverage of the literature. Both Winch and Lord Robbins (*Robert Torrens*, pp. 144–81) discuss the acceptance by the Classical economists of the Smith–Wakefield thesis; and for a somewhat different view see E. R. Kittrell, 'The Development of the Theory of Colonisation in English Classical Political Economy', *Southern Economic Journal*, 31 (1965), 189–206; 'Wakefield's Scheme of Systematic Colonisation and Classical Economics', *American Journal of Economics and Sociology*, 32 (1973), 87–111; 'Bentham and Wakefield', *Western Economic Journal*, 4 (1965), 28–40. The Wilmot–Horton schemes are well covered in Winch. For further details see R. N. Ghosh 'Malthus on Emigration and Colonisation: Letters to Wilmot-Horton', *Economica*, 30 (1963), 45–61, and 'The Colonisation Controversy: R. J. Wilmot-Horton and the Classical Economists', ibid., 31 (1964), 385–400. McCulloch supported Horton but remained the most faithful to Smith's position —see O'Brien, *J. R. McCulloch*, pp. 331–44 and 'McCulloch and India', *Manchester School*, 33 (1965), 313–17. Smith's own treatment is in *Wealth of Nations*, Bk. IV, Ch. 7. For a final Classical view of colonies which essentially showed a return to that of Smith see J. E. Cairnes, *Political Essays* (London, 1873), 'Colonisation and Colonial Government'.

# Index